The Cambridge Companion to Roman Satire

Satire as a distinct genre of writing was first developed by the Romans in the second century BCE. Regarded by them as uniquely "their own," satire held a special place in the Roman imagination as the one genre that could address the problems of city life from the perspective of a "real Roman." In this Cambridge Companion an international team of scholars provides a stimulating introduction to Roman satire's core practitioners and practices, placing them within the contexts of Greco-Roman literary and political history. Besides addressing basic questions of authors, content, and form, the volume looks to the question of what satire "does" within the world of Greco-Roman social exchanges, and goes on to treat the genre's further development, reception, and translation in Elizabethan England and beyond. Included are studies of the prosimetric, "Menippean" satires that would become the models for Rabelais, Erasmus, More, and (narrative satire's crowning jewel) Swift.

THE CAMBRIDGE
COMPANION TO
ROMAN SATIRE

EDITED BY
KIRK FREUDENBURG

*Professor and Chair, Department of the Classics, the University of Illinois
at Urbana-Champaign*

CAMBRIDGE
UNIVERSITY PRESS

CAMBRIDGE UNIVERSITY PRESS
Cambridge, New York, Melbourne, Madrid, Cape Town, Singapore, São Paulo

Cambridge University Press
The Edinburgh Building, Cambridge CB2 2RU, UK

Published in the United States of America by Cambridge University Press, New York

www.cambridge.org
Information on this title: www.cambridge.org/9780521803595

© Cambridge University Press 2005

First published 2005

Printed in the United Kingdom at the University Press, Cambridge

A catalogue record for this book is available from the British Library

Library of Congress Cataloguing in Publication data
The Cambridge companion to Roman satire / edited by Kirk Freudenburg.
p.   cm. – (Cambridge companions to literature)
Includes bibliographical references (p.) and index.
ISBN 0-521-80359-4 – ISBN 0-521-00627-9 (pbk.)
1. Satire, Latin – History and criticism.   2. Rome – In literature.   I. Freudenburg,
Kirk, 1961–   II. Series.
PA6095.C36   2005
877′.010932376 – dc22   2004057024

ISBN 13 978 0 521 80359 5 hardback
ISBN 10 0 521 80359 4 hardback
ISBN 13 978 0 521 00627 9 paperback
ISBN 10 0 521 00627 9 paperback

Dedicated to all the self-deluded emperors, ideologues, bullies, and buffoons who make satire possible, pertinent, inevitable.

It's hard to not write satire. For who is so long-suffering towards this lopsided city, who is so iron-hard that he can hold himself back?

Juvenal, early second century CE

Here . . . the daily panorama of human existence, of private and communal folly . . . is so inordinately gross and preposterous . . . that only the man who was born with a petrified diaphragm can fail to laugh himself to sleep every night.

H. L. Mencken, 1922

If you aren't completely appalled, then you haven't been paying attention.

Election-year bumpersticker, *Everywhere USA*, 2004

CONTENTS

NOTES ON CONTRIBUTORS

ALESSANDRO BARCHIESI teaches Latin Literature at the University of Siena at Arezzo and at Stanford University, and is editor of the journal *Studi Italiani di Filologia Classica*. His research interests are Latin poetry, Roman culture, and literary theory. He has recently co-edited the three miscellaneous volumes *Ovidian Transformations* (1999), *Iambic Ideas* (2001), and *Rituals in Ink* (2004), and published a collection of essays entitled *Speaking Volumes* (2001), and contributed to various Cambridge Companions.

COLIN BURROW is Reader in Renaissance and Comparative Literature and Director of Studies in English at Gonville and Caius College, Cambridge. His publications include an edition of *The Complete Sonnets and Poems* for the Oxford Shakespeare (2002), and *Epic Romance: Homer to Milton* (1993), as well as numerous articles on the reception of classical literature in early modern England.

CATHERINE CONNORS is Associate Professor in the Department of Classics at the University of Washington, Seattle, and the author of *Petronius the Poet: Verse and Literary Tradition in the Satyricon* (1998). She has published articles on Roman epic, Roman comedy, and the ancient novel, and her current research focuses on representations of nature and geography in literary texts.

ANDREA CUCCHIARELLI is a fixed-term researcher at the University of Siena at Arezzo. He has published articles on Lucretius, Virgil, Horace, and Petronius, and he is the author of two books: *La satira e il poeta* (2001), and *La veglia di Venere–Pervigilium Veneris* (2003, intro., trans., and commentary).

KIRK FREUDENBURG is Professor and Chair of the Department of the Classics, at the University of Illinois at Urbana-Champaign. His published works focus on the social life of Roman letters, and they include two books on Roman satire: *The Walking Muse: Horace on the Theory of Satire* (1993), and *Satires of Rome: Threatening Poses from Lucilius to Juvenal* (2001). His current projects are a commentary on Horace, *Sermones* book 2 (for Cambridge University Press), and a study of libraries and literary histories in the Greco-Roman world.

EMILY GOWERS is University Lecturer in Classics at the University of Cambridge and a Fellow of St. John's College. She is author of *The Loaded Table: Representations of Food in Roman Literature* (1993), and is working on a commentary on Horace, *Sermones* book 1 for the Cambridge Greek and Latin Classics series.

FRITZ GRAF is Professor of Greek and Latin and a Director of the Center for Epigraphical and Palaeographical Studies at the Ohio State University. He works mainly on Greek and Roman religions. His publications include *Nordionische Kulte* (1985), *Greek Mythology* (1985; English trans. 1993), *Magic in the Ancient World* (1994, English trans. 1997) and *Der Lauf des rollenden Jahres. Zeit und Kalender in Rom* (1997). He is currently working on a book on Apollo (to appear 2005) and on a study of Greek and Roman festivals in the eastern half of the Roman empire.

ERIK GUNDERSON is Associate Professor of Greek and Latin at the Ohio State University. He is the author of *Staging Masculinity: the Rhetoric of Performance in the Roman World* (2000) and *Declamation, Paternity and Roman Identity: Authority and the Rhetorical Self* (2003).

THOMAS N. HABINEK is Professor of Classics at the University of Southern California. His research focuses on the intimate relationship between Latin literature and the political and cultural practices of ancient Rome. He is the author of *The Colometry of Latin Prose* (1985), *The Roman Cultural Revolution*, co-edited with Alessandro Schiesaro (1997), and *The Politics of Latin Literature: Writing, Identity, and Empire in Ancient Rome* (1998).

JOHN HENDERSON is Professor of Classics at the University of Cambridge, and Fellow of King's College. His recent books on Latin literature include *Morals and Villas in Seneca's Letters* (2004), *The Roman Gardening Book* (2004), *Aesop's Human Zoo: Fables from Phaedrus* (2004), *Pliny's Statue* (2002), *Fighting for Rome* (1998).

DAN HOOLEY is Chair of Classics at the University of Missouri. He is editor of the journal *Classical and Modern Literature*, and author of *The Classics in Paraphrase: Ezra Pound and Modern Translators of Latin Poetry* (1988),

The Knotted Thong: Structures of Mimesis in Persius (1997), *Roman Satire* (forthcoming), and a number of articles on Roman poetry, classical reception, and translation studies.

DUNCAN KENNEDY is Professor of Latin Literature and the Theory of Criticism at the University of Bristol. A leading expert in the application of modern literary theory to the study of ancient texts, he is the author of *The Arts of Love: Five Studies in the Discourse of Roman Love Elegy* (1993), and *Rethinking Reality: Lucretius and the Textualization of Reality* (2002).

CHARLES MARTINDALE is Professor of Latin at the University of Bristol. He is the author of *John Milton and the Transformation of Ancient Epic* (1986), *Redeeming the Text: Latin Poetry and the Hermeneutics of Reception* (1993), and co-author of *Shakespeare and the Uses of Antiquity* (1990). He is editor of *Virgil and his Influence* (1984), *Ovid Renewed* (1988), and (with David Hopkins) *Horace Made New* (1993). His forthcoming works include *Shakespeare and the Classics*, co-edited with A. B. Taylor, Cambridge University Press, and *Latin Poetry and the Judgement of Taste: An Essay in Aesthetics*, Oxford University Press.

ROLAND MAYER has produced a range of commentaries on Latin authors (Lucan, Seneca, Horace, and Tacitus), as well as numerous articles and reviews on literary and philological issues. For seven years he was an editor of the *Classical Review*. He is currently researching into the Roman value-concept of *gloria*.

FRANCES MUECKE, Senior Lecturer in Latin at the University of Sydney, is the author of *Horace: Satires II* (1993). She has written a number of articles on aspects of genre in Latin literature and is currently working on Humanist scholarship in late fifteenth-century Rome.

ELLEN O'GORMAN is Lecturer in Classics at the University of Bristol. Her published works include *Irony and Misreading in the Annals of Tacitus* (2000) and articles on Horace, Lucan, Ovid, Statius, Plutarch, and Helen of Troy. She is currently working on a book about the representation of Carthage in Roman literature, for readers interested in history, cultural history, myth, aggression, trauma, and narrative.

JOEL C. RELIHAN is Chair of the Classics Department at Wheaton College in Norton, Massachusetts. His published works include *Ancient Menippean Satire* (1993) and a new English translation of Boethius' *De consolatione philosophiae* (2001). *The Prisoner's Philosophy*, his literary study of

Boethius' *Consolation*, will appear shortly from the University of Notre Dame Press. He is currently at work on a new translation of *The Metamorphoses* of Apuleius.

VICTORIA RIMELL is *Professore a contratto* in Latin literature at the University of Rome, La Sapienza, and was previously lecturer in classics at Girton College Cambridge, and Junior Research Fellow at University College Oxford. She is the author of *Petronius and the Anatomy of Fiction* (2002) and is currently writing books on Ovid and Martial, as well as editing a volume of *Ancient Narrative* on speech and writing in the novel.

ACKNOWLEDGMENTS

Now that this project, for so long just a rumor, has stepped into full public view, rather proud of its multi-colored jacket and mismatched pair of ISBNs, the book that it has become runs the risk of seeming considerably better adjusted and more "inevitable" than it really was, or ever could be. Pauline Hire proposed the idea of a Cambridge Companion to Roman Satire to me years ago, an idea that I regarded skeptically at the time, as a conundrum and a curiosity, certainly interesting, perhaps even worthwhile, but not terribly likely. Now that it is finished, I remain a skeptic, but fairly pleased with the end-result, glad to have done it, especially since the process of putting this act on paper has put me in touch with a good number of smart colleagues and friends, both old and new, who have caused me to rethink some of my own grand assumptions about what matters crucially to the study of Roman satire.

The standards set by the Cambridge Companion series are high, and a suitably serious attempt was made to meet them by the contributors of this volume. That said, I should make clear from the start that this book intends to serve its one most important purpose not as Roman satire's last word, but as a stalwart companion to those setting out to explore for themselves the genre's various regions, its topographical contours, and even its final frontier. Where you end that quest is your own business, and this book certainly does not propose to take you there. At best, it proposes to start you on your way, helpfully, along this line or that, if only to have you jettison it (let us hope inconspicuously) once you have found a route more direct, meaningful, and true. To do just that is good enough for us, and the stuff of a worthy companion. To do more would perhaps be too much, especially for an editor who has no truck with unilateral, empire-building schemes, such as this Companion could have easily become.

I cannot begin to recall in print the names of all who helped conceive, write, edit, and produce this book. But there are some whose impact demands special thanks, however terse. As always, Dan Hooley was much too nice

for his own good. Not only did he write a crucial chapter of the volume –
not even the one he wanted to write – but he worked hard to improve the
volume's contents from beginning to end. The same can be said for Erik
Gunderson who, though fully capable of keeping himself busy without any
help from me, read whatever I asked him to read, sometimes repeatedly,
and generously provided not just critical comments, but blisteringly smart
insights that he alone has the brains to think up. Watching him, and John
Henderson, think satire out of its classical box has been one of the more
rewarding aspects of the behind-the-scenes work of this volume. Charles
Martindale, a veteran of Companions past, was called upon for help of
every kind, intellectual, technical, and bibliographical. He has been most
patient with me, and gracious in providing help at every stage.

Much of the work for this volume was done during my year as National
Endowment for the Humanities Rome Prize Fellow at the American Academy
in Rome. Sincere thanks are owed to the Academy, to the College of Humanities at Ohio State University, and to the National Endowment for the
Humanities for supporting my cause. Andrea Cucchiarelli, Sergio Casali,
and Alessandro Barchiesi all did their best to ease me into *l'altro mondo* of
Italian classics. On behalf of my entire family, I extend to them my sincerest
thanks. Paulo Brozzi kept me well supplied with books, besides doing his
utmost to improve my Italian. Finally, sincerest thanks are due to all the volume's contributors (thanks for your patience), and to Sinead Moloney and
Michael Sharp at Cambridge University Press. By now, Michael, you should
know better than to support my dubious cause. Mostly I behaved myself this
time. Which isn't to say that this book is exactly what you had in mind.

EDITIONS AND ABBREVIATIONS

Editions of Greek and Latin Works Frequently Cited

Astbury, R. (1985) ed. *M. Terentii Varronis Saturarum Menippearum Fragmenta*. Leipzig.

Bieler, L. (1984) ed. *Anicii Manlii Severini Boethii Philosophiae Consolatio*, 2nd edn., Corpus Christianorum, Series Latina, XCIV. Turnhout.

Clausen, W. V. (1959, rev. 1992) ed. *A. Persi Flacci et D. Iuni Iuuenalis Saturae*. Oxford.

Degani, E. (1983) ed. *Hipponax*. Leipzig.

Eden, P. T. (1984) ed. *Seneca Apocolocyntosis*. Cambridge.

Holder, A. (1894, repr. 1979) ed. *Pomponi Porfyrionis Commentum in Horatium Flaccum*. New York.

Keller, O. (1967) ed. *Pseudacronis Scholia in Horatium Vetustiora*, vol. II. Stuttgart.

Christian Lacombrade, C. (1964) ed. *L'Empereur Julien: Œuvres complètes*, vol. II, part 2. Paris.

Malcovati, H. (1930, revised 1955) ed. *Oratorum Romanorum Fragmenta*. Turin.

Mynors, R. A. B. (1969) *P. Vergili Maronis Opera*. Oxford.

Olson, S. Douglas, and Sens, Alex (2000) *Archestratos of Gela: Greek Culture and Cuisine in the Fourth Century BCE*. Oxford.

Pfeiffer, R. (1949) *Callimachus, vol. I: Fragmenta*. Oxford.

Radermacher, L. (1907–65) *M. Fabi Quintiliani Institutionis Oratoriae libri XII*. Leipzig.

Shackleton Bailey, D. R. (1985) *Q. Horati Flacci opera*. Stuttgart.

Skutsch, O. (1985) *The Annals of Q. Ennius*. Oxford.

Vahlen, J. (1903) *Ennianae Poesis Reliquiae*. Leipzig.

Warmington, E. H., ed. and trans. (1935–40) *Remains of Old Latin*, 4 vols. Cambridge, MA/London.

Wessner, P. (1931) *Scholia in Iuvenalem Vetustiora*. Leipzig.

West, M. L. (1989–92) *Iambi et Elegi Graeci*, vols. I–II. Oxford.

Abbreviations and References

ANRW Haase, W., and Temporini, H. (1972–) *Aufstieg und Niedergang der römischen Welt*. Berlin.

CIL (1863–) *Corpus inscriptionum Latinarum*. Berlin.

GLK   Keil, H. (1857–80) *Grammatici Latini.* Leipzig.
OCD   Hornblower, S., and Spawforth, A. (3rd edn., 1996) *Oxford Classical Dictionary.* Oxford.
OLD   Glare, P. G. W. (1968–82) *Oxford Latin Dictionary.* Oxford.
RE   (1893–1980) *Realencyclopädie der classischen Altertumswissenschaft.* Leipzig.
ROL   Warmington, E. H. (1935–40) *Remains of Old Latin,* 4 vols. Cambridge, MA/London.
Sk.   Skutsch, O. (1985) *The Annals of Q. Ennius.* Oxford.
SVF   von Arnim, H. (1903–24) *Stoicorum Veterum Fragmenta.* Leipzig.
TLL   (1900–) *Thesaurus linguae Latinae.* Leipzig.
W   Warmington, E. H. (1938, repr. with corrections 1979) *Remains of Old Latin* III. *Lucilius, the Twelve Tables.* Cambridge, MA/London.

KIRK FREUDENBURG

Introduction: Roman satire

Origins: Lucilius

Near the beginning of the tenth book of his *Institutes*, midway through a list of readings recommended for the orator in training, Quintilian, Rome's most prolific theorist of rhetoric after Cicero, takes a tendentious step towards satire's terrain by claiming that this particular genre can be accounted "totally ours."[1] The claim is tendentious because extreme, and true only in a highly qualified sense. For ancient critics had long since sought to establish the genre's Greek pedigree by tracing its development past its most obvious early practitioners in Republican Rome (Ennius and Lucilius, both of whom wrote in the second century BCE) all the way to fifth-century Athens. Claims of satire's Greek provenience, although they could easily be stretched to an opposite extreme, are defensible and seem to have at least some narrow basis in fact.

Horace, writing more than one hundred years before Quintilian, was aware of both extremes. Perhaps to goad those in his audience who adamantly defended the idea that satire sprouted entirely from Roman soil, but perhaps also to mimic those who wanted to believe that any good thing in Roman literature just had to come from the Greeks, Horace went so far as to assert that Lucilius did not a whit more to invent satire than to rework the meters of Greek Old Comedy ("having changed *only* their meters and rhythms," *mutatis tantum pedibus numerisque*, *Sermones* 1.4.7). Referring to Aristophanes, Eupolis, and Cratinus, the three canonical comedians of fifth-century Athens, Horace says "Lucilius relies on them *entirely*" (*hinc omnis pendet Lucilius*, *Sermones* 1.4.6).[2] So much for satire's being at all "ours," let alone "totally" so.

---

[1] For Quintilian on satire, see *Institutes* 10.1.93–5. The difficulties surrounding the claim *satura quidem tota nostra est* are neatly summarized by Hendrickson (1927).

[2] These sentiments have long been regarded by commentators as suspiciously overdone; see, for example, Rudd (1966) 89. I suspect that such patent exaggerations sample and send up the hard-line views of certain of Horace's critics; see Freudenburg (2001) 18–19. That such

Actually, when Quintilian makes his famous claim, just a few years before the publication of Juvenal's first book, he does not say *satura tota nostra est* ("satire is totally ours"), although he is often quoted that way. He says *satura quidem tota nostra est* ("satire *at least/if nothing else* is totally ours"). His particularizing and emphatic *quidem* matters, for it is emotionally charged; a way of breathing a sigh of relief, midway inside a long list of Roman generic enterprises, all modeled after Greek precedents, themselves reviewed earlier in the same book, and saying "here, for once, and just this once, we Romans have something, *at least this one thing* that we can claim as our own and *not* derived from the Greeks." That is the fuller tale told by Quintilian's not-so-innocent *quidem*. It announces that we are now inside a pleasant myth, *tota nostra est*, one that was taken very seriously in some sectors, it seems, already a century and a half before in Horace's day. And clearly there were critics in Quintilian's day, too, who took the basic gist of this assertion a good deal more seriously than he himself did. For before he can make any significant headway into his discussion of satire's best practitioners and habits at *Institutes* 10.1.93 Quintilian must first dispute the rankings of certain critics who, still in his own day, stubbornly maintained (he is annoyed with them) that Lucilius was not just Rome's first writer of satire, and a very fine one at that, but Rome's greatest writer of all time, in all genres – not Ennius, not Horace, not Virgil: Lucilius!

Failing to make Quintilian's list in the late first century CE is Quintus Ennius (239–169 BCE), the poet usually accounted Rome's first writer of satire. Best known to us as the author of the *Annales*, Rome's finest national epic before the *Aeneid*, he is well represented in a number of genres where he merits mention by Quintilian as an author worthy of study.[3] The great majority of these poetic enterprises Ennius modeled directly after Greek precedents. But in among his lesser-known efforts there have survived a few scant remains of a four-book collection of poems that he entitled *saturae*. That title, the plural form of Latin *satura* (with each book apparently comprising one *satura*), is unknown before Ennius, and has been the subject of much debate.[4] Apparently it derives from the Latin adjective *satur*, meaning "chock-full."

exaggerations could actually rate as respectable theory in certain sectors (especially, it seems, among Greek scholars working in Rome) can be seen from the comments of Porphyrio and Pseudacron *ad Sermones* 1.10.66, where both claim that satire lacks a Greek precedent only in the sense that no Greek had written it in hexameter verse. Both scholiasts are quick to point out that Roman satire's hexameter scheme is itself a Greek metrical invention.

[3] Quintilian ranks Ennius among Rome's best writers of epic at *Inst.* 10.1.88. His tragedies do not make Quintilian's preferred list, but they are cited for critical comment (sometimes positively) on several occasions.

[4] For various possibilities, see Knoche (1975) 7–16.

It seems, then, that Ennius used the term to designate his poems as things chock-full of this and that ("miscellanies"), for what little remains of them (a mere thirty-one lines of verse) suggests that they have far more in common with collections of Hellenistic occasional poems, such as Posidippus' grab-bag of epigrams known as *Soros*, "The Pile," or Ennius' own *Hedyphagetica*, "Delicatessen," than they do with the later poems of Lucilius and Horace that go by the same name.[5] For this reason it is perhaps best not to refer to them as "satires" at all. That is their title, but not really their genre. Satire, in that sense, "our" sense, had yet to be invented.

Quintilian knew of the existence of these pre-Lucilian "satires."[6] But he carefully sidesteps mentioning them in his review of satire by claim-ing that "Lucilius was the first to achieve distinction" in satire. Not, in other words, the first to write satire, but the first to do it well. This is in keeping with Horace, who had named Lucilius his chief predecessor in the genre (*Sermones* 1.4 *passim*), even calling him satire's *inuentor* "discoverer/innovator" (*Sermones* 1.10.48), and "the one who first dared to compose poems in this manner" (*Sermones* 2.1.62–3), even though he, too, was cer-tainly aware that, in addition to Lucilius, "certain others" (*quibusdam aliis*, *Sermones* 1.10.47) had preceded him in satire.[7] Like Quintilian, he does not think they merit mentioning by name. For Horace, Ennius is an epic poet, linked to satire as a frequent target, never as a writer of satires.

Later scholars, such as Porphyrio in the second century and Diomedes in the fourth, are less reticent about Ennius' role in the history of Roman satire.[8] Although they make explicit room for Ennius (and for his nephew Pacuvius, also a writer of *saturae* in the Ennian manner, not a line of which survives) in their studies of satire, they are always quick to draw a hard and

---

[5] Gratwick (1982) lays out the Hellenistic background of Ennius' four *Saturae*. See also Muecke in this volume.

[6] He cites Ennius *in satura* at *Inst.* 9.2.36.

[7] Horace, *S.* 1.10.66 makes reference to an author of purely indigenous Latin poems. Though the reference is best taken as generic ("an author") rather than specific (definitely not Ennius, see Fedeli (1994) 524–5), the description of these poems as *Graecis intacti* lets us hear what is at stake in the world of contemporary satire criticism. The phrase is politically loaded, implying not just that the poetry in question was "untried" by the Greeks, but that it was "unspoilt/untainted" by them. I suspect that in the phrase *Graecis intacti* the poet adopts a momentary, "deviant" point of focalization. In essence he is quoting his critics (without the benefit of quotation marks) to send up one of their favorite ideas, that of the pure Roman essence that precedes, and is undone by, the Greek. On deviant focalizers generally, see Fowler (2000) 40–63.

[8] Porphyrio mentions both Ennius and Pacuvius among the "certain others" who preceded Horace in the writing of satire at Horace, *S.* 1.10.47, and he names Ennius with Lucilius and Varro as writers of *saturae* in his introduction to *Epistles* 1.3.

fast line between what counted for satire before Lucilius, and what became of it after him. Typical is Diomedes, who defines satire as (*GLK* 1.485):

> a poetic work belonging to the Romans [*apud Romanos*] that *now*, at any rate, is written to abuse and to attack the vices of men in the manner of old comedy, the sort that Lucilius wrote, then Horace, then Persius. But *in a former time* a poetic work that consisted of a smattering of different poems was called satire, the sort that Pacuvius and Ennius wrote.

The great divide here, as in every account of satire's history in Rome, is Lucilius. Before him, the story goes, the genre existed in a certain *Ur*-fashion, and it possessed certain elements that it would retain throughout its history, such as variety, comic situations, and low diction, fables, autobiography, lively dialogue, and so on. But it did not have the basic elements that Lucilius permanently attached to the genre as its most pronounced and consistent features: namely, personal abuse and social criticism. Such innovations, Diomedes suggests, did not spring fully armed from Lucilius' head, but came to him by way of precedents in Greek Old Comedy. Obviously, this is to give the Greeks a good deal of credit for Roman satire. And yet, inside his reference to the genre as something practiced specifically *apud Romanos* we can detect telltale traces of an alternate ideal, that of the genre's being exceptionally and/or completely Roman. Or in Quintilian's words, "totally ours."

Quintilian wants us to believe this about satire, so he leaves Ennius and Pacuvius unmentioned. He has to. To include them in his account would severely compromise his idea (one that had been bandied about for more than a century) of the genre's Roman indigeneity, for this is an idea that cannot survive Ennius' notorious philhellenia, his status as a *semigraecus* ("half-Greek"), and the fact that his literary career focused so heavily on adapting Greek literary precedents (especially epic, tragedy, comedy) into matching Latin forms. In the end, if this genre is to be defended as entirely Roman, that defense has to be put in terms of what Lucilius did to it, not how Ennius first developed it.

But the problem of satire's being unproblematically Roman, whether we take Quintilian's deeming it "entirely ours" to refer to the genre's origins or to its developed habits, is not simply a matter of specific social desires having inched their way into the criticism of satire from the outside. Rather, the overstatement of the genre's Romanness is a direct consequence of the way that satire was made to speak by Lucilius, and the social and political uses to which he put it. For Lucilius' genre-chartering performance (his thirty books of satires) is, from start to finish, an aggressive overstatement of what it means to be a genuine Roman in second-century Rome. His performance is, in great measure, deeply conditioned by a crisis in Roman identity that came with Rome's second-century economic and imperial successes, especially its subjugation of Greece, and the city's wholesale "translation" of Greek cultural materials and habits into the lives of the Roman elite.[9] And it is from within that rapidly globalizing cultural milieu, with so much burgeoning Roman invention consisting of rapid "translation" from the Greek, that Lucilius "first dares" to impress his audience with his being comfortable in his own, home-made, south Italian shoes. As Fritz Graf points out in his contribution to this volume, rapidly giving way to forces of modernization (= Hellenization) in this period are certain traditional instruments of social control that the Roman upper classes had long employed to shame themselves into behaving properly. Lucilius' brand of extra-legal verbal violence may well have drawn on certain of these dying, and utterly Roman, institutions (especially that of *conuicium facere*) to produce a voice skeptical of the law, capable of judging for itself, and full of regret for the loss of native values and old Roman ways.[10] It is precisely this manner of angry nostalgia for all that has been lost that Juvenal will bring back to life in direct imitation of his preferred model, Lucilius.

However much his satires may owe to the Greeks, and that is demonstrably quite a lot, and however Hellenized and high-brow Lucilius may have been in his personal life, the overall impression his poems make is that of being proudly home born. Their *romanitas* explodes off the poet's every page not by chance, but because that is largely their point, and how they mean to impress us. And that is one reason among many why the likes of Ennius and Pacuvius come in for such rough handling in these poems, and why, in turn, they get elided from so many ancient surveys of satire.[11] Catherine Connors (in this volume) points out that allusions to epic are not mere decorative enhancements: they are ways of defining, and reflecting on, the poet's political world. Lucilius parodies and pokes fun at Rome's epic poets not just because they were famous, and wrote infelicitous lines of poetry from time to time, but because doing so establishes the speaker as an authentic, unmediated Roman, unimpressed by two of the hottest and best paid of the city's second-century Hellenizers. Criticizing them, in other words, is not the point of Lucilian satire. It is a necessary means towards a different end: the performance of the poet's free-speaking, rugged, and utterly Roman self. That performance speaks "the satirist" into existence (his first appearance

---

[9] For the Hellenization of second-century Rome, see especially Gruen (1992).

[10] On the satirists' attitudes towards the law and legal institutions generally, see Marongiu (1977), Cloud (1989), Mazurek (1997), and McGinn (2001).

[11] Lucilius parodies writers of tragedy (especially) on numerous occasions. For specific cases, see Marx (1904–1905) 100, Skutsch (1985) 11–12, and the index of Krenkel (1970), vol. II, s.v. Ennius and Lucilius.

as such), marking him as "his own" creation in a vast sea of translations and imitations. And it structures criticism of satire for centuries to come, figuring it as a question of Roman self-possession, "ours" versus "theirs."

But if, as I have suggested, the underlying question posed by Lucilius in his poems is "what have we Romans to say *for ourselves* anymore?" the answer he gives is the vehicle through which he puts the question: his satires. Both in their formal design and in their content, poems of "his" kind stand in sharp opposition to the Greek-inspired poems-for-hire of Ennius, Pacuvius, and their ilk. Much the same can be said for satire's problematic relationship to the "alien wisdom" of Greek philosophy. Roland Mayer (in this volume) points out that Greek philosophical teachings, though ever present in Roman satire as materials that both structure and lend weight to the satirist's ethical and political arguments, are just as commonly deployed for purposes of parody and ridicule. The satirist keeps his distance, warily regarding his relationship to Greek philosophy, as to Greek things generally, as one of "ours" versus "theirs." But that should not deceive us. These poems, from Lucilius onwards, draw heavily on Greek precedents, especially diatribe, iambic poetry, and Greek Old Comedy. Many scholars, both ancient and modern, have seen this. Lucilius is demonstrably no hater of all things Greek. Rather, he plays one from time to time, as he has to, to place himself at a healthy, critical distance from his society's philhellenic enthusiasms. His first satire of his first book (it may have been the entire first book) begins with what looks like a xenophobic rant, attacking not Greeks *per se*, but Roman enthusiasms for all things Greek. These enthusiasms, he has the gods in heaven complain, found Romans wearing underwear from Lydia and racing to buy up all sorts of gorgeous, Greek luxuries. Even the most mundane of practical items, mere lamps and bed-feet, were called by their Greek names, *luchnoi* and *klinopodes*. The silliness and snobbery of it all sends the poet into a righteous Roman rage.

This poem is a genre-defining first act. Later satirists, most famously Seneca (ca. 4 BCE–CE 65) in his *Apocolocyntosis*, remind us of it repeatedly and pro-grammatically, as if to demonstrate what they can and, more importantly, *cannot* do while performing within Lucilius' clearly marked terrain. This is a generic space that stubbornly resists being reoccupied, plowed under, or improved. Strangely, it remains always fundamentally *his*, guarded by Lucilius as if by the former owner's jealous ghost (a nasty curmudgeon who does not take kindly to strangers).[12] Each satirist after Lucilius, by

---

[12] Hendrickson (1927) 54:

> Early Roman literary theory, dealing not yet with a literary genus, but merely with the personality of Lucilius (*character Lucilianus*), emphasized in him his freedom and

moving onto his terrain, is set with the challenge of speaking the way he once did. But none does. None can. Instead, by reminding us of the vast differences that separate Lucilius' free-wheeling "then" from their own restricted "now," Rome's post-Lucilian satirists produce radically different senses of the Roman self, in versions of Romanness that speak to, send up, or otherwise (satirically or perfectly) suit the times in which they themselves live.[13]

Post-Lucilian poses: Horace, Persius, and others

Like Lucilius, Horace was a south Italian, by reputation independent and rough around the edges. He wrote poems about life in the Big City, dwelling especially on its characters, trials, and annoyances. His poems treat us to the perspective of an outsider looking in, someone not altogether impressed. They complain. They gossip and criticize. And, above all, they urge us to laugh. Resemblances between the two authors, for the most part, stop here. For as Emily Gowers indicates, Horace projects a far different sense of himself in his "Conversations" than Lucilius did in his searingly nasty satires. He speaks in softer, more cautious tones, telling us that he means well by his criticisms, that he intends only to tell the truth, and that no one need take offense. Satiric poems, he tells us, are a touchy business, and hard to get just right. Like party-goers, they are fun to be around, but they sometimes get out of line and make everyone cringe from embarrassment and fear.[14] The way Lucilius did. Get them completely "soused" (another meaning of *satur*) and they turn nasty and belligerent, losing their feel for the finer qualities of irony, allusion,

> boldness of personal attack . . . when at a later time (in the early days of Horace) this *character Lucilianus* became generalized to cover the conception of a Roman *satura*, there came into the definition and idea of satire a notion of vehement personal attack which is in fact quite alien to all Roman satire subsequent to Lucilius. This point of view persisted curiously, so far as the name and theory are concerned, down to the latest times.

[13] For example Horace, in the first poem of his second book, tells of how Lucilius (again in that famous first satire) sank his teeth into the "Wolf," L. Cornelius Lentulus Lupus, a consular senator and former censor, *princeps senatus* in 131–25 BCE, whose death is the occasion for the mock *concilium deorum* in Lucilius' first book, later imitated by Seneca in his *Apocolocyntosis*, and Juvenal in his fourth satire. For satire's subsequent imitations of this scene see Connors in this volume. Horace, in his turn, takes on foes of a different, less threatening type, the "Deer" (Cervius) and "Dog" (Canidia), to whom he hesitates to show his teeth (S. 2.1.39–49).

[14] See especially Horace, S. 1.4.81–9. Ruffell (2003) makes clear that these lines distinguish the practices of a politely conversational, Epicurean satirist (Horace's own invention) from those of a Late Republican political lampooner in the traditions of Pitholaos, Calvus, and Catullus.

and fair play. But friends who are both direct in their criticisms and sensitive to the company at hand (besides being aware of their own deficiencies) comport themselves differently. They open up to one another in clever and revealing ways by drinking "just enough" (*satis*) and knowing when to stop.[15]

Horace's introduction of bad characters (drunken, belligerent, malicious) into the theorizing of good satire draws heavily on Greek rhetorical theories that treat criticism and jest as matters of gentlemanly comportment.[16] These theories insisted that jokes and critical jabs had to be used with utmost care because they were direct and open expressions of one's nobility and worth. Certain men of high standing, operating within certain highly delimited, ritualized contexts – such as the orator in his peroration, or the censor in issuing his decrees – were expected to rail at vice and, when called for, to belittle and poke fun. Doing so spoke to the speaker's innate nobility, and to his having the full legal wherewithal to practice a rite that few could access. But there were many others who practiced less savory brands of humor in the ancient Greco-Roman world: the pratfallers and facial contortionists of the mime stage, parasites in their cups, buffoons of farce, scandal-mongers and levelers of anonymous lampoons.[17] These degraded sorts had served as handy points of reference for rhetorical theorists since Plato, helping to define the gentleman by way of what he was not: namely, the low-bred "other" who veers overboard in jest because he is *by nature* extreme, backbiting, licentious, and crass.[18] Thomas Habinek points out that the satirist's self-performance depends on his staging these figures, repeatedly and in bold

[15] This is to apply Callimachean aesthetic principles to the writing of satire; see Hubbard (1981) and Dufallo (2000). It is also to apply the rules of the Greek symposium (and sympotic poetry) to the writing of satire. See Compton-Engle (1999) 326: "In sympotic poetry, the avoidance of polemical subjects is directly related to the desire to avoid drunken violence at the symposium itself."

[16] See Freudenburg (1993) 52–108.

[17] For Aristotle's theory of the liberal jest, see especially *Rhetoric* 3.1419b2–9. Cicero's rhetorical works are the most important source for the theory's subsequent deployment in Rome. See especially *De oratore* 2.216–90, *Orator* 87–90, and *De officiis* 1.103–4. For the later development of these theories in eighteenth-century England (with special emphasis on print satire) see Donald (1996) 1–74.

[18] Typical is Cicero, *Orator* 88: "the orator will use jest in a manner that is not too profuse, lest he come off as a buffoon. To avoid the mime actor's role, he will avoid obscenity. Nor will he take relish in abuse, like a rogue, and he will not laugh at disaster, which is inhuman." The citing of wicked and misguided humorists is deployed as a standard means of legitimation for satirists and theorists of satire from Horace's picture of a tattling and malicious dinner-guest (*S.* 1.4.81–9) and Persius' superficial satirist (*lusco qui possit dicere "lusco"* Persius 1.128) to Addison's "circumforaneous wits" (*Spectator* no. 47 [1711], Richard Payne Knight's "Pindars, Pasquins, sketchers and reviewers" (*The Progress of Civil Society* [1796]), and Pope's "dark anonymous Writers . . . deeply immers'd in dirty work" (*Dunciad* [1729] in

colors, as objects of ridicule, parody, and "play." For to play with them this way is to articulate the satirist's own sense of fair play. And that, Habinek insists, comes not from handbooks and literary traditions, but from social practices of long standing, mostly of a non-literary sort. Told this way, satire "belongs to the history of practices as well as to the history of texts," and it can thus be studied as much for what it does (its social life, especially in the area of self-production) as for what it says.

Dovetailing with Habinek's study of satire's social life are Fritz Graf's essay on satire's ritual analogies (see above) and two studies of satire's bodily rhetoric. In the first of these, Alessandro Barchiesi and Andrea Cucchiarelli look at how satirists figure their works in bodily terms, thereby inviting us to step into the role of amateur physician/satirist and, as it were, to read their works for signs of life. The satirist's own body thereby becomes a shorthand for the values to which he holds, and a means for our envisioning his work as a set of bodily expressions. The second essay in this set, by Erik Gunderson, moves from the literary figuring of satire's bodies to the psychic costs and benefits of watching them misbehave. So many bad characters, he shows, are caught *in flagrante* between satire's permissive sheets. What is the point of their being staged for our viewing, especially when satirists offer no compensating models of bodily pleasures properly buttoned down? The point, Gunderson suggests, is not simply to define the sexual parameters of the élite Roman male and to declare him satire's, and his society's, regrettable winner – this is where so much scholarship on bodies in Roman literature is stuck. Rather it is a means of our desire's watching theirs, and thus of having one's cake while eating it. In satire we watch the forbidden acts of others who are happily abandoned to their desires. The speaker demands that we share in his disgust at their lack of moral conscience and self-control. We do that. And yet with him we relish the act of repudiating them – Roman satirists do not just refer to bad behavior, they leer at it, and wallow in it. Watching the satirist watch takes us into a world of forbidden, compensatory pleasures, where losing one's hegemony never felt so good.

Throughout the history of the genre satirists define themselves in contrast to these degraded others who fail to make the grade of "real Romans" by being, in turns, too prurient and cheap, malicious, too superficial, complacent, or droll.[19] Horace attempts to redefine satire as the carefully controlled

---

ed. James Sutherland, *Twickenham Edition of the Poems of Alexander Pope* [London and New Haven, revised edn. 1953]).

[19] For late instances, see e.g. Anthony Ashley Cooper, earl of Shaftesbury, "Sensus Communis: an Essay on the Freedom of Wit and Humor" (1709), in *Characteristicks of Men, Manners, Opinions, Times* (Birmingham 1773) vol. I, and Joseph Addison's *Spectator* essays nos. 35, 47, 58–63, and 249 in ed. John Loftis, *Joseph Addison: Essays in Criticism and Literary*

straight talk of an Epicurean friend, someone rather far down the social scale, but noble at heart. Lost in transition are the effusiveness of Lucilius, and his indifference to caution, decorum, and tact. Lucilius had targeted some of the most powerful of Rome's political elite, strafing them in piques of glistening rage. This would become the stuff of legend, Lucilius as the tooth-and-nail attacker, a partial truth that accrues to him as myth to hero. In her essay, Frances Muecke provides a much fuller account of what Lucilius' poems were about. But it is primarily his aggression, and his failure to check himself in any situation whatever, that his legend privileges (making failure, of a certain kind, the key to his success). Horace, in turn, targets type-characters, unnamed fools, and persons of no particular account.[20] Much closer to the bottom of the social ladder's acceptable range than to the top, Horace could not afford to make enemies. Again as Gowers points out, his guarded speech is both a condition of, and commentary upon, his vulnerable place within Roman society (a freed slave's son and fighter for "freedom's" losing cause at Philippi). Whereas Lucilius had played censor for all of Rome, thus filling an open slot on the Roman library's Latin shelves that corresponds roughly to the poets of Old Comedy on the Greek side (again see Muecke), Horace avoids the political fray. He privatizes the satirist's censorial gaze by routing its observations back on himself, telling on others, but only as a means of self-improvement, just as his father once taught him.[21]

According to his legend, Lucilius chastised not folly generally, but fools, wherever he saw them. He was reckless, named names, made enemies. Horace struggles to adapt this set of expectations to his own restricted situation in the company of powerful men. The mismatch of "genre" to "poet" is palpable throughout his *Sermones*. But the clearest evidence of satire's having taken an abrupt turn towards guardedness and introspection in Horace is seen not just in the poet's lack of political aggression, but in his use of his stylus's eraser end. Lucilius, Horace complains, never erased anything from his thoughts or from his page. But why should he? His thoughts were his page. He wrote whatever came to mind not just because he was unimpressed by Greek-style refinements, but because he could get away with stating his opinions bluntly. He was exceedingly rich, powerful, and well connected, and that luxuriance of self-possession and political wherewithal crams his pages chock-full. It makes them "satire." Horace does not have

Theory (Northbrook, IL, 1975) 18–29 and 53–82. For the larger critical and social contexts of these eighteenth-century debates concerning the proper uses and proportions of satiric humor, see Tave (1960) and Rawson (1994).

[20] For the names in Horace, see Rudd (1966) 132–59.

[21] See Horace, *S.* 1.4.103–39. For the fictional, New Comic coloring of Horace's father, see Leach (1971).

that political luxury, so he introduces an aesthetic refinement that the genre previously did not know or respect: the use of the eraser. Horace packages personal self-limits as aesthetic refinements expressed "in conversation" that keeps within strict bounds of decorum, in tone, topic, meter, and so on.[22] For certain of Lucilius' advocates in the first century BCE this move towards controlled expression was totally unacceptable. Lucilius' metrical and social brusqueness they considered inviolable. Such ruggedness spoke to his being impressively self-confident, a "real Roman" who had refused to measure himself in terms set by the Greeks. But Horace would have us regard Lucilius' brand of unchecked expression as out of date and in need of reform.[23] His scaled-down chats poke fun at big-talkers generally, taking special aim, on three separate occasions, at the man who had invented the genre itself as a kind of big talk: Lucilius. But the odds of Horace's having his way with the genre are unfavorable, for the "improvements" he introduces to satire are all too easily read in reverse (from aesthetics to socio-politics), as failures of the self. In Dryden's famous assessment, the "temporizing" adjustments of "a well mannered court slave . . . who is ever decent, because he is naturally servile."[24]

But this needs qualifying. Horace's friendly conversations are not always as friendly as they seem. They are littered with barbs of wit and aggression that hide in the silky folds of irony, innuendo, and allusion. Political commentary inheres there, too, felt especially as a nagging sense of regret for all that has been lost from the poet's life, from the genre of satire, and from the ideals of the Roman state. These poems, in other words, are not without their Lucilian undercurrents. But they repackage Lucilius' confident assertion of being self-made (in a word, a "satirist") as a struggle to be self-made, best as you can, given the times. And these are times that change drastically from Horace's first book (published in 35 BCE) to his second (30 BCE). Whereas *Sermones* book 1 charts the poet's sometimes comical attempts to make his way back from catastrophe after Philippi and into the good graces of Maecenas, whose influence with Octavian in the 30s and 20s BCE was second to none, book 2 finds the poet ensconced in the company of Rome's political élite, but not altogether happy with his transition from "outside" to "inside."[25] If the first

---

[22] For a fuller account of Horace's 'limiting' efforts, see Freudenburg (2001) 15–124.

[23] Ironically, it is Horace who puts restrictions on the use of Greek vocabulary in satire in the interests of good Latinity. Lucilius had freely included both colloquial Greek and the lettered Greek of high Roman society in his satires.

[24] John Dryden, *A Discourse Concerning the Original and Progress of Satire* (1693), in *John Dryden*, ed. Keith Walker (Oxford 1994) 258.

[25] For the satirist's transition from outsider to insider in *Sermones* book 1, see Zetzel (1980) and Oliensis (1998b).

book is about striving to survive, the second is about surviving success, with the change in the poet's personal and political surroundings expressed vocally in his now having so little to say for himself and, conversely, his having to put up with so much big talk from others. A great deal of what Horace has us consider in book 2 thus concerns the high price of getting what one thought one wanted, as the poet steps back to look at, and listen to, some of the most annoying aspects of the life he now leads. How awful it is, he tells us, to do Maecenas' bidding morning (2.6.20–6) and night (2.7.29–35), especially when it comes to the task of keeping the conversation polite and meaningless at one of his gorgeous dinner parties. To not make the guest list of one of these parties is horrible. To attend, all too often, even worse. There, in the company of those who can make or break you, it is always best to keep to the topic that wafts right under one's nose, to that one area where a rich man's lackey can be expected to have strong opinions and talk the big talk of someone self-confident and in the know: food. Just listen in (*passim*, but especially *Sermones* 2.4 and 2.8) and you will know just how bad it can get. How nice it would be to escape to a place (a genre) that one could call "one's own" (*Sermones* 2.6), a pleasantly appointed country estate where "conversation" could be conducted at one's own discretion (as villa owner and host rather than tag-along guest), and kept as simple and edifying as the food itself! This is a dream that Horace chases in satire but cannot realize. His "ownership" of Lucilius' urban domain will always remain a matter of debate.

Persius (CE 34–62) was heavily influenced by Horace. He imitates him incessantly on his way to doing something completely different.[26] He is especially keen on turning the critical focus of satire further inward, as Horace started to do, from matters of the city, its persons, politics, enthusiasms, to matters of the soul. Which is not to say that Persius can be considered apolitical. One could not sneeze in Nero's Rome without being political. Deep under the surface, Persius is perhaps the most aggressively political of all Roman satirists. Whereas Horace's Epicurean friend was companionable and, to a respectable degree, a man of the world, Persius' satirist has no truck with polite society. He eats nettles for breakfast. And if he stays up late, it is only to study and memorize. He is, famously, the "Stoic satirist," a proudly uncompanionable ideologue whose lessons and language express the harsh ideals to which he holds. Straddling the roles of sluggard student and overbearing teacher, Persius' "Stoic satirist" is an unlikely combination.[27] Satirists, after all, were known for indulging in piques of strong emotion,

---

[26] On Persius' redeployment of Horace, see especially Hooley (1997).

[27] For the pupil as teacher in Persius, see Henderson (1999) 228–48.

laughter, rage, and disgust that Stoic sages regarded as outward signs of psychic turmoil. How does one express satire's expected measure of outrage in a Stoical demeanor of calm detachment? Moreover, how does one express oneself "freely," as both Stoic and satirist should (*libertas* is the one trait that they share in full) in an increasingly totalitarian state that fancied itself perfect in its every "golden" achievement? As Andrea Cucchiarelli points out, these are the central problems that Persius addresses in his first poem, where the poet agonizes less over the truth he must tell (everyone is an ass in Rome) than how he is to tell it to a society that is so utterly impressed with itself. His metaphor of secrets buried in a hole construes the satirist's social role as that of someone who cannot speak openly, so he hides things, the truths he must tell, in far-off places, under the surface. His language is wonderful to think with (bold in its metaphors, and amazingly rich in intertextual hues) but it is exceptionally hard to make sense of. Listen hard enough (he is quite sure that no one will listen) and these poems tell their truths, taking us past the glistening surface of Nero's Rome to its underbelly and soul.

His is a bitter potion, Persius tells us, but good for what ails you. Inside he has cooked a full measure of Greek Old Comic aggression: the "daring," "rage," and "enormity" of Cratinus, Eupolis, and Aristophanes (Persius 1.123–4). He also mentions Lucilius and Horace by name in his first poem, besides alluding to them on dozens of occasions throughout his satires as a way of further texturing and complicating his thoughts. The choliambic prologue makes clear that Hipponax and Callimachus, writers of Greek iambic poetry, belong on Persius' list as well.[28] The last line of his last poem reserves a place of special honor for the Stoic philosopher Chrysippus, whose ideas and expressions he has included freely from the start. This inclusion puts a curious strain on Persius' imitation of Horace, for Horace was very explicit in his first poem about wanting nothing to do with long-winded neo-Chrysippeans and their nit-picking.[29] Similarly, Horace was very careful to distance himself from the writers of iambic poetry and Old Comedy, although he does seem to concede that they belong on his list.[30] Virgil looms large in Horace's first book.[31] But some of the most noticeable points of imitation refer to writers who go unnamed, but whose presence is felt throughout. Chief among these are Lucretius, Terence, and Callimachus.[32] Mime

---

[28] For Hipponax and Callimachus in Persius' prologue and Persius 1, see Freudenburg (2001) 140–2, and Cucchiarelli (2001) 189–99.

[29] For Horace on the neo-Chrysippeans of his day, see Freudenburg (1993) 109–19.

[30] See Cucchiarelli (2001) *passim*.   [31] See Putnam (1995).

[32] For the influence of Lucretius, see DeWitt (1939), Glazewski (1971), and Freudenburg (2001) 16–17, 33–4. For Terence and New Comedy, see Leach (1971) and Hunter (1985). For Callimachus, see above, n. 15.

performances are factored in on several occasions. And by the time we reach book 2 of the *Sermones* Plato has made his way onto the satirist's list. Menander and Archilochus receive special mention there as well.[33] Aesop and Archestratus are not named, but they come to mind on several occasions. Menippus and Varro, who head satire's alternate "prosimetric" branch, can reasonably be thought to stand behind much of the learned nattering of book 2, especially the underworld consultation of *Sermones* 2.5.[34]

Genealogies of satire

Horace and Persius produce vastly different lists. But they are remarkably alike in the fact of their producing them openly and in detail. Compared to writers working in other genres, Rome's verse satirists are unusually expressive when it comes to laying out the genealogies of their works. They do this by inviting us to look into their bookbags to see what they have been reading. This is to put the satirist's legendary frankness to work at the level of his theoretical discussion. But it is also a necessary means of helping us place their works in reference to all the varied traditions that satire includes. For as the ancient *lanx satura* ("heaped plate") metaphor suggests, satire is less a thing in itself than it is a momentary, willed coherence of discrete materials cobbled together, this and that, messily contained. The cobbling *is* the thing, and each satirist's list constitutes his own unique recipe for it. To stray towards a library metaphor, their lists help us find a place for these books on our shelves, a task especially difficult in the case of Roman verse satire because throughout the genre's visible history (as even this quick glance at Persius and Horace suggests) shifts from one satirist to the next are, in every case, remarkably abrupt and disorienting. No two satirists produce the same list of models. In fact the only constant explicitly named on all the lists produced by Horace, Persius, and Juvenal is Lucilius. Naming him is thus not simply a cataloguing cue, it is a genre-constituting act. For in a genre so loose in its habits, where the parts are always showing *qua* parts and spilling off the plate, we know that we have "it" only when the satirist says (as he hands us the plate) "I'm writing satire now. You know, the kind of thing that Lucilius wrote."

It is only with Juvenal (*floruit* ca. CE 100–ca.130) that verse satire in Rome takes on the specific set of traits that would come to characterize the genre, and dominate so much conventional satiric theory and writing, in the genre's second major flourishing in Elizabethan England. For scholars of English satire especially, the zero-grade of Juvenal has long served as a kind of false

---

[33] Horace, *S.* 2.3.11–14.   [34] Rudd (1966) 237–9.

etymology for the genre itself. Roughly as follows: in satire, we have the complaints of an honest man, abused by, and indignant at, the corruption and folly that surround him on all sides. His poems take us on a tour of the city's highways, to its salons, back alleys, taverns, and so on, where the speaker stokes his indignation to treat us to the full measure of his honorable rage. A man of simple ways, the satirist is himself morally respectable and self-assured. Conservative, often to the point of being pig-headed, the satirist strays towards being laughably stuck in some far-off golden age. At times he is xenophobic and misogynistic, but he is funny, means well, and is always worth hearing out. Horace and Persius performed their roles very differently. But much modern scholarship since the 1950s has downplayed these differences to leave the impression that Juvenal's performative habits are generally those of the genre itself, as one exemplary part that stands suitably for the whole.[35] In his first poem Juvenal reaches past Horace and Persius to Lucilius, naming him satire's first and last "real Roman," the warrior whose sword he intends to take up and brandish as his own. Whether he does any decent moral slashing with it, or falls on it as the butt of his own joke, is the question he leaves us to ponder by being so un-Lucilian in his targets, so awkwardly out of date, loud, and extreme. As Victoria Rimell indicates, these are problems that are not always given their due weight in general studies of the genre, where scholars, especially in the field of British satire, have tended to feature a hard-and-fast, and sadly under-nuanced, "Roman background" on their way to describing something much more developed and complex in the sixteenth to eighteenth centuries. Such studies, of course, need a solid base to build on. This volume hopes to provide better, albeit less rock-solid, options for describing how the Roman satirists operated, the specific social and political conditions in which they wrote, and what they may have been about. Some of which, I hope, will make its way into future reconsiderations of the genre's later history.

Lucilius is at the top and center of Juvenal's list.[36] Horace and Persius are alluded to several times in Juvenal's first poem.[37] Some of epic's and

---

[35] For example, Kernan (1965) 36:

> The greatest satirists have always taken for their subject not mere petty stupidity but the more "heroic" and self-satisfied forms of vice and dullness, which, blind to reality, create grand inflated images of themselves and pompously attempt to reconstruct the world . . . the sonority of epic, the thunderous tones of Old Testament prophecy, the vocabularies of science and philosophy, the terms of wit and learning, the styles of refinement and morality are all appropriated – and mangled – by dullness attempting to enlarge itself.

[36] Juv. 1.19–20.   [37] See Woodman (1983) and Scivoletti (1963).

tragedy's most extreme habits are put on display from first poem to last.[38] But Juvenal's signature performance, that of the lovable, Greek-hating loser, born too late, and, by now, much too Roman for his own good, owes little to the influences named above. For this routine of a down-and-out Roman he has adapted not from Lucilius (certainly *not* Lucilius), but from his close friend Martial, whose *Epigrams* are fully "satiric" in our modern sense without being "satire" *per se*. As Gilbert Highet pointed out more than fifty years ago:

> Again and again, if we study the two poets together, we can see how a neat little epigram by Martial has been taken over, expanded, deepened, often cleaned up and given a moral purpose, and at last developed into one of Juvenal's most striking descriptions, sometimes into a whole satire. Thus, satire 3, with its main theme: *quid Romae faciam? mentiri nescio*, is essentially an elaboration of Martial's general complaints against the huge cruel city.[39]

Thus, as a specific cataloguing cue, Juvenal's naming Lucilius at the head of his list is only partially helpful. Perhaps even deceptive.[40] Martial's influence is much greater, and the importance of that influence to the larger history of the genre cannot be overstated. For it is precisely Martial's epigrammatic complaints against Greeklings, snobs, misers, freed slaves, whining poets, women, etc., that Juvenal makes into his signature performance. And it is this performance that poets such as Johnson will be drawn to and play upon in leveling their own "complaints against the huge, cruel city" of London.

Most English satirists of the sixteenth to eighteenth centuries were avid in their appreciation of Martial.[41] Although they knew him first as a writer of

---

[38] See Smith (1989), Hellegouarc'h (1992), and Braund (1996a) 21–4.

[39] Highet (1951) 370. Also Green (1974) 50: "Juvenal was a noticeably bookish writer . . . he must have known Martial's *Epigrams*, for instance, almost by heart, since there is scarcely one of the earlier satires but contains some echo of them." For detailed evidence of Martial's influence on Juvenal, and discussion of specific points of contact, see especially Colton (1991). A more manageable, general study of the same topic is Anderson (1970) 1–34. In addition, see Freudenburg (forthcoming) in *Rethymnon Classical Studies* vol. II.

[40] Among the more obvious differences between the two poets is Lucilius' open-handedness in providing us with autobiographical details. For Horace this was a defining feature of Lucilian satire (*S.* 2.1.32–4). Juvenal includes almost no autobiographical materials in his satires.

[41] In the sixteenth to eighteenth centuries epigram was generally regarded as "satire in brief." See Nixon (1963) 60–70; cf. Sullivan (1991) 289:

> Martial's satiric talent was his forte. This Sir John Harington and his fellows wished to refine into a contemporary serio-humorous weapon to criticize, or defend, the great . . . these epigrammatists accordingly furnished the prototypes of English satire as it would be practiced by John Oldham, John Dryden and their aristocratic coevals, and later by Alexander Pope and his successors. In this way, the literary friendship

epigrams in the tradition of Callimachus and Catullus, they were generally quite ready to accept him as one of their own; at heart, a satirist. But this raises the problem of what gets put into a Companion to satire as essential to it, and what does not. How does one judge "in" from "out" when it comes to satire's fringe players – most notably Martial, but there are many others with cases to make as well: Catullus (while we are at it), writers of iambic poetry, mime, Priapic literature, Fescennine verses, etc.? Martial gets no chapter of his own in this volume, but Petronius does. Can that possibly be right? Rather than address the question head on, I will simply suggest that this is the very problem that the satirists themselves both acknowledge and seek to address with their lists: that of satire's generic containability, and its distinction from enterprises that are generally "satiric" without being "satire" *per se* (see below). Martial chose to be known as a writer of epigrams, so I have chosen, quite artificially, to let him be that, leaving him off my list, while acknowledging that he perhaps should be there. Petronius makes this volume for reasons that are, in the end, both subjective and again suggestive of the genre's being willfully contained. Claiming him as a satirist, as Victoria Rimell points out, has always been difficult, and it has often involved titrating out an explicit moral authority from the lead character's first person narrative. Making Petronius a moralist renders him, in turn, a satirist, and the placement problem is solved. But this is to let the tail wag the dog, and it is to put strict limits on what the *Satyricon* may be satirizing. Rimell refuses to do this, and that is all for the good. Helping Petronius' cause *qua* Companion-worthy satirist in *my* book are the following: his naming his whatever it was (a novel, parodic romance, Menippean satire?) *Satyricon*, and his getting himself killed, in grand, festive style, by Nero.[42] But the more telling, hidden reason for his inclusion here is the fact that some exceedingly fine work has been done on Petronius in recent years, work worth featuring here.

Clearly mine is a personalized, politicized list. To tell *about* satire by means of such a list is not only to configure the genre of satire in a certain way (my way) and to constitute it as such, it is to assert, and tell on, myself.[43] At

---

between Martial and his younger contemporary Juvenal was reproduced in this similar relationship in English poetry between epigram and satire.

[42] See Tacitus, *Annales* 16.17–20.

[43] C. Martindale (1997) 9:

A canon is an assertion of what is valuable *for us*, and we need canons both because we cannot read everything and because we have no choice but to make value judgements about what we read. We organize the synchrony as a way of showing that our experience of the texts (which, to be sure, originated historically) is *our* experience.

the very least, my list lets you see what I have been reading and, scarily, what I have not, besides indicating what I have left out as failing to count. Moreover, as with any category-constituting list, mine is value laden by way of being hierarchically arranged, lending more emphasis to some "central" members (especially the verse satirists – but there are historical reasons for this, too) than to others.[44] And these are all key reasons why such lists tend to be fought over and vigorously, often preemptively, defended by satirists and Companion-writers alike. They let us see their compilers for who they are by way of how they draw the lines separating satire's core from its fringe, good humor from bad, sound moral criticism from spite, and so on. Laughter is generally thought to work this way, exposing the inner self by letting one's guard down. That is one reason why habits of humor are so often, and so easily, read collectively as expressions of national character, such as when Americans draw glib conclusions about the French from their continuing admiration for Jerry Lewis, or when we characterize "British humor" as its own discrete thing, fundamentally different from "American" by being more witty, self-reflexive and, at times, absurd, but at the same time, Americans are wont to insist, more repressed.[45] So the myth goes, the clear message being "be careful what you laugh at, when and where." For everyone (since Plato) is watching. And that makes naming satirists to one's preferred list an extremely tricky business, well worth watching and thinking about. Certainly I will include Fellini on my list of the modern world's real (Quintilian's "worthy") satirists. David Lodge, too, and perhaps H. L. Mencken.[46] But

[44] On membership gradience and notions of centrality within category-constituting lists, see Lakoff (1987) 12–57.

[45] Richard Wiseman, a British professor of psychology, recently concluded a year-long search for the world's funniest joke. His web-based experiment netted the further determination that there are, in fact, measurable and fairly predictable differences in national senses of humor. The results have been published by the British Association for the Advancement of Science in *Laughlab: the Scientific Search for the World's Funniest Joke* (London, 2002).

[46] For modern echoes of Juvenal in English, see Winkler (2001). Mencken's rantings about *boobus americanus* are themselves uncannily familiar to anyone conversant with Juvenal; cf. his essay "On Being an American" (*Prejudices*, third series, 1922, 12):

> here, more than anywhere else that I know of or have heard of, the daily panorama of human existence, of private and communal folly – the unending procession of governmental extortions and chicaneries, of commercial brigandages and throat-slittings, of theological buffooneries, of aesthetic ribaldries, of legal swindles and harlotries, of miscellaneous rogueries, villainies, imbecilities, grotesqueries, and extravagances – are so inordinately gross and preposterous . . . *that only the man who was born with a petrified diaphragm can fail to laugh himself to sleep every night.*

what about shock-jocks of the Howard Stern variety? How far can I go in that direction and still count with you? All the way to *Caddyshack* and *American Pie*? Conversely, how much will I tolerate in the opposite direction of the sophisticated and overly subtle? How far can I extend my list in that direction before I am written off as out of touch with real life, and a snob? This is what is at stake in producing a preferred list of what counts, and in deigning to laugh at this and not that. That list is a value-laden expression, less about what satire is than about its being willed into existence as an expression of the self, circumscribing the bounds wherein one can be reckoned a "real Roman."

Only late in the day were the big four of Roman verse satire canonized as the first and last of satire's real Romans, thereby giving rise to notions of satire's having a big picture that transcends the contentious posturings of individual satirists, their critics and their defenders, themselves.[47] This volume begins with Roman verse satire's standard canon not because that canon is beyond dispute, but because it is handy and, in a sense, what we have been left to begin with. By now it is clear that to contain Roman satire's most vital information between the covers of even a somewhat ample book is to tell a rather tall (dog-wagging) tale. But it is, at the same time, to be a decent and useful Companion, an office that sometimes finds one being strangely enthusiastic about obvious things, and overly deliberate in laying out the basics for those who have not traveled far in this direction before. None of which comes easily to scholars who know the pitfalls of generalizing too broadly about even a single poem of Roman satire, let alone about a book of poems or an author's complete works. Those who study these materials in depth know that there is a certain safety to be enjoyed in speaking narrowly, so it should come as no surprise that some of scholarship's most compelling finds lie hidden away from general view in the expert analyses of individual authors, poems, and lines of poetry. Part of the project of this volume will be to gather up some of what has been done exceptionally well here, in the specific, tucked away stuff of recent satire criticism, and make it accessible to a larger audience interested in "the field" as such. Which is to assume that such a field actually exists. My own sense is that it does not, but that certain lines of thought can be seen to run through the scholarship and, with a good bit of squinting, these lines can be shown to be heading, roughly, in the same direction (see my last three pages below).

---

[47] Porphyrio's introductory comments on Horace *Epist.* 1.3 point to the existence of a late first-century BCE anthology of Roman satire. He describes the letter's addressee, Julius Florus, as "a writer of satire, whose satires were selected from Ennius, Lucilius, Varro."

Menippean satire, Elizabethan brat-pack

This volume has been divided into three parts. The first introduces Roman satire's core practitioners and their practices, placing them within the contexts of Greco-Roman literary and political history, starting with what they wrote, when, to what end, and so on – basic questions that all readers are likely to ask. The second part looks to the question of what satire *does* within the world of Greco-Roman social exchanges, and the third part treats the genre's further development, reception, and translation in Elizabethan England (the most deliberate and sustained of Roman satire's several rediscoveries) and beyond. Besides the verse satirists named above, included in the first part are the prosimetric, "Menippean" satirists whose works, though little read today, were actively produced deep into late antiquity, and thus became the far more productive of satire's two principal branches. It is this branch, not that of verse satire, that we can trace forward from Rome (especially via Lucian) into the Renaissance and well beyond, e.g. to Rabelais, Erasmus, More, and (narrative satire's crowning jewel) Swift. Joel Relihan's essay helps us negotiate our way forward from prosimetric satire's obscure origins in Menippus and Varro, whose works have been lost, down along the genre's several divergent, sometimes re-intersecting, paths that take us first to Seneca, Petronius, and Lucian, then on to the "late arrivals" of Julian, Boethius, and others. From first to last, satires in this branch are parodic, and always, in that sense, late in arriving.[48] In her study of the habits of citation in Seneca's *Apocolocyntosis*, Ellen O'Gorman addresses the genre's failure to assert its own, unmediated authority, by preferring to self-consciously mimic the tropes of earlier genres. This she reads as more than just an admission of belatedness, but a means of establishing "the classics" as such, with citation gesturing towards authority to set off a body of materials worth quoting.

Menippean satires tend to feature know-it-all characters whose assertion of authority is hard to take seriously. At first glance this would seem to put them at odds with certain writers of formal verse satire who, in many cases, especially in Lucilius', look to be pinnacles of self-possession. But that is to credit them with too much too quickly. For the verse satirist's legendary authority is too often undone by his penchant for self-mockery and self-defeat. In the end, authorizing the satirist's words and allowing them to count as valid, incisive, and true to life is something that we do, often despite ample evidence to the contrary. And that act of authorization, as John Henderson has insisted elsewhere, and again in this volume, finds satire doing some of its most incisive work in the work it puts us to.

---

[48] On Menippean satire's strong penchant for parody, see especially Relihan (1993).

In the third and final part of this volume we face up to the fact that satire as we know it today in the West was not invented by the ancient Romans. Occasionally it has something to do with them. But discernible causal connections between modern and ancient forms and practices of satire are rare and never very easy to trace. As Duncan Kennedy points out in his contribution, they tend to be found wherever one proposes to go looking for them. For the most part Roman satire does not matter to us. It does not have to. And we are therefore justified in thinking that our satire is exactly that: entirely ours. For whereas Romans such as Quintilian treated satire as a specific set of generic enterprises totaling two in number, formal verse satire and the prosimetric or Menippean satire, we think of satire in functional terms, as something that satirizes; that is, not a specific form in itself, but an attitude or critical operation performed by a work that can inhabit a vast number of forms ranging from outraged Christian sermons (actually this is the form that can be traced most directly to the satires of ancient Rome via Jerome)[49] to comic strips, sit-coms, art exhibits, and adolescent films on the theme of losing one's virginity to a pie.

Because our satire has no one or two specific forms, we are less apt to say "this is a satire on X" than we are to say "this work satirizes X" (or if we say the former we really mean the latter). And it is the Greekness of that ending (-ize) that tells us just how far removed we are from Roman "formal" thinking about what constitutes a satire. For many an old-school etymologist has been right to insist that the English words "satire" and "satirize" have little if anything to do with one another: the first word derives from Latin *satura*, the specific term that the Romans used to name the literary form "invented" by Lucilius in the second century BCE; the second is calqued from Greek *satyrizo*, having to do with satyrs (literally "satyr-ize"), the goatish wild men of Greek myth. The same non-satiric etymology can, unbelievably, be cited for our words "satiric" and "satirist," neither of which has anything (etymologically) to do with satire, and everything to do with Dionysus' horny crew.[50] It is only late in the game, in the third and fourth centuries CE, long after Rome's last Lucilian satires had been written, that the latter terms began to be used with specific reference to the genre that the Romans, for some mysterious (food-related?) reason, named "satire."

The lines of influence connecting ancient satire to modern are tangled and flimsy. Work them too hard and they turn to dust. It is perhaps easiest and best then to admit up front that no Roman "stuffing" is baked into our *American Pie*. Which is not to say that the conceptual distance between satires past and present has always been vast, or that ancient and modern satires

---

[49] For Jerome as a satirist, see Wiesen (1964).   [50] See Hendrickson (1927) 59–60.

cannot, often powerfully, resemble one another in ways that really matter. On the contrary, in the third part of this volume we see that satire of a distinctly Roman stamp, verse satires that name Horace, Persius, and/or Juvenal (sometimes even Lucilius) as their most relevant precursors, began to be written in England in the 1560s, with an especially energetic burst of activity in the 1590s. But this aggressive, and absolutely unprecedented, resurgence of formal verse satire in imitation of Roman models should not be taken as evidence of continuity with a fixed Roman past. For while it is true that numerous medieval and early modern writers point to Juvenal, Persius, and Horace as their creative counterparts in a bygone age, it is equally true that there is little hard formal and thematic substance to be found inside these claims: Juvenal's influence was acknowledged by Chaucer and Skelton, but neither thinks of himself as Juvenalian in the same extreme way that Drant, Marston, Hall, and Nashe do.[51] But this is not to say that England's fresh crew of verse satirists and, by the 1590s, prose satirists and satiric tragedians and comic writers (e.g. Ben Jonson in his *Volpone*) agreed among themselves about what writing Roman-style satire entailed. The communities that sprang up around the public reconsumption of Roman satire were highly competitive and experimental, openly at odds not only with the current literary and moral scenes they describe, but with one another.[52] Charles Martindale points out in his essay that their habits and theoretical dispositions were never comfortably settled. Their general preferences for Juvenal in the Elizabethan and Jacobean periods and for Horace in the Augustan period are just that: general preferences. With them, Martindale shows, English satirists sought to legitimate their works by defining them against a hard and fixed Roman past that never really existed, in handy "translations" of Horace and Juvenal that are always more Horatian than Horace, more Juvenalian than Juvenal.

Colin Burrow points out that the resurgence of Roman satire in Elizabethan England happened not because it was inevitable (as if from telltale medieval rumblings), but because the Elizabethan satirists undertook to make it happen. Their reconnecting with Rome has something to do with the massive expansion of London in the later sixteenth century that allowed them to feel that they now knew exactly what Juvenal (usually Juvenal, but sometimes Horace) was talking about. Their published works develop and stretch to the breaking point the metaphor of (new) London as (old) Rome. Once the lid is taken off of this idea, there is no limit to the number of urban

---

[51] For satiric theory in the middle ages, see Minnis and Scott (1988) 116–19, 136–7. For medieval redeployments of Roman satire, see Highet (1967) 99–101, 305–10.

[52] For the highly competitive and experimental nature of this movement, see Corthell (1983).

and courtly experiences that can be curiously reconceived by being passed through a much older generic filter. This is what satire consistently "does" over the course of its several stops and starts in sixteenth- to eighteenth-century England. Its writers are not terribly interested in competing with the Romans in order to prove that they are good satirists themselves and that they have read their Latin both correctly and insightfully (straightforward *æmulatio*). These demonstrations, while socially valuable, are side effects of imitation rather than its end. Instead, they imitate the Roman satirists in order to reconfigure their present, putting it curiously, often disturbingly, by reference to an imagined past (allusion as metaphor). The tensions that exist between these two basic reference points become ever more complicated as the genre expands and develops into its own multi-referential field, so that by the time Rochester dons the mask of Horace criticizing Lucilius he can deploy that memory to have us think not only of Horace, but of Dryden's Horatian attack against Jonson, and Jonson's playing Horace to Shakespeare's Lucilius. As Daniel Hooley demonstrates, such multi-layered tensions between the present and a growing plethora of Roman pasts (Horace's, Jonson's, Dryden's) produce a fantastic range of meaningful effects, from promiscuity and emotional distance, to nastiness and sheer contempt. Understood this way, their deliberate imitation of the Romans does not impose strict limits on what the English satirists can say or do in their satires. Far from it. It gives them a limitless means for "configuring" their worlds (here with heavy emphasis on Latin *figura* "metaphor"). The end result, while incessantly "in reference to" Rome, is anything but "Roman." It is English satire *par excellence*. Always entirely "theirs."

Perhaps the genre's greatest theorist of the last century, Mikhail Bakhtin, promoted the idea that satire is somehow rooted in the local soils of medieval ritual.[53] In that sense, just like Quintilian centuries before, he found in satire something that he could appreciate as "totally ours." That is to say something home grown and real, and worth embracing as one's own. But, inevitably, to find what is uniquely one's own is, at the same time, to find oneself. Satire criticism, we have seen, has always been tightly wound with questions of identity, and thus it has tended towards the production of extreme pronouncements about what is "ours" versus what is "theirs." This happens still. Generally we see no need to trace our own satiric practices back to Elizabethan England, let alone to ancient Rome. And that is largely the truth of the matter. And yet, in making these claims, we should take a moment to appreciate the irony that inheres in our making them: by claiming to have invented our own forms and practices of satire, and to find ourselves in

[53] See Bakhtin (1984).

them, independent of the larger traditions to which satire belongs, we end up repeating claims that have been made for many centuries, even by the Romans themselves.

Naming satire "one's own": the recent social life of Roman satiric theory

The satire section of the Roman library was never out front, in a place well lit and heavily trafficked. For in its many guises, satire has never rated among the most companionable of public performances. The social cohesion it effects, when satirists opt to play rather than attack, tends to be momentary and easily fractured. For satirists always threaten, in an instant, to turn nasty and vindictive. Like uncouth dinner guests, mismatched to the rules of polite society, those who perform in this mode have a habit of overstaying their welcome. As Horace once observed, they drink too much, say too much, and eventually have to be shown the door.

Some rescue work and good humanitarian effort is always involved in introducing this mode of performance into polite society. The history of much scholarship on satire, whether ancient, early modern, or that of our own day, reads like a strained effort to land one's loutish, but fun-loving, brother-in-law a decent job. The man has had his reckless moments, we admit. The embarrassments he has caused are legendary, so there is no point in trying to hide them. And yet, we insist, this genre deserves a place, albeit a fairly low place, in the family of respectable performative enterprises. With a bath and a shave, and a sworn, twelve-step (programmatic) commitment to clean living, satire's level of respectability rises considerably, to roughly that of its moderately successful cousins, comedy, social commentary, and Platonic dialogue, but never to the ethereal heights of the family's decorated heroes of war, tragedy and epic.

Satire's social indiscretions are legion. They include a penchant for revealing secrets and telling tall tales. When in his cups, the satirist uses foul language, and his descriptions turn leering and pornographic. He exaggerates, goes on too long, and all the while he claims to have memorized vast reams of philosophy and technical lore at university. But when he trots it out for our bedazzlement he fails to impress us, jumbling the details and, too obviously, missing the point.

But there are even bigger challenges that this genre tosses in the way of its own companionability. Perhaps most notable of these is its strong penchant for passing judgment, and for conveying that judgment in fuming, hyperbolic tones – with raw sexual desire as its gutter-mate, anger ranks as the least sociable of human emotions; and it is precisely this emotion that is most commonly associated with satire.[54] And while it is true that satire's judgments are often put to us in friendlier packages, through innuendo, irony, and jest, its negative assessments are never far from the surface. Even when he swears, this time, to behave himself, this guest always threatens to ruin the party because, at some level, whether playfully or no, he is always intent on passing judgment against persons, literature, politics, religion, and so on.

There is much presumption in this, and much to be wary of. Here we have a guest/genre that thinks we all need to hear what he has to say about all he thinks is wrong with the world. And that act of judgment, always just that, an act, puts us in the role of the uncomfortably cornered victims of the satirist's bullying, or of our own compliance, or of our willingness to be played with and seduced. However we have come to this point, we have been handed a role to play, haled into the performance as players whose social sensibilities, religious and political convictions, and so on, are now squarely under the microscope. Like it or not, it is now our turn to respond. Our judgment is required. Sometimes we find ourselves in perfect agreement with everything that the satirist says, so we are free to weigh in with a heart-felt laugh. And yet, often, we find it difficult to second the satirist in his every (vengeful, leering, xenophobic, ironically smug) judgment. Even when we happen to agree with the gist of what he says, we commonly object to the way he says it. Perhaps we are put off by his sneering demeanor, his cartoonifying of complex issues, or his failure to keep his anger in check. Or sometimes he offends in the opposite manner, by not speaking critically enough, in words that are up to our high standards of being suitably bold and direct. These are just a few of satire's more commonly cited offenses.

A good deal of satiric theory, both ancient and modern, aims towards excusing satire of some or all of its indiscretions. Perhaps most famously, John Dryden, in his 1693 treatise "On the Original and Progress of Satire" set the course of satire criticism for the better part of three centuries by describing satire as a fallen enterprise that could be redeemed, to some extent, by moral purpose and art. When done right, Dryden insists, satire is a thing

---

[54] Kernan (1965) 16: "Satire always contains either an implicit or explicit set of values, which frequently takes specific form in judgments on such matters as what kind of food to eat, how to manage your wife and your household . . . and what kind of books to read, how to conduct political life." For anger, aggression, and judgment in satire, see Test (1991) 15–19, 27–36.

of fairly high character and purpose, in that it serves to identify and chastise society's wrongs. But in its "original" state, he says, satire is vindictive and unsavory and, as such, not satire at all. Not yet. For when Adam and Eve hurl their accusations at one another in the garden, each blaming the other for plucking the forbidden fruit, they are indulging in an urge that arises from man's fallen nature: the urge to berate and vindicate oneself in front of others. As such, this is an urge that does not lend itself to being perfected, only made the best of. In a perfect world satire does not redeem itself, it simply ceases to exist. However brilliantly crafted its form, and however heavily loaded it may be with moral purpose, its existence remains regrettable.

Satirists tell us, among other things, that humans need their diversions, and that satire, for whatever good it does not do, does precious little harm. Telling the truth with a laugh, they sometimes add, can actually do a world of good, however much it may hurt the bad characters who have it told to them and about them. Other excuses are added to reassure us that we are in good company when laughing along. Until well into the 1950s it was the standard practice of scholars of the genre to measure the satirists' practices against their programmatic apologies, their own and those of certain preferred others, as a means of assessing the satirist's respectability and worth. The emphasis was squarely on the author as a moral agent whose dirty work on the page needed explaining because it identified him as a moral character of a certain sort. Accessing and judging that moral character was the critic's task, with each new critic down the road excusing his preferred satirist(s) by means of a preferred set of programmatic values and excuses.

A different approach to satiric crudeness, and what we are to do with it, came with the publication of R. C. Elliott's *The Power of Satire* in 1960. Elliott traced the history of satire, in its developed literary form, back to proto-satiric activities practiced by cultures in remote parts of the world, as well as by figures of legend and distant history in the European West. His tools were collected reams of folklore and anthropologists' accounts of quasi-satiric practices observed in tribal cultures from Wisconsin to New Guinea and the Arctic Circle. The farther off the better. The result was a continuous, wide-ranging, comparative history of satire traced to its origins in magical rites the world around. By this reading, satire became a much bigger phenomenon than it had ever been before. Elliott's work had all the advantages that accrue to "science" that one is hard put to concede to the study of literature.

The Power of Satire remains a remarkable book, both for its findings and for the high place it holds in the history of satire's socialization. Other works of roughly the same period, especially Northrop Frye's *Anatomy of*

Criticism (1957) and Mikhail Bakhtin's *Rabelais and His World* (1968 in English) worked, in vastly different ways, to much the same effect.[55] Both made powerful arguments for moving satire to the center of literary study from the fringes by positing it, in Frye's case, as one of the four archetypal genre myths by which humans organize and understand their existence. More lasting and influential have been the theories of Bakhtin, who argued for a pre-history of satire in the medieval carnival. Satire, read Bakhtin's way, functions as an explosive force routinely applied to a culture's big, regulatory myths, something to stretch those myths, loosen their restraints, and make life livable. With these works especially leading the way, the study of satire moved decisively away from its fixation on the satirist as a moral agent, discrete and self-determined, to the role he played within a larger set of encoded social practices that both defined and regulated the culture to which he belonged. The satirist's work could now be said to help keep that culture vibrant, pleasing to the gods, disease free, and so on. And what better apology for one's existence could one want than that?

The gap Elliott opened between the satirist as a discrete, historical, moral agent and his "role" as society's lampooner was quickly picked up on and put to work by literary scholars who saw a tremendous advantage in particularizing satirists in this way. In effect, this helped solve, not once and for all, but in a different way, the problem of what one was to do with satire's crudeness. For no longer were scholars bound to focus narrowly on stated moral aims and practices as their best means of assessment, the method that left them to leave us with so many carefully argued hierarchies of greater and lesser satirists, all based on a time-bound and personalized, and often highly politicized, sense of what "worthiness" in satire entails. This could now be gotten around by separating the writer as historical fact from his satiric spokesman, or persona, on the page. Elliott argued that "the greatest satirists . . . recognize their own involvement in the folly of human life and willingly see themselves as victims, in obscure ways, of their own art."[56] And this opened the door for scholars such as Alvin Kernan to make way for the satirists' self-victimization. The critic could now let the satirists make fools of themselves openly, without referring us to the standard set of apologies for the toes they stepped on, or reminding us of the things that they would have us keep in mind. Moreover, the critics could work out the genre's larger form – something that really had not been done before – taking the satirist's

---

[55] Bakhtin's theory of carnival, though developed in the 1920s and 1930s, had little influence on studies of satire in English until the appearance of the first complete English translation of *Rabelais and His World* (one of his latest works) in 1968.

[56] Elliott (1960) 222.

persona as one element in that form.[57] There was now much new work to be done. Just five years after the appearance of Elliott's *Power of Satire*, Alvin Kernan, in his *Plot of Satire*, takes satire's buffoonery, and all its attendant indiscretions, not as an indictment of the practitioner's person, or as some sign of mental instability or physical distress, but as a performance put on, expertly, to achieve a certain effect.

Classicists were not slow to pick up on these findings. In fact, in his doctoral dissertation of 1954, and in two seminal articles on Juvenal of 1956 and 1957, William S. Anderson can be credited with anticipating Alvin Kernan, and informing his argument, on certain key points.[58] It was Anderson, above all, who put the case for Juvenal's not necessarily "being" an overblown xenophobe, but of his playing one to good effect. Juvenal could therefore be embraced without embarrassment as an artist and master of his craft. Similarly Horace's delivery of two vastly different sets of poems in books 1 and 2 of his *Sermones* could be explained as a deliberate change of roles rather than a crisis of confidence. And so on. Work of this kind has continued to the present day, most recently in Susanna Braund's *The Roman Satirists and their Masks* (1996a), and it still manages to provide useful insights into the trappings and operational cues of satire's many actors and their acts.

But this kind of study, by now, has perhaps gone on too long. Or, to put this more positively, the time is now ripe for it to be pushed farther and made to pay bigger dividends. For such studies in the field of classics especially, useful as they are, have tended to blunt satire's political edge by focusing on how certain effects are mechanically produced rather than on how they might have played in the highly tendentious political worlds wherein they

---

[57] Kernan (1959) 6–7:

> What is required is a more comprehensive method describing satire which will not limit our investigations to linguistic analysis or the location of single effects but will instead include all the major elements of composition used in the form . . . satire is, like comedy and tragedy, a very ancient form which appears to have its roots in primitive ritual activities such as formulaic curses and the magical blasting of personal and tribal enemies.

Although these observations pre-date the appearance of Elliott's *Power of Satire* by one year, Kernan authorizes them by referencing Elliott's article of 1954 ("The Satirist and Society," in his notes on p. 7).

[58] Especially on the matter of satire's "rhetorical" emplotment. See Kernan (1965) 98, n. 2. Both Anderson and Kernan wrote their respective doctoral dissertations at Yale in the mid-1950s. Both acknowledge the fundamental influence of two Yale professors of English, Maynard Mack ("The Muse of Satire," *Yale Review* 1951) and Martin Price (*Swift's Rhetorical Art*, Yale University Press, 1953). It cannot be overstated just how radical these ideas were in their day.

were produced. This is the downside of analysis fixated on form. It does no good to insist that Juvenal, or Swift, or whoever is "just" a persona if by that one means to imply that he had any chance of being anything else, or that his performance is just so much cleverly crafted entertainment devoid of political meanings and offenses.[59] The problem here is that the idea of writing as performance has to be taken the whole way, not just to the point of the author's person, the "scene" of satire and its "plot," but as far as the reader's/critic's/audience's own role in the production of the script. For, as mentioned above, the satiric act on the page floats a set of judgments that oblige us to commit ourselves as judges, critics, and fellow performers. Satire's "enactment" happens there, at the point of reception, always there, and not before.

Keeping this clearly in mind, we should recognize that persona theory has its further, hidden uses in the acts we put on as we reconsume Roman satire and "produce" it even today, one of which, perhaps the most important of all, is that of excusing satirists from their indiscretions and thereby making them into our good companions. By leaving our own critical operations unaccounted for, persona theory becomes just a different means towards the same old end, i.e. as the mechanism whereby scholars study rhetorical maneuverings to allow certain authors to win possession of the category "satire" and perhaps others not. But the side effect (or, I might suggest, the end result) of this act of authorization is the critic's own authorization as scholar and judge (the possession of *that* hotly coveted category). This is the critical work that satire always sets us up to perform. It is what I am doing as I write these words – in fact, I would not dare suggest that the same old thing can be gotten away from. At best, it can be recognized for what it is.

Classicists generally do not read satire this way, though John Henderson does, and has done so since the early 1990s.[60] He, more than anyone else working in the field, has taken the lead in insisting that the point of critical closure is where things really open up. That is why he gets the last say in this book, his turnabout being fair play. Other recent trends in the study of satire are harder to sloganize, but the works of several scholars, many

---

[59] Cf. Green (1998) xxviii:

> If Highet tried to discount the persona, too many contemporary critics have done their level best to eliminate the author . . . what concerns me is the effect on Juvenal, which has been to turn the *Satires* into a series of contrived, semi-dramatic performances, structurally exotic and wholly removed from real life, performed by a literary quick-change artist with a bundle of formal masks behind which to hide.

[60] The articles on satire now constitute part III of Henderson (1999) 173–273. For an easy introduction to Henderson on satire, see the two-page preface of Henderson (1997).

of whom are represented in this volume, hover around the idea that satire is culturally laden stuff, and only meaningful as such. The emphasis in this kind of analysis is on what writing does, not what it says, and especially not (just) what it says it does. To put the idea differently, satiric writing, on the surface, looks like a thing apart from the culture that proposes to look at culture and comment critically upon it. The writing's non-materiality seduces us into thinking of it this way, but that is to ignore the complex ways in which satiric writing is active inside the dialogue of values it proposes to judge. Satire's scripted judgments and complaints, like an article of clothing, a coffee-table, or a garden, possess powers to impress or offend that go well beyond stated aims and obvious functions. To use the Roman satirists' own favorite material metaphor, satire resembles a dish of food cooked up for a feast. And every Roman knows that food is not just something you eat to stay alive. Not in Rome. There it is the stuff of outlandish showmanship, a prop that helps one pose as a certain kind of moral agent by being brilliantly concocted and arranged and publicly consumed to gratify, seduce, and move ahead in the world. How odd that we should ever think of it as mere food. At one level Roman cooking would seem to be about nourishment, and satire about its stated moral aims. But these are fronts, and every "real Roman," both then and now, theirs and mine, knows it. Satirists use the metaphor of food to make a metatheatrical point. With it they expose a gap between what they say is true and our ability to validate it as the simple truth. This is where I see much of the work of this volume coming together. Not that we all agree among ourselves on most or every point. But we all concede that satire's act plays much bigger than its script.

I

SATIRE AS LITERATURE

I

FRANCES MUECKE

Rome's first "satirists": themes and genre in Ennius and Lucilius

Among the many intriguing aspects of Roman verse satire is the fact that it was such an early creation. Only a generation before, Latin literature had begun with the deliberate translation and adaptation not just of Greek genres, but of individual works, such as Homer's *Odyssey*. Paradoxically to modern perceptions, throughout the history of Latin literature acknowledgment of Greek predecessors was to remain a sign of high poetic ambition. Roman satire, on the other hand, although not totally without precedent in Greek literature, was destined to be the only kind of Latin poetry which had a Latin name and did not openly claim a Greek model.

Owing to the loss of most early Roman literature we simply do not have enough surviving evidence to trace the formation of Roman satire with exactness. To modern literary historians Quintus Ennius (239–169 BCE) represents the first phase in the development of the genre. For the Romans, however, it was created anew by Gaius Lucilius (*floruit* 130–103 BCE). It was the latter, not Ennius, who became the generic exemplar for Roman verse satire (Horace, *Sermones* 1.10.46–9, 64–7; Quintilian, *Institutes* 10.1.95 does not mention Ennius). In fact, it was perhaps not clear until after Lucilius had made *satura* a vehicle of mockery and invective that a new genre had been created.

Poetic genres in antiquity were defined by a characteristic subject matter and the type of verse meter they used. Each genre had its place in a relative hierarchy from high to low, and implied by the hierarchy were certain distinctions of tone (e.g. serious vs. comic) and stylistic register (grand vs. everyday). Such was the scheme set out, for example, in Horace's *Ars Poetica* 73–88. The reality of the poetry itself was infinitely more complex as each poet strove to create something new, within and against the limits of the genre as they were embodied in the work of his predecessors.

In the period before Ennius wrote his *Saturae*, the Hellenistic poets of the Greek cultural diaspora of the third and second centuries BCE had begun to exhibit a new attitude to generic convention. Inversions of the hierarchy, deviations of focus, new combinations of subject matter and meter, and crossing of borderlines were the order of the day. Experimental combinations sometimes "took" and new genres, such as the bucolic, came into being.

Given this background, and as an almost inevitable function of its secondariness, Roman literature from the beginning was generically self-conscious.[1] Roman satire, then, was not alone in making itself one of its important themes, but it does stand out as an inherently controversial genre. It is controversial in two respects: its literary status and its offensiveness. On the one hand it is a poetic kind that is regarded as so low as almost to verge on the prosaic. Lucilius speaks of his works as *ludus ac sermones* – "trifling and chats" (fr. 1039W) and, in a metaphor suggesting the rough and ready, *schedium* – "something thrown together," "an improvisation" (fr. 1131W, cf. Petronius, *Satyricon* 4.6, Apuleius, *De deo Socratis* 1, Horace, *Sermones* 1.4.47 *sermo merus*, "pure talk"). On the other hand, its free speaking of "the truth" about its victims is seen as likely to cause offense.

Therefore in our survey of the earliest Roman satirists we must follow two lines: textual features and polemical tone. Roman satire came into being through the combination of the negative critical element (satire as a supra-generic mode) with a kind of writing determined only by a very loose set of formal and thematic characteristics, a hybridization of genres, essentially a mixture of serious and comic, high and low. And, it must be added, in practice Roman satire was not always or necessarily "satiric" in tone, although its characteristic flavor was Roman.

In what follows we will attempt to situate early Roman satire within the system of genres already existing in Greek literature, and within the development of early Latin literature. This essay focuses on the internal dynamics of literary history. Considering the way in which early Roman satire was embedded in its historical context is beyond its scope.

Satire as a mode is to be found in a range of Greek literary genres. There are two Greek verbs which may be translated as "to satirize": *iambizein* and *komoidein*. The first, associated with abuse, invective, and lampoon, that is, personal attack, not primarily intended to amuse, belonged to iambic, a word which denotes a genre and a meter of the same name. (Iambic meter had wider uses, being also employed for the dialogue of tragedy and comedy.) The verb *komoidein* initially was coined for a specific aspect of the genre of comedy. From the noun *komoidia* ("revel-song") was created the verb "to ridicule" (Aristophanes "ridiculed the city," *Acharneis* 631). Then the verb was extended from the ridiculing practiced in comedy to ridicule and

---

[1] Fraenkel (1957) 124.

joking in other circumstances.[2] The shift of meaning from "revel-song" to "ridicule" is analogous to that undergone by the Latin noun *satura*.

Greek iambic and comedy, then, as genres, provided parallel cases when Roman satirists and theorists wished to account for their own genre and for the presence in it, or in Lucilius, its founding exemplar, of scathing attack. For instance, Diomedes (*GLK* 1.485.11–17) and Apuleius (*Apologia* 10) describe Lucilius as a writer of "iambic" because of his employment of abuse. In the bookcase of the Augustan satirist Horace were the works of Eupolis, a leading writer of Old Comedy, and Archilochus, the seventh-century BCE inventor of iambic (*Sermones* 2.3.12). In his first book Horace asserted the dependence of Lucilius on Old Comedy (*Sermones* 1.4.1–6): the Roman poet showed the same freedom of speech as the writers of Old Comedy in attacking those conspicuous for their crimes.

At this point we should draw some general distinctions. "Savage" iambic was primarily believed to be motivated by a desire for personal revenge, while comic satire was funny as well as political. Iambic, as personal poetry, was closer in form to Roman satire, while Old Comedy, totally distinct in generic form, provided a model for critical engagement with society as a whole; Lucilius, in Horace's words, "scoured *the city* with plenty of salty wit" (*Sermones* 1.10.3–4, cf. Persius 1.114). Fragment 1145–51W, cited below, which depicts "people and senators alike" indiscriminately as shady characters, well illustrates Lucilius' freedom from inhibition. Therefore, neither Greek iambic nor Old Comedy sufficiently furnishes the "determinative repertoire"[3] of Roman satire, since the linking of the satiric impulse with a new set of textual elements must be attributed to Lucilius, the "inventor" of the genre (Horace, *Sermones* 1.10.48).

Compared with the original extent of their works the earliest satirists' remains are few and fragmentary. Of Ennius' satires (that is, a collection conventionally called *Saturae* – an individual book may originally have been a single *satura*, "mélange," "medley") we have only isolated lines (thirty-one in *ROL*). The collection was extensive enough to be divided at a late stage into four (or six?) books.[4] The differences between lines cited from individual books (e.g. book 3) are such as to show that a book contained separate poems in differing meters. This metrical variety was what distinguished Ennius' satire in antiquity (Diomedes *GLK* 1.485.33–4): "Formerly *satura* was the name for the kind of poetry which consisted of a variety of poems, such as Ennius and Pacuvius wrote." The poems were probably written in the later part of Ennius' career, and collected by him, if the title *Satura(e)* is his own.

---

[2] Silk (2000) 63–4.   [3] Silk (2000) 67.
[4] Waszink (1972) 102, 105, Courtney (1993) 7–8, 12.

Ennius, in origin a Messapian from the Sallentine peninsula in the heel of Italy, was brought to Rome in his mid-thirties after serving in the Roman army. Settling in Rome, he acquired Roman citizenship and earned his living as a teacher. As a professional writer, he both modernized and expanded the range of literature in Latin. He composed in all the public genres already imported from Greece into Rome – tragedy, epic, and, less importantly, comedy. The satires, for us perhaps his most original and interesting creation, belong to another sphere of his activity, and are classed among the more experimental "minor works," most of which were closely related to, or based on, Greek writings of the fourth or third centuries. For example, in the *Sota* he adopted the Ionic meter of the Hellenistic poet Sotades (first half of the third century BCE). In the satires, with his use of iambic meters (among others), variety of subject matter, personal expression, "autobiography," incorporation of elements of popular poetry such as fables in a more sophisticated environment, Ennius wrote in the spirit of that Hellenistic poetry which had begun to unravel the traditional generic links between meter, tone, and subject matter.

Iambic meter, which had always had a greater range than its characterization as "abusive" suggests, especially lent itself to such generic experimentation. It became the meter for monologue and dialogue in Attic drama. It also had a long history in personal poetry, where it was used not only for satirical abuse (Archilochus, Semonides) but also for amusing narrations and more serious reflections. Solon (*floruit* 600 BCE) transformed it into a vehicle for vivid personal expression and political justification. As examples of Hellenistic extension of the iambic (both from the mid-third century BCE) we can cite Machon's anecdotes about notorious Athenian parasites and courtesans in iambic trimeters and Herodas' *Mimiamboi*, comic sketches of low-life urban characters. Both of these exhibit comic–iambic combinations but are formally much more homogeneous than the earliest Roman satire. So are Cercidas' slightly later *Meliamboi*, which combined lyric form with satirical, iambic content. Callimachus' *Iambi*, which in theme range beyond the iambic narrowly defined, highlighting the poet's individuality, can be mentioned as a parallel, if not a direct model, for Ennius' satires.[5] Ennius himself does not appear to have acknowledged a close dependence on Callimachus' *Iambi*, or any iambic predecessor.

The variety of Ennius' subject matter and meters distinguishes his *Saturae* from these Hellenistic iambic experiments (his polymetric collections are perhaps more like those of Archilochus or Solon), yet the satires are to be situated in the same category of the realistic and low – which, in ancient terms,

---

[5] Waszink (1972) 124–6, Gratwick (1982) 160.

usually means colloquial and even obscene language (apparently avoided by Ennius himself), an urban setting, a concentration on characters and affinity with comedy. Indeed, the meters of Ennius' satires – iambic senarii, dactylic hexameters, trochaic septenarii, sotadeans, trochaic tetrameters – were for the most part dramatic meters or also used in drama.

The Roman comedy contemporary with Ennius was *fabula palliata* (Latinized New Comedy) dominated by the verbal brilliance of the prolific Plautus. As a practitioner of tragedy Ennius must have been close to the comic stage and its language. A large proportion of the satiric fragments suggest comedy, in style or situation.[6] Stage language and meter predominate in the fragments, which have a strong dialogic feel. The portrait of a parasite (fr. 14–19W), for example, may be put in the mouth of the fellow himself. Coffey remarks that "It is sometimes impossible to tell the difference between the description of a situation from real life and the retailing of a speech or scene from comedy":[7] this is because low genres such as satire tended to stylize "real life" as comedy. Throughout the history of Roman satire, comedy and the even less respectable mime were to remain sources of both low realism and fictional displacement.[8]

Other comic–satiric types appear in snatches of dialogue – the glutton (fr. 1W) and the slanderer (fr. 8–9W). A fragment in the style of a comic list of verbs in asyndeton (cf. Lucilius, fr. 296–7W) *restitant occurrunt obstant obstringillant obagitant* ("they stand stock still, come against one, get in the way, impede, harass") (fr. 5W) has a close parallel in Plautus (*Curculio* 291) *obstant obsistunt incedunt . . .* ("they get in the way, block the street, move along . . ."). In the play the parasite enters at a run describing how the street is blocked by groups of Greek philosophers conversing among themselves, laden with books and baskets. Ennius' "busybodies," "meddlesome people drawn straight from the Roman forum"[9] may anticipate the crowded street scene so emblematic of satire (see Horace pushing his way through the crowd at *Sermones* 2.6.27–31; Juvenal 1 and 3). The repetitive word play on the subject of the deceiver deceived (fr. 28–31W) is a stylistic device shared with Roman comedy.

Apart from comedy, the best-represented sphere is that of popular moral teaching. Animal fable, of course, was prominent in Greek iambic (Archilochus, frs. 172–81 and 185–7West, Callimachus, *Iambi* 2) and was later to become a characteristic subject matter of Roman satire (see the fable of the ant in Lucilius [fr. 586–7W] and Horace [*Sermones* 1.1.32–5], that

---

[6] Waszink (1972) 110, 130–3. [7] Coffey (1976) 29.

[8] See Freudenburg (1993) 27–51 for what Horace makes of the legacy of popular comedy.

[9] Van Rooy (1966) 41; cf. Coffey (1976) 29.

of the fox and the sick lion in Lucilius [fr. 1111–20W] and Horace [*Epistles* 1.1.73–5], and, in Horace, the calf and the frog [*Sermones* 2.3.314–20], and the town and country mouse [*Sermones* 2.6.79–117]). In Ennius as well as the fable of the crested lark (*ROL* 389) and the piper and the fish (fr. 20W, cf. Herodotus 1.141), there is the debate between the personified abstracts Life and Death (Quintilian, *Institutes* 9.2.36, *ROL* 395), also with folk-tale origins. Likewise typical of popular moral teaching are the exhortation (fr. 2W), the proverb (fr. 27W), and the animal comparison (fr. 23W) – with etymological word play.

Of great interest for determining Ennius' stance, if it could only be pinned down, is another line using animal imagery: *non est meum ac si me canis memorderit* ("it is not my wont as if a dog has bitten me") (fr. 22W). If the fragment suggests that Ennius does not "bite back" even when attacked, it could be situated in the metaphorical complex of the dog as an image of the iambist or satirist (cf. Horace, *Epodes* 6, *S.* 2.1.84–5, Persius 1.108–10 (?)) or the purveyor of cynic abuse (Horace, *Epistles* 1.17.18).[10] The contrast with Lucilius (fr. 1000–1W) where the speaker identifies with an angry dog ("from there let me fly at him with a dog's grin and eyes") would be telling, if this indeed gives us Lucilius' own attitude.[11]

That Ennius himself was a frequent subject of his satires will be suggested below from external evidence. From the extant fragments again we have his quip in an unplaced line *numquam poetor nisi [si] podager* ("I never poetize except when I'm gouty")[12] (fr. 21W). When Horace remembered this he associated it with Ennius' epic poem (*Epistles* 1.19.7 "Father Ennius himself never sprang to the singing of arms except when drunk"). More serious are the fine lines:

> Enni poeta salue, qui mortalibus
> uersus propinas flammeos medullitus
> (fr. 6–7W)

Hail, poet Ennius, you who from your innermost being pledge fiery verses to mankind.

This fragment from book 3 in which Ennius is addressed by name as "poet" (the term *poeta* is that borrowed from Greek, and is absent from the extant Lucilius) expresses pride in his own achievement, as the reincarnation of Homer (ὁ ποιητής) and the author of the *Annales*. Here he borrows from its

---

[10] Anderson (1958) 195–7; cf. Muecke (1985) 113–33.   [11] Gratwick (1982) 159.

[12] Gout, a painful ailment of the extremities, is associated with good living (cf. Aristophanes, *Plutus* 559–61).

symposiastic setting the metaphor of the "cup of poetry" (Dionysius Chalcus fr. 1 Diehl). Some other associations may point to the frank and free expression of satiric verse (cf. Lucilius fr. 670–1W, *ego ubi quem ex praecordiis | ecfero uersum* ["when I bring forth any verse from the depth of my heart"], Horace, *Sermones* 1.4.88–9).[13]

The hexameter fragments are different again (frs. 3–4W and 10–11W). If he is parodying his own *Annales* Ennius may have already introduced into satire this very characteristic satirical technique.[14] That Ennius' meters in the satires included the dactylic hexameter is noteworthy, as this, the meter of Greek epic and didactic poetry, was to become Roman satire's canonical meter. It was introduced to Rome by Ennius himself, as the proper meter for heroic epic (*Annales*) and, less grandly, for the *Hedyphagetica* ("Delicatessen") (Ennius' translation of Archestratus' *Hedypatheia*), a didactic gastronomic tour of the Mediterranean. Occasionally in this poem Ennius introduces epicisms that make piquant clashes with the subject matter. But arguing that Ennius' adaptation should not be thought of simply as epic parody, Skutsch concludes "to him the mundane and everyday subject matter may well have suggested a metrical as well as a linguistic style close to comedy."[15]

When we consider why Lucilius eventually chose the hexameter as the standard meter of his satires, the precedent of such "low epic" as the *Hedyphagetica* may not be the only influential factor. Ennius included in his historical epic the *Annales* un-Homeric themes which Virgil was to exclude from the surface of his epic – autobiography, literary polemic, grammatical erudition, philosophical speculation – but which, on the other hand, were major themes in Lucilius' hexametric satire.[16] As an example of such "satirical" material in the *Annales*, which at least shows Ennius' strong didactic and moral interest, and at most might be a disguised self-portrait, we can cite the digression which describes the relationship of a great man with his trusted, and more lowly, companion (Ennius, *Annales* fr. 268–86 Sk.):[17]

> Saying this he summoned him with whom he pretty often shared his table and his talk and his consideration of his own private affairs, as he liked, when he was tired after devoting a great part of the day to settling matters of the highest concern in the forum and the holy senate; to whom with confidence he might speak of great and small matters, and jokes, and pour out to him if he wished things good and bad to say and put them in a safe place . . .   (268–75)

---

[13] Jocelyn (1977) 131–51, Waszink (1972) 113–19.
[14] Jocelyn (1972) 1026.   [15] Skutsch (1985) 4.   [16] Mariotti (1963) 108–16.
[17] Mariotti (1963) 127–30, Van Rooy (1966) 40–1, Badian (1972) 181, 206.

Such friendships between unequals, important as they were in Roman society, became a theme in Roman satire (with an increasing emphasis on inequality), from the easy intimacy of Lucilius and Scipio Aemilianus (when Scipio and Laelius "had withdrawn from the crowd, leaving the public stage for a private place, they used to fool around with him [Lucilius] and play in casual clothes while waiting for the vegetables to cook," Horace, *Sermones* 2.1.73–4) through Horace's less comfortable position as Maecenas' companion (*Sermones* 1.3.63–6, 2.6.40–6) to the perversions of the relationship in Juvenal 5 and 9.

Ennius' satires also present their author as an individual – another urban character. The frequency of first and second persons suggests that Ennius staged scenes or encounters involving himself or other characters. From other sources it can be conjectured that in the satires Ennius told humorous anecdotes of his own life. For example, Cicero refers to Ennius' account of a walk with his neighbor Servius Sulpicius Galba (Cicero, *Academica* 2.51), and recounts the witty *beffa* turned against Ennius by his friend Nasica after he had heard Ennius instructing the maid to say he was not at home: when Ennius objected to being turned away later by Nasica himself, Nasica said "I believed your maid when she said you weren't at home. Won't you believe me in person?" (Cicero, *De oratore* 2.276).[18]

In a small compass many continuities with the multifarious variety of later satire have been detected. Of these the most important thematically are the comic, moral, and autobiographical elements. As to form, the strong presence of dialogue hints at the aspect later highlighted by the designation *sermo*, "conversation," "chat." At the same time it should be stressed that Ennius' satiric fragments, in tone and content, have much in common with his other minor works. This observation confirms the absence not so much of moralizing as of that note of self-assertion and that element of criticism of individuals which, in later eyes, was the distinguishing characteristic of Lucilius.[19]

If with Ennius we were more concerned with what *satura* was made from, with Lucilius we gain a somewhat better idea of what was made. Nonetheless, we still have no whole poems, and minimal context to make sense of Lucilius' vivid and lively detail, the heart of his enterprise. Fragments of 1300 lines or part-lines remain of thirty books. The longest fragment is 1196–1208W, the famous definition of virtue.[20] Three collections are represented: books 26–30 are the earliest (131–ca. 129 BCE), and books 1–21 cover the rest of Lucilius' career. Standing apart from, but transmitted with, the main *œuvre*

---

[18] See Skutsch (1990) 25–7, Leeman, Pinkster, and Rabbie (1989) 312–13.
[19] Waszink (1972) 111–12. [20] See Mayer p. 152 below.

are books 22–5, consisting of epitaphs and perhaps other occasional poems in elegiac meter.

In the beginning Lucilius, following Ennius, used dramatic meters. The first two books were in trochaic septenarii, the next two contained satires in trochaic septenarii, iambic senarii and hexameters respectively. The hexameter may have been used in book 28 for the sake of epic parody (cf. frs. 845W and 848W). The subject of the satire is obscure. In book 29 the hexameter was appropriate for a didactic treatment of the topic of choosing a woman (cf. fr. 910–11W). Finally in book 30 Lucilius settled on this meter exclusively, and made it the sole meter of his second collection. The decision was momentous for the establishment of the genre and its nature. A stable meter of its own gave the genre a recognizable status, as did the fact that Lucilius made his reputation as a poet in this kind of poetry alone.

The hexameter itself was a suitable vehicle for what has been dubbed stylistic "mobility,"[21] the comic or ironic switch from one stylistic register to another, exploited by all the Roman verse satirists. Writing in this meter allowed them to adopt, if they wished, the technical advances of the writers of serious hexameter poetry (epic, didactic), and to parody their style. Lucilius himself created a casual, conversational tone, in opposition to the more formal, literary medium. His looseness, like his prolixity, was to provoke Horace's criticism (cf. *Sermones* 1.10.56–61, *S.* 1.4.9–11).[22] For example, from the famous journey of book 3 (fr. 102–5W):

> uerum haec ludus ibi, susque omnia deque fuerunt,
> susque haec deque fuere inquam omnia ludus iocusque;
> illud opus durum, ut Setinum accessimus finem,
> αἰγίλιποι montes, Aetnea omnes, asperi Athones.

But there all this was child's play, nothing to worry about [lit. both up and down], all this, I say again, was nothing to worry about, fun and games. That was hard work, when we came to the region of Setia, goat-deserted mountains, Etnas all, rugged Athoses.

Earlier we pointed to the occasional untraditional themes of Ennius' *Annales*. These were now taken up at greater length and in other forms by Lucilius and his contemporary Accius, tragedian and literary historian. Satire and its associated material, which was a minor part of Ennius' *œuvre*, for Lucilius was a *raison d'être*. In him again, autobiography is a mode and source of material for satire (Horace, *Sermones* 2.1.30–4):

---

[21] Silk (2000) 110. See Petersmann (1999) 291, 296.   [22] See Rudd (1966) ch. 4.

In the old days, he entrusted his secrets to his books, as though to faithful friends, having no other outlet whether things had gone well or ill. The result is the man of old's whole life is open to view as if sketched in a votive tablet.

Right from the beginning Lucilius was a vivid presence. In books 26–30 his name appears six times in confident (frs. 650–1, 763–5 and 791–2W) and joking (fr. 929–30W, "that rascal Lucilius," cf. frs. 1077 and 865W) assertions of his identity as a man and satirist (fr. 1075W). He drew material from such personal experiences as a journey (book 3, cf. Horace, *Sermones* 1.5), an illness (book 5), and his love affairs (fr. 892–9W, etc.), although everything he touched received the stamp of his individual outlook.

Lucilius' self-assertion and polemical stance, which transformed the mode of comic realism he took up from Ennius, must be linked to his higher social position. If Ennius acquired a certain status from his writing, he remained in modest circumstances, socially dependent upon the politically powerful figures who were his patrons. One of these was M. Fulvius Nobilior, on whose staff he went to Aetolia in 189 BCE and whose deeds he celebrated in a play as well as in book 15 of the *Annales*. The tradition that the poet's statue was placed in front of the tomb of the Scipios well illustrates the subordinate nature of the position he acquired (Cicero, *Pro Archia* 22, Livy, *Ab urbe condita* 38.56.4). In contrast, when Lucilius died, we are told, he was honored by a public funeral (Jerome, *Chronicles* p. 148eH), the prerogative of the rich and powerful senatorial class to which he belonged. Although he had chosen not to pursue his natural career as a statesman, Lucilius maintained a proprietorial engagement with Rome's political life. As a member of the élite, he could address his peers as equals and range freely over all levels of society, "people and senators alike" (fr. 1146W). That such a man should address himself self-confidently and polemically in the fiercely competitive world of the Roman aristocracy is not surprising. What is extraordinary is that he should do so through his verse, for poetry, especially of this kind, was not a mode of élite self-expression. The writer and his writing, then, become a topic of some prominence.

Literary polemic provides the peg for generic self-definition. The satirist as literary critic is also defender and definer of his own rôle and status. Books 26–30 present the satirist as writer, conscious of his audience, and aware of the need to demarcate his genre (traces in books 26, 27, 29, 30). In some difficult fragments (frs. 632–4 and 635W), which Warmington puts at the beginning of book 26, Lucilius said he wished to be read by neither the very learned nor the very ignorant. In fact the primary audience for which he wrote was a group of friends – his interlocutors are often "friends" – and many of his themes reflect the cultural and political concerns of the governing class (cf. Horace, *Sermones* 2.1.62–74).[23] The need for the satirist to negotiate a delicate course between friends and enemies, inclusion and exclusion, made friendship itself one of satire's themes (frs. 694, 695, 859–78, 957–8 and 959–60W, cf. Horace, *Sermones* 1.3, 1.4; cf. Ennius, *Annales* 268–86 above).

Self-conscious apology and justification for polemic or revealing outspokenness appear predominantly in the early books, combined with parody of higher genres such as tragedy, as a way of implicitly defining the genre. It is in these books that Horace has Lucilius "exposing each man's inner foulness" and "smothering Metellus and Lupus with slanderous verses" (cf. Horace, *Sermones* 2.1.64–8), yet their preserved fragments do not present many examples of this sort of attack. Metellus' speech on the unfortunate necessity of marriage was ridiculed in book 26 (frs. 644–5 and 646W), and Lupus' harshness as a judge made fun of in book 28 (fr. 805–11W). Other leading themes are comic, philosophic, or to do with social behavior in matters such as sexual relations, business affairs, and dining.

In the second collection, literary polemic provides the peg for grammatical erudition. In books 9 and 10 Lucilius discussed literary and grammatical questions, arguing against Accius on the rules of good spelling, defining poetic terminology (fr. 401–10W), criticizing other writers, and laying down principles of composition (fr. 417–18W). The scholarly and theoretical nature of the treatment may well have given the "very uneducated" pause. But before we make the easy assumption that such material was not "satirical," we should remember that Persius (according to *Vita Persi* 51–2) was inspired to compose satire, especially his first satire, by reading Lucilius book 10. Evidently the link to contemporary literary controversy of the theoretical discussions was marked and memorable (see Horace, *Sermones* 1.4 and 1.10, *Ars Poetica*, Persius 1, Juvenal 7).

Beside grammatical studies a significant theme was philosophy, another topic in which an aristocratic, Hellenized audience might be expected to take an interest. The two were not entirely unrelated, as Elizabeth Rawson reminds us: "Abstract discussion of problems of literary aesthetics was something for which the impulse came on the whole from philosophy."[24] In the 140s Panaetius, the Greek Stoic philosopher, had moved to Rome where he benefited from the patronage of Lucilius' friend, the great general and politician Scipio Aemilianus. We do not find Panaetius' name in the satires,[25] but other Greek philosophers are mentioned; for example, in book 1 Carneades for the power of his argumentation. His recent death was topical and suited

---

[23] Puelma Piwonka (1949) esp. 74–80.
[24] Rawson (1985) 279. [25] But see Cichorius (1922) 75–7.

the subject of the satire (fr. 35 W). In book 28 the doctrines and leading personalities of the Epicurean and Academic schools were discussed at a Greek symposium (frs. 815, 820, 821, and 822–3 W).

When criticizing the judicial rigor of Lupus (fr. 805–11 W), Lucilius incongruously played on the terminology of natural philosophy, saying that Lupus would deprive the defendant of all four elements: fire, water, earth, and air. The comic point, I believe, lies mainly in the juxtaposition of the unrelated spheres of activity. Such comparisons, through metaphor or simile, were part of Lucilius' comic charm. Another striking instance is the simile of the victorious fighting cock raising itself on its toes, applied to a good wife (?) (fr. 328–9 W).

So far we have seen Lucilius' development of distinctive themes that linked early Roman literature and culture with aspects of Hellenistic literature, scholarship, and thought. If we now turn to examine generic continuity between Ennian and Lucilian satire, we must highlight as well the associations with comedy, in theme, dialogic form, and style. Earlier I adopted Waszink's proposition that Ennius was influenced by "existing drama . . . the then already flourishing Roman comedy."[26] When Lucilius was writing, tragedy and comedy were still the most important public and popular genres in Rome. As Elizabeth Rawson stated, "it is becoming more and more widely recognised that . . . theatre was one of the central institutions of Roman culture."[27] Accordingly, drama was the main target of Lucilius' literary parody and criticism in books 26 and 29.

Similarly, in the early books, apart from the use of stage meters, we find a vivid account of an attack by citizens and slaves on the house of another man (a pimp?), in search of a woman (fr. 793–814 W). The threats in direct speech are linguistically very reminiscent of comedy (e.g. *malo hercle uestro, confectores cardinum* ("be it to your harm, hinge-smashers") (fr. 795 W cf. Ennius, *Saturae* 1), *orationem facere conpendi potes*; | *salue, dum saluo in tergo et tergino licet* ("you can spare your speech; off with you, while you can get off with your back and the whip intact") (fr. 796–7 W, which is put in another context by Krenkel).[28] The house-attack scene must be based on an episode of New Comedy (cf. Menander, *Perikeiromene* 467–85, Terence, *Adelphi* 88–91, *Eunuchus* 771–816). In a similar scene in book 29 of a lover's attack on a house (937–48), the Menandrian-Terentian name Gnatho is used (*Gnatho, quid actum est? Depilati omnes sumus* "Gnatho, what is up?" "We've all been fleeced," [fr. 945 W]; *Caede ostium, Gnatho, urge. Restant, periimus*, "Chop down the door, Gnatho, use force!" "They won't

[26] Waszink (1972) 130.   [27] Rawson (1987) 88.   [28] Krenkel (1970) II 430–1.

move; we're finished," [fr. 946W]; compare Plautus, *Curculio* 395–8 with fr. 943–4W). The stereotypical depiction of nagging and scheming wives and greedy courtesans must also be linked to comedy (e.g. fr. 640–1W (the grotesque exaggeration of the coinages is comic), fr. 642–3W, cf. Plautus *Aulularia* 478–524, especially 508–22, *Truculentus* 52; with fr. 296–7W (a comic list), cf. Plautus *Poenulus* 220).[29] The following fragment is a good example of a comic character sketch (fr. 278–81W):

> He who has no mule, no slave, nor any companion, himself keeps with him his satchel, with whatever cash he has; he eats, sleeps and bathes with his satchel; all the fellow's goods are in the one satchel; this satchel is tightly tied to his shoulder.

Satire and comedy also share Greek popular moralizing, and the use of proverbial expressions. Elizabeth Rawson argued that the moral lessons and sententious utterances in Roman comedy were meant both to be approved for their own sake, and laughed at when put into incongruous mouths.[30] Roman satire adopted a similar ambivalence.

Whereas relatively few direct verbal borrowings from Plautus, Caecilius, and Terence have been identified – and perhaps they should not be expected – the stylistic influence is pervasive, both in the creation of a racy colloquialism and in the use of comic coinages, vulgarisms, and other devices of popular comedy.[31] For example, the metaphorical "identification" of fragment 746W *Quae pietas? Monogrammi quinque adducti; pietatem uocant!* ("What sense of duty? Five outline sketches were brought in; duty they call it!"). In connection with the coinages of fragment 640–1W, Rudd comments, "This is Lucilius the heir of Plautus."[32] Dramatization of narrative and anecdote by the extensive use of direct speech (see books 1 and 2, the council of the gods and the trial of Scaevola) is an important technique – so much so that we should always reckon with the possibility that someone other than the satirist is speaking. Nor should we forget those (admittedly rare) passages in Plautus which address life in Rome directly. The passage in Plautus (*Curculio* 466–85; cf. *Curculio* 285–98, 499–515), where the Choragus locates unsavory types in the Roman Forum, provides a precedent for that of Lucilius on the corruption of modern ways of life, so emblematic of Roman satire (fr. 1145–51W):[33]

---

[29] Gruen (1993) 286–7.
[30] Rawson (1987) 83–4. See also Freudenburg (1993) 21–39 on the "moralizing buffoon."
[31] Petersmann (1999) 296–310.   [32] Rudd (1966) 104.
[33] See Marx (1904–1905) I XVI.

Now indeed from dawn to dusk, on holidays and workdays, all the people and all the senators alike busy themselves in the forum, never leaving it. All have given themselves over to one and the same study and art – to be able to swindle without getting caught, to fight by cunning, to compete by smooth talking, pretend to be a fine fellow, to lay traps as if all are enemies of all.

Terence retreated from Plautus' satiric involvement with Roman social and political issues. It was, however, the direct response to contemporary personalities or events that typified Lucilian satire, even if it cannot fully account for it.[34] In book 1 a savage political and moral attack on the recently dead Lupus (*princeps senatus* 131–25 BCE) was worked into a parodic council of the gods (based on the divine council in Ennius' *Annales* 1). There the gods, as a heavenly version of the Roman senate, discussed the degraded state of Roman morals – luxury, debauchery, gluttony – for which Lupus might have been held responsible. Lupus' arrival among the gods seems to have caused consternation: *Quae facies, qui uultus uiro? – Vultus item ut facies, mors, icterus morbus, uenenum* ("What is the man's look, and his expression?" – "His expression is the same as his look, death, jaundice, poison.") (frs. 36 and 37W, cf. Horace, *Sermones* 1.7.1, Seneca, *Apocolocyntosis* 5.2–3; on Lupus again see fr. 1138–41W).

In book 2 Lucilius exploited the satiric and comic possibilities of a battle in court between Q. Mucius Scaevola the "Augur" (praetor 120, consul 117) and Titus Albucius, who accused him of extortion after his governorship of Asia (119/18). An enmity had arisen between the two when Scaevola had made fun of Albucius' extreme philhellenism (fr. 87–93W). The satire depicted vicious attacks on either side, typical of the often slanderous (and factitious) invective of the Roman courtroom (frs. 54–5, 57 and 67–9W; cf. Horace, *Sermones* 1.7). The Neronian satirist Persius remembered these two books as examples of Lucilius' hostile attacks on Lupus and Mucius: *secuit Lucilius urbem, | te Lupe, te Muci, et genuinum fregit in illis* ("Lucilius lacerated the city – you, Lupus, and you, Mucius – and broke his molar on them") (1.114–15, cf. Juvenal 1.153–4), and Cicero spoke of Lucilius being "annoyed" at Mucius (*De oratore* 1.72). It is not surprising that ancient readers attributed the hostility to Lucilius himself, but we should distinguish between the satirist and the scurrilities he retailed, while noting nevertheless the satirist's freedom to include them.[35]

The accusations of debauchery (frs. 33 and 63W) and gluttony (frs. 46, 50–1, 67–9 and 70W) which are found in these two satires are standard subjects for the blackening of an opponent's character, in politics or the courtroom. In censuring and exposing the stains on others' lives (frs. 852–3

---

[34] Fraenkel (1957) 79–80.   [35] Gruen (1992) 290–1.

and 1070W) satire finds considerable scope for itself in the stuff of corporeality – sex and food. Longer episodes are preserved as well as isolated coarse
comments (e.g. frs. 61, 361 and 1182W). Disquisitions on food give scope
for philosophizing and moralizing (or the parody of it) (frs. 200–7, 1022–3,
and 1234W), and descriptions of dinner parties for retailing amusing and
no doubt indiscreet conversation. L. Licinius Crassus' dinner at the home of
Granius the auctioneer was a splendid and sumptuous affair (fr. 601–3W),
but Granius was also a very funny man (fr. 448–9W, Cicero, *Brutus* 172).
The consumption and offering of food must be emphasized as one of satire's
enduring themes, and a rich source of tropes and self-reflexive metaphors.[36]

The freedom and confidence of Lucilius' expression made a deep impression on later readers. He was of high social standing in Rome, and though he
himself did not pursue a political career, at a period of crucial social, political, and cultural developments, he was close to, but critically detached from,
Rome's political and intellectual life.[37] In a rare expression of the positive
purpose of his writing, possibly from an *envoi* or a dedication, he portrays
himself as working for the general good, so aligning satire with Rome's most
dominating social value (fr. 791–2W):

> Rem, populi salutem fictis versibus Lucilius
> quibus potest inpertit, totumque hoc studiose et sedulo.

To the verses he has written as best he can, Lucilius imparts the people's pros-
perity, a matter of importance, and all this with zeal and earnestness.

Further reading

Studies of Ennius and Lucilius may be found in the general books on Roman satire.
Particularly comprehensive is Coffey (1976). Gratwick (1982) 156–71 is an adven-
turous and stimulating treatment. For those with Latin, Petersmann (1999) 289–
310 illustrates the linguistic variety of both satirists and Lucilius' great artistry in
language.

For more on Ennius see Mariotti (reprinted Urbino, 1991), Jocelyn (1972) 987–
1026, Waszink (1972) 99–137.

Apart from the specific treatments of Lucilius, much of value will be found in
the many studies of the later satirists' works. For a thorough survey of work on
Lucilius see Christes (1972) 1182–239. Rudd (1986) is an attractive presentation of
Lucilius in the context of Roman satire overall. Fiske (1920) is more detailed and
more speculative. For Lucilius in his contemporary context see E. S. Gruen, *Culture
and National Identity in Republican Rome* (Ithaca, 1992) 272–317 and for the Late
Republican reception Rawson (1985) and Freudenburg (1993).

[36] Gowers (1993a) ch. 3, Griffin (1994) 190–7.   [37] Gruen (1992) ch. 7 *passim*.

EMILY GOWERS

The restless companion: Horace, *Satires* 1 and 2

Horace's two books of *Satires* have always lurked in the shadow of the *Odes*.[1] Aside from such favourite anecdotes as the much-translated encounter with a literary gatecrasher on the Via Sacra, or the "granny's tale" of the town mouse and the country mouse,[2] they have for the most part been found strange, profoundly unsatisfying poems, whose self-deprecating tone has condemned them to neglect. They are also, by most standards, astonishingly unsatirical. The first book, published in 36/5 BCE, is Horace's poetic debut, an "integrational"[3] book in which a freedman's son marks his miraculous arrival in society (after being proscribed and fighting on the wrong side at Philippi), and justifies his envied niche as a civil servant (*scriba quaestorius*) and poet in the "pure house" of the millionaire Maecenas.[4] The second, published in 30 BCE after the battle of Actium, is tense with all the increasing restrictions of the new regime; Horace virtually gives up the right to speak, and directs his satire mostly against himself.

Some of the most important changes in civil liberties in the history of Rome are spanned, then, by the two books. By positioning himself as a satirist in the footsteps of his aristocratic Republican predecessor Lucilius (d. 102 BCE), Horace was drawing attention to the difficulty of writing full-blooded satire in a changed political climate. He was also demonstrating how even the most casual and messy of genres could aspire to new standards of composition. By promoting technical improvements such as restraint, flexibility, and inoffensiveness, Horace made a literary virtue out of a political necessity.[5] In recent criticism the *Sermones* have been steadily rehabilitated: not just as a socio-political document of one citizen's cautious progress through the mean

---

[1] The *Satires* traditionally follow the *Odes* and the *Epodes* in many editions of Horace's works.
[2] *Sermones* 1.9; 2.6.79–117.   [3] Kennedy (1992) 33.
[4] Pure house: 1.9.49; Horace's life: Suetonius, *Vita Horati*; Fraenkel (1957) 1–23; Horace's post of *scriba quaestorius*: Suetonius, *Vita Horati*; Armstrong (1986); Horace and Maecenas: Reckford (1959), Lefèvre (1981), DuQuesnay (1984) 24–7, Evenepoel (1990).
[5] Freudenburg (1993) 86–92.

streets of Rome and a meditation on freedom, both personal and generic, but also as a deceptively sophisticated and allusive literary artefact.[6]

Horace alternates between calling his satires *Satirae* and *Sermones*, "Conversations," a title which suggests that they were simulating companionable speech, with its aimless starts, slack inner logic, and throw-away endings, the kind friends tolerate and enemies overlook.[7] They are addressed primarily to his patron Maecenas, which makes everyone else into jealous eavesdroppers, but Horace is also by implication conversing with the small poetic coterie, including Virgil and Varius, to which he belonged (and which he puts on display in a triumphant rollcall at the end of book 1), as well as being in constant intertextual dialogue with the wider community of poets, dead and alive.[8]

Book 1 experiments with different kinds of *sermo*: diatribe (primarily a Hellenistic form associated with neo-Socratic or Cynic ranting on moral themes),[9] gossip, literary chitchat. *Sermones* 1.1–3 are moralizing sermons, the basic rules for life Horace claims to have learned at his father's knee – how to be undemanding and play safe in the areas of material consumption, sex, and social relations; 1.4 and 1.10 are defenses of Horatian satire; 1.5 is an account of an uncomfortable journey from Rome to Brundisium in the train of a peace-making expedition; 1.7–9 are anecdotes (7 is about a *cause célèbre* in Brutus' camp in Asia, 8 is a comic aetiology spoken by a statue of Priapus, in 9 Horace meets his nemesis, a literary poseur trying to penetrate Maecenas' circle); 1.6 is a conversation with Maecenas, a confident approach to a great man from a nobody who has chosen a quiet life away from politics.

It is a big joke, of course, that a man whose profession was that of a civil servant or private secretary (*scriba*) should set himself up as a conversationalist, and there is play throughout on the notions of writing and speaking,[10] as well as the idea of having anything to say at all. Lucilius had bared his soul

---

[6] E.g. DuQuesnay (1984), Henderson (1999) 202–5, Oliensis (1998a) 17–63; Freudenburg (1993) *passim*; (1996); (2001) 1–124.

[7] Cicero, *De officiis* 37 on the theory of *sermo*; on the alternative titles see Van Rooy (1965) 50–89.

[8] E.g. Horace and Lucretius: Merrill (1905), Murley (1939), Freudenburg (1993) 19–20; Horace and Virgil: Van Rooy (1973), Zetzel (1980) 66–7, Putnam (1995); Horace and Callimachus: Wehrli (1944), Wimmel (1960) 148–67, Benedetto (1966), Cody (1976), Scodel (1987), Freudenburg (1993) 104–7; Horace and Lucilius: Fiske (1920); Horace and Philetas: Gigante (1993).

[9] Oltramare (1926), Wimmel (1962).

[10] *Charta* ("paper"): S. 1.4.36, 101, 139; 1.5.104; *subscribe libello* ("add this on to the bottom of my book"): 1.10.92.

to his books "like faithful friends," but his "open tablet" becomes Horace's closed book.[11] Dangerous personal and political gossip is largely censored, even though the satires leak with a constant stream of real and type names.[12] The speaker of the *Sermones* represents himself as naturally reticent, while the real bogeys are people who talk too much: windy Stoics, divas who do not know when to stop, vicious dinner guests, garrulous satirists like Lucilius, pushy and pretentious literati, squabbling litigants, and loud-mouthed salesmen.[13] *Sermones* 1.6 contains a tiny sketch of Horace's first interview with Maecenas, a "non-conversation" between a stammering youth and a laconic aristocrat, which works as an ironic background for the book as a whole.

The state of "talking to Maecenas" is Horace's *fait accompli*, the place where he has ended up, but are these "conversations" really any more than a kind of smokescreen, with their banal philosophizing, damp-squib jokes, holiday slides, and shaggy-dog stories? Horace appears to be trying to white-wash his reputation and refute the charge of social climbing by having nothing whatsoever to say for himself. If we do learn anything significant from the poems, it is only in the most indirect way. Larger hostilities are recorded through the minor frictions of personal relations or duels between nonentities (a legal battle in Brutus' camp in Asia Minor in 1.7; a slanging match between two clowns in 1.5). The central portrait of *amicitia* between two former enemies, Horace and Maecenas, stands in for the entire peace process; the discord between Octavian and Antony is dismissed as a tiff between friends; Horace's own involvement on Brutus' side in the civil war is reduced to a pardonable gaffe like entering a room in the wrong way.[14]

One can, of course, read between the lines and understand Horace's apparently casual but discreet dialogues with Maecenas as a blueprint for how to behave as a new arrival in post-Republican Rome, where freedom of speech and movement are permitted within fixed guidelines, both external and self-imposed.[15] The first three so-called "diatribe" poems are really an account of the moral survival course which has kept Horace afloat, with a consistent emphasis on lying low and demanding little, an ethics of self-preservation and contentment.[16] Impersonal sex with anonymous women is deemed

---

[11] *S.* 2.1.30–34; Harrison (1987).   [12] Rudd (1966) 132–59 on Horace's names.

[13] *S.* 1.1.13–14, 120; 1.3.1–8; 1.4.86–91; 1.4.12; 1.4.14–16; 1.9.12–13, 33–4; 1.10.90–1; 1.7.7, 26–9; 1.6.42–4.

[14] E.g. *S.* 1.5.29; 1.3.140. See Hunter (1985) 486–90, and Kennedy (1992) 31–4 on the "domestication" of political terms like *amicitia* and *libertas* in *Sermones* 1.

[15] Freudenburg (1993) 86–92 on Horace's reining in of *libertas* against the background of the civil war; Hunter (1985) on its reinvention as constructive frankness between friends.

[16] Links between the diatribe satires: Armstrong (1964).

preferable to fighting one's way through barricades of bodyguards and hair-dressers to test the hidden charms of famous men's wives, and risking one's reputation and bodily parts in the process.[17] Social relations should be a matter of give and take, where one errs on the side of indulgence, like fathers who give their bandy-legged and birdy sons fond pet names.[18]

The first satire sets the tone for the collection as a whole, opening with a quizzical enquiry addressed to Maecenas ("Why is it that no one is content with his lot but always envies other people?") and ending with a simile about a satisfied dinner guest (suggesting Horace's own contentment with his small sufficiency). Throughout, images of greedy capacity – granaries, stomachs, money chests, measuring jugs – make the poem not just a sermon against avarice, but a thinly veiled program for Horatian satire, where moderate consumption of material things goes hand in hand with moderate consumption of words.[19] Horace ends with the promise: "That's enough [*iam satis est*]: I shan't add another word." This is nothing less than a radical reshaping of a traditionally open-ended genre into a slimmed-down, modest form, sweetening the pill of moral correction with humor instead of souring it with malice and envy.

There are many ways in which this opening poem is surprising. First, it avoids reference to contemporary Rome in favor of a timeless, generalized discussion of human nature, which draws on different strands of Hellenistic tradition: the moderation of Epicurean philosophy, the streamlined literary aesthetics of Callimachus, the ingredients of Cynic diatribe – animal fables, thumbnail vignettes, anonymous objections[20] – and the negative example of heavy-handed Stoics. Secondly, it conspicuously avoids personal abuse[21] and puts the blame for resentment and ill will squarely on other people, not the satirist himself (actually this so-called "disclaimer of malice" was a characteristic maneuver of satire right from its origins).[22] Even so, the name "Maecenas" immediately gives the poem a historical context. The book's publication coincided with tense negotiations in the war with Sextus Pompeius and a fragile entente between Octavian and Antony. Horace represents himself and Maecenas as the stable exceptions looking down on an anthill of scurrying, disaffected human beings from the high ground of a post-revolutionary status quo. These outlines of a philosophy can be read as a "back to basics" campaign, while Horace's blend of Callimachean and Epicurean economics contrasts pointedly with the accusations of moral excess hurled between both sides in the recent civil war.[23]

---

[17] *S.* 1.2.44–6, 97–100, 133.   [18] *S.* 1.3.43–8.   [19] Hubbard (1981).
[20] Oltramare (1926).   [21] LaFleur (1981).   [22] Dickie (1981), Bramble (1974) 190–204.
[23] For the political background to *Sermones* 1: Du Quesnay (1984).

To have a satirist as a friend is a risky business, and *Sermones* 1 really concerns the impossibility, recast as *undesirability*, of writing vitriolic satire in the new conciliatory climate. As Lucilius' low-born successor tries to become a companion to his former enemy, and to negotiate awkward collisions in the streets of Rome, some of the old associations and freedoms of satire must be shed in the process. Instead of the archetypal figure prowling around the forum with venomous fangs and squinting eyes, or "smearing filth onto paper," the new satirist is, most unsatirically, diplomatic and accommodating.[24] Horace characterizes his satirical activity alternately as meaningless doodles, metrical prose, pious self-improvement, a child's moral ABC learned at the knee of a stern father, or, as in the picture of the frenzied toilette of pruning and scratching that precedes his casual literary appearances, a kind of perfectionist self-laceration (the only live victims of contemporary satire are the quicks of the writer's own fingernails).[25]

The flavor of satire has changed too. The acerbic salt and vinegar of Republican invective commemorated in 1.7 is now toned down to suit the sweet-tempered rhetoric of the new civility. When Horace speaks as a statue of Priapus guarding Maecenas' revamped pleasure gardens in 1.8, he plays gamekeeper rather than poacher to the new regime, and frightens away trespassing witches with a comic fart rather than sexual aggression.[26] When he is pursued down the Via Sacra by an ambitious poet (1.9), he keeps his dislike within the bounds of politeness, and eventually allows the law to extricate him rather than indulging in open abuse. A cynic's history of civilization in *Sermones* 1.3 (99–117) doubles as a history of the civilizing of satire: tooth-and-nail fights between grunting, promiscuous cavemen give way to the civic branding of thieves and adulterers, followed by deference before the law, and finally mellow philosophical discrimination and forgiveness.

But Horace's *Sermones* are not just a sunny promenade over the burial grounds of the civil war.[27] First, this social upstart and freedman's son is still uncertain of the liberties he can take in a city "where sharp-toothed resentment thrives," where a *libellus* is not just a choice little book of poems but a prosecutable lampoon or a court writ, where Caesar is the ultimate authority (*Sermones* 1.3.4), and where the satirical urge to brand or label, to point one's finger (*notare*), can backfire on the aggressor.[28] Secondly, the framework of

---

[24] *Rhetorica ad Herennium* 4.62; Horace, *S.* 1.4.36.

[25] Doodles: *S.* 1. 4.138–40; 9.2; metrical prose: 4.48; self-improvement: 4.134–7; moral ABC: 1.25–6; 4.105–26; self-laceration: 10.69–71 (71 *uiuos . . . unguis*).

[26] Anderson (1982) 74–83 on this poem as a poetic statement.

[27] *S.* 1.8 is set in Maecenas' public park built over the former Esquiline cemetery.

[28] *S.*1.3.60–1; *libellus*: *S.* 1.4.66; cf. *S.* 1.4.71; 1.10.92; *notare*: *S.* 1.4.5, 106.

the satires is never completely amicable. The threeway relationship between
a potentially offensive speaker (Horace the satirist), a potentially hypercrit-
ical listener (his fastidious patron Maecenas), and a potentially offended
eavesdropper (the general reader) is always a triangle of possible paranoia
and irritability.[29] Every poem in the book could be summed up as an exercise in warding off *inuidia*, malicious resentment, and disowning the satirical
impulse: the sermons against material envy (1), sexual ambition (2), and vin-
dictiveness (3), and the disavowals of literary outspokenness (4 and 10), hob-
nobbing with the great (5), political ambition (6), venomous invective (7),
sexual aggression (8), pushiness and self-promotion (9).[30] Many poems wriggle out of a proper ending with a humorous riposte, a pun, a fart; Horace's
ideal satirist, personified by his mocking friend Aristius Fuscus in *Sermones*
1.9, is an escape artist. Easygoing on the surface, Horatian satire has been
more appropriately named "a restless genre."[31]

Horace later refers to his satires as poems which "creep along the ground,"
inspired by a "pedestrian muse."[32] Yet they are more ambitious than they
seem, and less casual. He boasts openly that his unpretentious life allows
him to travel unencumbered and at his own whim, and to sleep with women
whose names he can make up himself, but the one exception to these relaxed
rules is the perfectionism which ties him to new standards of literary composition.[33] Lucilius' sloppy, spontaneous-seeming "improvisations," which
exemplified aristocratic Republican freedom, are rejected in favor of a calculated refinement.[34] The new satire, like the new civility, is sensitive and
flexible in its approach to a touchy audience:

> You need brevity, to let the thought run freely on without
> becoming entangled in a mass of words that will overload the ears.
> You also need a way with words which is sometimes solemn,
> sometimes humorous, sometimes playing the role of an orator or
> poet, sometimes that of a witty talker who keeps his strength in
> reserve and carefully plays things down.[35]

[29] Muecke (1990), Gold (1992) 162–75 on the ambiguous range of "the audience"; Seeck (1991), Lyne (1995) 142 on Horace's moralizing as touchy for Maecenas; Richlin (1992) 184 for the *Satires* as "irritating."

[30] Hubbard (1981) 319 on *inuidia* as the subject of *S.* 1.1.   [31] Labate (1981).

[32] *Epistles* 2.1.250–1, *sermones . . . /repentis per humum*; *S.* 2.6.17, *musa . . . pedestri.* See Freudenburg (1993) 183–4, 206–7 on walking and mule-riding metaphors; Freudenburg (1993) 201–3, Gowers (1993b) on *S.* 1.5, the journey to Brundisium, as a realization of these metaphors.

[33] Traveling light: *S.* 1.6.104–6; anonymous sex: *S.* 1.2.126.

[34] Rudd (1966) 86–131, Freudenburg (1993) 100–3 on Horace's refinement of Lucilian satire.

[35] *S.* 1.10.9–14.

As if working a passage through the city at Maecenas' side, Horace adapts *sermo* to protect his patron from mud, noise, and crowds, and faces up to the onslaughts of anonymous objectors in his path.[36] What look like clumsy signposts ("Where is all this leading?" "To cut a long story short," "That's enough of that") are a kind of X-ray of his conversational maneuvers, always geared to self-improvement and to sparing the reader delay or boredom.[37]

The literary principles laid out in 4 and 10 – brevity, variety, amenability, inoffensiveness – are put into practice in poems which draw attention to narrowly avoided pitfalls of composition, and clean the mud off Lucilius' energetic but sloppy models. Horace's journey south to Brundisium (1.5, based on a similar journey poem by Lucilius) is hampered by real mud, noise, and crowds, but he whisks his readers through at top speed.[38] His collision with the pest in 1.9 is full of discomfort and meandering, but he makes it fast moving with zigzagging choreography and snappy dialogue.[39] The three "diatribes" (*Sermones* 1.1–3) verge on triteness, long-windedness, and illogicality, as they swerve from one topic to another on the twist of one word: in 3 *aequus* (the central paradox is that it is not "consistent" or "fair" to regard all sins as "equal"); in 2 *medius* (it is "moderate" to enjoy the "middle" regions of the "middle" class of woman who is "easily available" – *in medio*).[40] At the start of 1.1, Horace cuts short a reasonably small catalogue of discontented human beings with a preemptive "et cetera, et cetera – I don't want to wear out even loquacious Fabius" (13–14) – as though he is only just avoiding the irritating insistence of the sermonizing genre.[41] He ends by shunning the example of philosophers like Crispinus, who pillage the stockpile of Hellenistic philosophy endlessly.[42]

As a personality behind his "conversations," Horace presents himself as similarly well intentioned and self-improving. One prominent element of the *Sermones* is autobiographical. That is not to say that we should take Horace's account of his humble origins and reluctant emergence completely literally.[43]

---

[36] Compare the instructions to the solicitous client at *S.* 2.5.16–17, 88–98 to shelter his patron in the street and tailor his speech to the mood required.

[37] *S.* 1.2.23; 1.1.14; 1.1.95; 1.1.120.

[38] Freudenburg (1993) 201–3; Gowers (1993b) 57–8.   [39] Rudd (1966) 76–85.

[40] Lejay (1911) 1, 60 on the "logic of conversation"; Coffey (1976) 70.

[41] *Delassare*, "to wear out" (14), looks like a translation of Greek *diatribein*, "to wear out, pass time," from which "diatribe" comes, though Jocelyn (1982) is skeptical whether there was ever a classical concept of this form.

[42] *S.* 1.1.120–1.

[43] Armstrong (1986); Williams (1995) for an ingenious theory that Horace's father was only temporarily enslaved; Schlegel (2000) on the father scenes as evoking a generic ancestry for Horatian satire.

Recent criticism has identified the portrait Horace gives us of himself as a composite of comic types – the cowed son, the parasite, the slipshod, bumbling Cynic philosopher – proper for the decorum of satire, whose origins Horace traces from Old Comedy and father figures like Lucilius.[44] This is a personality attuned to the character of the genre – low key, quotidian, and, on the surface at least, deferential to authority. An unthreatening pose is not simply a literary device, however, but part of Horace's calculated public "face," designed to disarm, to elude precise pinning down, and to exemplify the modest front of the new regime.[45] His seemingly casual revelations in the manner of Lucilius are in fact the controlled self-presentation of a self-made man.

Horace rehearses many different roles in relation to Maecenas and society at large. The ranting figure who plucks personalities from the crowd (*Sermones* 1.4.25) in the first four satires resembles some Cynic street philosopher: Horace, the blunt and abrasive "cat who may look at a king," is playing Bion to Maecenas' King Antigonus, Aesop to his Xanthus, Diogenes to his Alexander.[46] This is the rough, man-of-the-world voice of the speaking penis (*Sermones* 1.2.68–71), Cato egging on a young man outside a brothel (1.2.31–5), or the earthy Priapus statue (1.8).[47] However, there are more private scenarios for *sermo* too: the closet in 1.3, for example, where a gauche Horace bursts in on Maecenas' silence or quiet reading "to annoy him with some conversation or other."[48] More withdrawn still are the moments in 1.4, where Horace rehearses encounters and moral dilemmas in private, and in 1.9, where he is absorbed in solitary reverie. The image of Horace talking to himself on a sofa or in a portico "with pursed lips" (4.138) suggests that satire has finally abandoned the public stage where it began in democratic Athens for the enclosed spaces of agoraphobic Rome.[49]

Horace presents himself as an imperfect moralist, a Socratic ironist all too aware of his own minor faults.[50] While he claims to steer the middle path through the extremes of social behavior, there are intermittent caricatures of his rusticity, his naked ambition, or his bad conversational manners which put him back among the crowds of eccentric characters from which he has emerged: exhibitionists, prima donnas, interlopers, small-town civil servants, philanderers, *enfants terribles*.[51] While he claims to lead a

---

[44] Reckford (1969) 35; Zetzel (1980) 62; Freudenburg (1993) 3–51, 198–235; Turpin (1998).

[45] Oliensis (1998a) 1–16.

[46] *Epist.* 2.2.60: "conversations in the style of Bion"; Kindstrand (1976) 21–87 on Bion's legacy.

[47] Henderson (1999) 184–91 on *S.* 1.2 and 1.8 as "man's talk."   [48] *S.* 3.65.

[49] Oliensis (1998) 26: "an oxymoronic portrait of satiric silence."

[50] Anderson (1982) 13–49.

[51] Henderson (1999) 214–15 notes the similarity between the pest's calculations at *S.* 1.9.56–60 and Horace's own at *S.* 1.4.134–7.

"pure life" himself, images of the filth he has left behind – stinking broth-els, dirty bath-oil, chamber-pots, flute-girls, quacks, and buffoons – give the satires an essential token staining. The satirical body with which Horace fleshes out his "disembodied voice"[52] centers on the nether regions, the stomach or the groin (rather than the "uplifted head" of *Odes* 1.1); it is unkempt, and spotted with minor blemishes equivalent to the poet's own overlookable peccadilloes. Horace's most notorious affliction in the *Satires* is conjunctivitis: when he smears black cream onto his sore eyes on the jour-ney south in *Sermones* 1.5, this is a kind of cautionary inoculation against other people's blackening or accusations of moral shortsightedness, as well as a solipsistic act of defiance (it makes him blind to the arrival of Maecenas).[53] Similarly *Sermones* 1.7, the vicious court case in Brutus' camp, is a blot on the book, a concentration of all the festering sores remembered from Caesar's murder, Philippi, and the proscriptions.[54]

Throughout the book, there is a tension between being part of the crowd and being sifted out of it (thanks to the discrimination of Maecenas), being a nobody or a somebody, a loner or a companion, free or tied. This is an essen-tial aspect of the power relations between satirist and patron.[55] When Horace describes a typical day in his life, he spends it in conspicuously solitary fash-ion, hovering on the edge of city crowds and not dancing attendance on Maecenas. In *Sermones* 1.4 his maneuvers suggest ambivalence about being "in" or "out" of any circle: he perversely removes his "prosaic" satire from the category of real poetry, and shuns publicity – the promiscuous world of billboards, singing in the baths, and "smearing filth onto paper"; yet at the end he issues a threat from the center of a crowd of poets who want to bully everyone into joining their ranks. In *Sermones* 1.9 Horace starts off in a world of his own, but is forced by the end to play his part as one of the crowd, and to recognize his civic obligations.[56]

It is important that Horace leaves traces of resistance throughout the book, both to make his friendship with Maecenas seem rocky and therefore more genuine, and to emphasize what satire has lost in being sweetened and toned down. Full-blooded satirists – Attic comedians, the witch Canidia, prowl-ing informers, sparring entertainers in southern Italy, the squabbling liti-gants of Brutus' camp – still haunt the poems, their malice not yet stamped out. In any case, Horace's restraint is thrown into doubt by some of the

---

[52] Zetzel (1980) 68.

[53] See Cucchiarelli (2001) 66–70 on bleary eyes as a political and scribal handicap.

[54] Henderson (1998) 91.

[55] Oliensis (1998a) 17–63 *passim* on the mixture of deference and independence in Horace's relations with Maecenas.

[56] Mazurek (1997) on the law in Horace's *Sermones*.

book's structural devices. Many of the poems end prematurely, as if playing safe – a freeze-framed chariot race (1.1), *coitus interruptus* (1.2), the end of the line at Brundisium (1.5), a stay of execution (1.7). And yet the "That's enough now" (*iam satis est*) that is the catchword of Horatian satire comes at the end of only the first poem out of ten.[57] Horace then immediately breaks his promise not to add another word by launching into 1.2. The last poem, 1.10, looks at first like a recantation of the criticisms of Lucilius in 1.4, but turns out to be an emphatic restatement of them. For example, the demure phrase "I would not dare to remove the crown *sticking* to his head with abundant glory" (1.10.48–9) reminds us teasingly of the mud-slinging of 1.4.[58] In this poem the phrase "It is not enough" (*non satis est*) is applied to Horace's perfectionist standards of literary composition (1.10.7). The last words, "Go, boy, and tack this on to the bottom of my book" (1.10.92), added on like a stop-press or postscript, open the way for book 2 and end the book on a defiant note of "publish and be damned."

There was a five-year interval between the appearance of book 1 and that of its companion volume, book 2. Post-Actium, the sinister encroachments of imperial machinery make themselves felt: committees of civil servants, foreign campaigns, tax revenues, lobbyists, documents to be signed and sealed. Everywhere there is less room for maneuver. Horace has consolidated his position with Maecenas and satisfied his goals with a country seat, the Sabine farm, yet his movements are cramped by all the petitions and interference that go with the life of a celebrity. The law, in book 1 a convenient, depersonalized means of disposing of one's enemies, has become an arcane system one needs to know inside out in order to survive.[59] Other obscure branches of knowledge, like cookery, legacy hunting, and court protocol, now compete with moral philosophy as routes to the good life.

Book 2, even more than book 1, is attuned to the reactions of its touchy audience. It opens by immediately confronting the contradictory criticisms of people who think the first book was too sharp (*nimis acer*) or too spineless (*sine neruis*) – a somewhat ironic note of despair, because this is exactly the kind of mixed reception a satirist would expect![60] This supplementary volume is a rewriting of book 1 (*Sermones* 2.3.2, "unweaving everything you've written"), a readjusting of Horace's social mask (cf. 2.8.84, "you return with your outward appearance changed"), a return to Maecenas (2.6.31, "you run

[57] Dufallo (2000).
[58] As the word "muddy" in the very next line indicates.   [59] *S.* 2.2.131.
[60] Or a perfect fusion of the humor and sharpness recommended at *S.* 1.10.14–15: Freudenburg (1990).

back to Maecenas"), a refashioning of a self-fashioned man (cf. 2.5.55–6, "a civil servant cooked up from a minor magistrate"). With only eight poems, book 2 is shorter than book 1. However, this is partly deceptive, as the third poem, the monstrous sermon by the Stoic convert Damasippus, is the length of three poems put together – a three-pound mullet (2.2.33–4) in itself.[61] The book as a whole offers a strange impression of overload and selling short (*satura* versus *quod satis est*). Cooking, which in Latin shares so many terms with moral vocabulary – good, bad, sweet, bitter, healthy, sick, rotten[62] – becomes, in its new pretentious form, the supreme agent of social malaise, with emphasis on the dyspeptic stomach, replacing the sore eyes of book 1.[63] Horace himself suffers from an embarrassment of riches, his own material gains (2.6.4, "I ask for nothing more") mingled with dissatisfaction (2.8.18, "wretched wealth").

There are two new frameworks for the poems of book 2. One is the symposium or *con-uiuium*, the high-minded gathering of friends, once a model for a perfect society, and now the ideal from which this collection, with its frequent allusions to Platonic dialogue and eight-poem structure (following the eight speakers at Plato's *Symposium*), is such a falling off.[64] Companionship, one of the ideals of book 1, is now a nostalgic memory attached to the past or the uncorrupted countryside: the horseplay of Scipio and Laelius before an informal supper (in line with the "impromptu" character of Lucilian satire), a dinner guest released from crazy rules, the carefree herbs of a country mouse, the good old days of the unexpected guest and pot luck.[65] The pests and hangers-on who dogged Horace in *Sermones* 1 (cf. 1.6.102) have been replaced by an abstract, generalized anxiety (2.7.115, "the dark companion presses close and follows you as you run away"). The repressed civilities of 1.9 become naked abuse in 2.6, as Horace collides with anonymous ill-wishers in the street; "living with the great" (2.1.76), a recipe for contentment in *Sermones* 1, is now an unwanted responsibility (exposed in 2.5–8). By the end of book 2 Horace is still looking for a *conuiua*, a dinner companion – or someone to live with.[66]

The only ideal *sermo* in the book is the ethical conversation which bubbles up at a dinner of beans, greens, and bacon on Horace's Sabine farm in *Sermones* 2.6. Otherwise, his choice of speakers is hardly utopian, and the disproportion between them and their host is grotesque. Horace symbolically

---

[61] Jamie Masters first pointed this out to me.

[62] Gowers (1993a) 132–3.   [63] *S.* 2.2.43, 77–8; 2.8.5.

[64] Cicero, *Ad familiares* 9.24.3; *De senectute* 13.45: the *conuiuium* is so-called because it is the occasion when we most truly live together. Platonic allusions: Anderson (1982) 41–9.

[65] *S.* 2.1.71–4; 2.6.68–9; 2.6.117; 2.2.90–92.   [66] *S.* 2.8.2.

relinquishes the power of speech to a series of self-appointed pundits and cranks: a jurist, a dispossessed farmer, a bankrupt antique dealer turned Stoic, a gourmet, the mythical prophet Teiresias, a slave, and a comedian.[67] Many of these could be termed "losers," disenfranchised and down at heel, but born again through new philosophies.[68] Horace (except in 2.6) positions himself as listener to his own *sermones* and sufferer from writer's block (2.2.2, "this talk isn't mine"; 2.3.2, "you write so seldom"). After the confident dictation that ends book 1 (1.10.92, *subscribe* – "take this down"), he returns to his childhood role as a pupil taking instruction (2.1.5, *praescribe* – "dictate to me"), and preaches and practices silence.[69] Although original oracular speech is privileged over the written record, the founts of wisdom, following Platonic precedent, are often drained only at second hand, from eavesdropping janitors or lecturers' groupies.

As in book 1, Horace's consumption of words is infected by his speakers' ambitions. Old lessons in contentment have not been properly learned. Contrast the boatman's words at 1.5.12 ("Squeeze in another three hundred; whoa! that's enough"), where even a practical reckoning embodies Horace's Callimachean program, with Damasippus' relentless greed for figures at 2.3.116: "A thousand jugs full – that's nothing: make it three hundred thousand!"[70] The gourmet Catius is similarly insatiable in his pursuit of the different branches of culinary knowledge: "It's never enough to spend all your attention on just one area" (2.4.48).

But these second-hand speakers nevertheless enable Horace to get something said. Trebatius the jurist, advising Horace to lead a quiet life (*quiescas*) in 2.1, reformulates the position for the imperial satirist, who is incapable of writing fulsome military epic, but still slashes his sword in gestures of malice towards his perennially offendable audience, and is still inspired by his familiars – witches and vindictive judges. Although Horace is protected by his friendship with Maecenas, this is a case of "a sensible man preparing himself in times of peace for future outbreaks of hostility" (2.2.110), as well as an ironic re-entry into the satirical tradition.[71] The countryman Ofellus tells us about the triumvirs' rural dispossessions. Damasippus' hectorings about human folly and inconsistency blow up in Stoic format many of the ethical themes of book 1. Catius' rules for cuisine (a "subtle system of flavors," 2.4.36) are a disguised "recipe" for Roman satire, encoding Horace's

---

[67] Labate (1981) 26.   [68] Oliensis (1998a) 51–63.

[69] 2.5.90–1: "Beyond 'No' and 'Yes,' be silent"; 2.6.53: " 'Have you heard anything about the Dacians?' 'Nothing at all.' "

[70] Oliensis (1998a) 56 notes the second of these.

[71] Anderson (1984), Clauss (1985), Freudenburg (1990).

innovative literary-critical principles – tasteful variety, discrimination, refinement – in a suitably irreverent portrait of an obsession.[72] In 2.5 Horace tells us the new rules for insinuating oneself as an efficient courtier and legacy hunter (via a satirical Ulysses intent on rebuilding his fortunes), without openly endorsing them. And, to match these excessive or warped discussions, he offers virtuoso parodies of imbalanced *compositio* – the self-conscious placing of words.[73]

The second frame for the book is the topsy-turvy festival of the Saturnalia, which allows two speakers, Davus and Damasippus, freedom of speech (exceptional, it is implied) to remove the smug mask Horace manufactured in book 1, and to undo all his strategic disavowal there of parasitism, hypocrisy, and ambition.[74] The slave and the Stoic expose inconsistencies in Horace himself, who plays town and country mouse by turn, or self-inflating pneumatic frog;[75] in their distorting mirror, his vices appear outsize. Instead of overblown panegyric or courtly praise (2.5.98), the book is stretched out with the abuse of self-directed satire. In 2.7 Horace the casual *flâneur* is called a jittery puppet on a string and a slave to a grand master; once self-sufficient, he is unable to spend a moment by himself.[76] In 2.3 his "Be quiet" comes not quite in time to conceal disproportionate revelations about his philandering, materialism, and choleric temper.

Although Horace and his companions profess a desire to learn throughout the book,[77] there is also great emphasis on the futility of learning. Book 1's images of the child under instruction are replaced in 2.3 with Brueghelesque images of children's games – leapfrog, riding a stick, doll's houses, pinning a tail on someone else's back – which reduce Horace to the stature of a pretentious pygmy, and the philosophical hobbyhorse itself, with its absurd exaggeration and crazy repetitions, to child's play.[78] Fortune becomes the supreme games player (2.8.62–3, "How you always love to make sport of human affairs"), while Horace's trivialized relationship with Maecenas (2.6.48–9: watching and playing sport together) becomes a model for the reception of satire.

As the slave Davus says in 2.7, "Feasts go sour if they go on too long" (107), and it is appropriate that the unexpectedly premature ending of *Satires* 2 is a dining-room farce which encapsulates the mixture of overabundance

---

[72] Gowers (1993a) 135–61.   [73] Freudenburg (1996) on S. 2.3 and 2.4.

[74] S. 2.3.5 *Saturnalibus*; S. 2.7.4 *libertate Decembri*. McGann (1973) 72–84 on the crazy aspects of *Sermones* 2; Evans (1978), Freudenburg (1993) 211–23 on the Saturnalia.

[75] S. 2.7.29–37; 2.3.314–20.   [76] S. 2.7.82; 2.7.75; 2.7.112–13.

[77] E.g. S. 2.8.19; 2.3.33; 2.2.52.

[78] Huizinga (1949) 10, 143 on repetition and exaggeration as functions of play.

and dissatisfaction in the book so far.[79] Horace is not invited to the party, but there are aspects of him in several different *personae* on the inside of this tragicomic drama: the narrator, the contemporary comedian Fundanius, the pretentious host, Nasidienus, and the satirical guest, Balatro, who accompanies Maecenas and, unlike the frank dinner guests denigrated in book 1, blackens his host's name through muffled imperial sarcasm and hypocritical flattery. Nasidienus' elaborately devised menu invites the same verdict as Horace's satires at the start of 2.1: everything is either bitter or spineless (acrid *hors d'œuvres* which lash the stomach; arrangements of lacerated limbs). The host's running commentary only provokes dyspepsia and, ultimately, disgust in the guests, who shun the food as if it had been poisoned by a witch. And yet fiascos like a collapsing curtain provide them with satisfactory *unintended* entertainment at Nasidienus' expense ("There are no games I'd rather have watched than these"). Satire, Horace seems to be suggesting, has come a long way from its healthy social rôle. However, while it will never please its perpetually irritable audience on its own terms, it can, through self-parody and a hint of poison, achieve a kind of dysfunctional success, which is perhaps the most that can be hoped for from this unsatisfactory genre.

Further reading

The fullest commentaries on Horace, *Satires*, are Lejay (1911), Kiessling and Heinze (1957), Fedeli (1994). The most useful English editions are Brown (1993) and Muecke (1993); Palmer (1891) is not to be sniffed at. Essential reading includes Fraenkel (1957) 76–153, Rudd (1966), Anderson (1982) 13–150, Coffey (1989) 63–97 and Labate (1981) 5–45. Also recommended are the neat summary of Braund (1992) 16–25, and the milestone articles of McGann (1973), Zetzel (1980) on the slipperiness of *Satires* 1, and DuQuesnay (1984) on its political dimension. Recent stimulating work includes Freudenburg (1990; 1993; 1995; 1996) for pioneering investigations of literary-critical elements (see also Nilsson [1952] on metrical variety and Cartault [1899] for a catalogue of stylistic features); Henderson (1998) 73–107 and (1999) 171–227 combining new theoretical approaches with virtuoso close reading; Oliensis (1998a) 17–63 for a sophisticated socio-literary discussion of Horace's deference and independence in the *Satires*. There is a good prose translation by Rudd (1973); see Stack (1985) and Carne-Ross and Haynes (1996) for earlier translations. Martindale in Martindale and Hopkins (1993) 1–25 discusses the supreme adaptability of "Horace" for later generations; Burrow (1993) in Martindale and Hopkins (1993) is excellent on the appeal of Horatian elusiveness and rootlessness for sixteenth-century European court culture. There is a full, but not up-to-date, bibliography in Kissel (1981).

---

[79] Rather than that Horace was simply running out of ideas: *pace* Fraenkel (1957) 145. On 2.8: O'Connor (1990–1), Gowers (1993a) 161–79, Freudenburg (1995), Oliensis (1998) 57–61, Caston (1997).

3

ANDREA CUCCHIARELLI

Speaking from silence: the Stoic paradoxes of Persius

Persius is hard to read. He wants it that way. "If you do not wish to be understood, you should be left unread" (*si non vis intellegi, debes neglegi*) asserts a famous sentence of Ambrogius (some attributed it to Gerolamus) that would become the rallying cry of certain of Persius' modern detractors. Difficulty, though an inescapable fact of reading Persius,[1] ought not to be made a cause of censure in his case, but a necessary point of interest for his interpretation. In fact, any interpretation that would propose to uncomplicate an author so obviously enamored of contradictions and short-circuitings of meaning might well be regarded as suspect.

One of the chief reasons for Persius' complexity is that two of the principal components of his satire, the imitation of Horace and Stoic philosophy, are naturally in conflict with one another, and thus he toggles between opposite poles of outspokenness and silence, public engagement and disengagement, and so on. Paradox and conflict operate at many levels in Persius' satires, found in what his poems assume, what they assert, and in the political context that they put us in mind of. Horace, Stoicism, and the question of freedom (satiric and political) are for Persius diverse aspects of the same search.

Persius' imitation of Horace

We begin with the question of Horace's influence. Allusions to the classic satirist of the Augustan age are both frequent and hard to make sense of in the poems of Persius: not one of his six hexameter satires lacks a model in one or more Horatian poems. In the first of these (Persius 1), to which we will return shortly, Persius refashions, intensifies, and fits to his own times the censure that Horace had turned against the literature of his day, taking aim at its neoteric "softness" (*mollitia*) and its epic/tragic bombast. The second satire, dedicated to a friend, Macrinus, is a lengthy reproach of

---

[1] It is significant that the first exegetical commentary on Persius is attributed to a near-contemporary, the grammarian Valerius Probus.

human desires delivered in the manner of a Stoic diatribe, such as Horace had reproduced in certain of his satires (e.g. the first three poems of his first book, and poems 3 and 7 of book 2).

In his third and fourth satires Persius imitates the favored mode of Horace's second book by packaging diatribe as conversation: Persius 3 is a lively interchange between a young pleasure-seeker, stirred from a drunken sleep, and a preachy friend (perhaps the poet himself) who puts the wastrel in mind of his Stoic training by means of a straightforward protreptic to philosophy. Persius 4 reworks a pseudo-Platonic dialogue, the *Alcibiades 1*, with a Socrates character exhorting the young politician, Alcibiades, to put no confidence in external flatteries that distract from true introspection. In Persius 5, the longest (191 verses) and most complex in the book, we again encounter the reserved and confidential poet of Horace's *Sermones* and *Epistles*, here in a celebration of freedom (*libertas*), the highest of the Stoic virtues. The sixth and final satire matches a Horatian theme (the "golden mean") to Horace's signature epistolary style, to address a friend who is himself decidedly Horatian (Caesius Bassus, a scholar of Horace's poetry and active imitator of his *Odes*).

But Horace is not simply a resource for themes, expressions, and rationales in Persius. Rather he is the "lens" through which Persius views the tradition of satiric poetry that precedes him. Persius writes in dactylic hexameters, a formal decision that puts him in line with Horace, who had strictly separated the forms of "satiric" and "iambic" in his *Sermones* and *Epodes* respectively, as a reaction against the polymetry of Lucilius. The same "bifocal" view is evident in Persius: his six hexameter satires, Persius 1–6, are written in a "pure," post-Horatian variant of the classical Latin hexameter. But he also experiments with the iambic mode in his prefatory *Choliambs*. While it is not certain that Persius wrote his fourteen-line *Choliambs* as a preface to his book of hexameter satires,[2] these Hipponactean (later Callimachean) "limping iambic" verses reproduce, in a parodic key, the language and structure of a traditional proem. And yet the first hexameter satire, Persius 1, also follows the course of a programmatic preface and can easily be thought to open the collection.[3] The actual layout of the text thus suggests that the two poems

---

[2] The *Choliambs* occupy the place of a prologue in the majority of manuscripts. But in certain codices the lines are positioned as an epilogue.

[3] Cf. Kenney (1962). According to ancient sources, Persius' book was published posthumously, under the direction of his friend Annaeus Cornutus. We therefore cannot be certain that the traditional arrangement of individual poems is Persius' own. Decisive for the preservation of the text of Persius was the late antique recension, from which part of the extant manuscript tradition extends: the so-called *recensio Sabiniana* was prepared in CE 402 in Barcelona and, perhaps, Toulouse, by an imperial functionary, Flavius Julius Trifonianus Sabinus.

function as separate but related components that divide the work of a proem between themselves.

The *Choliambs* give an iambic version of the theme of the first satire. They dwell on the decadence of contemporary literature, the product of "crow poets" enslaved to the most basic of needs, most notably, "the belly." Both the *Choliambs* and Persius 1 present us with a satiric poet who stands at, and speaks from, his society's margins: his failure to communicate is the problem with which Persius 1 opens: "who will read these things?" "you asking me? nobody!" (2); so too in the *Choliambs* the poet calls himself a "half-rustic" (*semipaganus*, 6), one of the most disputed terms in all of Persius, but signifying at the very least his alienation from the contemporary scene of poetry, and its commonplaces and practitioners.[4] This juxtaposing of two distinct forms, satiric hexameters and iambs, with both entailing a prefatory function and developing themes that are deeply analogous, cannot help but express a distinction; that is, the recognition of a double register through which to look upon the poetic tradition, fully in keeping with the split vision (satiric/iambic) of Horace.

Persius likewise displays a decidedly Horatian attitude in the way he looks to the great authorities of satire. Horace had problematized the writing of satire by several times reflecting on differences between himself and satire's *inuentor*, Lucilius (in *Sermones* 1.4, 1.10, and 2.1). Near the conclusion of his programmatic first satire, Persius reminds us of these earlier discussions of "free speech" and "style": at verses 114–15 the *auctor* Lucilius returns dressed as he was by Horace in *Sermones* 1.4 as a raging castigator of vice. Horace himself then follows in lines 116–18, caught by Persius in the private act of ironically needling a famous friend (one thinks here primarily of Maecenas): "Flaccus applies an expert's soft 'touch' to his laughing friend's every vice and, once let inside, he jibes close to the heart. He is an old hand at suspending the crowd from his well-blown nose." To fill out the list of his models, Persius then names the poets of Greek Old Comedy, Cratinus, Eupolis, and Aristophanes, with the last of these designated by a periphrasis (123–4).

It is here, at the end of the first hexameter poem, that Persius reaches his highest pitch of self-reflexivity: he thinks back on Lucilius by way of Horace's reflections upon Lucilius. He also thinks back on those whom Horace had designated as Lucilius' poetic predecessors, the poets of Old Comedy. And it is exactly here, amid these programmatic reflections, that Persius finds the

---

4 The basic idea can be found already in Horace's *Sermones*, or at *Epistles* 1.19.39–40: *non ego . . . /grammaticas ambire tribus et pulpita dignor.*

context ripe for expressing his two most decisive symbols for the kind of satire he himself writes: it is a "pit" or "hole" (*scrobis*) for him to speak into, and a concentrate or distillate, thick and "cooked down" (*decoctius*).

Buried words

As we have seen, the first satire opens with the crisis of satiric communication: after the first (Lucilian?)[5] verse, the poet asks, "who will read these things?" A few verses down (8) the nasty revelation to which we were headed is cut off by a question: "for at Rome who isn't ... ah, if only I could say it!" Forced to take a different direction, the satiric discourse doubles back on itself and looks instead to the matter of poetry and poets. But the hundred or so verses that follow (9–106) cannot escape the question of "satiric freedom" that was broken off in verse 8 and resurfaces in an instant in verse 107: "but why scrape tender little ears with biting truth?" An explicit prohibition follows: "'I forbid anyone to make a stink here', you say. Paint two snakes: 'This is a holy place; piss outside, boys!'" (112–13). At this point Persius speaks a word that has the power to close all discussion: "I give up" (*discedo*, 114). The satire thus threatens to end with the satirist's surrender. But instead of stopping, Persius makes another start with the sudden re-appearance of Lucilius at the end of line 114 ("Lucilius attacked the city"), followed by Horace, as we have just seen.

Having looked at Lucilius and Horace, Persius then asks: "But, for me, it's forbidden to mumble? Not in private? Not even in a hole? Nowhere at all!? Still, I'll dig right here" (119–20). Thus Persius closes the circle by returning to the *fas/nefas* opposition introduced in the poem's first lines, with *si fas dicere* (8) recalled by *muttire nefas* in line 119. But by this point we have been presented with a fresh alternative, that of burying one's secret in a hole (*cum scrobe*). This hole is the "little book" (*libellus*) itself, the

---

[5] Horace's obsession with his predecessor, Lucilius, is perhaps expressed already in the poem's first line by way of a direct citation: the scholiast asserts that the line is quoted directly from Lucilius, a claim not necessarily dubious, but impossible to verify. According to Persius' *Vita*, it was when he read Lucilius that Persius was inspired to write satire. But this agreement between the biographical tradition and the commentary tradition is suspect, perhaps stemming from a circular logic of the following type: Persius begins with a citation of Lucilius, so his decision to write satire must somehow begin with Lucilius too (or vice versa). At any rate, a reference to Lucretius 2.14 *o miseras hominum mentes, o pectora caeca*, suffices to achieve a lofty, moral-didactic level at the beginning of Persius 1. In general, since Lucilius' work is nearly all lost, it remains impossible to establish with certainty if, and in what measure, his work operates in the text of Persius.

receiver of secrets "freely" spoken ("I've seen it, seen it, my book, that . . ."). The solution seems both to activate and answer the question left dangling earlier in the poem, with "is there anyone without ass's ears?" in verse 121 completing what was left off in verse 8 ("for in Rome who is there without . . ."). The satirist has found his own paradoxical way to speak his "truth": just bury it in a hole.

First comes Lucilius, a public "club-wielder" (*fustigator*) against vice. Then Horace, the intimate friend and "confidential" satirist. These are the satiric heroes we are given to consider in Persius 1, in a line of discussion recuperated from Horace's own *Sermones* 2.1.[6] But in recasting the question of the satirist's freedom, to indicate that it has been gradually shut down in the successive stages of the satiric tradition,[7] Persius puts before us a peculiar symbol not found in Horace: that of "the hole" (*scrobis*), which is the extreme and final expression of the public/private opposition. Lucilius was free to move across the entire "open" space of the city, Persius says, whereas Horace locates his needlings of vice within the heart of his (famous and powerful) friend (a protected spot, certainly, but also conspicuously political and social). And yet Persius, in his turn, has no option but to dig his own hole; that is, to close himself off in secretive repartee with his *libellus*.

The image is highly paradoxical, for the book is a peculiarly "leaky" kind of confidant. As a book, it cannot keep the satirist's secrets safe and out of the public domain. In fact, it is one of the most potent means for their diffusion. On this point the clear intertextual engagement with the myth of Midas leaves no doubt: stunningly, Persius' *libellus/scrobis* recalls the hole into which Midas' barber "hid" his secret about the king's having sprouted the ears of an ass. This is the secret of Persius 1.120–1, "I've seen it, seen it, my little book: is there anyone without little ass's ears?" And it is in what follows this "speaking into a hole" in the Midas myth that we come to view the full potential of Persius' hole as an image of speech and revelation

---

[6] In *S.* 2.1, near the reference to Lucilius the club-wielder (62–70: esp. 69, *primores populi arripuit populumque tributim*), he is referred to as the jesting friend of the powerful élite, Scipio and Laelius, taken into their private counsel (71–4). It is to this latter picture that Horace refers in 75–8, esp. 75–6 . . . *me / cum magnis vixisse*. But the gradations are leveled out by Persius, who attributes only to Horace the role of the "confidential" satirist. The question of satiric *libertas* must have appeared already in Lucilius, and there remains for our inspection one fragment of Lucilius that Persius perhaps worked into his (largely Horatian) intertext: fr. 454 W. *non laudare hominem quemquam neque mu facere unquam* (cf. 119 *me muttire nefas?* – *mu facere* is onomatopoetically analogous to *muttire*). The verb *muttire* occurs in Lucilius' programmatic book 26 (fr. 672–3 W), again in the context of speaking/not-speaking.

[7] On this point, see Freudenburg (2001) 178–81.

rather than of silence: the reeds that grow over the hole whisper the barber's secret. So, too, Persius' *libellus*/hole holds its secrets, but only as so many "seeds" of free speech, seeds that will soon sprout and burst into view.[8]

But even this paradox of words sprouting from silence may well draw upon a remembered precedent in satire. For in the assertion that "no shop has my books for sale, nor any sale-rack" (*Sermones* 1.4.71), Horace had already hinted that his *libelli* were not intended for general publication. Given that his freedom of speech was entirely of a private kind, the satirist saw no reason for anyone to fear his pen: "why should you fear me?" (*Sermones* 1.4.70).[9] And yet Horace opens the first poem of his second book with a reference to a reading public much broader in scope and, at least in some measure, hostile: "There is a whole class of people who think I'm too harsh in satire, and that I am stretching the genre past its legal limit" (*Sermones* 2.1.1–2). If the poems were not, in some manner, published, the claim makes no sense.

Horace tells of satire's power to expose the life of its author by reference to the "confiding" habits of his predecessor: "Lucilius confided in his books just as if entrusting trade-secrets to his trusted associates . . . and so it happens that the old man's entire life is on public display, like a painting on a temple wall" (*Sermones* 2.1.30–4). As if sharing private secrets with trusted friends, or, more precisely, *because of this* (*quo fit*), Lucilius' entire existence was in the public domain, as if painted to the last detail on a votive panel. In poetry (and in literature more generally) writing brings personal exposure, even the exposure of one's private life.[10] Persius, who began with the problem of communication, found a solution to the free speech problem in the ambiguous nature of poetry that "converses" with a static, "receptive" object (the book) that is bound to be read by many.[11] The biographical

---

[8] Already in vv. 24–5, in the satire's first critical volleys, the expansive force of satire's "seeds" are perhaps hinted at (though admittedly in reference to trivial poetic pursuits) in the image of the wild fig: *quo didicisse, nisi hoc fermentum et quae semel intus/innata est rupto iecore exierit caprificus?* For the biographical tradition it is the myth of Midas that hides an important satiric truth; cf. below.

[9] On the particular nature of Horatian *sermo*, also constructed of silences and the absence of communication, see Gowers in this volume.

[10] The same is true for Sappho and Alcaeus, famous earlier poets who considered their books "friends" (Porphyrio on *S.* 2.1.30 *Aristoxeni sententia est. ille enim in suis scriptis ostendit Sapphonem et Alcaeum volumina sua loco sodalium habuisse*).

[11] Here again Persius resembles the Horace of *Sermones* 1.4, who only recited to friends when "constrained" (73 *nec recito cuiquam nisi amicis, idque coactus*). This hesitation towards his own profession returns in the biographical tradition of Persius: *scriptitavit et raro et tarde* (*Vita Persi* l. 41). For the biographical information we are almost entirely dependent upon a *Vita Persi* that perhaps originally appeared in the commentary of Valerius Probus, dedicated

tradition asserts that his satires were published only after his death through the initiatives of his friends, Cornutus and Caesius Bassus, and that his book was madly snatched up just as soon as it was published. And praise of the book would continue a generation later in the writings of Quintilian and Martial.

The concentrate (*decoctius*)

After naming as his immediate models Lucilius and Horace, Persius moves on to the "retro-models" of Greek Old Comedy, whom Horace had brought within satire's generic bounds in *Sermones* 1.4, pointing to them as Lucilius' authorities in free speech. It is within the context of this retro-modeling that Persius produces yet another key symbol for his work, the "distillate" or "concentrate" (*decoctius*): "whoever you are, inspired by Cratinus' daring, when you grow pale over enraged Eupolis and the giant Old (Comic) Man (Aristophanes), cast a glance at *these things* too, if perchance you have an ear for anything more boiled down" (Persius 1.123–5). Commentators are divided over the crucial word: is it a concentrated potion? A thick broth? A kind of infusion slowly boiled down?[12] Or is it a medicine infused into the ear?[13] All that remains clear is that, at the heart of the notion, and thus of Persius' aesthetic ideal, is the idea of intensification/condensation (though what that specifically implies – stylistic pungency? rhetorical richness? intertextual density? – is far from certain), and that the idea is somehow connected to the poets of Greek Old Comedy.

The motivation for connecting condensation with Old Comedy quite possibly derives, as usual in Persius, from Horace. For over against the assertion of *Sermones* 1.4 that Old Comedy stands as an archetype for Roman censorial power, Horace counterposes in 1.10 a scenario in which Greek Old Comedy figures as an exemplar of the serio-comic style. He asserts: "quite often laughter slices through knotty disputes both better and more forcefully than harshness" (1.10.14–15). He then follows with a reproof of his detractors, such as Hermogenes, who have not bothered to read the poets of Old Comedy at all. And just before, but within the same line of argument, he

to Persius' works shortly after Persius' death (*De Commentario Probi Valeri sublata* is added to the title of the *Vita*). Some scholars have hypothesized an origin of the *Vita* in Suetonius. If the *Vita* seems reliable in its substance, it remains probable that certain details may have been added in accordance with the regular procedure of antique commentators who freely sought out biographical details of the poet from the poetic works themselves.

[12] The various options proposed by scholars are gathered in the commentaries of Kissel (1990) and Harvey (1981). Cf. also Bellandi (1996) esp. 132 and n. 210.

[13] Cf. Freudenburg (2001) 181–2.

had exalted the value of brevity as the stylistic virtue that avoids assaulting the listener's ear with superfluous verbiage: "there is need of brevity to keep the thought moving along, and to avoid loading down the listener's tired ears with cumbersome words" (9–10). Thus already in Horace's tenth satire we have the several elements that return in a different combination near the end of Persius 1: the poets of Greek Old Comedy, the listener, his ear, and brevity (expressed as *decoctius*). At this point, after detailing the qualities of his ideal reader in contradistinction to readers oppositely disposed, Persius is motivated once more (as in v. 114 above) to affirm strongly his satire's value. His parting assertion, a complete hexameter, stands on its own in the manner of an autonomous epigraph: "for them [sc. readers enamored of lighter fare] a dose of playbill in the morning. After lunch, the *Callirhoe*" (134).

Persius the Stoic

While it is true that the genre's inventor, Lucilius, had shown certain affinities for Stoic philosophy, e.g. in the cultural myth of the "Scipionic Circle" (an idea promoted especially by Cicero), and also, as far as we can tell, in the textual concretization of his *Satires*, Horace, in his *Sermones*, on several occasions takes pains to detach himself from the rigors of Stoicism.[14] His ironic "conversations" written for a restricted circle of friends, poems thriving on the strength of the poet's urban wit (*urbanitas*), permitted Horace, already in his first book, to counterpose an antitype to his own work in the preachy tirades of Stoic diatribe. Subsequently in book 2 Horace lets others run the risk of preaching Stoic doctrine.[15]

In contrast, Persius expresses himself as a Stoic deeply committed to his philosophical beliefs. The biographical tradition provides us with the famous image of the young poet who, having lost his father at a tender age, passed his early days with his mother, an aunt, and a sister. He then seems to have found a father substitute in the person of his Stoic teacher, Cornutus, under whom he studied at Rome after moving from his native Volterra in Tuscany. Whereas Horace had poked fun at the excessive verbiage of Stoic preachers, Persius invested his ample fortune (he was not poor) in outfitting a vast personal library that perhaps held, according to his *Vita*, as many as 700 volumes of the Stoic Chrysippus. But it is exactly this kind of book-mongering that Horace had once attacked in his Stoic rivals and detractors: "and so you don't think I've ransacked the bookracks of that blear-eyed Crispinus, I'll add not a single word more" (*Sermones* 1.1.120–1).

---

[14] Cf. Mayer's contribution to this volume.
[15] See esp. Labate (1981) 33–44; also Gowers in this volume.

This said, one ought not to think that Persius regarded Stoic teaching as a mere storehouse of wisdom, complete and irrefutable. It was perhaps the example of Horace, *Epistles* 1.1.14 ("I swear upon the words of no teacher"), that dissuaded Persius from knee-jerk fundamentalism[16] and urged him towards more subtle modes of playfulness and irony. This can be seen, for example, in his third satire. The poem opens with a teacher berating his student (Persius 3.1–4):

> So, busy as always, I see! Already the morning's clear shine penetrates the shutters and widens its narrow cracks with light. We keep on snoring, enough to defroth (last night's) unmastered Falernian, until the sundial's shadow touches high noon.

The situation bears a clear resemblance to an earlier third satire, Horace, *Sermones* 2.3.1–2, which opens with Damasippus, a recent convert to Stoicism, complaining to Horace: "you write so infrequently that in a whole year you call for parchment less than four times." Comparisons can be drawn out in detail: Horace is lazy, overfond of wine and sleep (3); rattled by his slow rate of production he chastises his writing instruments (7). So, too, the wastrel of Persius 3 (12–14 and 19).[17] But despite these analogies, a clear difference stands out to loosen the connections that bind the two poems. For the voice of Persius' preacher is laced with none of the irony that makes Damasippus, to some degree, the butt of his own abuse. Rather, the voice is that of an authoritative Stoic teacher, not an unlikely, impromptu diatribist forced into philosophy by financial failure. And the listener in the poem is no longer the poet, but a young, dissolute apprentice to philosophy.

But the complexity of Horace's design is not entirely lost in Persius 3. For it is quickly revealed that the young disciple bears a distinct resemblance to Persius. He, too, is a member of the Etruscan nobility and enjoys equestrian rank (Persius 3.27–9). We thus begin to wonder whether he is a stand-in for Persius himself, especially since Horace had once played the part of victim in *Sermones* 2.3 (he is berated again by Davus in *Sermones* 2.7). These suspicions intensify in lines 44–7, where the speaker recalls a specific moment from the wastrel's youth that one might readily refer to Persius himself: "I remember wiping my eyes with olive oil when I was a small boy," and

---

[16] Cf. Mayer in this volume.

[17] It is significant that *S.* 2.3 and Pers. 3 open with opposed temporal coordinates: respectively *raro*, "rarely", and *adsidue*, "always"; and again a certain time is "set" at the beginning of *S.* 2.7, where Davus again lays claim to the satiric voice with *iamdudum ausculto*, "I've been listening for quite some time." The designation of time draws a base, a space, and a personal context. For the connection between the two satires see esp. Harvey (1981) 77–8 and, more recently, Hooley (1997) 202–29, Reckford (1998) 337–54, and Bellandi (2002).

so on. As the discourse proceeds Persius names the Athenian Stoa, just as Damasippus once had, but it is only at the end of the poem that he recalls the specific concepts and words of Damasippus (Persius 3.116–18): "And now, when the torch is set under you, your blood starts to froth and your eyes to spark with wrath, and you say and do what even crazed Orestes would swear was crazy." The same set of ideas (ignorance synonymous with folly, wrath, and, as if on cue, the mythological example of Orestes) had been worked up much more diffusely by Damasippus at *Sermones* 2.3.132–41.[18]

In his third satire Persius seems to have "redeemed" the Stoic teacher from his ironic send up in Horace.[19] But within this game of "distantly" appropriating a model in Horace we find not only emulation (inevitably desacralizing), but a deeper, "integral" understanding of the author emulated. For within the larger domain of his *Sermones* that includes his *Epistles*, Horace had conceded far more space (terrain less obviously ironic) to Stoic doctrine. Persius would have us take full account of these *Epistles*, for he concentrates into his satires the entire scope of his predecessor's poetry and life (again exemplifying the poetics of *decoctius*). On the other hand, as a post-Horatian satirist who found in Stoicism a means to originality, he was able, to a certain degree, to bring to the fore and liberate the Stoic element of his predecessor's thought that Horace himself had largely hidden in folds of irony.

Stoicism and Persius' "condensed" style

It was through the peculiar inroad of satire that Persius made his mark upon the "new" poetry of the Neronian age. But it was primarily through his cultural upbringing, exploiting clear advantages of his status, that Persius came into contact with the city's brightest poetic talents. At Rome he completed his studies in grammar under the guidance of Remmius Palaemon, whose open-minded approach to the interpretation of classical texts was well

---

[18] The specific connection is not acknowledged as meaningful by Harvey (1981)104 (who cites the end of S. 2.7), or by Kissel (1990) 492. Hooley (1997) 226–7 concentrates instead on connections with another passage of S. 2.3, namely vv. 321–3. Other mythological exempla in Horace, S. 2.3 include 193–204 and 211 (Ajax); 303 (Agave).

[19] Persius seems to recover the high-handed bearing of Damasippus, but in profoundly modified form in the programmatic Pers. 1.123–5 *audaci quicumque adflate Cratino/iratum Eupolidem praegrandi cum sene palles / aspice et haec, si forte aliquid decoctius audis*: cf. Horace, S. 2.3.77–8 *audire atque togam iubeo componere, quisquis/ambitione mala aut argenti pallet amore*. The redeployment of Horace is not limited to his *Sermones*, but extends to his *Epistles* and *Carmina*. Other authors of special importance for Persius include Catullus, Propertius, and Virgil (esp. the *Aeneid*); see Bellandi (1996) 119–55.

known. Close to the so-called "circle of the Annaei," Persius also enjoyed intimate ties with the poets Caesius Bassus and Lucan from a very young age (the latter was an ardent admirer of Persius' poetic talents). It is from inside this "modern" poetic scene, where Augustan classical materials were ever present in profoundly altered forms, that one can best grasp the specific ideal of "condensation" implied by Persius' *decoctius*.[20]

Closely connected with this "new poetic" tradition we once again find Stoic philosophy as Persius came to know it through the city's aristocratic coteries. Stoic philosophy is directly relevant to the form of Persius' satires, and it is indispensable for our understanding of his poetic and stylistic choices – and not simply because the diatribes and treatises of the Stoic sect were often stylistically extreme.

Stoic doctrine asserted a direct and "natural" connection between words and things, teaching that language is itself "by nature": because reason (*logos*) is a universal principle penetrating every level of reality, thought and expression must necessarily resemble one another.[21] In Persius these ideas are joined to a basic principle of comic representation, already widely used and explicitly theorized in ancient comedy, according to which there should exist a precise correspondence between linguistic expression (especially in poetry) and the nature of the individual speaker.[22] The combining of these two powerful cultural components leads to a series of satiric consequences in Persius: his notoriously difficult manner of expression (linguistic violence) functions to expose Roman society's warped and unnatural state.

One project of Persius' investigation is to understand how to interpret these, always tricky, connections between speech and reality. The poet's own expertise in this matter he credits to his teacher, Cornutus, saying of him: "you take care to distinguish that which rings hard and true from a plaster cover on a painted tongue" (Persius 5.24–5).[23] This emphasis upon expert philosophical insight helps to specialize the idea of moral "exposure" that shoots through the poems of Persius ("for at Rome who does not. . . . ah,

---

[20] The idea of "condensation" helps explain, for example, the dialogic complexity that so often confuses the text of Persius in the superimposition of multiple voices that are difficult, at times impossible, to disentangle. This is to push to its furthest potential, right to obscurity's edge, the *sermocinatio* of diatribe, as well as the rapid-fire dialogue of comic drama.

[21] See Baratin (1982) 9–21; and Long (1971) 75–113.

[22] One recalls, for example, Aristophanes, *Thesmophoriazusai*, 167 ὅμοια γὰρ ποιεῖν ἀνάγκη τῇ φύσει; cf. Barchiesi–Cucchiarelli in this volume. The principle is voiced in one of the most important Stoic texts of Persius' day: Seneca, *Epistles* 114, with its epigrammatic formulation *talis oratio qualis uita*; see Bramble (1974) 23ff.

[23] Persius has a physician's eye: he examines the body to pronounce a diagnosis; again see Barchiesi–Cucchiarelli in this volume.

if only I could say it," 1.8; "I've seen it, seen it, little book: is there anyone without ass's ears?" 1.120–1). This same "expository" project Persius
consistently turns from persons and sensible experience, back upon himself,
as if to shift satire's focus towards a consideration of the conscience, and
towards knowing how to probe into the deepest secrets of the heart ("so
that my words might unseal the whole of what hides unsayable in its secret
fold," Persius 5.28–9).

Precise comparisons can be made with Stoic teaching in the matter of
Persius' most distinct symbolic expression, i.e. his "concentrate" (*decoctius*,
literally "thing more condensed"). "Conciseness" (Latin *breuitas* = Greek
suntomía) was a virtue of Stoic eloquence. Zeno, the founder of the Stoic
sect, took this idea to the point of saying that even individual syllables,
if possible, should be kept short (Diogenes Laertius 7.20 = *SVF* I, p. 70,
fr. 328).[24] This extreme view of style was made known at Rome by Cicero,
who recognized *brevitas* as a feature of "archaic" style in Cato, Pictor, and
Piso (*De oratore* 2.53), and who expressed his relation to the Stoics in these
terms:

> There is the further point that they [sc. the Stoics] maintain even a style of
> discourse that, while it is perhaps subtle and certainly pointed, is for an orator
> bland, unfamiliar, jarring to popular sensibilities, obscure, empty and starved,
> and of such a type that can never be put to effective use in public.
>
> [*De oratore* 3.66]

"Difficulty," "obscurity," etc. are characteristics that might well describe,
from a negative perspective, Persius' "pointed" and "subtle" style. Elsewhere, to describe the style of Spurius Mummius, Cicero finds a descriptive
term that, while it has no specific gastronomic or medical connections, well
approximates the idea of *decoctius*: "Lucius, for his part, was simple and
archaic. Spurius, while no more elaborate, was more restrained [*adstrictior*],
for he was an expert in Stoic doctrine" (*Brutus* 94). And further below, "the
speech of the Stoics is more restrained" (120).[25]

---

[24] For bibliography see Moretti (1995) esp. 52–70; and, for Roman culture, 71–105.

[25] Other relevant *loci* include *Brutus* 113–14, *Rutilius autem in quodam tristi et severo genere
dicendi versatus est . . . Sunt eius orationes ieiunae . . . Panaeti auditor, prope perfectus
in Stoicis; quorum peracutum et artis plenum orationis genus scis tamen esse exile nec satis
populari adsensioni accommodatum; De orat. 2. 159, Hic nos igitur Stoicus iste . . . genus ser-
monis adfert non liquidum, non fusum ac profluens, sed exile, aridum, concisum ac minutum;
De fin. 4. 24, mihi vero – inquit* [sc. Cato] – *placet agi subtilius et, ut ipse dixisti, pressius*
(on this last passage, see Moretti [1995] 112). Already Horace had regarded brevity and
obscurity as part of the same nexus: *brevis esse laboro,/obscurus fio* (*Ars Poetica* 25–6).

In another passage of explicit metapoetic interest, at the beginning of the poem addressed to his Stoic teacher, Cornutus, Persius looks past any obvious models in Augustan poetry to align himself directly with Stoic teaching. The particular image of "a mouth moderately opened" (*ore teres modico*, 5.15) finds its counterpart in the words of Zeno, who said: "one engaged in dialogue ought to comport himself like an actor. He should speak loudly, but not open his mouth too far; that is what chatterboxes do, but their words have no effect" (Diogenes Laertius 7. 20 = *SVF* I, p. 70, fr. 327).[26] In addition, the concept of the *semipaganus* in the *Choliambs* seems well-matched to the "uncultured" aspects of Stoic rhetoric (at least in the image of it left to us by Cicero).

Cicero had said of the Stoics (*De finibus* 4.7): "they invent new words and neglect those in use." Images, metaphors, and examples drawn from daily experience, especially from physiology, were apparently the stock-in-trade of Stoic discourse. One thinks of how Zeno once responded to a student: "if you don't steep your tongue in thought, still more will you err in your words" (Stob. *Ecl.* 3.36.23, p. 696 Hense = *SVF* I, p. 67, fr. 304), which might remind Persius' reader of the "painted tongue" image of Persius 5.25 (cited above). As a Stoic thinker, Persius puts numerous physiological metaphors and images to work in his investigation of the connections binding spirit to body: "(the Stoics) compare philosophy to a living thing, by making logic correspond to bones and nerves, ethics to fleshy parts, and physics to the soul. Another analogy is to an egg: logic corresponds to the shell, ethics to the white, and physics to the yolk" (Diogenes Laertius 7.40 = *SVF* II, p. 16, fr. 38).[27]

The term "expressionistic" has been used with good reason to describe Persius' peculiar style. His is a satiric language that strengthens and intensifies the means of expression already tested by the Augustan poets.[28] Stoic presuppositions motivate this particular expressionism, making it into a game of discovery: strained connections between words stimulate reflexion, causing the reader to negotiate the difficult path that goes from things to words, and vice versa. Related to this is the phenomenon so frequent in Persius of his "showing" us images that seem abrupt and riddling because heavily

---

[26] For the standard comparisons, such as Horace, *S.* 1.4.43–4 *os/magna sonaturum*; Horace *Ars* 94, *tumido . . . ore*; 323–4, *ore rotundo/ . . . loqui*; etc., see Harvey (1981) 131; Kissel (1990) 589–90.

[27] Once when he was going to the theater to hear the cithara-player, Amoebeus, Zeno said to his students: "let's go and see how this man's insides, his bones and nerves, imbued with reason and rhythm, oversee the fixed arrangement of his vocal expression" (Plutarch, *Moralia* 443a = *SVF* I, p. 67, fr. 299).

[28] Cf. La Penna (1979) 5–78, esp. 60–78; fundamental are Bramble (1974) and Bellandi (1996).

burdened by background content that is suppressed. The result is a style that one might call "conceptual": "singing . . . Pegaseian nectar" (*Choliambs* 14, that is, producing honey-sweet poetry that, legend asserts, comes from the spring Hippocrene ("horse-spring"), so-called because it sprang from a stroke of Pegasus' hoof); "to swallow . . . pure Anticyras" (Persius 4.16), that is, to drink pure hellebore extract, a cure for insanity, produced in the Greek city of Anticyra; the metonomy of city-for-product had already been used by Horace at *Sermones* 2.3.82–3, but in a much more explicit way). Examples multiply from line to line and poem to poem, leaving us to reflect on our own, and to account for the mysteries of "stony gout" (Persius 5.58); "purging the night" (2.16); "yanking old grannies from your lung" (5.92); "Mercurial spit" (5.112), and so on. Again, as instances of his expressionism, Persius makes frequent use of low onomatopoetic terms, many of which are still commonly found in modern languages of Latin descent (*scloppus*, "pop," *lallare*, "lullaby," *papa*, "pappa"), as well as interjections or diminutives typical of colloquial language: *Hercule, nugae, uetulus, rancidulus* ("by Hercules," "twaddle," "gramps," "stinky"). Grecisms and words of non-Latin origin are not avoided, but the general impression is that Persius is quite vigilant about not admitting into his poems diction that is not already in wide use in the city of Rome. It might be said that between Persius and the freewheeling bilingualism of Lucilius stands the restriction of Horace (especially *Sermones* 1.10.20–30). In the end, common language ("words of the toga") constitutes the satirist's prime materials for exercising his stylistic inventiveness.

Stoic "brevity" must have influenced Persius in developing his poetics of *decoctius*. It can be said, then, that Persius likely found in his own Stoicism the means to overcome the restrictions and idiosyncrasies of Horace, his teacher in satire, for whom there existed in Stoicism (and diatribe) only the opposite defect: that of the garrulity of unbearable preachers, such as Fabius and Crispinus. It is therefore one of Persius' own Stoic paradoxes that he should advance "past" Horace in realizing the aesthetic criteria that are, by legacy, derived directly from him.

Persius and *libertas* ("freedom/free speech")

Stoicism carried precise anti-imperial connotations in the age of Nero. Persius frequented the Stoic circle(s) that collected around such high-profile figures as Seneca and Thrasea Paetus, both of whom would soon enter into direct conflict with Nero (the majority of Persius' teachers and friends would be forced to commit suicide or to go into exile). His *Vita* relates that Persius was deeply attached, as son to father (*coluit ut patrem*), to Servilius Nonianus, the anti-Neronian historian who would become one of Tacitus' sources. The *Vita* also informs us that Persius dedicated certain verses to the memory of the Elder Arria, the mother-in-law of Thrasea Paetus, to whom he was distantly related. She had committed suicide in anticipation of her husband's death, after he, Caecina Paetus, had been involved in a conspiracy of CE 42 against the emperor Claudius (the episode, which soon became an exemplary tale of Republican defiance, is found in Tacitus, Pliny the Younger, and Dio Cassius).[29]

By undertaking to write poetry that formally defined itself as an expression of "free speech" (*libertas*/ Greek *parrhesia*), Persius would seem generically bound to express political views. The grand political invectives of Lucilius had shown the way. And Persius cannot avail himself of the excuse that Horace once used to justify his political reticence, by claiming to be inferior to Lucilius in wealth and social standing (*Sermones* 2.1.74–5). And yet it remains a fact that one cannot find in Persius' satires clear allusions to the persons and events of contemporary political life in Nero's Rome. In his case, the encounter between Stoicism and satire has not produced the expected attitude of political opposition.

Instead, Persius expresses himself on the impossibility of voicing criticism directly: "to tell" (*dicere*) is not "allowed"(*fas*), he says; and even to "mutter" (*muttire*) runs the risk of a "criminal offense/sacrilege" (*nefas*). The point is driven home, as we have seen, by corresponding passages near the beginning and end of his first satire. But it is exactly in relation to the second of these passages that we are informed of the possibility of our reading Persius' satires politically. The *Vita* tells us that verse 121 may originally have contained an allusion to "King" Nero, but that Cornutus, Persius' post-mortem editor, decided to suppress the reference prior to publication. Thus the first part of the verse may originally have read "King Midas has ass's ears," only to be "corrected" to read "who is there without ass's ears?"[30] The story is suspect, especially since it occurs in a section of the *Vita* that seems to have been inserted as a later expansion. It is unlikely that Persius would have wanted

---

[29] These verses, along with Persius' other non-satiric works, were destroyed by the poet's mother, on the advice of Cornutus. Nothing definite can be said about the *praetexta* of uncertain title (transmitted by the MSS as †*uescio*†; S. Mariotti conjectured *Veios*). But it should be observed that clear anti-imperial sentiments animate the only *praetexta* that has come down to us, the *Octavia*, likely composed shortly after the death of Nero.

[30] "His verse, since it was aimed at Nero as follows: 'King Midas has the ears of an ass' [*auriculas asini Mida rex habet*] was corrected by Cornutus, just this one, in this way: 'who is there without ass's ears?' [*auriculas asini quis non habet?*], so that Nero would not think it was spoken against himself."

to make the reference to the myth of Midas so utterly explicit. And the existence of an alternate original version of the line seems also to be undercut by the discernible interplay between verses 8 and 121 (studied above). The story perhaps originates with a misunderstanding of a commentator's gloss on verse 121. But if, as is probable, the story was first circulated just after, or even contemporaneously with, the book's initial publication, it must still count as a valuable testimony to the open "legibility" of the text of Persius 1 within, or near, its original setting. The inevitability of certain readers finding an allusion to Nero, the consequent risk of censure, and the necessity of an intervention into the text, work to bring the satires of Persius inside the anti-imperial frame of the opposition. Perhaps the senatorial, Stoic circles in which Persius lived and wrote were inevitably inclined to interpret his poems in a political key. They may have wished to see a political act, a denunciation, in Persius' attempting to muzzle a genre that had been set up to express free speech: "but for me it's forbidden to mumble?" But apart from tendentious interpretations (perhaps willful mis-appropriations), free speech of an overtly political kind does not appear in Persius' satires. Only philosophical "freedom," the emancipation of the individual from the constraints of vice and desire.

Horace, Persius, and Stoicism

In his programmatic satire, Persius 1, Persius chooses the last of Horace's several reflections on the satiric genre as the place from which to set out upon his own satiric discourse. He might have started from some other, more likely, place (say, from *Sermones* 1.1), but Persius resumes the discourse of *Sermones* 2.1, with all its radical questions: why write satire? What are the limits of free speech in satire? What pressures do one's predecessors apply, especially Lucilius, but also Horace?

In choosing to start here, Persius is forced to expose his own attitudes towards his models as both their reviver and imitator. On the one hand, he constantly keeps us in mind of Horace (chiefly of his *Sermones*, but of other poems as well). But those Horatian memories commonly bring tension along with recognition, as we have seen. For along with the simple pleasure that comes from recognizing a pre-existing source in Horace, comparisons and reckonings of differences between these two textual surfaces inevitably arise, sometimes to chafe the reader's sensibilities. These complications of sense operate at every level of the text and can be found even in matters of diction and style. A telling example is the case of Persius 5.14: "you follow the toga's words, a skilled old hand at rough joinings." The evident model for this difficult image is the maxim of Horace, *Ars Poetica* 47–8: "your speech will excel if a skilled joining [i.e. collocation] renders a known word new." But here the Horatian memory, activated already in lines 10–13 immediately preceding (recalling Horace's bellows of *Sermones* 1.4.19–21), elicits more than a simple nod of recognition. It draws us to account for some obvious differences: the "joining" (*iunctura*) is no longer "skilled" (*callida*) in Persius, as it had been in Horace. Rather it is "hard" (*acris*), and the poet himself is now "skilled" (*callidus*). Thus, at the same time as he remembers Horace's maxim, Persius puts it to work to achieve new effects: his refashioning of Horace's "skilled joining" is thus itself a *callida iunctura*, rendering (in Horace's punning words) a "known" (*notum*) Horatian expression "new" (*nouum*).

As we have seen, innovation, the loading of images with expressionistic force, and the intensive use of the tools of rhetoric confer upon Persius' satires an experimental color. It is in Callimachus, especially in his *Iambs*, that we can reasonably posit a point of reference for Persius' striving for complexity with little fear of obscurity: if Persius' *Choliambs* seem to make a return to the polymetry of Lucilius, they have an earlier referent in Callimachus' first *Iamb* (in fact also written in the choliambic meter). Comparisons with this poem may be extended to various specific themes, perhaps especially to the caricature of contemporary poets as squawking birds. But the poems are also comparable, above all, on the level of style. Both are marked by brevity, density that tends towards obscurity, and an intractability of language that is both deeply learned and colloquial.[31]

Thus Callimachus, a maestro of self-reflexivity, adds yet another lens to the complex optical machine that Persius uses to look upon Horace (and upon Lucilius, the satiric tradition, the Old Comic poets, but also upon many others, such as Virgil). His satiric communication, at the moment that it reaches its highest level of intensification, is overloaded by the memories it activates, and short-circuited by its own ambiguity. The intense memories activated by the text and its very interpretability are found to collide, and to generate irresolvable contradictions.

It was not, in fact, an easy task to "imitate" Horace, and not just because imitating a classic is always difficult. Horace himself undertook to discourage imitators; or better, he wanted to indicate the dangers of producing a superficial imitation that failed to capture the deeper levels of poetry. He makes the point through a physiological reference to his own body at

---

[31] On Callimachus and Persius, see Sullivan (1985) 74–114, Koster (1990) 155–63, and Freudenburg (2001) 140–2. On the dialogue (and contradictions) in Persius between high-brow Callimacheanism and the poetics of the *semipaganus*, see Bellandi (1996), with bibliography.

Epistles 1.19.17–20:[32] "the model imitable in its defects deceives. But if I should, by chance, turn pale, they would down draughts of cumin to drain their blood. Oh imitators, you slavish sheep, how often your blusterings make me rage and laugh!" If Persius avoids such charges of "slavish" imitation, it is because he takes seriously the lesson that follows directly in lines 21–5 of the same letter, where Horace recalls the manner in which he himself had imitated Archilochus in his rhythms and moods (he adds "modes" and "art of song" in v. 27), but not in his specific themes. Therefore, having been enjoined not to reproduce his predecessor's themes in slavish detail (this is strictly the forbidden "surface" mode of imitation), Persius must seek to access him more deeply, in the secrets of his art.

This is precisely how Persius comports himself in relation to Horace. He demonstrates that he has deeply absorbed the lessons taught by his predecessor, even at the technical levels of diction and verse. But he avoids imitating him at the level of "themes," choosing here to chart his own new path. For while it is true that words and turns of phrase return from Horace, and the ear attuned to Horace is constantly put in mind of his "conversations" (*sermones*) by the hexameters of Persius, the gestures and attitudes of the Horatian persona do not return, unless in a form deeply modified.

Persius is constantly looking to Horace, as to an image in a mirror, to model himself in his satires. But the image that he finds there (and thus the image we perceive of him) is distorted and ambiguous, combined from elements utterly disparate and, at times, contradictory. And yet this unlikely image of the "Horatian Stoic satirist" brings with it a stunning new insight into the workings of imitation *as* originality: the paradox that even the most minute and excessive practices of imitation can produce an utterly original expression when that imitation is, like the "wild fig" (*caprificus*) of Persius 1.25, bursting with potential and "uncontainable." By claiming to hide his words in a hole, Persius ensures that they will break to the surface and speak in full voice.

Further reading

The most detailed commentary on Persius is the monumental German commentary of Kissel (1990). Though much older, still indispensable is Jahn (1843), which includes the ancient scholia. The easiest and most reliable guide in English is Harvey (1981). Among the best Latin editions of Persius are A. Cartault, *Perse: Satires* (Paris 1951); W. Clausen, *A. Persi Flacci et D. Iuni Iuvenalis Saturae* (Oxford 1959; 2nd edn., Oxford 1992); and D. Bo, *A. Persi Flacci Saturarum Liber* (Turin 1969). The most useful editions with commentary and English translations are J. R. Jenkinson, *Persius: the Satires* (Warminster 1980); and G. Lee and W. Barr, *The Satires of Persius*

---

[32] Cf. Barchiesi–Cucchiarelli, in this volume.

(Liverpool 1987). Older, and rather frayed in some of its judgments, is J. Conington and H. Nettleship, *The Satires of A. Persius Flaccus* (Oxford 1893 = Hildesheim 1967), with translation and commentary. In the Loeb series (with text and English translation) is G. G. Ramsay, *Juvenal and Persius* (London/New York 1918; 2nd edn. 1940). More recent English translations include W. S. Merwin, *The Satires of Persius* (Bloomington 1961); and Rudd (1973).

Among the older critical studies that remain fundamental to the study of Persius are Reckford (1962) 476–504, Bramble (1974), and the two articles on Persius in Anderson (1982). For Persius' satires taken individually, see D. Korzeniewski, *Die erste Satire des Persius*, in D. Korzeniewski, ed. *Die römische Satire* (Darmstadt 1970) 384–438. For a general profile of Persius as author, see R. G. M. Nisbet, "Persius," in Sullivan (1963) 39–71. Large-scale critical studies of Persius include Dessen (1996), and, in Italian, Bellandi (1996). The most important recent, large-scale study, with special attention to Persius' intertextual techniques, is Hooley (1997). Freudenburg (2001) contains numerous stimulating interpretations delivered in a lively style. For Persius as an imitator of Horace, with bibliography, see Cucchiarelli (2001) 189–203.

For an overview of bibliography see M. Saccone, "La poesia di Persio alla luce degli studi più recenti (1964–1983)," *ANRW* II, 32.3 (1985) 1781–1812, and (following in the same volume) the fine critical discussion of E. Pasoli, "Attualità di Persio," 1813–43. For a (by now dated) bibliographical review, see W. Anderson, "Recent Work in Roman Satire," *Classical Weekly* 50 (1956) 37–8; *Classical World* 57 (1964) 344–6 and 63 (1970) 191–9.

4

VICTORIA RIMELL

The poor man's feast: Juvenal

Juvenal is the satirist of comparatives and superlatives. In exploiting hexameter satire's partnership with epic, he sets out to look bigger, denser, ruder, slyer, angrier, fleshier, more sophisticated and bilious, to the power of ten, than all the other satirists before him put together. Next to this heavyweight, Horace's bitter-sweet social commentary, or Persius' harsh medicinal concentrate, should begin to taste like very thin soup. Juvenal rejects outright Callimachean principles of slenderness, compression, and refinement, claiming instead to be driving his chariot "down the track which great Lucilius blazed" (1.19–20).[1] Horace's irony lite, or Persius' short sharp shock therapy, is to be replaced by behemoth-scale onslaughts inspired by the bellicose Republican freedom fighter. Whereas Horace buries Lucilian rage beneath manicured lawns, Juvenal digs up a century of pent up angst, yet only to hurl it at corpses who cannot answer back.[2] This is war, and there is no escape, either for his victims or readers (and we may well suspect that they are one and the same in his book). The dysfunctional morass of contemporary Rome incites antirationalistic gibe, not spiritual inner journeys or jocular reflection among friends. "Today every vice has reached its zenith," he announces in his opening poem (149); "doesn't it make you want to cram wax tablets with invective right there on the street corner?" (63–4). As he prepares to hoist every last inch of his mock-epic sails (1.150), he warns his readers of impending conflict: they risk blushing beetroot, or sweating themselves ill with guilt, once he starts swinging his satirical sword (165–7). But by the end of the first satire, we realize that the warning may not have come soon enough: "once the soldier dons his helmet, it's too late to chicken out of war" (168–70). This satirist shames his audience into tasting the bile that spurs

---

[1] See Courtney (1980) on what Horace, Persius, and Juvenal have in common. Note in particular that Juvenal mentions Horace as one of his models at 1.51.

[2] *Sat.* 1.170–1. Note that this is nothing new: Persius and Horace also appeal to the precedent of Lucilius in their programmatic satires (*S.* 2.1 and Pers. 1).

his verse[3] (*facit indignatio uersum*, 1.79), talks down from his lofty pulpit to taint readers with his own humiliation as social outcast. In doing so, Juvenal is constantly force-feeding readers the experience of empire itself, as illustrated in satire 10, where every talent and success (from the gift of the gab to beauty and fame) is ultimately twinned with failure and deterioration, just as imperial power is doomed to self-destruct. The heights of pseudo-epic pomp are scaled, it seems, only to stage a more sensational fall from grace.

This chapter will race thematically through Juvenal, painfully aware of what it cannot cram in. Along the way I will be flagging and responding to some central ideas in contemporary criticism of Juvenal. For instance, while it is safe to say that we have long stopped labeling this satire as documentary type "realism," the problem of how sincere (or how self-satirizing) the Juvenalian persona is at any point has remained a dominant concern: do we recognize in Juvenal the fervent conservative moralist, or the prejudiced, hamfisted hack constantly sending himself up, and is it always simply either/or? Can anyone slash their way through the fogs of deception to tell genuine from faked, as Juvenal asks in satire 10.2–4? Much has been written on Juvenalian anger, and on the shifting emotional tone of the satires: *indignatio* seems to wane after book 1, yet to what extent is this a ruse?[4] Similarly, critics have disagreed over how to read the looseness, inconsistency, and messiness of Juvenal's style and structure: is it a mask that slips to reveal Callimachean precision, and if not, does it signpost "bad" art?[5] Scholars have long tried to nip and tuck the awkwardness of Roman satire to fit the equilibrium of a "classical aesthetic,"[6] and until recently there has been strong resistance to reading sardonic self-consciousness into Juvenal's "superficial" and "undisciplined" posturing, not least because this would risk making *us* his victims. Yet one of the things I will be stressing is that the satirist is always knee deep in his own muck. We'll see that Juvenal turns inside–outside distinctions inside out and back again, to implicate everyone and everything in Rome's flabby, edgeless empire.

---

3 On *indignatio* as a feature of Juvenal and other writers of the period, see Ramage (1989).

4 Braund (1988) is the lengthiest work on anger in Juvenal, arguing that "irony" replaces *indignatio* as the dominant mode in the third book.

5 On Juvenal's notorious "loose construction," see especially Kilpatrick (1973).

6 See discussion in Freudenburg (2001) 6. Dryden's discussion (1900, 84–5) inadvertently demonstrates the difficulty of making Juvenal presentable, satisfying reading: comparing Juvenal to Horace, Dryden writes that the former "fully satisfies my expectation . . . he drives the reader along with him; and when he is at the end of his way I willingly stop with him. If he went another stage it would be too far." Yet in the same paragraph, "he is sometimes too luxuriant, too redundant; says more than he needs . . ."

Thinking big

Juvenal's sixteen satires, split into five books (1–5, 6, 7–9, 10–12, 13–16), begin in the monstrous cosmopolis of Flavian Rome, and expand to zigzag to the ends of the earth and back again, if only as a journey of the mind. In satire 2, Juvenal wants to escape to the North Pole, imagines a trip to Hades, and traces the map of imperial conquest west to Ireland and the Scottish highlands, and east to Ardaschan. We do not need to travel far to live the Greek life in Rome in satire 3, plunge the depths of the frozen sea of Azov to spy the origins of a prize turbot in satire 4, and visit everywhere from Corsica, Egypt, Asia, and the Sahara to the mythic paradise of Phaeacia in satire 5, before Juvenal dumps his victim back in the slums of the Subura where he belongs. The opening lines of satire 10 appeal to readers to scour the globe from Cadiz to the Ganges to find a man who can distinguish true from false. Satire 15, the last complete poem, spins out the adventure holiday of a lifetime through the cannibalistic heartland of Egypt, stopping to scan imperial conquests in Spain, Britain, Germany, Poland, Romania, and Iceland. These xenophobic satires all boomerang back and forth between the cultural stewpot of urban Rome and the sites of provenance and destination for its kaleidoscope of imports and exports. The point is that in Juvenal Rome *is* the world: it has become so saturated with people, influences, vices, that it has both devoured the entire globe and come to represent it in freakish concentrate. Juvenal's transformation of the satiric recipe sets out to expose, indulge, enact, and even to outdo this excess. In other words, these poems perform imperialism, are as piggishly stuffed as Rome itself.

The most virulent vice in Juvenal's landscape is the crazed pursuit of fortune, fame, and Hollywood-style scale, and his caricature with the most screen time is the corpulent millionaire or wannabe aristocrat. This creature boozes, feasts, and belches his way through the day, wolfing seven courses alone (1.94–5), gobbling up legacies, waddling to the bathroom holding a belly swollen with undigested meat (1.142–3).[7] The emperor Domitian fulfills all the criteria for sickening greed in satire 4, as does his courtier Montanus with his "slow, gross paunch" (4.107), and the gourmand host in 5.114–15 dining on foie gras made from a liver as big as the goose itself; or the woman in satire 6 (428–32), who drinks until she spews from her bloated gut and almost drowns in her own vomit. Husbands' bodies are blackened and bloated with poison in satire 1 (69–72); the eel caught in the River Tiber for satire 5's dinner party is fat with sewage (*pinguis torrente cloaca*, 105), alongside the prize turbot presented to the emperor in satire 4, which is

---

[7] Compare Persius' "death in the bath" scene at 3.98–106.

"torpid with sloth" from its icy hibernation (*longo frigore pingues*, 44). In satire 6, a modern Medea poisons her two children with "steaming black pies" (631): "Two kids, in one meal?!" (641).[8] Lawyers are puffed up with self-importance, and strain their lungs until they burst (7.108–12), while the blue-blooded advocate needs eight stout Thracian slaves to carry him through the forum (7.132). In satire 8, we see fat Lateranus, the consul turned muleteer, boozing himself into a stupor in the baths, low-class cabarets, and seedy taverns (173–8). And the bull Juvenal would have wanted to sacrifice to celebrate the return of his friend from a mock-epic sea voyage in satire 12 is so well fed that he can hardly move, with a neck so massive only the heftiest priest could slash through it at a stroke (10–16).

Eating disorders

This is satire which aspires above all to satiety, to fulfillment of the grossest hunger, ambition, and wickedness. Like Persius and Horace before him, Juvenal plays on the etymology of satire: *satur*, meaning full, and *satura*, meaning mixed platter. But the idea in Juvenal is always that Roman satire is now allowed to run rampant, to pack so much in at such an emotional pitch that it becomes unsurpassable. Nevertheless, Juvenal's characters and satiric personas are perpetually dissatisfied, their bellies painfully hollow even after the feast, just as in satire 1 Juvenal resigns himself to paining readers with the same indigestible mishmash. Fullness to the point of bursting frustrates the desire for more, a desire which may have been the point of eating to begin with. These satires constantly imagine the problem of what happens when a gluttonous empire has no more room to distend, in terms of a physical satiety which paradoxically registers as a hunger with nowhere to go. As we will see, Juvenal's constant play on contradictory perspectives is rooted in this dilemma of empire and appetite.

In satire 7, which bemoans the fate of today's unfulfilled writers, the contemporary poet is the epitome of greed: "of course it comes cheaper to keep a lion than a poet: poets have bigger bellies" (78–9). In the dinner party of satire 5, the host eats *haute cuisine* while guests are served inedible scraps; poor man Trebius leaves the dining room even hungrier, and his "empty rumbling belly" is pure pantomime entertainment for the well fed: *quis melior plorante gula?* "what better than a whimpering gullet?" (158). In satire 15, the Egyptian rabble tears apart its victim raw, bones and all, but so many

---

[8] The cannibalistic connotations here (we are reminded of Procne's and Philomela's murder and barbecuing of Itys) represent the limits of sick fantasy, the "ultimate" sin. Compare with Juvenal 15.

want a bite of the action that each man gets only a morsel, and the last in line are left to scrape blood off the ground with their fingernails (89–92): cannibalism, already a perverse hunger (one analogous to the satirist's own parasitism), fails to satisfy. When, at the end of satire 14, the speaker predicts that the maxim "wealth does not bring happiness" needs updating, that the "minimum wage" needs to rise, he sets a trap for the domino effect of ambition: even if he doubles, triples the amount, you will not be self-fulfilled (14.327–9).

So on one hand Juvenal seems to reject the simple diet advocated by Horace and Persius in favor of aspirational, hedonistic cuisine, while on the other he pillories the conspicuous consumption of the corrupt upper classes, from which he himself is excluded. So in satire 1, Juvenal's verse is introduced as a *farrago*, a pigswill made up of the rancid scraps of humanity it feeds on (85–6), minced up literary culture for an audience with no taste. Yet Trebius in satire 5 is a figure of fun, and satire 3 makes the pauper an "eternal butt for bad jokes" (147–53). If you are poor and cannot afford private transport, you get beaten up in the street *and* get sued for damages, such is your "freedom" (3.297–9), although in satire 10 (21), only the penniless citizen escapes the highwayman and is happier owning nothing. Juvenal's strategy is disorienting polarization and juxtaposition. Outrageous extremes dizzy the perspective, and are then exposed as fissured or on the verge of collapse. The poor man and the rich man dine together, eating foods at opposite ends of the social spectrum (satire 5), yet the dining room is never so simply divided: even on first reading, we taste the irony that the gloating maitre d' dines on a dubious "dish of mushrooms such as Claudius guzzled, before the one prepared by his wife" (146–8), while the frustrated guests have been vaccinated by the filthy salad dressing ("a prophylactic against venomous snakes," 91).

Perspectives and disorientation

There are several points at which Juvenal spells out his strategy of blowing things up out of all proportion only in order to achieve maximum deflation or disorientation. The edifices of gargantuan Rome itself, which stand as a constant allegory for this satire, are built on very shaky foundations and continually threaten to topple (3.193–6). In satire 8, similarly, the speaker warns that to lean on borrowed glory is foolish, as "the pillars may fall, and the house collapse in ruin" (8.76–7). Sejanus' pursuit of excessive wealth and honors "built up a towering edifice, storey by storey, so that his final downfall was that degree greater, the crash more catastrophic" (10.104–7), while the satirist in 11 sneers that the more broke greedy gourmands are, "like some house about to collapse, with daylight showing through the cracks," the better they dine (11.12–13).

Sometimes structures founder or shrink if only you look at them from another angle: if you view a beehived lady from the back, you see a sawn-off midget forced to stand on tiptoes for a kiss (6.502–7). Planet earth was not big enough for Alexander, yet in death "a coffin was measure enough to contain him" (*sarcophago contentus erit*, 172). Frequently too, Juvenal cranks up the scale: if his friend is distraught on losing a couple of hundred bucks, imagine what it must feel like to be robbed of 5K or more, a pile so big "even the largest strong-box can scarcely contain it" (13.74). And all too often, we are hit with two opposing perspectives at once: the vices of Rome are unimaginable in number, yet all this can be "contained in one courtroom" (*sufficit una domus*, 13.160). The pitched battles between Thracian cranes and Ethiopian pygmies would look hilarious in Rome, but deadly serious in a land where soldiers stand about one foot high (167–73), just as women with breasts as big as their babies look normal sized in Egypt (163).

It is Juvenalian rhetoric which really ensures that these *exempla* hit home. His satire claims tragi-epic stature and gutter street-cred all at once, and this is communicated in a jagged contrast between grandiloquent, archaic rhetoric and poeticisms, and the biting vernacular (obscenities, Grecisms, diminutives, slang, neologisms) which constitutes satire's fast food. The defamiliarizing antithesis we have seen working on the level of narrative or subject matter is even more striking on the level of poetics: overtly lofty registers that destroy any semblance of Horatian *sermo* (conversation) are twinned with colloquialisms. Or they are partnered with un-Latin Hellenisms whose harsh consonants grate the Roman ear, often jammed at the end of the line, or slipped in at the beginning of the next for maximum impact (e.g. *bulbuco* at 7.116). The hyperbolic is lined up with the microscopic, prompting critics to compare Juvenal to a film director or miniaturist, painting in epigrammatic flashes or zooming in for a close up before panning out for the skyline shot.[9] In the middle-distance, Juvenal's poems often look like they split halfway, or come apart like a concertina. He has regularly been charged with incoherence or "loose construction," and classicists have debated whether the introductions of poems 4 and 7, for instance, were written and tagged on afterwards.[10] Yet it is Juvenal's tactic to accumulate illustrations without a clear logic or sense of unity (indeed, contradictions and shifts of opinion are often designed to expose where *you* draw the line between tough talking and vile prejudice), so that the reader is often forced to weigh up the relative

---

[9] See e.g. Ferguson (1979) xix–xxii; Kenney (1963).
[10] See Anderson (1957) and Kilpatrick (1973).

strengths and weaknesses of characters and arguments, to pursue a continual project of "compare and contrast" without the guiding light of any consistent authoritative voice. Juvenal is the most impersonal and elusive of the Roman satirists.[11]

Satire 4, poised just as the first book is cranking up to its culinary climax, is probably where this collage of effects packs the most punches. This satire looks like it folds in two: the first section of narrative (v. 1–27) concerns Crispinus, the Egyptian freedman come good whom we also met in 1.26. He is the cradle-snatching monster of iniquity who bought a huge red mullet for sixty gold pieces, to eat by himself. The second, apparently unconnected section, amplifies the first (and not only in its length). The emperor, implicitly, is Crispinus blown up in epic caricature, a sickening glutton who is flattered when a fisherman presents him with a gigantic turbot, and summons his courtiers as if to an emergency war cabinet to decide how it should be cut up and cooked. The debate over an outsize fish, which cannot fit even on the largest platter[12] (*orbs* = "round body," as well as "globe," 132), is a trivial event which suggests the full magnitude of Domitian's tyranny:[13] Domitian cuts throats as easily as he slices his dinner, can whip up the terror of his courtiers over a recipe, never mind a *real* issue. Paradigmatically here, Juvenalian bathos is a boom and bust affair, vacillating histrionically from horror to farce, and from world to plate, until the scale that measures big, small, bigger, biggest, threatens to snap. Line 17, *ut perhibent qui de magnis maiora locuntur* ("as those who talk up big things bigger would say") describes the satirist's machinations; line 11, *sed nunc de factis leuioribus* ("But now onto a lighter topic"), is a sardonic dig. When the speaker announces *malim fraterculus esse gigantis* ("I'd prefer to be a giant's little bro," 98) to mean "I'd rather be a nobody," this is clearly in the eye of the beholder, as even the younger sibling of a giant is huge. The *sinus* in which the turbot is snared in line 41 could mean (big) bay or (small) net; the (huge) fish is caught in a (tiny) skiff (*cumba*, 45). Juvenal combines snappy, short sentences with overblown periods (e.g. 28–33), and the sharpest lines jigsaw opposing textures and scales (see 131–2, or 109–10: *saeuior illo* | *Pompeius tenui iugulos aperire susurro*, "more ruthless was Pompeius, whose tender whisper slit men's throats"). The vocabulary of magnitude abounds (*tanto*, 18; *magnae*, 20; *magna*, 32; *maiora*, 66; *magnae*, 74; *saeuior*, 109; *grande*,

---

[11] Declamatory satire was an unsuitable medium for autobiographical criticism, and we know next to nothing about Juvenal's life.

[12] Compare Horace S. 2.4.75/77, where his advice was not to cram too large a fish onto too small a plate.

[13] This point is developed in Gowers's reading (1993a) 202–11.

115; *magis*, 119; *plurima*, 119; *ingens*, 124; *magni*, 125; *magnis*, 133; *magnus*, 145, etc.).

Up close, the perspective verges on the hallucinogenic. We start off with comparison: Crispinus is a *monstrum* (2), but so is the emperor's fish (*monstrum*, 45); Crispinus is already appearing *iterum*, "again," in line 1, but Crispus and Crispinus are also two of Domitian's courtiers at 81 and 108. Crispus and the turbot have both survived winters by being mild and sluggish (*mite ingenium*, 82–3; cf. *tardos et longos frigore pingues*, 44), never swimming upstream (*numquam contra torrentem*, 89–90; cf. *torrentis*, 43); the courtier Montanus' flesh is also as lethargic as the turbot's (*Montani quoque uenter adest abdomine tardus*, 107). In the first Crispinus narrative, the speaker comments that he could have bought the fisherman for the price he paid for the fish (25–6), and when the fisherman in the second story offers the turbot to Domitian, he says *propera stomachum laxare sagina | et tua seruatum consume in saecula rhombum* ("purge your stomach of its last meal and eat this turbot, served to adorn your reign," 66–7). *Sagina* is a strangely unflattering word to use, being the kind of small fry fed to bigger fish. The "flattery" makes Domitian's imperial crest rise (*et tamen illi surgebant cristae*, 69–70), and later on the courtier Veiiento flatters the fish (or is it Domitian?) in precisely the same terms, saying *cernis erectas in terga sudes?* ("do you see the row of spines sticking up along his back?" 127–8). Identification of perpetrator and victim, or the extent of each character's wickedness, splinters at the first stages. All the figures in this satire blur into the belly of the fish, which, although too fat to swim, "wanted to be caught" (*ipse capi uoluit*, 69): is Domitian a cut-throat, or a pathetic sucker for sycophancy, is the fisherman also the fish, are the victimized courtiers passively in control? This confounding of our perspectives on scale and blame pulls its punchline at 154: "the man whose hands were wet with the Lamiae's blood was done for." The Lamiae personify the senatorial class suffering under Domitian's tyranny who will eventually get their revenge,[14] yet the threat is magnified if we think bigger and remember that they are also bloodsucking bogeys of Greek myth, victims turned avengers who seize and kill the offspring of other women.

Thus on one hand satire 4 teaches us to think like Juvenal, Crispinus, and Domitian, to think big, mythical, epic, imperialistic, anarchic, to let our imagination loose on a grand scale. Like the courtiers coping with a gigantic fish, we learn that Juvenal's verse demands a deeper casserole than

---

[14] Domitian executed Aelius Lamia, a consul, in CE 80. He was murdered by his niece Domitilla's steward Stephanus, an officer called Clodianus, a freedman named Maximus, a chamberlain, Satur, and an unnamed gladiator (Suetonius, *Domitian*, 17).

any predecessor. Yet reading Juvenal may be more like riding the whims of a tyrant than studying the *National Enquirer*, as this satire actively undermines our objectivity and sense of scale, letting us glimpse a tyrant's glee only to position the reader as a courtier, aristocrat, or civilian forced to realise that the despot's crazy, unpredictable perspective is the only one that counts.

Contagion and carnival

Nobody and nothing escapes Juvenal's poison pen. His satire continually emphasizes that its writer is immersed in the vice he censures, that everything is sullied. Corruption is contagious ("Infection spread this plague . . . just as in the fields a single scabby sheep or pig destroys the entire herd," 2.78–81). Even the innocent stroller is constantly at the mercy of slops, falling pots, and roof tiles in the Rome of satire 3; in satire 6, the morning after whores relieve themselves in the streets, their "innocent" husbands splash through the stale urine on their way to work (6.309–12). In the rhetorical schools of satire 7 (the breeding ground for Juvenal's hybrid of low and high literature), the canonic texts of Virgil and Horace are stained black with lamp oil (7.226–7). We have already seen how the rich host of satire 5's feast does not escape his own dirty trick, just as Juvenal's parallel dinner party at satire 11, set up to look like a pure organic experience, turns out to be a yuppie farce held within earshot of the Circus, possibly the epicenter of urban filth.

Juvenal's satiric persona is a performer, speaking to or at his readers, nagging and jabbing them with rhetorical questions and anaphora. As we have seen, it is our guilty consciences and red faces which are to take center stage in his war of words. A key feature of all our Roman satire is its carnivalesque role-swapping (writers and readers, teachers and pupils, patrons and clients, giants and pygmies), but in no other Roman satirist is this more aggressively staged. Satire 1 begins *semper ego auditor tantum?* "must I always be in the audience?" Juvenal has begun by acting as his own scathing critic, getting his audience's retaliation in first. He has been bored to death by Cordus' ranting speeches, that over-dense *Orestes* overflowing the margins of its roll, he is tired of stale mythological themes and clichéd rhetorical tropes (here Juvenal looks much like the obnoxious heckler of Persius 1, lashing out at the Lucilian-style trash which the satirist is setting out to write: *quis leget haec?* 1.2). Yet if you can't beat 'em, he reasons, join 'em: his audience will have to suffer not only the torment of yet more of the same, but also the frustration of having their own reactions flaunted as predictable. And unlike the fired up poet, they will have to listen "calmly and reasonably" to this performance (*si uacat ac placidi rationem admittitis, edam,* 21). The bait of solidarity Juvenal offers here is a devilish trap, his initial change of sides a failsafe alibi for bad poetry: he is just parodying, and self-consciousness can lift him ranks above the likes of Cordus. Moreover, the dense allusiveness of the opening spiel on contemporary literature ensures that it will always be the reader, especially the educated one, who will be caught out untangling citations, never the satirist himself, who knows these mythical landscapes "like his own back yard" (7).[15]

A similar role reversal is developed in satire 7, although as critics have emphasized, by his third book Juvenal looks more slyly than aggressively ironic. In lines 150–70, today's teachers are the sorry victims of their students, who churn out an insufferable bubble and squeak (*crambe repetita*, 154), which looks synonymous with Juvenal's *farrago* of 1.86, and drives the abused teacher to the gladiatorial arena. To read Juvenal, do we too have to stoop to (lower than) his level?

Satire 9, Juvenal's only dialogue poem, dramatizes the ambiguous and dangerous position of the listener. Here, Juvenal plays aloof, Socratic audience to gigolo Naevolus' tale of woe, butting in only to request further detail or give snippets of advice. Naevolus is depicted as a sophisticate turned brute, a cyclopic, coarse figure (he has a single slave, just as Polyphemus had a single eye, 64–5) lashing out against his tight-fisted customer Virro. Apparently, the satiric speaker just has to sit back and let Naevolus sketch his lifestyle in grotesque detail, send himself up as a despicable victim no better or worse than his shadow, Virro. But once more, it is the twist of the knife in the last lines that makes us rethink. Naevolus implicitly compares his speech to the Sirens' bewitching song, which makes Odysseus' crew jump overboard to their deaths if they listen to it (9.148–50). Fortune may have blocked her ears, but what happens to the audience in the poem, or even to us as readers (again, Juvenal seems to be "on our side")? Can the satiric speaker really be so remote, so unmoved, so unseduced? Juvenal's wry reaction to Naevolus' excitement in line 102 alludes to Virgil, *Eclogues* 2, where Corydon, who is in love with his master's favorite, Alexis, asks himself "O Corydon Corydon, what madness has seized you?"(2.69). Of course the fact that this is "parody" provides the perfect cover for implication or sincerity, but this is a dangerous game. Is Juvenal engaged in a dialogue with himself, does he set *himself* up to look like Virro's rival for Naevolus' affections, is he a surrogate Virro on which Naevolus can test out his argument? His opening line "you look more depressed than Marsyas after his flaying" (1–2) imports a frisson of (poetic) competition (Marsyas was a satyr who was flayed after losing to Apollo in a musical contest), and the satire as a whole replays discussions of the perverted patron–client relationship which dictates the career

---

[15] See Henderson (1999) on this aspect of Juvenal 1.

of poets as well as gigolos (Naevolus is a *cliens*, line 59). Lines 9–10 ("you used to be a dinner-table wit") look like a classic *poetic* put-down coming from a satirist. In lines 35–6 ("however much Virro may have drooled over your naked charms") *te* might well refer to Juvenal rather than being used impersonally, designed to prick his speaking partner's empathy, and by line 46, it is a moot point who *tu* is (is this Virro speaking to Naevolus, Juvenal to Naevolus, or Naevolus to Juvenal?).[16] Modern editions which insert quotation marks and speakers in the margins elide this insecurity. Now Juvenal can always play Odysseus in this dialogue, the epic hero who escapes the Sirens unscathed: Naevolus' song is told for him alone (*soli tibi*, 93). Yet we might also recall that the Siren song in *Odyssey* 12 is made up of "twin voices": is it Juvenal's readers who risk being bewitched by this double act? Listening to sordid gossip is painful, and unavoidable: there will always be some drunk ready to pour it into your wretched and reluctant ear (*nolentem et miseram uinosus inebriet aurem*, 113).

Mirror shields

At this point, you might not recognize the "serious moralist" that many critics until recently have found in Juvenal.[17] The satirist is never a well-adjusted saint, more a self-implicated leech. Hence the sticky layers of Juvenal's humor, which goes far beyond farcical hyperbole, acid rhetoric, or hilarious juxtaposition. Nor does the "irony" which critics have argued marks the later satires (when Juvenal's trademark *indignatio* becomes passé)[18] start at satire 7. Throughout the satires, the victim is usually also the villain, the satiric persona alternately (and indecipherably) our ally and adversary, even within the same poem. Characters who might at first sight look like the common-sense preacher, the purveyor of home truths with whom we agree and identify, turn out to be bigoted freaks or superficial no-hopers who end up confusing readers over *which* ideas they should and should not agree with. It is a fine line, and the trick is that there's no opting out (that's the catch-22 of tyranny): *everyone* is invested in social politics, everyone (today, too) has an opinion on immigration, homosexuality, heredity, prostitution, adultery . . .

Hypocrisy will always get Juvenal a laugh.[19] The deflating punchline of satire 1, after Juvenal has claimed to be regurgitating Lucilian bombast, is

---

[16] See Habinek (in this volume) for discussion of how Naevolus resembles the archetypal satirist/Roman, while also being a figure for ridicule.

[17] E.g. Courtney (1980) 31: "Juvenal presents himself as a serious moralist and critic of society."

[18] See Braund (1988).

[19] On Juvenal's "double irony" and self-exposure, see Fredericks (1975; 1979).

that freedom of speech is more curtailed than ever, and that therefore he will only dare to slander ghosts (1.170–1). Umbricius, Juvenal's "friend" of satire 3, flees to Cumae (like Daedalus) to escape the lascivious Greek actor-types who have colonized Rome; yet those oiled-up Greeks are epitomized by the same mythic master craftsman who is also a well-worn figure for the wily poet in Latin literature (3.79–80). Pots calling kettles black is the subject of satire 2, which attacks those "serious moralists" oblivious to their own faults. But Juvenal dresses up as courtesan Laronia to make the bulk of his moralizing speech (2.36–63).[20] She argues that women, unlike the men who slander them, do not pretend to be experts in law or philosophy, or spin epic yarns (the accusatory spotlight is already bent back on the satirist here), or cross-dress in chiffon while they prosecute. Like this image of the lawyer in a négligée, Juvenal's joke at his own expense is transparently obvious: he is himself a man wearing a woman's cloak as he speaks. How do we read the rabid misogyny of satire 6 now? When Juvenal goes on to explain that the man who dresses up like a woman ends up like emperor Otho, who uses his shield as a mirror to check his reflection before battle (v. 99–103), this becomes the ultimate metaphor for the Juvenalian pose: the weapon which deflects criticism in satire's epic arena is also the tool for indulgent self-exposure.[21] We might compare the vanity of Juvenal-as-Lucilius at the end of satire 1, swinging satire's naked sword at mere ghosts, overdressed and overdone. As the subsequent line of satire 2 (which could read as this satirist's aphorism) claims, "it takes a citizen of superlative guts to win Palace spoils on the field of Bebriacum *and* plaster his mug with face-pack" (105–6).

The middle poem of book 3, satire 8, is a minefield for readers.[22] Its subject of ancestry and the significance of names, triggered by the rhetorical question, *stemmata quid faciunt*? "what good are family trees?" (1), is all encompassing. The speaker's argument proves tricky to follow. First the message is that noblemen cannot rely on ancestry to win respect if they are not virtuous in their own lives. Names are highly unreliable tokens of status, as they can always be used ironically (we call the scabbiest cat "Tiger," so when a man labels you "Lord," be suspicious). Yet the protreptic at line 20, *nobilitas sola est atque unica uirtus*, can be read two ways: either "virtue is the one and only nobility," or "nobility is the one and only virtue." For at the same time

---

[20] On the figure of woman in Roman satire, see Henderson (1999) and Braund (1995). On Juvenal, *Sat.* 2 also see Gunderson in this volume.

[21] See Gunderson's discussion (in this volume) of the satirist as a pervert who gets pleasure from lambasting the pleasures of others.

[22] On this satire, read Henderson (1997).

the addressee Ponticus is told to model his conduct on the patrician heroes (a Paulus, Cossus, or Drusus) whose *names* mark their illustrious military careers. The argument for ancestry's irrelevance, the analogy that the race-horse wins on speed, not birth certificate, is muddled by contradiction: we should not lean on borrowed glory, yet this satire is imbued with tradition, with political and literary history. Its roll call of heroes, all the great families of Rome from the Aemilii (3, 9) to the Iulii (242) takes its cue and (mock-) *gravitas* from epic texts;[23] the very idea that nobility consists in virtue not birth is a well-worn philosophical and rhetorical theme: *fama nobis tradit* (71), "fame/reputation handed this story down." The seediest tavern in town, where "privilege is abolished, and all men are free and equal" (177–8), is where the speaker's iconoclastic fantasies really wind up. No noble can retain his dignity: if he ditches his title, rebels against establishment pretense, he enrols among the low-life of Lateranus' local; yet if he brandishes his ancestry (even if he proves himself virtuous, as Juvenal previously advises), the satirist can still expose him as a fake, for all Romans, like the scrawny cat named "Tiger," are mongrel offspring of Romulus and the convict mob he drew to swell the city of Rome (272–5). This poem displays how the satirist is split between his ambition to discredit predecessors to bolster his own prestige, and the necessity of buttressing poetic inheritance in order to define himself against it. He fractures dynasties and dismantles faces in stone (see 11. 4–5, 18, 53, 77) at his own expense, as well as ours. And because questioning heredity, that is, delving into cultural values and identities, is so inflammatory a pastime, we might read Juvenal's advice to "set some curb on your anger" (*pone irae frenum modumque*, 88) as a patronizing ploy to let his audience's indignation replace the satirist's malice of satires 1–6. As critics have commented, despite the marked change of tone in the final three books, the veneer of Horatian restraint and politesse frequently cracks to reveal the old satiric fury.[24]

Juvenal makes it very difficult for readers to sum him up. As his satire rollercoasters through history and empire, and the decayed past meets a crumbling present, or a future doomed to rot, profound pessimism and even nihilism still make for a rollicking good read. Juvenal makes a "heads I win, tails you lose" politics serve as a recipe for seducing his captive audience: the more you get of him, the more you want (he brings out the imperialist in you), even if, like Trebius in satire 5, you are a fool to endure him more than once. Inevitably, it is the hope of a good meal that lures you on (*spes bene cenandi vos decipit*, 5.166).

[23] In particular Horace, *Odes* 1.12 and Virgil, *Aeneid* 7.756–886. See Henderson (1997).
[24] E.g. Conte (1994) 477.

Further reading

Peter Green's Penguin translation (1974) is excellent, and Latinists will probably find a combination of Courtney's (1980) and Ferguson's (1979) commentaries most useful. Also see commentaries by Braund (1996b), and on satires 1, 3 and 10 see N. Rudd and E. Courtney, *Juvenal: Satires I, II, X* (Bristol 1977). Excellent general works include Freudenburg (2001) 209–77, J. Bramble, "Juvenal and Martial," in Kenney and Clausen (1982), Gowers (1993a) 188–219, Anderson (1982) 197–254, and Braund (1996a): for a detailed explanation of stylistic features, with examples, see 17–29. On the later satires (7–16), see Braund (1988), and Henderson (1997). The following are illuminating articles on individual satires, in order of the satires they deal with: Kenney (1962) 29–40; Motto and Clark (1965) 267–76; Kilpatrick (1971) 229–41; J. G. Griffith (1969) "Juvenal, Statius and the Flavian Establishment," *Greece and Rome* 16: 134–50; P. F. Wilson (1995) "A Complete Catalogue of Sexist Slur: Juvenal's Sixth Satire and Bob Dylan's 'Just Like a Woman'," *Liverpool Classical Monthly* 20: 4–9; S. H. Braund (1992) "Juvenal: Misogynist or Misogamist?," *Journal of Roman Studies* 82: 71–86; Rudd (1976) 84–118; W. S. Anderson (1962) "The Programs of Juvenal's Later Books," *Classical Philology* 57: 145–60; M. Morford (1973) "Juvenal's Thirteenth Satire," *American Journal of Philology* 94: 26–36; W. S. Anderson (1988) "Juvenal Satire 15: Cannibals and Culture," in A. J. Boyle, ed. *The Imperial Muse: Ramus Essays on Roman Literature of the Empire*, 203–14 (Victoria, Australia).

5

ELLEN O'GORMAN

Citation and authority in Seneca's *Apocolocyntosis*

Seneca's Menippean satire, often entitled *Ludus de morte Claudii* ("Funning with the death of Claudius"), offers a sort of interlude from the play of the Roman satirists and their critics. Indeed, many features of this branch of satire seem to preclude its being comfortably set alongside Horace, Persius, Juvenal, or even Petronius (which is not to imply that these four are at all comfortable set alongside each other . . .). While all satirists (sometimes angrily) celebrate their belatedness, their parasitic reliance upon the tropes of earlier genres and their mimicking even of these very celebrations, the Menippean satirist, eschewing indignation, turns to self-conscious mimicry – parody. Within this play of parody is created the image of an author both in control and not in control of the work he calls "his own." Joel Relihan has elegantly formulated it thus: "Menippean satire, *one may say*, opposes the word-centered view of the universe, and is a genre that, in words, denies the possibility of expressing the truth in words."[1] How Seneca positions Roman culture, Roman emperors, and Roman *authority* within this generic view is the subject of this essay. By reading the *Apocolocyntosis* as a text engaged in the reception of classical literature, I hope to draw out the extent to which this satire, gleefully after every event, offers to subsequent writers and scholars a mode of expression which is more than just an admission of belatedness. The project of quotation and citation, as pursued in this paper, plays a fundamental role in the creation of classical literature as quotable, as worth alluding to.

The story of the *Apocolocyntosis* is concerned with the death of Claudius, followed by a senatorial debate in heaven over the question of whether he should be deified (during which the text breaks off). Claudius is eventually expelled from heaven, and descends to hell via earth, where he witnesses his own funeral. In hell he is placed on trial for the murders of many Roman

---

[1] Relihan (1993) 11, my emphasis. That "one may say" is an important feature of this reading; despite the undermining of the word's authority, one *may*, nevertheless, continue to speak.

citizens, and is eventually handed over to his predecessor, the emperor Gaius, who claims him as an escaped freedman.

Seneca's fantasy of the Emperor Claudius' first day in the afterlife (CE 54, 13 October, sometime after lunch) highlights for us the difficulties of reading quotations as quotation without the benefit of quotation marks. The text is a farrago of voices and soundbites, rarely explicitly referenced and drawing on styles and genres from the proverbial to the high tragic. Much of what goes on in the *Apocolocyntosis* is language at play, and even when quotation and allusion make a wider point there is still a strong sense of fun underlying the verbal play here.[2] I hope in what follows to explore some of the wider points, while continuing to collude.

As well as employing a range of quotation and allusion, the *Apocolocyntosis* is also *about* quotation, what it means to quote, and what relationship with the past is configured by, within, the act of quotation.[3] At this level Seneca may seem, at first glance, to be sending a clear message about his chosen victim, Claudius, and about the hierarchy of understanding within which Claudius, his satirist, and his readers are to be situated. Consider the following exchange between Claudius and Hercules, as narrated by Seneca.[4]

accessit itaque et quod facillimum fuit Graeculo, ait:
τίς πόθεν εἰς ἀνδρῶν, ποίη πόλις ἠδὲ τοκῆες;

Claudius gaudet esse illic philologos homines: sperat futurum aliquem historiis suis locum. itaque et ipse Homerico uersu Caesarem se esse significans ait:
Ἰλιόθεν με φέρων ἄνεμος Κικόνεσσι πέλασσεν

So he went up to him and said, what is very easy for a little Greek:
"Of what race of men are you? Where is your city and your parents?"
Claudius was very pleased that there were philologists there: he hoped there would be some place for his own histories. So he too said in Homeric verse, meaning that he was Caesar:
"From Ilium the wind carrying me drove me ashore at the Kikonians"

(5.4)

---

[2] The idea of allusion as play is in general more modern than ancient (Derrida (1981) 219). But the title of Seneca's work as *ludus* evokes the idea of a mocking mimicry (cf. *OLD ludo* 6b) which is overlooked by the more common and po-faced term *imitatio*. As I will argue in this paper, Seneca's satiric voice offers a particular take on the process of allusion, different from what is articulated by Seneca in, for example, *Epistle* 114.17–20.

[3] The practice of Greek quotation among the educated classes of Rome seems to have had a variety of motives, sensibly outlined by Wardman (1976) 46–50 and 65–7. Berthet (1978) examines Suetonius' use, for characterization, of episodes where emperors quote Homer. Laird (1999) examines quotation as, among other things, intertextuality.

[4] The text of the *Apocolocyntosis* is that of Eden (1984). All translations are my own.

The initial point of this exchange seems to be precisely to set up this hierarchy of understanding, based on each character's capacity to select an appropriate Homeric tag to communicate what he means to say.[5] Hercules' question is easily put, both because he is a Greekling and because what he really wants to know is encapsulated in a formulaic line.[6] Claudius' answer is more allusive; he chooses a line in which Odysseus refers to his point of departure, the start of his homecoming. In order to read it as an answer to Hercules' question, the reader has to recontextualize it, first within the story of Aeneas (for whom Ilium was not only a point of departure but also a homeland) and secondly within the Julian family's legend of descent from Aeneas. As an acknowledgment to the allusiveness of Claudius' tag, the narrator gives us the "actual" meaning *before* he gives us the allusion: *Caesarem se esse significans ait*. Claudius thus appears as a more subtle manipulator of quotation than Hercules; the philologist scores points over the native Greek in control of a Greek cultural possession (but we will return to this hierarchy below). But the narrator intervenes at this point to cap Claudius' quotation.

> (erat autem sequens uersus uerior, aeque Homericus:
> ἔνθα δ' ἐγὼ πόλιν ἔπραθον, ὤλεσα δ' αὐτούς).

> (But the following verse was more true, equally Homeric:
> "and there I sacked the city and killed the people")   (5.4)

In the "knowing your Homer" competition this speaker scores under three headings. "Spotting the reference": he recognizes exactly where Claudius' quotation comes from, and adds the next line. "Following up the allusion": he presses the allusive link between Odysseus and Claudius to a point where it begins to tell against Claudius. "Choosing a more apposite tag": Claudius, related to the Julian family only by marriage, is indulging in a fiction about how he came to power. The narrator's reference to sacking a city reminds

---

5 Many of the details in the *Apocol.*, such as this one, play on the details of Claudius' character and reign. Part of the joke here has to do with Claudius' enthusiasm for scholarship and antiquarian studies, which appears in the historical accounts as a distraction from the "real business" of ruling.

6 Kirk Freudenburg has pointed out to me that we could see Hercules here as speaking rather than quoting: "because he's a Greek hero from the old days and because that's the way Greek heroes talk – Homer is quoting 'them' in a sense." This would allow for a different way of pointing up the gap between Homeric and post-Augustan discourse (even when they look the same); from the belated perspective, even the *real* archaic hero is read as an imitation. Seneca as well as Claudius sees Hercules from this perspective, when he calls him a *Graeculus*. As a description of this most muscle-bound of heroes it is woefully inept, but the diminutive term also inscribes Hercules into the discourse of the belated, as the degenerate contemporary Greek is often termed by Romans *Graeculus* (notably by Juvenal 3.77–8). Note, too, that Hadrian's Hellenophile tendencies earned him this title (*Historia Augusta* 1.5).

the reader that Claudius "actually" came to the throne on the shoulders of the Praetorian Guard. By the end of the exchange, then, we have a situation where Claudius, learned as he is, is put firmly in his place as a less able manipulator of quotation than his narrator. More than this, the question posed by Hercules has, in the course of the answers offered, become a question about how Claudius came to be emperor: by (legal) inheritance, alludes Claudius; by (illegal) force, alludes the narrator.

This is all at first glance, but the hierarchy which seems so certain in the above paragraphs depends upon an assumption to which I now return: which is the more successful quotation? Why should Claudius' tag, which requires so much work on the reader's part before it will make sense, win out over Hercules', which appears to say exactly what Hercules "really" means? If, after all, the point of quotation is to pick a line which says what you *really* mean . . . but this leads us to the question "why use *another's* words to say what *you* mean?" We will return to this question. But first let us consider what other criteria of successful quotation operate in the exchange examined above. As I have just remarked, Hercules' tag appears to say exactly what he means, in which it might be said that it wins out over Claudius', which says something other than what is meant – the gap between words and meaning must be bridged by unspoken stories/analogies and an explicit narrative gloss. If the competition is over control of the Homeric quotation, the native Greek, whose line may be read alone, scores over the philologist, whose line needs a footnote or a lemma. With these competing views in mind the hierarchy is no longer stable, and the narrator's "capping" intervention is as a consequence less obviously the triumphant final word. The narrator claims to match Claudius' learning (his tag is "equally Homeric") and to surpass him in appropriateness (*this* line is "more true").[7] But a quick scan of the lines (or a glance at Eden's commentary) will reveal that the narrator here follows Claudius *non passibus aequis*, not with equal feet. His line is missing one word, so that it is not *equally* Homeric, word for word. If the missing word were restored – Ismaros, the name of the actual city sacked by Odysseus – the line would be equally Homeric, but the allusion to the city of Rome would be at best clumsy and at worst unworkable. In short, it would no longer apply; it would no longer be "more true." The narrator's dilemma here is about the fit between the truth he wants to tell about Claudius and the Homeric words he wants to use in the telling.

---

[7] The competition over appropriateness here is elided into the competition over truth. That is, if Claudius' quotation is seen as entirely appropriate, as signifying that he is Caesar, the distinction between "appropriate" and "true" will no longer hold. In questioning the appropriateness of his quotation, the narrator challenges the truth of what Claudius "really" means.

The gap between speaking the truth and quoting Homer (and perhaps the latent silliness of the entire exchange)[8] is explicitly set out for us in plain prose in the next chapter. This narrative, which "properly" answers Hercules' question, is, "appropriately" enough, spoken by the goddess Fever, Claudius' only companion to the afterlife.[9] Like the narrator, the goddess first grounds the superiority of her answer in truth. She begins "*iste mera mendacia narrat*", "this guy's telling unadulterated untruths" (6.1). Her version, by contrast with what went before, is free of quotation: she gives us the place of Claudius' birth, which is impossible for those speaking in Homeric lines; she repeatedly reminds Hercules that *she* is the speaker ("*ego tibi dico . . . quod tibi narro . . . hunc ego tibi recipio*", "I'm telling you . . . what I say to you . . . I guarantee you") and she concludes her speech with a comment on the inappropriateness of Homeric quotation in representing Claudius and his background: "*You* (Hercules) ought to know that many miles lie between the rivers Xanthus and Rhône" (6.1). The gap between Homeric quotation and what it is being made to mean is here at its widest, and the hierarchy of understanding has now been reconfigured to privilege not the one who knows Homer, but the one who knows the difference between "Homer" and "now."

But, not to succumb to the delirious notion that the plain narrative gives us the transparent truth, let us return to the centre of Fever's short speech, where she iterates that Claudius, born at Lugdunum, is a native Gaul: "*itaque quod Gallum facere oportebat, Romam cepit*", "And so he did what a Gaul should do, he captured Rome" (6.1). Despite Fever's reliance on her *own* authority throughout her speech, here she employs citation of a "source text" – this comes early in Roman history – in order properly to represent Claudius. Here direct quotation of a specific text is not employed, but rather a semi-absurd elevation of a historical event to the level of a general truth. "The Gauls once captured Rome (390 BCE); therefore *all* Gauls always eventually capture Rome." This could well be a parodic sideswipe at the historical *exemplum* and its alleged usefulness; certainly Fever's procedure here creates a text in the moment of citation. Her final criticism of the "Homerists" needs to be read in the light of this; it seems that Fever is, like the narrator, attacking an allusion not because it *is* an allusion but because it is less appropriate than another allusion. It is also significant that Fever's preferred "source

---

[8] Suetonius tells us that Claudius employed Homeric quotation continually, even in such inappropriate contexts as the lawcourt (*multum uero pro tribunali etiam Homericis locutus est uersibus*, Suetonius, *Claudius* 42.1); the silliness of the dialogue here may in part be sending up this feature of Claudius' character.

[9] This is another joke based on the details of Claudius' life, which seems to have been plagued by sickness (Suetonius, *Cl.* 2.1, 31.1). The unseemly nature of Claudius' ill-health, in the historical record, is another sign of his unfitness for rule.

text" portrays Claudius in the same light as the narrator's tag: whether as "a Gaul" or as "Odysseus", Claudius is always sacking the city of Rome.

Or does it make a difference? Many miles lie between the Xanthus and the Rhône. Can we *really* disregard Fever's last words to such an extent as to claim that these two sentences "*really* say the same thing"?

> ἔνθα δ' ἐγὼ πόλιν ἔπραθον, ὤλεσα δ' αὐτούς.
> And there I sacked the city and killed the people

> itaque quod Gallum facere oportebat, Romam cepit
> And so he did what a Gaul should do, he captured Rome

Or ought we, like Hercules, to know better? This is not the only or even the first episode in the *Apocolocyntosis* to raise questions about whether the same thing can be told in different words. This comes in early in the piece with Seneca's exercise in how to tell the time. There are two stages in this process. I will here discuss only the first:[10] establishing the date of Claudius' death.

> iam Phoebus breuiore uia contraxerat arcum
> lucis et obscuri crescebant tempora Somni,
> iamque suum uictrix augebat Cynthia regnum,
> et deformis Hiems gratos carpebat honores
> diuitis Autumni iussoque senescere Baccho
> carpebat raras serus uindemitor uuas.

puto magis intellegi si dixero: mensis erat October, dies III idus Octobris.

> Now Phoebus' arc a shorter course had drawn
> Increasing hours to Sleep conceded Dawn,
> Now Cynthia, triumphant, spreads her sway,
> And Winter robs the glorious Autumn's day.
> The god of wine doth age at Time's command;
> The harvest late, the sparser grape yields to the vintner's hand.

I think it will be better understood if I say: the month was October, the day the third one before the Ides.   (2.1)

The plain prose statement, juxtaposed with "the bombastic *circumlocutions* of times of year . . . beloved by poetasters,"[11] is funny in itself, but

---

[10] The second stage (where the time of day is seen as something which *demands* poetic treatment, and which is not properly served by the "unnuanced" plain narrative) reverses the tenor of the first stage, where prose undermines verse. Hence, the apparent elevation of history at the expense of poetry, which could be inferred from the two examples I discuss in the main text, is only half of Seneca's story.

[11] Eden (1984) 68, my emphasis.

after the questions I have raised about Fever's speech we might look further at the claim made for the statement, that of intelligibility. The narrator thinks prose here will be "better understood," but that depends upon what he wants to be understood from the statement. The prose gives us the date, which the verse does not. What does the verse give us to understand about the date of Claudius' death? The seasonal imagery of these six lines conveys darkness, deformity, limitation and belatedness – how much of this is "circumlocution", speaking *around* the point, or is it speaking precisely *to* the point of Claudius' reign and death, a point which cannot be understood simply from the statement of a calendar date? "*nimis rustice*", someone may protest, "*surely* it's *just* a parody?" Can Seneca, poking fun at poetasters, not in the same words make a point about Claudius? This is an analogous problem to that posed by "his" praise of Nero in chapter 4: does he *really* mean it?[12] My question here is, how *does* he say what he "really" means? (How we answer that question then determines who we think "he" is.)

The quotation (or the citation) in one context seems primarily designed to point up the incongruity of its own application. Using Homer to talk about Claudius' origins, for example, does not obscure but rather highlights the unheroic aspect of this emperor. This way of reading quotation sets up another hierarchy between texts and worlds: the "straight" text and the text that ironically, parasitically, plays off the straight text; the world of heroes and the world of unscrupulous freedmen; the world where every speech is one's own and the world where each word uttered is a quotation. Satire, the genre that is "always already too late", might be seen as the writing which sets these worlds in motion. But satire confounds this simple progression from primary text/world to secondary, by engaging in a two-way process. The Homeric quotations bandied about by the characters in chapter 5 are intended (by the characters) to authenticate the exchange, though they serve instead to point up the inanity of a comparison between Claudius and an epic hero. But the process of authentication does not stop there. As the Homeric tag fails to invest "Caesar" with the presence and authority that he intended to derive from it, so the inanity of his attempt rebounds upon the quotation itself. "Homer" becomes de-authorized.

This has implications for the second context in which quotation/citation is used, as the explicit guarantor of truth. In historical or scholarly discourse the quotation is precisely used to authorize the claims that are made by the

---

[12] There is much discussion of this question in the secondary literature on both Seneca and his nephew Lucan: yes, he really means it; no, it is ironic; it is irony in which the emperor Nero himself would pleasurably collude. Diverse positions within this range are taken by Sullivan (1985), Rudich (1997), and Masters (1994).

quoter. Why use *another's* words to say what *you* mean? The answer, for the scholar, is "because it is only *elsewhere* that truth is guaranteed." Crucial to this is the concept of the *auctor*, the authority, the one whose words are not quotations, or rather the one whose words are always quotations, for the *auctor* is constituted in and by "quotation" of his work.[13] At the beginning of the *Apocolocyntosis*, in Seneca's homage to the historiographical preface, the *auctor* appears as a debased Cassandra figure ("since then . . . nobody has believed what he says he saw" [1.3]) who only speaks to an audience of one. Partly what Seneca plays with here is the paradox of presence and absence at the heart of the authorizing quotation. The words must be another's, not mine (truth as absent, only present elsewhere), but the words must be rendered *exactly* as they were rendered by the other (truth as present, immanent in the precise rendering of these words).[14]

This gets played out in full in the Olympian debate on "what is Claudius and where should he be put?" Chapters 9 to 11, the speeches of Janus, Diespiter, and Augustus on the deification of Claudius, filter this question through the related ones of where Claudius fits into the tradition and which tradition he fits into. The debate, while apparently centered on a ridiculous figure, becomes bitingly relevant to the Roman and the modern reader when it hinges upon the use of quotation to configure one's relationship to the past, and which past that might consequently be. Seneca begins the ordered speeches in the celestial curia with another swipe at the historians; only part of Janus' speech can be given, since he spoke so fast that the stenographer could not keep up, *et ideo non refero, ne aliis uerbis ponam quae ab illo dicta sunt,* "and so I won't report it, not to put down in other words the things that were said by him" (9.2). Seneca outdoes the historians in scrupulousness, since even the austere Thucydides was quite happy to render in speech "the kinds of things that might have been said."[15] But Seneca immediately goes ahead and does what he just claimed he would not do, rendering in indirect speech a *six*-word paraphrase of Janus' "*many*" words. Of course, both Janus' and subsequently Diespiter's speeches are already *aliis uerbis*, as each

---

[13] The most authoritative account of the *auctor* in Roman society, and the consequent weight of the term *auctoritas*, is Galinsky (1996) 11–15. See esp. 13: "[An *auctor*'s] *auctoritas* comes from special insight and is so weighty that the person seeking advice will almost certainly accept it."

[14] Throughout this piece (and here most obviously) I have been thinking through the arguments of Derrida (1981), esp. 175–226.

[15] Thucydides' explanation of his practice in representing the "general sense" of the speeches of others (*Histories* 1.22) is discussed by most Thucydideans; see, for example, Hornblower (1987) 45–60. The Roman historians, when researching senatorial debates, would have had recourse to the archive, the *acta senatus*.

one presents his view of the past through the quotations he chooses. As in the earlier competition between Fever and the Homerists, Diespiter chooses his quotations precisely to engage in dialogue with Janus. So Janus presents a "Homeric" version of mortals who should not be deified – "*censeo ne quis post hunc diem deus fiat ex his, qui* ἀρούρης καρπὸν ἔδουσιν *aut ex his, quos alit* ζείδωρος ἄρουρα," "I move that from this day on nobody should be made a god from those who 'consume the fruit of the land' or from those whom 'the grain-giving land' sustains" (9.3). Diespiter matches this with a "Lucilian" version of an earlier deified mortal who needs some company – "*sitque e re publica esse aliquem qui cum Romulo possit 'feruentia rapa uorare'*," "and it is in the state's interest that we have someone who can 'munch on boiled turnips' with Romulus" (9.5). Diespiter's satiric capping of the Homeric quotation, replacing epic grain with satiric roots, also obliquely answers Janus' first complaint about the degeneration of god-making: "becoming a god used to be a big deal: now you've made it into a bean farce" (9.3). In effect Diespiter counters the sharp distinction between then and now by offering the example of an archaic, respectable and *already satirized* god: the founder of Rome.

But the climax of the piece is Augustus' indictment of Claudius, a fantasy of a past which speaks out against its misuse in the present. Augustus stands as the ultimate *auctor* for Claudius, as the founder of the imperial role which Claudius is seen to have usurped and perverted.[16] "Appropriately" enough, this *auctor* is very careful about the transmission of his words; his motion in the senate is written down in advance. "'I put this motion as my considered opinion:' (and then he read out (*recitauit*) from a note pad)" (11.4). This conclusion to the debate forms a frame with its opening, the absence of Janus' words from the record. Whereas Seneca there balked at rendering the speech *aliis uerbis*, here the scrupulousness of Augustus ensures that we will get his exact words. And this fits with a well-known biographical detail of the emperor Augustus, that "he made a practice of reading everything aloud [*recitare omnia*]. In conversation with individuals and even in more serious chats with Livia he said nothing except what was written in his notebook, in case he said more or less than he intended on the spur of the moment" (Suetonius, *Life of Augustus* 84.2). Augustus believes that he cannot say the same thing in different words. His awareness of the presence commanded by the exact words is part of what makes him such a weighty authority. We will return to this point later.

---

[16] The name "Augustus" comes from the same semantic root as *auctor*, "source/author", and *auctoritas*, "authority." Indeed, this name seems to have been chosen for precisely this significance.

From this position of authority Augustus launches an attack on Claudius precisely for failing to measure up to either the heroic or the historic models he aspires to emulate. This is analogous to the earlier competition over which lines of Homer to use when describing Claudius – or whether to use Homer at all. One of the models for Claudius' rule, his "source text", is Augustus himself, so that the dialogue between "quoter" (Claudius) and "quoted" (Augustus) here becomes explicit. In fact, the source text dominates the dialogue, with Claudius' only contribution ("quoted" by Augustus) being the word *"nescio"*, "I don't know" (11.1). Augustus represents Claudius' assumption of the title "Caesar Augustus" as *"sub meo nomine latens"*, "hiding under my name" (10.4), a representation which makes visible the quotation marks around the title, and sees the title as failing to signify Claudius to such an extent that he is entirely concealed by it. The sections of Augustus' speech where he remarks on Claudius' "citation" of him, then, offer us a vision of the place of Claudius in history, from the perspective of that history. Augustus quotes his own *Res Gestae*, a document produced at the end of his life and offering a strongly retrospective view of his achievements,[17] but he reinscribes that document within a new context, where his actions have a new and unworthy *telos*:

> in hoc terra marique pacem peperi? ideo ciuilia bella compescui? ideo legibus urbem fundaui, operibus ornaui, ut –?

> Was it for this that I made peace by land and sea? For this that I settled the civil wars? For this that I grounded the city in its laws, and adorned it with public works, so that –?
> (10.2)

The repeated *in hoc . . . ideo . . . ideo . . . ut* harps on the new context of Claudian Rome within which Augustus' efforts appear now to be all for nothing, or worse. Seneca's conjuring of Augustus to indict Claudius here parodies Cicero's famous impersonation of Appius Claudius in his attack upon Appius' descendant Clodia. "Appius" ends his speech thus:

> Was it for this that I broke the peace treaty with Pyrrhus, so that you could daily strike the most disgraceful bargains with your lovers? Was it for this that I built an aqueduct, so that you could wash yourself after sex? Was it for this that I built the Appian Way, so that you could hang out there with your various male friends?
> (Cicero, *In defence of M. Caelius Rufus* 14.34)

This "paradigm" highlights the absence of an indictment in Augustus' version, since he effectively fails to complete his sentence and tell us what offense Claudius has committed.

---

[17] The text and translation are available in Brunt and Moore (1967).

History, by the authority of the *auctor* Augustus, fails to indict Claudius of any precise crime. Moreover, as with the inanity of quoting Homer discussed above, the past does not remain untouched by the present in which it appears as citation. Augustus' spluttering over this unforeseen, degenerate end to his *Res Gestae* prompts the question "what *did* he do all this for?"[18] And is any of the possible answers to that question any loftier than the specimen he now sees petitioning for godhead? The insufficiency of the *Res Gestae* in itself to indict Claudius without indicting its author as well is acknowledged by Augustus, who fails to come up with anything to follow *ut*,[19] and has recourse instead, tellingly, to the words of another.

> quid dicam, p.c., non inuenio: omnia infra indignationem uerba sunt. confugiendum est itaque ad Messalae Coruini, disertissimi uiri, illam senten-tiam "pudet imperii".
>
> I am at a loss, elders of the senate, as to what I should say: all words fall short of my indignation. I must have recourse to that saying of the most eloquent Messala Corvinus, "my power shames me." (10.2)[20]

Augustus' own words, so important for his authority, as we have seen, fall short of his *indignatio*. The term is an important one, configuring as it so often does the satirist's attitude towards his subject. *Indignatio* is what Augustus *really* means, but his own words are insufficient to convey this. Ironically, our central *auctor* here demonstrates that when he wants to say what he *really* means he has got to use another's words. And the words of Messala Corvinus indict not only the principate insofar as it is open to abuse by someone like Claudius, but also potentially the principate itself and its chief architect, Augustus. The quotation, once more, indicts the quoter.

Satisfying as it is for us to scupper Augustus with his "own" words, the quotation of Messala Corvinus does not disrupt a certain privileging of past greatness over present degeneracy. It simply caps Augustus' moral high ground with an appeal to idealized Republican virtue, and adds one earlier

---

[18] The passage of the *Res Gestae* which seems most germane to this discussion is its conclusion, where the *telos* of Augustus' actions appears to be his own pre-eminence in *auctoritas* (discussed by Galinsky (1996) 11). That authority, as we now see, is not quite so stable.

[19] Interestingly, Augustus *can* represent Claudius' crimes elsewhere (10.4–11.6); it is only when they are semantically linked to his own actions that he finds himself lost for words.

[20] Messala Corvinus (64 BCE–CE 8) was another aristocrat rehabilitated after opposing Octavian in the civil wars. His words originally seem to have constituted his refusal to serve as city prefect in 26/5 BCE, on the grounds that his powers were excessive for a citizen in a so-called republic, and their deployment here could be read as an indictment of Augustus. Yet Messala also proposed the bestowal on Augustus of the title "Father of the Country" . . .

element to the well-known history of decline and fall. But if we return to where Augustus does *not* rely upon *alia uerba*, to where the authority of his words seems absolute, we can see that the very action of authorizing in the same movement de-authorizes. As I remarked earlier, Augustus sets himself up as an *auctor*. An *auctor* is one who is quoted, and Augustus quotes himself – a self-made man. The presence and authority of Augustus' motion in the senate is in part an effect of his quotation of himself: "and then he read out from a note pad" (11.4). At the same time, the act of quotation here *fails* to invest these words with presence, since their original conception is posited elsewhere. And thus the Augustus present in senate is de-authorized, since he speaks *aliis uerbis*, in the words of another (Augustus).

The process of establishing Claudius' place in the afterlife entails also establishing his place in multiple traditions (literary, political, mythical) but the questions which the many quotations/citations raise indicate that "tradition" is not passively applied here but rather engages in a dialogue, and becomes transformed in the process. The "tradition" to which the *Apocolocyntosis* give us access is, like the afterlife itself, a synchronous babble. In this virtual chat room the truth about Claudius is to be found not in words nor in what lies behind them, but in what stands in for them – *pro uerbis, prouerbium*. Claudius, Seneca begins, is "the man who made the proverb true [*uerum prouerbium*] that you should be born a king or a fool" (1.1).

Yet Seneca's denial of a simple relation of truth to words does not condemn representation to an afterlife of meaningless play.[21] This can perhaps be best exemplified by a glance at the reception of Seneca by two authors who take on this project of speaking meaningfully, with a dislocated authority: Publius Cornelius Tacitus and Robert Graves.

Seneca's many swipes at the historians have been noted, as has his extended parody of historiographical prefaces. Part of the joke of the first chapter is his notoriously shaky authority for his story. Tacitus, writing a generation later, does not overlook Seneca's mimicry, but instead reincorporates it into his historical discourse, making his claim for the truth of what he says serve simultaneously as a parodic homage to the *Apocolocyntosis*:

> I am not entirely unaware that what I am going to relate will seem fantastic, that *anyone* could be so complacent (in a city where everyone knows and gossips about what's going on), *still less* that the consul-elect should marry the emperor's wife, having sent out invitations and summoned witnesses (like they're planning to have a family), and that *she* listened to the sermon, made the vows, went through the whole ceremony; *and* that they had the full wedding

---

[21] Cf. Derrida (1981) 219 (his emphasis): "As its name indicates, allusion *plays*. But that this play should in the last instance be independent of truth does not mean that it is false . . ."

breakfast, kisses and hugs, followed by the honeymoon night – conjugal relations. But I'm not making this up to shock you, I'm just reporting what was
heard and written by older men [*senioribus*].

The emperor's wife is, of course, Messalina, and the ensuing chapters of
the *Annals* book 11 (this is chapter 27) constitute the raciest episode in this
tale of the Julio-Claudians. Indeed, with its reversals and absurdities it clearly
resembles a Saturnalia that ends badly;[22] the influence of Seneca is pervasive.
But here in his "preface" to the account Tacitus appears to allude obliquely
to the shaky historical authorities of the earlier satire. His worthy *seniores*
seem at first to lend weighty authority to even the most fantastic tale, but
that depends on whether one *always* values the talk of old men. The men of
the previous generation who wrote about Claudius and Messalina include
Seneca (who may be obliquely pointed to by the play on *senior/Seneca*);
indeed, Seneca's list of Claudius' victims in chapter 13 of the *Apocolocyntosis*
is closely followed by Tacitus' account of executions in *Annals* 11.35–6.
But Tacitus' reception of the parody makes a more important point, that
recognizing the impossibility of precisely locating truth does not preclude a
writer from making an ironic claim to truth, and a concomitant demand to
be believed.[23]

In the nineteenth and twentieth centuries the location of this ironized
claim was more firmly – and problematically – located in the genre of the
novel, and in particular of the historical novel. Graves' highly successful
Claudius books (*I, Claudius* and *Claudius the God*) draw on both Tacitus
and Seneca as sources, and introduce us to the emperor as a first person
narrator, who admits to us early in the first novel that his memory is not at
all reliable. The influence of Seneca is, again, pervasive, but the appearance
of the *Apocolocyntosis* within this text once more raises questions about
citation and authority. After Claudius' voice falls silent ("Write no more
now, Tiberius Claudius, God of the Britons, write no more")[24] his death is
narrated three times, by Suetonius, Tacitus, and Dio. But the novel sequence
as a whole is further framed by the entire text of the *Apocolocyntosis*, translated by Graves, just as he has "translated" Claudius' "autobiography."
Seneca's farrago of quotations is finally itself framed in quotation marks,
and appears, along with other *real* texts from antiquity, to authorize the
fiction of the novel's text as a whole. Graves's reception of Seneca, then,

---

22 This trope in the historical understanding of Claudius is explored by Dickison (1977).
23 On irony in Tacitus more generally see O'Gorman (2000) 10–14. For a provocative exploration of the relationship of irony to truth and belief, see Haynes (2003).
24 Robert Graves (1934) *Claudius the God*, London, 418.

inscribes the *Apocolocyntosis* within the logic of its own reception of the classical tradition.[25]

Further reading

There are few pieces devoted exclusively to the *Apocolocyntosis*, though it is briefly discussed by most writers on Seneca's life and work: see M. Griffin's biographical study *Seneca: a Philosopher in Politics* (Oxford 1976). The structure of the work, its context and general considerations are all covered by M. Coffey in *Roman Satire* (Bristol 1989) 165–77. A lively short essay on repetition is A. L. Motto and J. R. Clark, "Satiric Plotting in Seneca's *Apocolocyntosis*," in *Essays on Seneca* (Frankfurt 1993) 197–208. For a more provocative political reading, see Eleanor Winsor Leach (1989), "The implied reader and the political argument in Seneca's *Apocolocyntosis* and *De Clementia*," *Arethusa* 22: 197–230. The best discussion of Menippean satire in general is Relihan (1993): the chapter on Seneca is at 75–90. More generally, a good introduction to parody in literature is M. A. Rose, *Parody: Ancient, Modern, and Post-modern* (Cambridge 1993). Further work on how allusion configures an appropriate authority for poets can be found in Hinds (1998). On ancient historiographical conventions see John Marincola, *Authority and Tradition in Ancient Historiography* (Cambridge 1997) and C. S. Kraus and A. J. Woodman, *Latin Historians* (Oxford 1997).

[25] My ideas about the *Apocol.* were kick-started by discussions with Kirk Freudenburg and with members of the Seneca class at Ohio State University, spring 2000, for all of which I am very grateful. Thanks next to the Bristol Satire Reading Group, summer 2001 – Paul Duffus, Duncan Kennedy, Genevieve Lively and Charles Martindale – for their challenging and refreshing thoughts. Finally, thanks to Kirk Freudenburg (again and again) and Joel Relihan for reading and commenting on this piece.

6

JOEL RELIHAN

Late arrivals: Julian and Boethius

Readers of this chapter may be surprised by its Greek content. Verse satire
is certainly a Roman genre, but Menippean satire (as a generic term no
older than the Renaissance) is a Greco-Roman phenomenon.[1] Its founder
and patron saint is the Greek Menippus, a Cynic of the third century BCE;
the Roman Varro names his literary experiments *Saturae Menippeae* after
his Greek muse. But if we are to understand Menippus at all, we need to
speak of Lucian, the prolific Greek belletrist of the second century CE. This
Lucian is both a student of Greek literature and an observer of the Roman
scene; the fourth century Roman emperor Julian, who writes in Greek and
who is influenced in one of his satiric productions both by the Roman Seneca
and by the Greek Lucian, helps to illumine both Seneca and the traditions
of Menippean satire in late antiquity. These Greeks have a crucial place in
this Roman book, for without them the history of Roman satire, both in late
antiquity and in the Renaissance, cannot be written.

To extricate a history of the genre of Menippean satire in the classical
period from our intractable welter of testimonia, fragments, and imperfectly
preserved literary experiments – Varro's *Menippeans*, Petronius' *Satyricon*,
and Seneca's *Apocolocyntosis* are all to varying degrees incomplete – is to
acknowledge that our data, as frustrating as they are, have also overwhelmed
the texts that gave them birth.[2] The little that we can know about Menippus
the author, combined with the literary uses to which Lucian puts Menippus,
as character as well as author, leads me to the following conclusion: that
Menippean satire is a useful name for the epicenter of a range of phenomena, both stylistic and thematic, that in fact evolve over time. The essence
of Menippean satire is an otherworldly fantasy in which a naive experimenter travels to an impossible realm in order to learn that the truth is not
to be found at the edges of the world but at home and under one's own

---

[1] See Relihan (1984) 226–9.
[2] See Relihan (1993) 12–36 (ch. 2: "A Definition of Menippean Satire").

feet; the one who would preach this truth is made comic because, in accordance with good Cynic principles, one cannot be dogmatic even about one's anti-dogmatism, and the challenge to accepted authority and received truths cannot honestly take the form of a new authority and a new absolute truth. The mixture of prose and verse which is so obviously a part of Varro, Seneca, and Petronius must be read as a provocative crossing of generic boundaries and as a stylistic impropriety, for the author who writes in such an incoherent way invites us to challenge the claim to authority which is inherent in the act of writing itself. The fictional character who makes the discovery about the superiority of common sense may himself be abused; the genre may be said to be most internally self-consistent when the author presents himself, not merely as the narrator, but also as the actor, in his own self-mocking drama.

One problem with taking Lucian as a source for what may be known about Menippus is that Lucian's own position in the history (that is, in the ongoing development) of the Menippean genre can easily be overlooked or misestimated. The multiplicities of Lucian's own output, as well as his excellence in the one genre that he claims for his own, the comic dialogue, make it clear that while there may be much that is Menippean in Lucian, it does not follow that there are many Menippean satires.[3] The two works that stand out as Menippean satires are his *Necyomantia* ("Menippus, or The Consultation of the Dead"), in which Menippus travels to the underworld to consult Teiresias about the best way to live one's life, and its companion piece *Icaromenippus* ("Menippus the New Icarus, or Over the Rainbow"), in which Menippus flies to heaven via the moon and witnesses a debate on what may be done to silence the philosophers and their unwarranted speculations. In creating two journeys for Menippus, Lucian does in a diptych what Seneca does in a single work: create a fantasy on many levels, in which the comic hero sees all of the universe.[4] But note this difference: whether or not the reader is willing to see in the grotesque Claudius the naive narrator who puts the other world to the test by demonstrating that it cannot contain him, Seneca's *Apocolocyntosis* is actually less universal than Lucian's pieces. The focus of *Apocolocyntosis* is the buffoon Claudius and the Roman institution of imperial apotheosis that even dares to raise the question of whether this unworthy

---

[3] I have also argued that Varro's 150 *Menippeans* would not, if we could read them entire, fall all comfortably under the same generic label.

[4] Further on this diptych and its literary influence in Relihan (1996) 265–93 and esp. 277–80; see also Relihan (1993) 76–7, 104–14. For Seneca's work as the paradigmatic Menippean satire, see Riikonen (1987).

candidate can be made a god.[5] But while Lucian's infernal fantasy raises social and ethical questions, his heavenly fantasy raises intellectual ones: the philosopher and the nature of philosophical speculation in the abstract are the butt of the humor here, as is the inability of the Olympian gods to do anything effective about them. Philosophers and their ideas here transcend the social world of mortals; they are topics appropriate for heaven because heaven is the realm into which pretentious philosophers try to obtrude themselves and their intellectual systems, as if human beings were the sum of their thoughts.[6] But in general terms, in the century that separates the Latin Seneca and the Greek Lucian we see a passage from more generally social concerns (a Roman talking to Romans about Romans) to more abstract and intellectual concerns (the nature of the gods and the universe, and the difficulty that all mortals have in their attempt to locate themselves within the ultimate order of the world). The satirist will not try to keep people out of hell, though he will try to keep them out of heaven; but Seneca's expulsion of Claudius from Olympus is for reasons quite different from those in play in Menippus' ascent and return in *Icaromenippus*.

Lucian's practice, in evidence here as well as in others of his comic dialogues, of presenting unworthy philosophers as the object of the reader's as well as the gods' disdain, is consistent with some of what can be attributed to Varro's *Menippeans* and to his inspiration in Menippus himself. We do not need to imagine the influence of the Roman Varro on the Greek Lucian; the example of Menippus is sufficient to inspire them both. But what needs to be stressed is Lucian's own removal of himself from the humor of his pieces. Varro's *Menippeans* are linguistic extravaganzas, Lucian's pieces are models of Attic purity and restraint.[7] Further, Varro the author is certainly one of the philosophers abused in the course of some of his pieces, but Lucian does

---

[5] The examination of unworthy applicants for godhood is a Hellenistic motif which may have found its way into Menippus and which is certainly in evidence in Lucian's *Council of the Gods*.

[6] Northrop Frye continues to be crucial to this discussion: "The novelist sees evil and folly as social diseases, but the Menippean satirist sees them as diseases of the intellect, as a kind of maddened pedantry which the *philosophus gloriosus* at once symbolizes and defines": Frye (1957) 309.

[7] Even granting that the late grammarians who preserve the scraps of the *Menippeans* for us have done so in order to illustrate archaic vocabulary and neologism, there is no escaping the conclusion that the excesses of an academic language pushed to and beyond its limits are crucial to the humor of the pieces in general and to the characterization of the author, the narrators, and the participants in the fantasies and dialogues contained within them. Similar conclusions may be drawn about Apuleius' *Metamorphoses*: who would have thought that an ass could speak and write like that?

not really mock himself at all. He prefers to put on Menippus the burden of the humor; he will mock his mocker, or import other mockers: Momus, for example, or Silenus in *Deorum Concilium* ("The Council of the Gods") and *Jupiter Tragoedus* ("Zeus the Tragic Actor"). In one piece, Lucian has Dialogue protest that the author's humor and stylistic experimentation (most notably, the mixture of prose and verse) have made him unrecognizable (*Bis Accusatus* ["The Author Twice on Trial"] 33); but Lucian is too elegant, and too calculating, to write in a way that would justify these claims. In Lucian there is a mixture of elegance and intellectual criticism which is something essentially new in the history of Menippean satire, and it is this habit that he will pass on to the Emperor Julian, 200 years after his own time: intellectual fantasy at the expense of others, but not at the expense of the author himself, in which self-parody is kept to a minimum, and the superiority of author or observer to what is observed is stressed.

But after Lucian the traditions of Menippean satire diverge along two separate lines, roughly defined as the neo-Varronian (encyclopedic and inwardly intellectual) and the Lucianic (outwardly social). The second path, connecting Lucian to Julian, even given Julian's willingness to borrow from Seneca, is probably the less interesting, and certainly the less productive, of the two ways in late antiquity. But it is this particular strain that will animate the Latin Menippean satires of the Renaissance, and which will seem from a twenty-first century perspective to be the most up to date.[8] The other path is that of the Varronian revival, in which Varro's love of self-parody, intellectual parody, linguistic excess, encyclopedic content, and innovation in verse will find willing students in Martianus Capella, Fulgentius, Ennodius, and Boethius. Excepting Boethius, these authors are not much read, and their works are, like Julian's *Caesars*, appreciated more for the encyclopedic material which they contain than for the form which surrounds it. But the desire of these neo-Varronian satires to enclose all of the world within the confines of a single book, to doubt the ability of human reason to comprehend what it means to be human, to suggest that there is a form of uncommon knowledge which transcends the earthly wisdom, even the very Philosophy, of the narrator or author – this is the path that leads to the twelfth-century Renaissance: in particular, *De Cosmographia* ("A Map of the Universe") of Bernardus Silvestris and *De Planctu Naturae* ("The Complaint of Nature")

---

[8] Conventions of philologues on Helicon, flights to Parnassus, dream visions of the embarrassments to which pretenders to learning may be put in the other world, can be found conveniently assembled in the great Renaissance collection of classical and neo-Latin Menippean satires: the two-volume *Elegantiores Praestantium Virorum Satyrae* published in Leiden in 1655. See Relihan (1996) for a full discussion of these trends; see also Haarberg (1998) 177–243, and Blanchard (1995).

of Alan of Lille.[9] By opening the door to certain kinds of abstract knowledge rather than undertaking to discredit them all, these works veer away from the genre's Cynic origins toward a conviction in superior wisdom. The trail they blaze, however rich, dies out in the middle ages, so its stopping places always seem much more time bound and quaint to the modern world than do those of the genre's alternate, Lucianic route. But it is along this path that Boethius and his *Consolation of Philosophy* lie.

The history of Menippean satire in late antiquity needs to be appreciated for its dynamics, its differing emphases, its long and multi-form influence. Four particular elements mark the change from the Menippean satires of Seneca and Petronius: an increasing interest in intellectual, rather than social, criticism, possibly reflecting ultimately the concerns of Menippus himself; an increasing factual content, the legacy of Varro's *Menippeans* and their interests, leading to that most curious creation of late antiquity, the ironic encyclopedia (cf. Julian's anecdotal *Caesars*, a biographical history of the Roman empire, and Martianus' textbook of the seven liberal arts); an increasing willingness to regularize and to expand upon the role that poetry plays, so that the text itself begins to mirror its encyclopedic content by its universal form, containing all things within all structures; and the dramatization of the process of writing itself, often taking the form of an author debating with his Muse over the form that the work should take and how it should be interpreted. These elements are not all present in all works, and Julian's disengagement from self-parody has already been mentioned, yet together they form a coherent package, a bundle of compositional and thematic tactics that help to define an inward turn of Menippean satire. Now the subject is not so much the world outside as the world of the mind, and the world of the written word as an expression of the mind. While these late texts attempt to describe the boundaries between rational and supra-rational thought, *Consolation* actually attempts to describe the process of thought itself.[10] Ultimately, the Menippean satires of the late period try to indicate the existence of two worlds: one, the mortal world that cannot be explained by rational thought because it is full of irrational human

---

[9] See Relihan (1993) 179–97, for a brief discussion of Boethius' *Consolation* as a Menippean satire and its influence in the twelfth century and its prosimetric fantasies in which Theology, presiding over the decline of Christian Platonism, becomes the answer to the problem of the limitations of philosophy. For a strongly dissentient view, see Pabst (1994). I will address the medieval influence of the Menippean Boethius more fully in *The Prisoner's Philosophy: the Limitations of Pagan Thought in Boethius's* Consolation (South Bend, IN, forthcoming).

[10] Curley (1986) 253: "Boethius does not believe that philosophy's proper medium is a succession of simple declarative sentences but a highly wrought text, the many voices and tones of which interact so as to produce a pattern mirroring the complexity of the cosmos."

beings; the other, present more outside of the text than within it, a world of eternal truth, the realm of true divinity or (in Martianus Capella's formulation) the Unknown or Undefinable Father. This is the transmutation of Cynic common sense into the new common sense of a new world: a scholar's hidden heaven, a mystic faith, or even a Christian truth. Such new common sense is a reflection of a new era, not merely an "Age of Anxiety" but an age whose abiding concern is to define the relation of body and mind, and so define the self.[11]

Julian's *Caesars*

Julian's *Caesars* is a heavenly fantasy which resists a number of the comic elements of the Menippean satires of Lucian on which it is based. The interlocutor demands a story from the narrator, but the narrator is no ridiculous figure just returned from the other world as in Lucian's *Necyomantia*, and the reason for the request for the story is that now it is the Saturnalia (Seneca's *Apocolocyntosis* also has a Saturnalian setting), and a comic story is appropriate for the festivities. The narrator plays a bit with the expectations of his interlocutor; after raising the possibility that this story (the word is *mythos*) may be Platonic, Aesopic, or purely fictional, the narrator is told by his exasperated friend to get on with his story, whatever it may be. Ultimately, the narrator does not return to earth in some comic way, as Menippus does in Lucian; rather, at the end of the secondhand story that Hermes told to him, the narrator reveals that he was given a special encouragement from the god: he should attend to the commands of Mithras in his own life, so as to find a kindly guardian god for himself in the next. In context, this is a denial of the value of the story that has preceded it, and to this extent we see Julian firmly within the traditions of the Menippean genre.

Briefly, the story is this. The Saturnalia allows for a banquet in heaven at which the past emperors of Rome are invited to dine with their social superiors, the Olympian gods. This temporary equality is the occasion for a contest, an appropriate sympotic activity; the winner will be elevated to divine status permanently, in order to be a companion for Romulus, the founder of the feast. The chronological parade of the emperors into the dining hall allows Silenus (appropriately a satyr, and thus given to "satyric" taunting and play – see Freudenburg's volume introduction) to mock them all, frequently in

---

[11] See Chadwick (1999) 60–81. Chadwick never mentions Boethius in this article despite his familiarity with him (*Boethius: the Consolations of Music, Logic, Theology, and Philosophy* [Oxford 1981]), yet this article is an excellent introduction to the issues raised by *Consolation*. See also the introduction to my translation of *Consolation*, Relihan (2001) x–xxvii.

rather trivial ways; not only does Julian go Seneca's *Apocolocyntosis* one better, by thus abusing all the emperors, but he does so in an encyclopedic fashion, thus aligning the work with one of the traditions of later Menippean satire. We get a brief, comic encapsulated history of Rome in the guise of a symposium; it does not much matter for our purposes that this catalogue shows that Julian has no very deep knowledge of his predecessors, if only because a display of deep knowledge was surely not his goal.[12]

We proceed to the contest, for which six men are chosen as the original plan is somewhat expanded: three for their virtues, selected by Hermes (Caesar, Octavian, Trajan); one for his philosophy, selected by Cronus (Marcus Aurelius); Heracles calls for a Greek, Alexander the Great; Dionysus wants Constantine, so that a libertine can balance such a virtuous list, and he is allowed to compete so long as he stands only at the threshold of the dining hall and does not actually come in. The competition is in two rounds: first, each gives an account of his reign; second, each describes the goal of his life. Silenus insults only Trajan, Marcus, and Constantine in the first round; in the second, after Hermes asks the main questions, Silenus insults them all during an investigation of certain details. The gods convene and vote in secret. The victory of Marcus Aurelius seems a foregone conclusion, as Julian would reasonably want to champion another philosophic Roman emperor who wrote in Greek, but Julian is operating entirely within Menippean traditions by casting doubt on this victory. The victor is never announced; Zeus speaks to Hermes, who issues a proclamation allowing all six contestants into heaven, each to find his own guardian god. As in Alice's caucus-race, all are winners and all must have prizes; as in the myth of Er, these souls make both noble and laughable choices. Trajan does not pick an Olympian god, but clings to his fellow contestant Alexander; Constantine runs off after Indulgence to Jesus, seen granting easy absolutions to unrepentant sinners.

The change in the rules of the contest reveals that the heaven which tries these souls does not judge fairly or respect merit. Seneca's afterworld in

---

[12] This is unfortunate, as no other Roman emperor leaves a written account of his thoughts about his predecessors; see Bowersock (1982) 159–72. The nature of these criticisms is illustrated by Smith (1995) 13–14:

> If there are passing jibes at a Pius or an Alexander Severus, that hardly suffices to disclose an intellectually isolated author; it may simply show one willing to twit the great and the good to amuse the reader. By the same token, Augustus is a chameleon, Trajan a *macho* with an eye for a pretty boy, Plotinus' patron Gallienus a mincing transvestite, Alexander the Great a tearful drunk who seeks to exculpate himself when criticized by dextrous "tricks of logic."

Apocolocyntosis is susceptible to the same charge. In this light, Julian's receipt of special instructions, to aim for Mithras as his guardian god, shows that he imagines for himself a different heaven and a different reward.[13] His is not this comic Olympus; Julian, the Mithraic initiate, aims for some more noble realm for his life after death. There is no need to deny that there are serious issues at and below the surface in Julian's *Caesars*. Julian surely establishes himself as the true and just ruler, and the parade of former emperors is an ironic Mirror for Princes, showing how not to think, how not to worship, how not to rule. But as we will see in Boethius as well, Menippean satire is here in the service of autobiography, and the inward turning of the genre in late antiquity has as prideful subtext, that Julian alone is the true believer, that Julian alone is the true emperor, that history converges on him and that he is the focal point of the divine gaze.

Boethius' *Consolation*

Consolation of Philosophy is typically a sticking point in a discussion of Menippean satire: its satiric affiliation has been difficult to maintain because it seems so ponderously serious. But the satire of Menippean satire means mixture, a jumble of things that do not go together, a stylistic and thematic incoherence: the mixture of prose and verse, of heaven and earth, of earnestness and jest. What has happened in *Consolation* is that the mixture, the satiric mess, which is in origin emblematic of the confusion and incomprehensibility of human life, becomes sublime when the totality of the timebound world, life and death, justice and injustice, is given meaning when seen through the eyes of God.

Philosophy, who is here the personified other voice of the dialogue, encourages the prisoner to forget his earthly life, to ignore the wrongs done to him and fly away with her to heaven so that he can look down and see that tyrants

---

[13] *Caesars* 336C, translation from Relihan (1993) 126:

> Now speaking to me, Hermes said: "But to you I have granted knowledge of your father Mithras. Keep you therefore his commandments, preparing for yourself a mooring cable and a safe harbor while you are alive; and, whenever you must come away to this place, having established for yourself, with Good Hope, a kindly guardian god."

Commenting on this passage, Athanassiadi-Fowden argues "that the tone of Hermes to Julian in 362 suggests that by that time the emperor was a fully saved Mithraist – one who had exhausted the springs of spiritual knowledge." See Athanassiadi-Fowden (1981) 40. But Smith (1995) 126 makes the necessary observation that there is nothing particularly Mithraic about the fable itself.

themselves, and not their prisoners, are the ones who are truly exiles.[14] This process, she imagines, will result in a proper definition of what a human being is; she has diagnosed her interlocutor's root problem as a forgetfulness of self at the end of book 1, and this is the specific motivation for the process of her cure (*de consolatione* 1.6.17–19). But the prisoner refuses to go away with Philosophy, and I would argue that he redirects her arguments. Books 4 and 5 represent not what Philosophy intended to talk about but the prisoner's own concerns. In response, *Consolation* ends with Philosophy defining not man but God, showing how the phenomenal world is rational in terms of the nature of God's vision and knowledge, even if mortals cannot understand it, or explain how their actions are free and not constrained by necessity (in the lengthy argument of *de consolatione* 5.6). The world that Philosophy wants the prisoner to transcend has been given value by God; divine vision makes sense of the confusing phenomena of the world, even that most baffling thing of all, the punishment inflicted on the virtuous and the just.

Consolation ends with a pointed paradox. The prisoner forces Philosophy to admit that there is a kind of necessity imposed on human actions by the fact of God's unerring knowledge of them.[15] But the last words of the dialogue are Philosophy's and she turns the tables on the prisoner when she speaks of the necessity of virtuous action, even though this is a conclusion she surely never expected to reach when she began to reeducate the prisoner in book 1 (*de consolatione* 5.6.48: "Unless you want to hide the truth, there *is* a great necessity imposed upon you – the necessity of righteousness, since you

---

[14] Cf. 4.m.1.19–30 (all translations from *Consolation* taken from Relihan (2001); accent marks aim to preserve the meter of the original):

> Hére with the scéptre and reíns of the úniverse
>   In hánd, is foúnd the Lórd of kíngs,
> A´nd he, unmóving, contróls the swift cháriot,
>   As fíery júdge of áll the wórld.
> Nów if your páth takes you báck to this pláce again,
>   Which nów you loók for únrecálled,
> Yoú will say, "Nów I remémber my fátherland –
>   Here wás I bórn, here sháll I stánd."
> Thén should it pleáse you to víew on the eárth below
>   The níght that yoú have léft behínd –
> Pítiless ty´rants, whom désolate peóples fear,
>   You wíll behóld as éxiles thére.

[15] As Philosophy says at 5.6.25:

> Now if you should say at this point that what God sees will happen cannot *not* happen, and that what cannot not happen is contingent by necessity, and if you bind me tight to this word "necessity," then I will admit that it is indeed a thing of the most steadfast truth, but one which scarcely anyone but a contemplator of the divine has approached.

act before the eyes of a judge who beholds all things"). In *Consolation*, God becomes the heavenly viewer (*kataskopos*). The cynical view of Menippus on the moon, the chance to see the world in its totality and to note the puniness of human endeavors, is now reserved for God himself. Philosophy earlier wanted the narrator to achieve this height and this vision and laugh (the standard cynical/Menippean response). But by the end it is reserved for God, who does not laugh. The prisoner was encouraged to take up Menippus' challenge and mock human strivings and his own impending death, but on this side of the grave he must look to God's vision, which does not negate but positively ennobles the human actions it perceives. Real death, not Lucianic/Menippean fantasies of death, will be the prisoner's route to the heaven from which he can see these things for himself; but this vision is not in our text.

But even here there are comic structures and clear Menippean elements. Boethius does not write in a vacuum: not only is there reason to presume that Boethius was aware of some of Varro's *Menippeans*, but his immediate predecessors in the genre have clearly worked their influence on him.[16] From the early fifth century is *The Marriage of Philology and Mercury* of Martianus Capella, an encyclopedia of the seven liberal arts in which the personified Liberal Arts present themselves as bridal gifts for Philology once she has arrived on Olympus for her wedding; the story is narrated to the author by the genre of the work, Satura, although he will argue with her and she will abandon the work at its end in disgust. But during her ascent Philology glimpses another world; she prays to the Sun as the first emanation of the Unknown Father in august epic hexameters (2.185–93), a poem which is the direct model for the epic central poem of *Consolation* (3.m.9). The wedding takes place on a lower heaven; ultimate reality is not depicted. From the late fifth century is *The Mythologies* of Fulgentius; here Calliope, the Muse of epic poetry, initially appears to redirect the narrator's work, his proud reduction of classical mythology to moral allegory. Calliope first appears to debate with the narrator as to who will direct the encyclopedia of allegories which follows, and later returns with Satura in tow, only to find the narrator on his bed, babbling in verses in his sleep like a madman, just as Philosophy finds the prisoner in *Consolation* weeping over the dictation he takes from his Muses. *Consolation*'s initial disparagement of the narrator's abilities, the redirection of the initial work, the dramatized debate between author and Muse for control of the work, and the problematic ending are all elements of a Menippean satire that seeks to illustrate Philosophy's limitations, not her absolute power to answer questions.

---

[16] For Varro's *Menippeans* in the fifth and sixth centuries, see Shanzer (1986) 272–85.

Conclusion: politics, pride, and satire

In the history of Menippean satire the self-parodying role of the author-narrator is subject to considerable changes. We may well believe that Menippus was himself engaged in self-parody in the broadest possible terms, depicting himself as a man back from the dead, wearing an Arcadian cap woven with the signs of the zodiac, tragic boots, a full beard, and carrying an ashen staff.[17] But when Lucian applies himself to writing Menippean satire he sends a re-animated Menippus in place of himself on a journey to the Underworld, dressed in Odysseus' hat and Heracles' lion-skin, carrying Orpheus' lyre, so that he would have ease of access. Varro, I believe, would have often depicted himself as the fantastic experimenter of Menippean satires, whereas Seneca in the *Apocolocyntosis* arranges not only to be the narrator and not the actor in his drama, but also sends Claudius on a journey to a hell from which he will not return. Seneca, as I have argued, is willing to use the grotesque Claudius to point out the grotesquerie of the Roman afterlife in which the divinification of a Claudius is even a possibility; but Seneca the author is above the fray, and whatever critical points he wishes to make about the apotheosis, religion, and the cult of emperors, he is himself master of, not part of, the humor. He puts to comic use the skills he has honed as a dramatist and poet in creating some of the scenes and poetic effects, but the goal of the *Apocolocyntosis* is not to make fun of Seneca. Lucian is also cleverly in control, as in his *Dialogues of the Dead*, which manage to take the Menippus who wants to be superior to the fantasies with which we populate the land of the dead and force him to take his place in it, never to return.

In late antiquity we see two different approaches to the question of an author's self-parody, one essentially related to Menippean predecessors and the other essentially new. The first is that of Julian, who, like Seneca and Lucian, his models in matter and form, is not really part of the humor of the piece. He does not make the trip to heaven even as a simple observer, but is told a tale by Hermes, here the psychopomp. (It is to be noted that Menippus is related to Hermes in the role of one who knows the ways of the dead; in Renaissance Menippean satire, we generally see a devaluation of the person of Menippus himself, as his functions are largely apportioned to the mocker Momus and to the infernal Mercury; Julian's *Caesars*, with its Momus and Silenus, is in this tradition and is part of the general transmutation of Menippus in the Renaissance.)[18] But the other method of self-parody

---

[17] So we are told in the *Suda*, *s.v.* φαιός; cf. Relihan (1993) 45.

[18] Relihan (1996) 278–80. The *Momus* of Leon Battista Alberti, written between 1443 and 1450, is a good illustration of this sublimation of Menippus; the work is now available in the English translation of Sarah Knight (Cambridge, MA 2003).

is in evidence in Martianus Capella, Fulgentius, and Boethius. The author is engaged in a debate with his Muse, whose wisdom is insufficient for explaining what is central to human experience. True wisdom is championed by the humble author who rejects the theoretician's claims to absolute knowledge in favor of a simple piety that trusts God himself to know what the author, in this life, cannot. This is truly Cynic, in a way, and a worthy descendant of the thoughts and habits of Diogenes and his followers. But whereas both the Cynic satirist and Boethius are obsessed with questions of how life is to be valued and lived, Boethius refuses simply to reject or even to transcend Philosophy in favor of common sense *per se*.[19] Rather, he offers the promise of an all-knowing God who may be approached by humble prayer.[20]

But there is of course in such a posture a great deal of pride. The author who sets out to subvert the wisdom of Philosophy cannot do so without a great deal of confidence. The pride of a Julian, who has his own Mithraic heaven waiting for him, who feels himself to be the superior to all of his predecessors on the throne and in the field, is obvious; the pride of a Boethius is less so. But it is clear that in the composition of *Consolation of Philosophy* Boethius the author, with a great deal of nostalgia, looks over the history of philosophy and sees nothing between Plato and Socrates and his own time except for schismatic Hellenistic philosophers and a few martyrs who died in the reigns of tyrants, much as Julian sees primarily shameless self-seeking and abuse of power in the emperors leading up to himself. Philosophy comes for the prisoner because the prisoner is the last philosopher. But the prisoner is the author, and just as the author is the last true Roman poet, he is also the last true Roman Republican and patriot.[21] Death is the reason

---

[19] For Julian's own obsessions with fate and fortune, with piety, and with his relations with his predecessors, see Athanassiadi-Fowden (1981) 198–201.

[20] As the prisoner says near the end (5.3.34):

> Therefore: That one and only avenue of exchange between human beings and God will be taken away, the avenue of hope and prayer for deliverance; provided, of course, that for the price of our rightful humility we deserve the return of divine grace, which is beyond price. This is the only way by which human beings seem to be able to speak with God – by the act of supplication – and to be joined to that inapproachable light (cf. 1 Timothy 6:16) even before they succeed in attaining it.

[21] One of the reasons for the composition of so many poems in so many meters is to demonstrate that Boethius has all of the strings of the ancient traditions in his own hands. He is not writing contemporary poetry. And while in all of his castigations of Nero can be seen the realities of the contemporary Theoderic, responsible for his imprisonment and shortly to be responsible for his death, in the exempla that dot the prisoner's arguments there are frequent references to the Republican heroes: Cato, Fabricius, Aemilius Paullus. Philosophy tries to make the point that these great men of old are dead, and that death swallows up much of what is meaningful.

why the prisoner should come away with Philosophy; Philosophy is herself here playing the Cynic, harping on the reality of death, seeking to negate what the prisoner prides himself on. But the prisoner refuses to yield to these arguments. Instead, he sees that by keeping Philosophy talking he can keep himself alive and thus, rather than rushing off with Philosophy to the realms beyond, can preserve himself for a death that will come soon enough, and for a later revelation.

Further reading

Those interested in Menippean satire in late antiquity should first read the brief prologue of the *Mythologies* of Fulgentius, translated in Appendix B of my *Ancient Menippean Satire* and discussed in ch. 10; the excellent monograph of Bradford Gregory Hayes, *Fulgentius the Mythographer* (dissertation Cornell 1996) should now be consulted (esp. ch. 4). A translation of Martianus Capella's *Marriage of Philology and Mercury* is available in the two volumes of William Harris Stahl, Richard Johnson, and E. L. Burge, *Martianus Capella and the Seven Liberal Arts* (Columbia 1971, 1977). Whether these prosimetric texts and the *Consolation* together exert a satiric instead of a merely rhetorical and encyclopedic influence in the middle ages is contested. Berhard Pabst's *Prosimetrum* (1994) is resoundingly negative; Joseph Harris and Karl Reichl, eds., *Prosimetrum: Crosscultural Perspectives on Narrative in Prose and Verse* (Cambridge 1997), may offer the reader an interesting and broader context for a more sympathetic approach. Peter Dronke (1994) shows prosimetrum at play in a wide range of forms of popular medieval literature and in effect describes, though he does not say so explicitly, the importance of this form in the history of autobiography. For a Menippean revival in the twelfth century in the aftermath of Christian Platonism, see Alan of Lille's *Plaint of Nature* (James J. Sheridan, trans., Toronto 1980), Bernardus Silvestris's *Cosmographia* (Winthrop Wetherbee, trans., Columbia 1973), and my *Ancient Menippean Satire*, ch. 12.

The emperor Julian still does not excite as much interest as he should in purely literary terms. The recent edition of Friedhelm L. Müller, *Die beiden Satiren des Kaisers Julianus Apostata* (Symposion oder Caesares und Antiochikos oder Misopogon) (Stuttgart 1998) does not raise the question of genre at all. Julian's personal and religious history fuels most monographs. See most recently Adrian Murdoch, *The Last Pagan: Julian the Apostate and the Death of the Ancient World* (Stroud 2004); pages 212–14 contain a fascinating account of the uses of the example of Julian and his *Caesars* in Catholic–Protestant polemic in the Renaissance. Boethius receives more attention, though students of his vast medieval influence in literature and philosophy are skeptical of the literary claims made here for Menippean satire in *Consolation*; see now John Marenbon, *Boethius* (Oxford 2003), and his three elegant chapters on the content and interpretation of *Consolation* (96–163). The bibliographical guide to *Consolation* by Joachim Gruber, "Boethius 1925–1998 (2. Teil)," *Lustrum* 40 (1998), 199–259, has only just appeared; the third part of this bibliography, which will also deal with *Consolation*, remains to be published. Ann W. Astell, *Job, Boethius, and Epic Truth* (Cornell 1994), while dealing with the influence of Boethius in medieval secondary epic, documents the surprising ways in which philosophical dialogue can inspire other genres, and is a good avenue for approaching *Consolation* and its influence in purely literary terms.

Is Bakhtin's approach to the definition and history of Menippean satire the best way to understand the genre as a phenomenon of Renaissance and modern literature? My feeling is that Bakhtin's theories have receded from the high-water mark of their influence. Their characterization of ancient literature is too broad, and their representation of the virtues of Russian literature are too parochial; see H. D. Weinbrot, "Bakhtin and Menippean Satire: Soviet Whiggery, Bion, Varro, Horace, and the Eighteenth Century," *Classical and Modern Literature* 22/2 (2002) 33–56.

7

CATHERINE CONNORS

Epic allusion in Roman satire

One of the things Lucilius, Horace, Persius, and Juvenal have in common is their pleasure in a nice bit of epic furniture about the place. It is easy enough to install, since epic and satire both use the dactylic hexameter. It is fun to hear Horace describe the city mouse and the country mouse going to Rome in the kind of night that falls in Roman epic (Horace, *Sermones* 2.6.98–101). It is amusing to see a decadent Roman aristocrat as a "boy Automedon" (Achilles' charioteer, Juvenal 1.61), or to see the admirable Pyrrha, who helps repopulate the earth after the flood by throwing stones over her shoulder, through Juvenal's jaundiced eyes, looking like a procuress setting out her girls (Juvenal 1.84). And of course everyone enjoys a nice swipe at bad epic poets now and then. But the function of epic allusion in Roman satire should not be understood as exclusively decorative. In many genres, poets use allusions to define their poetic projects and to articulate important themes.[1] It is well understood that the Roman satirists use allusions to or descriptions of their satiric predecessors to articulate their poetic projects.[2] What has been less appreciated is how precisely each poet chooses his allusions to epic to define his poetic project and its political dimension.[3]

Each satirist inhabits a different set of political circumstances. Lucilius, born into a wealthy family as Rome becomes ever more avid in its pursuit of the luxurious prizes of conquest during the second century BCE, plunges into the cut and thrust of Republican politics with direct attacks on a number of important political figures. Horace, son of a freedman, who has had the luck to make his way into the circle of Maecenas, looks back at years of civil war and forward to better times under Octavian and eschews famous names in favor of benighted nobodies as targets of his satire. Seneca, hailing from

---

[1] Hinds (1998).

[2] On satirists' programmatic allusions to their predecessors see Kenney (1962) and Bramble (1974) 16–23.

[3] Freudenburg (2001) places politics in the foreground of his readings of the satiric tradition.

an extremely wealthy and well-connected family and holding the position
of tutor and advisor to Nero, disdains Claudius' arbitrary and high-handed
dealings and can hardly contain his glee at Claudius' death. Persius cryp-
tically suggests to his circle of friends that it would be dangerous to speak
too openly of Neronian folly. Juvenal portrays himself as in need of a good
patron and rails against the tyranny of Domitian for all to hear, once it is
safely over. A relatively limited number of epic motifs – mainly from battle
scenes and scenes of the gods meeting in council – are the basis of most of
satire's epic allusions. Each poet exploits his scraps of epic in different ways,
and the differences reflect not just their stylistic choices but their political
worlds.

Fish, Politics, Hexameter – and satire

Fish occupy a special category in ancient thinking about food. Not as basic
or homegrown as grain and vegetables, fish is unlike meat too: it is not
sacrificed, nor need it be consumed communally. The smallest and cheapest
fish nourish the poor man, while the rich man can afford the most delicate
flavors and exotic varieties. Like satire itself, fish is a private indulgence,
not a public shared undertaking. Talking about the fish men eat is in effect
talking about the money they spend on themselves for themselves – and this
can be a good way of getting at a political target.[4] Ennius' translation of
the gourmandizing poem on food – and especially fish – by Archestratus of
Gela (in Sicily) should be viewed as part of the literary and cultural context within which Roman satire takes shape. In his *Hedypatheia* ("life of
pleasures"), written some time between 390 and 350 BCE, Archestratus used
vaguely Homeric hexameters to tell readers where to go to buy the best food
and drink in the Mediterranean. During Archestratus' lifetime, Sicily was
famous for its rich and elaborately spiced cuisine, which was publicized in
the Greek world in several notorious cookbooks.[5] While Archestratus was
derided as something of a glutton by some later readers, his recent editors
make beautifully clear that he prizes above all simple preparations of high
quality ingredients and deplores social climbers who hire (or buy) specialized
professional cooks to provide them with the latest fancily spiced Syracusan
dishes. As Olson and Sens argue, Archestratus seems to write for an élite,
like-minded audience; the easy mastery of Homer his poem displays in its
hexameter form and vocabulary marks them all as men educated in a traditional way. While the poem is not exactly satire, it does seem to set an "in
group" of truly luxurious people who eat exquisitely simple food and joke

---

[4] Cf. Davidson (1997) 3–35.   [5] Olson and Sens (2000) xxxvi–xxxix.

about Homer (perhaps a traditional aristocracy) against an "out group" of conspicuous and uninformed consumers (perhaps a newly affluent middle or commercial class).[6]

Only one eleven-line fragment survives of Ennius' hexameter translation of Archestratus, the *Hedyphagetica* ("Delicatessen"), but it is a tantalizing one. Skutsch has argued that Ennius makes changes to his model that may reflect his experience in the entourage of Fulvius Nobilior as he waged a military campaign in Aetolia in 189/8.[7] In line 3 of the fragment (Ennius fr. 33–44 Vahlen, which translates Archestratus fr. 7 Olson and Sens = Athenaeus 3.92d–e), Ennius adds *Caradrum*, which seems to be a town name, to describe a precise location in Ambracia where good scallops are found. This detail is not found in the corresponding line of the original Greek, and the place itself seems to have been rather obscure. Ennius may be one-upping his Greek source with the results of his own experience there in Ambracia on the ground. Nobilior's campaign brought heaps of Greek stuff back to Rome. He appropriated statues of the Muses and housed them in a Roman temple of Hercules. He had in his entourage Ennius, a poet who in his *Annales*, which tell Rome's history, up to and including Nobilior's exploits, brings the Homeric hexameter – and the kind of panegyric favored by Hellenistic kings – into Latin. Nobilior's Muses and the hexameters of Ennius' *Annales* are imperial artefacts which celebrate Rome's ability to put the spoils of conquest to its own uses. Ennius' translation of Archestratus, too, transforms a Greek artefact into a document of Roman conquest even in details as small as the scallops at Charadros: the world of the Mediterranean is no longer merely the place where a Sicilian gourmet travels to eat, but from where a Roman general comes home in triumph.

Turnips in heaven

It would be nice to know whether Ennius used mock epic elements in his poems in various meters called *saturae*, but the limited fragments do not show clear evidence of this. Much more important for understanding connections between epic and satire is Ennius' epic *Annales*, for satirists often pluck their epic allusions from its grand history of Rome. In the first book of the *Annales*, the gods meet as a divine council to discuss Romulus' fate and are told that he is destined to join them in heaven (*unus erit quem tu tolles in caerula caeli/ templa*, "there will be one whom you [Mars] will bear aloft to heaven's blue

---

[6] Olson and Sens (2000) xliii–lv; see also Wilkins (2000) ch. 6, on representations of luxurious eating in Greek comedy, esp. 292–304 on fish, and ch. 7, "The Culinary Literature of Sicily."

[7] Skutsch (1968) 38–9.

realms," *Annales* 54–5 Sk.). Another Ennian fragment, also assigned to the first book of the *Annales*, represents Romulus among the gods (110–11):

> Romulus in caelo cum dis genitalibus aevom
> degit
> Romulus spends his life in heaven with the gods who created him

The picture of the once mortal Romulus among the gods, which seems not to have been part of the story before Ennius, was a powerful one, and it came in for mockery from several later poets. In Seneca's *Apocolocyntosis* (to which I shall return below), the motion proposing the deification of Claudius concludes that "the republic needs someone else who can *gobble steaming turnips*" (*ferventia rapa vorare*) with Romulus (Seneca, *Apocolocyntosis* 9.5). The emphasized words are the end of a hexameter; Lucilius is their most likely author. An epigram of Martial likewise vividly pictures Romulus living on cooked turnips (Martial 13.16):

> These turnips [*rapa*] which we give you, delighting in the winter cold,
> > Romulus is accustomed to eat in heaven [*in caelo Romulus esse solet*]

The Lucilian line can thus be reconstructed with what Skutsch describes as almost mathematical certainty:

> > *Romulus in caelo ferventia rapa vorare.*
> > Romulus . . . gobbled steaming turnips in heaven . . .

In response to Ennius' picture of Romulus *living* in heaven (*Romulus in caelo*), a satirist – presumably Lucilius – produces an earthy picture of Romulus *eating* in heaven, and not nibbling at ambrosia, but gobbling the very mundane turnip. The vision of Romulus in heaven also happens to survive in graffiti at Pompeii. The phrase *Romulus in caelo* appears four times on walls in the city (*CIL* IV 3135, 7353, 8568, 8995). Skutsch suspects this line was used (much as the *Apocolocyntosis* used *ferventia rapa vorare*) in some kind of skit mocking the deifications declared by the Julio-Claudian emperors, and he compares Vespasian's deathbed joke *vae puto deus fio* ("alas, I think I am becoming a god," Suetonius, *Vespasian* 23) on June 23, CE 79, just prior to the eruption of Vesuvius on August 24.[8]

Romulus' satiric feast takes on new meanings as political circumstances change. During the Republic, before deified emperors have even been dreamed of, to picture Romulus over his turnips in heaven would be to mock Ennius' gravity and to joke about the role of the *Annales* as an authoritative version of Rome's history by asking what Romulus is *really* up to up there.

---

[8] Skutsch (1985) on *Annales* fr. 110; Skutsch (1968) 109–12, 30–1.

The picture is funny, and it also resonates with contemporary debates about Roman-ness. The turnip is the most rustic of foods, grown, not purchased, native, not imported. Plutarch reports that the Elder Cato was inspired by the story of Manius Curius Dentatus' conviction that a man who could be satisfied with turnips did not need gold (Plutarch, *Cato Major* 2.2). By eating turnips, even in heaven (where does he *get* them anyway?), Romulus embodies the qualities of sturdy incorruptibility which Cato and those like him had praised so highly – no Greekish nectar and ambrosia for him! But the turnips make that rigid version of Roman-ness – and the passages of Ennius' *Annales* which promoted it – look ridiculously, hopelessly out of date in the cosmopolitan Republic. When deification becomes a regular feature of imperial succession, quoting the epic phrase *Romulus in caelo* becomes a joke about the implausibilities of deification – especially if you remember the Lucilian turnips, as Seneca and Martial evidently expected their audiences to do.

Death by fish sauce

The context in which Lucilius joked about Romulus and his turnips is not known. More can be understood about the ways Lucilius parodies Ennius in an epic council scene modeled on the Ennian discussion of what will become of Romulus. Lucilius' target is Lucius Cornelius Lentulus Lupus, a leading senator, criticized for a decadent lifestyle and for corrupt practices as a judge.[9] From the fragments it is possible to see that the gods assemble to condemn Lupus' luxurious tastes and decide upon his fate. Similar council scenes by Seneca, Juvenal, and Julian introduce – and send up – the deliberators individually; Lucilius likely did this too. Various extravagant luxury objects and practices are mentioned: Lydian cloaks (fr. 12W), soft coverlets (fr. 13W), the use of Greek words instead of Latin (frs. 14 and 15–16W). Lupus' name means "wolf," but it also is used for the bass, known as a rather large and especially voracious (that is, wolfish) fish (cf. Varro, *Res rustica* 3.3.9; Columella, *De re rustica* 8.16.4, Martial 10.30.21). The decision of the gods is framed as a pun on this fishy sense of *lupus*; the *ius* (judicial decision, plural *iura*) is a *ius* (sauce) made from smaller fry (Lucilius, fr. 46W, with Warmington's note): "The juices [*iura*] of the saperda and the silurus [both little fish] destroy you, Lupus." Where Romulus ascends to the heavens to dine with the gods (albeit on turnips), Lupus is to be submerged in the sauce of lesser fish. Persius savors the edible fishiness of Lupus' identity when he says "Lucilius cut the whole city to pieces – you, Lupus, and you, Mucius – and broke his jaw bone on them" (Persius 1.114–15). Lucilius'

---

[9] Marx (1904–1905) on fr. 3M, fr. 4M; Coffey (1989) 42–3.

council scene has a slapstick side: Apollo objects to being called *pulcher*, apparently sensitive to the epithet's debauched overtones (fr. 28–9W); Lactantius reports that in the council of the gods Lucilius made fun of the fact that all the male gods are called *pater* (fr. 24–7W, = Lactantius, *Divinae Institutiones* 4.3.12). And someone seems to take Apollo to task for speaking in an obscure oracular fashion (fr. 30–32W). Someone even recollects an earlier (more dignified?) assembly (frs. 19 and 20–22W): "I would wish, o dwellers in heaven, we had been present at the council, the earlier council [*priore concilio*], which you say was once held here. . . ." Here, Lucilius may exploit a strategy Ovid later revels in, in which characters in a later poem "remember" what had been said or done in an earlier poem. Indeed, Ovid's most elaborate example of the game may take its cue from Lucilius, for it refers precisely to the Ennian assembly on the fate of Romulus which is evoked in the trial of Lupus. In both the *Fasti* and the *Metamorphoses*, Ovid has Mars remind Jupiter of the promise to raise Romulus to the heavens which had been made in the *Annales*, and in both versions Mars goes so far as to repeat what Jupiter said to him in the *Annales*: *unus erit quem tu tolles in caerula caeli | templa* ("there will be one whom you [Mars] will bear aloft to heaven's blue realms," *Annales* 54–5 Sk.; cf. Ovid, *Fasti* 3. 487 and *Metamorphoses* 14.814, where Mars introduces the quotation with "For I noted [*notavi*] your virtuous words in my memory [*memorique animo*] and I remind you of them now").[10] A participant in Lucilius' divine assembly, called to solve the latter-day Lupus problem, wishes he had been present at an earlier divine assembly. Which one could be more prominent in readers' minds than Ennius' scene of the gods' discussion of the fate of Romulus? The joke would be even more pointed if the speaker who regrets not being at the earlier council was Romulus himself.[11] It is even possible that the description of Romulus and his turnips belongs in this council scene.

What was Lucilius' purpose in making a meal of Lupus?[12] Even without viewing the surviving fragments as evidence of a narrowly partisan agenda it is still possible to understand them as having a political dimension. Clearly the attack on Lupus' luxurious excess, like the mocking picture of Romulus and his turnips, participates in contemporary discourse about how much

---

[10] On Ovid's allusions to Ennius, see, with further references, Conte (1986) 57–63 and the response of Hinds (1998) 14–16.

[11] On Romulus' presence in the Lucilian council scene, see Krenkel (1970) vol. 1, 109, Charpin (1978) 201–2, Gratwick (1982) 169–70, Coffey (1989) 43.

[12] Though some have seen Lucilius' satire as designed to advance the political agendas of his patron Scipio Aemilianus (see the remarks of Coffey [1989] 47–8), Gruen (1992) 272–317 argues that Lucilius' attacks on wealth and the excesses of Hellenism are not constrained by narrowly political agendas.

Greek culture is too much for Roman identity to withstand. It may also be useful to consider the trial within the political context of the last decades of the second century BCE. At various points there were proposals to redistribute public lands from aristocrats who held them in excess of legal limits to veterans and the urban poor.[13] Against this background, defining a society-wide problem (the conflict between traditional if not strictly legal aristocratic prerogatives and the immediately pressing needs of veterans and the urban poor) as the foibles of a single wealthy individual of luxurious tastes and corrupt judicial practices could help to make the broad limitations on aristocratic prerogatives that land reform proposals would represent seem an unnecessary and undesirable break with tradition. Despite this fundamentally conservative aspect of the poem in its original context, for Lucilius' satiric successors, attacks such as this one on Lupus and on other leading figures in Rome came to embody Republican *libertas*, the ability to speak freely without fear of undue reprisals, a quality whose loss under tyrannical, paranoid, and vindictive emperors was much lamented.

Lucilius' sword

Lucilius' successors like to think of him as a poet who uses his pen like an epic hero's sword. In the first satire of his second book, Horace stages a dialogue between himself and Trebatius, who recommends against writing satire and suggests that Horace compose an epic in praise of Caesar instead. Horace stubbornly rejects epic and clings to satire, claiming that it pleases him to write "in Lucilius' manner" (*Lucili ritu*, Horace, S. 2.1.29). In response to Trebatius' warnings that poets can get in trouble if their satires offend the wrong people, Horace says he'll rely on his pen: "it will protect me like a sheathed sword [*et me veluti custodiet ensis / vagina tectus*]; why should I bother to draw it if I am safe from attackers?" (*Sermones* 2.1.41–2). So Horace imagines the deterrent effects of the aggressive satires he might write if provoked.[14] Of course, implicit in Horace's reference to a sheathed sword

---

[13] For detailed discussion see Astin (1967) 161–74, 190–210; Stockton (1979) 40–60.

[14] Horace even claims a historical precedent for his deterrent stance, for he explains in an otherwise oddly incongruous digression that his hometown, Venusia, was settled to prevent either Apulians or Lucanians from having an easy path of attack against Rome once the Samnites had been driven out of the area (2.1.34–9; see Dionysius of Halicarnassus, *Antiquitates Romanae* 17–18 for the foundation of the colony in 291 BCE). The Latin colonists at Venusia do not wage war, they merely plow their fields on the border between Apulia and Lucania (S. 2.1.35) in such a way as to deter attacks on Rome (this – pointedly? – whitewashes the fact that in 90 BCE during the Social War Venusia alone of Roman colonies and Latin allies joined the opposition to Rome, cf. Appian, *Bellum Civile* 1.39). So, too, Horace as satirist deters attackers without waging actual war.

within his comparison of Lucilius and himself is the notion that Lucilius did wage war, brandishing his satiric pen like a sword.[15]

Juvenal takes the notion of Lucilius as epic hero implicit in Horace and makes it explicit when he announces in his first satire that he follows in Lucilius' path (Juvenal 1.19–21):

> I will explain why it pleases me to traverse the ground,
>   over which the great hero [*magnus*] born at Aurunca drove his horses,
>   if you have time and listen calmly to my account.[16]

By naming Lucilius by his birthplace in this indirect way (just as epic poets like to name their heroes) and by figuring his writing as the sweep of a chariot across a battlefield, Juvenal at once alludes to Lucilius' social status as an *eques* (which literally means "horseman" and designates a political class of substantial property holders), and casts Lucilius as an epic hero.[17] Later on in the same poem Juvenal again describes Lucilius' satirical attacks as battles of epic proportions. Here the sword is out of its sheath (Juvenal 1.165–7):[18]

> Whenever raging as though with sword drawn [*ense velut stricto*]
>   Lucilius bellows,
>   his listener, whose mind shivers over his crimes, blushes hot,
>   and his vitals sweat with secret guilt.

Though Lucilius is cast as an epic hero by Horace and Juvenal, it seems unlikely that he would have portrayed *himself* as an epic hero in any but the most ironic way. In the surviving fragments, Lucilius does represent the Roman forum as a battlefield, but it is not the scene of the single-handed swashbuckling sort of battles that Horace implies and Juvenal describes (Lucilius fr. 1145–51 W):

[15] On other aspects of Horace's engagement with epic models and with Lucilian critique of lofty panegyric in S. 2.1, see Freudenburg (2001) 87–92. Horace elsewhere associates Lucilius with the large-scale and continuous flow of epic poetry by comparing him to a muddy river in an image that alludes to Callimachus' programmatic description of large-scale epic as a muddy river (S. 1.4.11, S. 1.10.50–1; cf. Callimachus, *Hymn to Apollo* 108–9). Detailed discussion of Horace's strategy of defining his literary, social and political identity through contrasts with Lucilius in Cucchiarelli (2001), esp. 56–83, 84–118.

[16] Braund (1996b) on these lines and 21–2.

[17] On Juvenal's view of Lucilius in this passage, see further Bramble (1974) 169–70, Cucchiarelli (2001) 205, Rudd (1966) 110.

[18] On precise epic parallels for Juvenal's language here see Virgil, *Aen.* 10.711–15 and others discussed by Braund (1996b).

but now, from morning till night, on holiday and work day,
the whole people and likewise the senators too
flaunt themselves in the forum [*indu foro*] and never leave it;
and they dedicate themselves to one and the same pursuit and practice,
namely to be able to make false promises with impunity, fight deceitfully,
rival each other in ingratiating speech, act the good man,
and lay ambushes as if all of them were enemies to all men.

Lucilius' phrase *indu foro*, an archaic version of *in foro*, looks back to an important and well known passage of Ennius (*Annales* 268–86 Sk.). Ennius describes Geminus Servilius, a leading citizen who, "when tired from spending the greater part of the day in the direction of matters of highest importance by advice given in the wide forum and the sacred senate" (*consilio indu foro lato sanctoque senatu*), likes to relax with his trusted friend, a thoroughly admirable man thought to represent a self-portrait of Ennius himself (Gellius 12.4.4). As Skutsch remarks, the description of the two men exchanging conversation at table seems "more appropriate to Satire than to the Epic":[19] the patron would speak to his friend "without restraint of matters great and small and make jokes" (*res audacter magnas parvasque iocumque / eloqueretur, Annales* 273–4 Sk.) and he would "spew forth (*evomeretque*) things that are good and bad to say" (*Annales* 274–5 Sk.). Horace noticed the satiric qualities of Ennius' picture of patron and friend for he alludes to it in describing his own relationship with Maecenas (*Sermones* 1.3.63), where *saepe libenter* at line end echoes the same phrase and position at Ennius, *Annales* 268 Sk. (see Skutsch on this and on *Annales* 280). And Horace's picture of how Scipio and Laelius were "in the habit of exchanging trifles and witty remarks" (*nugari et . . . ludere . . . soliti*) in private with Lucilius after their public activities "while the cabbage was cooking" (*Sermones* 2.1.73–4) also seems to owe something to Ennius. Horace thus acknowledges the satiric qualities of the Ennian passage by incorporating allusions to it within his satiric descriptions of the relations of patrons and poets. By contrast, Lucilius reverses Ennius' satire-into-epic trajectory when he casts satire's forum as a version of an epic battlefield. Whether or not the phrase *indu foro* is felt as a direct allusion to the Ennian passage, the constant and universal bad behavior in Lucilius' forum pricks the bubble of Ennius' idealistic vision of great men ethically directing Rome's affairs.

Horace's road warriors

Allusions to epic allow satire to juxtapose the realm of high, important, national matters with the realm of low, trivial, and private matters. Lucilius

---

[19] Skutsch (1985) 451.

can make the trivialities of Lupus' private life into a matter of national consequence by having the gods discuss them. Horace moves in the other direction. Just as he gives the city mouse and the country mouse an epic night to walk through that makes them look all the smaller, he emphasizes his own lowly status and the privacy and intimacy of his satires with self-deprecating epic allusions. These allusions operate within an overall strategy of self-presentation, a project carefully designed to flatter Maecenas: what a discerning man he must be who can appreciate someone as understated and relatively unimportant as Horace.

When Horace takes the road to Brundisium in satire 1.5, lofty epic models are evoked along the way to ensure that Horace's journey looks humble.[20] The poem's opening, "Aricia welcomed me with modest hospitality when I set out from great Rome" (*egressum magna me accepit Aricia Roma / hospitio modico*) has been thought to evoke the beginning of Odysseus' tale to the Phaeacians ("the wind carrying me from Troy brought me to the Cicones," *Odyssey* 9.39).[21] At the next stop, he declares war – on his belly (*ventri / indico bellum*, 1.5.7–8). Night falls in a decidedly epic fashion: "now night was preparing to draw shadows over the earth and scatter the constellations in the sky" (*iam nox inducere terris/ umbras et caelo diffundere signa parabat*, 1.5.9–10. But the battle that ensues is one of abusive language (*convicia*) hurled back and forth by boatmen and the boys alongside the canal (1.5.11). Cucchiarelli makes the very appealing point that the frogs that disturb Horace's sleep at 1.5.14–15 evoke the comic version of the heroic descent into the underworld staged in Aristophanes' *Frogs*.[22] Later on, Caudium is the scene of an epic "single combat" between the Oscan rustic Messius Cicurrus and the urban Sarmentus which entertains the party. Horace plays Homer to their heroes (1.5.53–54):

> Muse, please recall also, born from what father did each engage in – dispute.

At Beneventum a kitchen fire of epic proportions (especially signaled by saying "Vulcan" instead of simply "fire") breaks out (1.5.73–76):

---

[20] On epic parody in Horace, S. 1.5 see Sallmann (1974) 200–6, and Gowers (1993b) 55–6, 59; Reckford (1999) 538–43.

[21] Ehlers (1985) 80–1. *Odyssey* 9.39 is quoted verbatim in Seneca, *Apocolocyntosis* 5.4.

[22] Cucchiarelli (2001) 25–33. Note too his observation at 23–4 that the names of the hosts Murena and Capito in S. 1.5.37–8 are both words that are used for fish: as he remarks, in a contrast typical of Horace's overall relationship to Lucilius, Horace's fishmen are benevolent friends while Lucilius' fish-man Lupus is a target of angry mocking attack.

for when Vulcan escaped [*dilapso . . . Volcano*], the flame darted through the old kitchen and hastened to lick the high roof. Then you could see the greedy guests and the frightened slaves snatch up the meal, and everyone wanting to put out the flames.

In the epic tradition the westward voyages of the Greek heroes are the sequel to the burning of Troy. In Horace's version of the tradition, after the epic-tinged fire at Beneventum he subsequently stops at Canusium, which he is careful to mention was founded by Diomedes after his return from Troy (1.5.91–92).

If in 1.5 Horace offers a portrait of the satirist as an Odyssean hero in miniature, in 1.9 he sketches an Iliadic scene as he playfully imagines his extrication from an annoying encounter in the street as a rescue by Apollo.[23] A certain man (*ille*) falls upon Horace as he strolls the Via Sacra and tries to use him to secure access to Maecenas; Horace tries unsuccessfully to escape. Finally, to the poet's relief, the man is summoned for a court appearance. In the poem's last line, Horace says "thus did Apollo save me" (*sic me servavit Apollo*, 1.9.78). The line alludes to Apollo's rescue of Hector from the attack of Achilles on the plain of Troy (*Iliad* 20.443), as was noticed by Porphyrio, an early third century CE commentator on Horace. Porphyrio also reports that Lucilius quotes the Homeric line in Greek in his sixth book (fr. 267–8W):

> nil ut discrepat ac τὸν δ' ἐξήρπαξεν Ἀπόλλων
> fiat
> so that there may be no dispute and it may become a case of "and Apollo rescued him"

This Horatian allusion to Homer via Lucilius has led some critics to see a Lucilian model in the background of Horace's street scene;[24] on this basis a fragment describing a street scene in which Scipio Aemilianus has sharp words for someone (fr. 254–8W) has also been ascribed to Lucilius' sixth book. It is especially tempting to see an allusive connection between this Scipio scene and Horace, *Sermones* 1.9 because the phrase describing Scipio's progress, *ibat forte domum* ("he happened to be on the way home," Lucil. fr. 258W), is so close to the opening of Horace's poem (*Sermones* 1.9.1–2):

> I happened to be on the Sacred Way [*Ibam forte Via Sacra*], as is my habit, thinking of something trivial [*nescio quid meditans nugarum*], all absorbed in it . . .

---

[23] On Horace's use of the imagery of the epic battlefield throughout 1.9 see Anderson (1956).
[24] Fiske (1920) 330–6, Fraenkel (1957) 118.

If indeed Horace frames his street scene with reminiscences of Lucilius, one in the first line and one in the last line, perhaps there is even a self-reflexive wink in "thinking over something trivial" (*nescio quid meditans nugarum*) in Horace's line 2; Horace was thinking of some light or trivial poetry (*nugae*) on the Sacred Way – Lucilius' (the word *nugae* is associated with Lucilius at Horace, *Sermones* 2.1.73). Unlike Scipio, who speaks boldly, embodying the concept of *libertas*, at the man in the street, Horace hurls no public abuse at the pest, ineffectually attempting to put him off and rolling his eyes; he has us watch him saving the scene to smirk over with Maecenas in private. The epic allusion allows Horace to cite Lucilius as a source and to "correct" his stylistic flaws by clothing the Greek line in decent Latin garb. Moreover, the Horatian rewriting of Lucilius in this poem, as elsewhere, redefines *libertas* as something to be enjoyed in private rather than embodied in frank public exchanges. As DuQuesnay has argued, Lucilius' close association with *libertas*, which had been appropriated by the Pompeian faction (Cicero, *Ad familiares* 12.16.3), becomes a valuable piece of political capital to be put to use in Horace's indirect but pervasive suggestions that Maecenas and Octavian – and not Octavian's defeated opponents, especially the supporters of Sextus Pompey – are the true protectors of *libertas*.[25]

In 1.5 and 1.9, allusions to epic contrast the heroic and national with the everyday and inconsequential. But even these inconsequentials have consequences. Every time Horace's epic allusions help make his relationship with Maecenas look private and ordinary, he fosters the impression that the world Octavian is building is a world where sensible men can enjoy sensible friendships – instead of the destructive factionalism of civil war.[26] The same strategy is at work in satire 1.7, a mock epic account of an exchange of insults. The half-Greek Persius engages in a battle of insults with Publius Rupilius Rex, a former praetor proscribed by Antony and Octavian, who took refuge with Brutus in Clazomenae in Asia Minor before the battle of Philippi in 42 BCE. Horace compares the contest to the epic encounters between Achilles and Hector or Diomedes and Glaucus on the plains of Troy (*Sermones* 1.7.10–18). But when Persius turns boldly to Brutus and tops Rex's insults with "why don't you kill this king [*rex*]?" (*cur non | hunc Regem iugulas*, *Sermones* 1.7.34–5), he jokes about the ancient Brutus' murder of the king Tarquinius Superbus and the present Brutus' participation in the murder of Caesar (amid rumors that he sought the title "king", Suetonius, *Julius Caesar* 79). Allusions to epic and distant history juxtapose the grand

---

[25] So argued by Du Quesnay (1984), esp. 27–32; and see too the further comments of Kennedy (1992) 29–33, and Henderson (1994) 81.

[26] See Cucchiarelli (2001) 84–118, esp. 100, 117.

with the trivial: if the Brutus joke is not grand, it must be trivial. But here again, something inconsequential has consequences: Horace was with Brutus in Asia, and therefore the inclusion of the Brutus joke in a collection dedicated to Octavian's friend Maecenas fosters the notion that even the conflict between Brutus and Octavian – and Horace's presence on the side of Brutus – ultimately has no lasting consequences for the poet's ability to make his way back from the side of Brutus into the circle of Octavian's intimates.[27] Now as then, a troublesome episode in the east (the Greeks in Troy, Brutus in Clazomenae) is merely one step on the way to Rome's eventual triumph (Rome's foundation by Aeneas and eventual refoundation by Octavian).

Satires 2.5 stages a mock epic version of Ulysses' conversation with Teiresias in the Underworld. Teiresias tells Ulysses how to flatter the rich into bequeathing him their wealth. The punchline of the poem is a prophecy of the unsuccessful legacy hunting of one Nasica, which will happen "when a youth, a terror to the Parthians, descended from ancient Aeneas, will hold sway over land and sea" (Horace, *Sermones* 2.5.62–4). Having a debased Teiresias prophesy the victories of Octavian "descended from ancient Aeneas" parodies a moment in the *Iliad* when Poseidon, as he decides to rescue Aeneas from Achilles, foretells a lasting and powerful future for the descendants of Aeneas (*Iliad* 20.302–8). The Homeric prediction does not mention Italy, and indeed this was felt to be a problem by those who sought to trace Rome's origins to Troy;[28] Horace's Teiresias clarifies the situation nicely by referring directly to Octavian's military success.[29] At first sight, the third person mock epic narrative of 2.5 seems quite different from the self-deprecating allusions in the first person narratives of 1.5 and 1.9 which measure little Horace against the epic heroes of the past. But Oliensis has recently argued that in this mock epic treatment of attempts at social advancement, Horace is satirizing his own ascent into Maecenas' inner circle as set forth in the first book of satires; he strengthens his position in the inner circle by being the first to make fun of how he got there.[30] Horace's satires share the multivalent qualities of other literature produced in the orbit of Octavian /Augustus.[31]

---

[27] Du Quesnay (1984) 36–8. Henderson (1994) 156, referring to the fact that Glaucus traded his gold arms for Diomedes' bronze arms, a trade Horace mentions at *S.* 1.7.15–18: "poem 1.7 offers us Horatian 'gold', the representation and its work of re-presentation, in lieu of the nasty Civil War 'bronze'." See too the perceptive discussion of Schlegel (1999), esp. 344–7.

[28] See Gruen (1992) 12–13.

[29] Horace may also be making an ironic reference to a famous story that when Octavian was born the astrologer Nigidius Figulus said "now is born the master of the world" (*dominus terrarum orbi natus*, Suetonius, *Augustus* 94.5).

[30] Oliensis (1998a) 57.

[31] Kennedy (1992) is a good starting point for embarking upon this vast topic.

Readers optimistic about the measures Octavian had taken to quell civil strife could find celebrations of *libertas* flourishing among friends in peaceful times. Those more paranoid, suspicious or caught up in their memories of war might see what Freudenburg (2001) calls "the totalitarian squeeze" (71) or "the hissings of compliance" (108).[32]

Persius and the battlefield of the soul

Persius writes during the reign of Nero, who himself liked to indulge in epic-tinged chariot racing and the extravagant composition of poetic treatments of mythological themes. Like Horace, Persius rejects the drawn epic sword of Lucilius and Juvenal. More secretive in his epic allusions than Horace, Persius seeks out epic descriptions of severe introspection and thwarted utterance to adorn his cryptic and crabbed verses. When he sets out to praise his friend Cornutus in the fifth satire, he disavows the poetic custom (which goes back to Homer, *Iliad* 2.488–90) of asking for many mouths to meet the descriptive demands of his topic (Persius 5.1–4).[33] After Cornutus interrupts to praise Persius' terse style, Persius resumes to say that he would ask for a hundred throats to say all that would otherwise remain unsayable about Cornutus. Both Homer and Persius use the topos to describe the limits on what they can say, but where the effect of the Homeric lines is to convey the grandeur and magnitude of their subject, Persius' lines convey the impression that it is nearly impossible for him to write at all.

In his third satire Persius stages a dialogue between a lazy writer and a friend who offers bracing advice to get to work. The poet narrator complains about the difficulty of working – even his pen gives him trouble! In one of his many rebukes, the friend castigates the narrator for sleeping late (Persius 3.58–9):

> you are still snoring, and hanging slack, its hinge loose, your head [*caput*]
> gapes [*oscitat*] in yesterday's yawn with jaws completely unfastened.

As Barr and Lee (1987) astutely note in their commentary, in this picture of a head released from its fastenings Persius reworks a famously gruesome Ennian line about a man decapitated in battle: "the head torn off from its neck gapes on the ground" (*oscitat in campis caput a cervice revolsum*, *Annales* 483 Sk.). A Virgilian decapitation imitated this Ennian line too ("then Aeneas knocks to the ground the head [*caput*] of the man begging in vain and getting ready to say more," *Aeneid* 10.554–5).[34] It is typical of

---

[32] See, too, Henderson (1994).   [33] On the many-mouthed topos, see Hinds (1998) 34–47.
[34] Cf. Skutsch (1985) 645–6 on Virgil's use of Ennius in this context.

Virgil's tongue-tied version of epic heroism that the warrior's decapitation is figured as an interruption of his speech. Ennian death on the battlefield, poignantly reworked as Virgilian thwarted speech, becomes the satiric version of thwarted speech, the lazy poet's snore. Persius elsewhere even makes Ennian epic itself the product of snoring. In his prologue he says he has not dreamed (*somniasse*) he was on Parnassus. This alludes to, among other things, the beginning of the *Annales* in which Ennius apparently said that he had a dream that revealed he was descended from Homer through a sequence of reincarnation that included a peacock (*Annales* 2–11 Sk., and see Skutsch [1985] 147–53 and 164–5). And in his letter to Bassus from his winter retreat in Luna on the Ligurian coast, Persius quotes an Ennian line, "Get to know Luna's port, citizens, it's worth it," with the footnote that "So Ennius' heart bid him, after he snored off (*destertuit*, only here in Latin as Barr and Lee [1987] note) being Quintus son of Homer descended from the Pythagorean peacock" (Persius 6.9–11).

Persius' fullest refashioning of epic motifs happens in his first satire.[35] Persius' poetry may have scant appeal, he admits, to audiences besotted with exotic treatments of mythological themes (Persius 1.1–5):

> O the cares of men! o what emptiness there is in the world!
> "Who will read these words?" Are you saying that to me?
> Nobody, certainly. "Nobody?" Two or nobody. "A wretched and pathetic
> thing." Why? That "Polydamas and the Trojan Women" should prefer
> Labeo to me? Not important.

Persius here measures himself against Attius Labeo, a Neronian poet who translated the *Iliad* and the *Odyssey* word for word. Only a line of Labeo survives (given by the scholiast on this passage) but from it we can get an idea of what Persius is so annoyed about: *crudum manduces Priamum Priamique pisinnos*, "you will chew on Priam raw, and Priam's little children" translates *Iliad* 4.35 (see Courtney [1993] 350). The words *manduces* ("you will chew on") and *pisinnos* ("little children," perhaps a piece of baby-talk, *OLD s.v.*) undoubtedly struck Roman readers as exotically "low" and everyday, creating a piquant contrast with Homer's epic grandeur. Calling the Roman audience "Polydamas and the Trojan women" alludes to the Homeric account of Hector's decision to stay and fight Achilles because he would feel shame before his brother-in-law Polydamas and the women of

---

[35] On Persius' rejection of epic in the choliambic verses which serve as a prologue to the collection, see Cucchiarelli (2001) 191–2; Freudenburg (2001) 134–5. On epic in Persius 1 see further Sullivan (1985) 92–114 (on the possibility that Persius is mocking Nero's own treatments of epic themes in his poem on Troy and elsewhere), and Freudenburg (2001) 151–8.

Troy if he yielded the field (*Iliad* 20.100, 105). The moment of epic Persius here imports into satire is not the battle itself but Hector's decision to stay and fight to avoid the shame of flight. Moreover, women are not regularly pictured as the audience for poetry; the reference to the women of Troy is Persius' nasty jab at effeminate customs popular among Roman men who like the poetic thrills that someone like Labeo has on offer.[36] Persius' lesson here: do not waste time putting the *Iliad* literally into (deliciously "low") Latin; transform it to attack what is wrong with Rome. His own book, even if he has to keep it completely secret, is worth more than any *Iliad* (Persius 1.119–23).

Juvenal's fire

Where Horace and Persius use allusions to epic to express how small, intimate, and personal their satires are, Juvenal uses epic allusions to make a claim to something big.[37] As Bramble puts it, when Juvenal rejected epic themes in his first satire: "Roman vice became as monstrous and portentous as anything in the fictions of epic or tragedy."[38] In his first satire, as noted above, he imagines Lucilius as a sword-wielding, chariot-driving epic hero. Unlike Lucilius, who satirized the living, Juvenal chooses targets who are dead; this will be safer, he says. But the scale of his poems and the totality of his denunciation of Roman life make satire into something that Juvenal, too, wages on an epic scale. Hardie has suggested that even the fury of Juvenal's denunciation of contemporary epic in the first satire shares epic's tendency to locate its beginnings in an explosion of rage he describes as "the energy of Hell."[39] Juvenal likes to assert the decadence of the present by measuring its distance from the epic past. In the fifteenth satire, Juvenal tells a tale of real-life cannibalism in Egypt so outrageous that Ulysses would have been laughed out of Alcinous' court as a "lying teller of tales" (*ut mendax aretalogus*, Juvenal 15.16) if he had tried to tell the Phaeacians any such thing. The stone-throwing violence which begets the cannibalistic excess is described with an epic footnote (Juvenal 15.65–71):

---

[36] Bramble (1974) 69 also sees an allusion to Virgil, *Aen.* 9.617, a denunciation of effeminacy among the Trojans.

[37] Braund (1996b) 21–4; see also Bramble (1974) 164–73, and, on Juvenal's use of mock tragic elements, Smith (1989). Scott (1927) offers a comprehensive approach to Juvenal's use of the grand style, though her distinction between "humorous" and "sincere" imitation is problematic.

[38] Bramble (1974) 172.

[39] Hardie (1993) 65. On Juvenal's detailed engagement with epic models in the first satire, especially with Valerius Flaccus' *Argonautica*, see Henderson (1995).

not the kind of stone Turnus and Ajax threw,
nor the kind with which Diomedes smashed Aeneas' hip,
but the kind today's right hands – different from theirs –
are strong enough to throw. For while Homer was alive the human
race was already in decline,
now earth brings forth wicked and puny men . . .

Homer's Diomedes smashes Aeneas' hip with a stone "no two men could carry such as men are now" – in Homer's time (*Iliad* 5.303–4). Men have weakened still further by Virgil's time: Virgil restages Aeneas' peril at the hands of Diomedes when Turnus hurls a stone at him which *twelve* latter-day men could not carry (*Aeneid* 12.899–900).[40] Juvenal impudently authenticates his tale of decline – even for Homer, things are not what they once were.

Juvenal's third satire has an especially detailed epic texture.[41] Umbricius meets the poet by the Capena gate at Rome (where the Camenae, Rome's spirits of poetic inspiration, who breathed life into its earliest epics, used to live, Juvenal 3.16) and declares his plan of moving to Cumae, gateway to the Underworld. His journey reverses Aeneas' foundational journey from Troy to Rome via Cumae, where the hero entered the Underworld and was shown the truth of Rome's future. Juvenal had just alluded to the heroic Underworld – and how its denizens would be shocked by modern Romans – at the end of the second satire (Juvenal 2.154–9). Where Anchises shows Aeneas a pageant of all that is admirable in Rome's history to come, Umbricius (whose name carries associations of *umbra*, "ghost") catalogues Rome's rogues, from shifty immigrants and hypocritical flatterers to street thugs and criminal aristocrats. In the *Aeneid*, a newly created Roman identity was forged in the flames of Troy. Juvenal makes everything go backwards: Rome burns with flames that are, in their allusion to Virgil, distinctly Trojan (Juvenal 3.198–202):

> iam poscit aquam, iam frivola transfert
> Vcalegon, . . .
> ultimus ardebit quem tegula sola tuetur
> a pluuia
> Now Ucalegon demands water, now he hauls out his worthless
> possessions. . . .
> He will burn last whom only the roof tiles protect from the rain. . . .

Juvenal designs his *ultimus ardebit* (Juvenal 3. 201) to create a satiric sequel to Virgil's lines (*Aeneid* 2.310–12):

---

40 See Courtney (1980) on 15.63–4 and 65 for further references.
41 Motto and Clark (1965), Staley (2000).

> iam Deiphobi dedit ampla ruinam
> Volcano superante domus, iam proximus ardet
> Vcalegon . . .
> now the spacious house of Deiphobus produced ruin,
> with Vulcan overwhelming it, now Ucalegon burns next . . .

In addition, these very lines of the *Aeneid* already have a connection to satire.[42] Virgil's *Volcano superante* is noticeably similar to Horace's *dilapso . . . Volcano* in his mock-epic account of the kitchen fire at Beneventum in *Sermones* 1.5 (quoted above).[43] Since Virgil is actually along for the ride in Horace's poem, there is every reason to think he nods to Horace in *Volcano superante*. In the flickering shadows around Ucalegon, Juvenal looks back with a fierce nostalgia to a time when epic was admirable and epic poets paid attention to satirists and they both enjoyed the support of powerful political friends.

The gods in epic – and in satire

Lucilius' trial of Lupus made a big impression on his poetic successors. Even epic poets paid attention. The ancient commentator Servius remarks that Virgil's whole account of a divine council in *Aeneid* 10.104ff. is "transferred" from Lucilius' council on the fate of Lupus. The politics of the Virgilian assembly are recognizably Augustan. Venus and Juno offer partisan complaints about the setbacks and difficulties of the Trojans and Italians whom they respectively favor; Jove announces that he is impartial, and that "the fates will find a way" (*Aeneid* 10.113). Virgil thus makes the entire history of Rome, from its earliest beginnings to Augustus' victories, look foreordained, and ensures that the king of the gods (or their emperor) is not

---

[42] So argued by Austin (1964) on *Aen.* 2.312.

[43] It may also be the case that in addition to using Horace as a source Virgil also has an Ennian source in common with Horace. When the fatal night falls at Troy (*vertitur interea caelum et ruit Oceano nox*, "meanwhile the heavens turn and night rushes from Ocean," *Aen.* 2.250), Virgil borrows from a line of Ennius' sixth book (*vertitur interea caelum cum ingentibus signis*, "meanwhile the heavens turn with their huge constellations," *Ann.* 205 Sk.). This Ennian line is plausibly attributed to a description of the night that Pyrrhus tried to take the Roman forces by surprise at Beneventum; in the darkness his troops lost the way. When the night ends they have lost the advantage of surprise, and their subsequent defeat by the Romans marked the end of Pyrrhus' campaigns in Italy (Plutarch, *Pyrrhus* 25). It would make sense for Virgil to allude to the end of this chaotic night (at the aptly named Beneventum, "it turned out well") at the beginning of the night of the fall of Troy. So perhaps Horace's chaotic kitchen fire at Beneventum is not just any old bit of mock epic but a latter-day version of chaotic night-time events there described by Ennius.

seen – at least here – to impose his will ruthlessly upon the world. In Ovid's *Metamorphoses*, Jove convenes the gods to hear the crimes of the egregious Lycaon, whose name derives from the Greek *lukos*, wolf, and who is turned into a wolf for offering human flesh to Jove (Ovid, *Metamorphoses* 1.163–243). By Varro's time, Lucilius' books 1–21 were circulating as a unit (distinct from two other units, books 26–30, composed before 1–21, and books 22–5).[44] Therefore, the wolf-men Lupus and Lycaon each appear as the first narrative episode in the first book of a large poetic work which is a collection of separate episodes. Each embodies a decadent age and by his crimes brings the cosmos itself into danger. Each is punished for excessive, inappropriate episodes of consumption – Lupus for his own excesses, Lycaon for serving human flesh to Jove. Where Lupus is singled out for destruction to ensure that the rest of Rome survives, Lycaon's crime comes to stand for all human decadence and wickedness and is punished by Jove with the universal flood. Hellenistic models perhaps lay behind Ovid's version of the Lycaon story as prelude to universal destruction in the flood; if they did, Lucilius likely knew them too, and they would certainly sharpen the cosmic dimensions of his tale of the gods deliberating how to punish Lupus without destroying Rome. Lucilius' gods exist in a fundamentally Republican world: there are speaking roles for Apollo (Lucilius fr. 28–9 W), Neptune (fr. 35 W, saying that even if the philosopher Carneades came back from the dead he would not be able to sort out the present question), and presumably Jove. Ovid's gods are definitely living in an empire. Jove consults the other gods not in a heavenly senate house, but in a "marble chamber" (Ovid, *Metamorphoses* 1.177) on the "heavenly Palatine" (the heavenly equivalent to Augustus' home on the Palatine, Ovid, *Metamorphoses* 1.176), where he sits above them (*celsior*, *Metamorphoses* 1.178). Their horror at Lycaon's crimes is compared explicitly to the way the whole world felt upon the assassination of Julius Caesar (*Metamorphoses* 1.199–203). In Ovid's version of divine deliberations, only Jove speaks and the other gods merely murmur in response to authorize his universal destruction of the human race.[45]

The transformation of the divine process of deliberation is taken even further in Seneca's *Apocolocyntosis* when the emperor Claudius arrives in heaven after his death and the gods meet as a senate to decide whether he should be deified. Jupiter sends Claudius away because non-senators are not permitted in the senate house (*curia*, Seneca, *Apocolocyntosis* 9.1) during

---

[44] Varro, *De lingua Latina* 5.17, and Gratwick (1982) 168.

[45] Feeney (1991) 199–200 describes Ovid's strategies for heightening the subordinate relation of the other gods to Jove, especially at *Metamorphoses* 1.244–5.

deliberations. Janus speaks against deification of any mortals. Diespiter speaks in favor of Claudius; in what is most likely a nod to Lucilius, he is the one who says that heaven needs someone who can "gobble steaming turnips with Romulus" and he adds that the deification should be appended to Ovid's *Metamorphoses* (Seneca, *Apocolocyntosis* 9.5). Finally Augustus himself, making his first ever speech in the divine senate (Seneca, *Apocolocyntosis* 10.1), denounces Claudius as a murderer and rails: "while you make such gods, no one will believe that you are gods" (*Apocolocyntosis* 11.4). Voting with their feet like Roman senators, the gods move to Augustus' side to express their support and Claudius is expelled from heaven (11.6). As Eden observes, the idea of projecting contemporary procedure in such full detail upon the divine assembly probably descends from the satires of Menippus, but in Seneca's hands it becomes a pointed commentary upon the actual senatorial proceedings in which Claudius was deified (Tacitus, *Annales* 13.2).[46] Politics and satire are inseparable when Nero's subsequent neglect and cancellation of the divine honors voted Claudius by the senate (Suetonius, *Claudius* 45) mirrors Seneca's satirical vision of him banished to the underworld.

Though it does not showcase the gods in council, Juvenal's fourth satire nevertheless stands firmly within the tradition of satiric divine councils established by Lucilius.[47] The poem begins with a denunciation of the decadent habits of the greedy Crispinus, especially his purchase of a fantastically expensive mullet. Juvenal brings the epic council scene down to earth as the emperor, not Jove, confers with advisors, not gods. Their subject is not the fishy Lupus, but an actual fish, a huge turbot. At the start of the turbot narrative, Juvenal invokes Calliope, the Muse of epic (Juvenal 4. 34–6):

> Begin, Calliope. It's ok to be seated; it's not a matter for
> singing, it deals with what really happened. Tell the tale,
> Pierian girls (may it do me good to have called you girls).

The fish's magnitude, its capture near Ancona, and its swift transport to Domitian's villa at Alba Longa, just south of Rome (where a temple of Vesta still preserved the flames of Troy, Juvenal 4. 61–2) are all described in expansive epic style, and Domitian's eleven courtiers are described in an epic catalogue.[48] The scholiast tells us that in the catalogue Juvenal is parodying an epic poem on Domitian's war in Germany, almost certainly Statius' *De bello Germanico* (*Scholia*, Juvenal 4.94; cf. Statius, *Silvae* 4.2.65–7, Coleman,

---

[46] Eden (1984) 98.   [47] Braund (1996b) 271.
[48] See Braund (1996b) for full details, and Anderson (1982) 237–44.

Statius Silvae IV, p. xvii). In Juvenal's version of the epic council scene, the political dynamics are different again from Lucilius' and from Seneca's. Instead of the open debate of Lucilius' senatorial gods, or the authoritative imperial pronouncements of Ovid's Jove before those he pretends are his peers, or Seneca's fully detailed mock senate, in Juvenal "the senators, shut out, watch the meal be admitted" (*exclusi spectant admissa obsonia patres*, Juvenal 4.64), courtiers are solicited for their advice, and the emperor does not speak directly at all except to ask whether the fish should be cut up (Juvenal 4.130). The fish becomes a figure for the city itself when Montanus says that what it needs is a specially made dish "which can enclose its huge circumference with a delicately worked wall" (*quae tenui muro spatiosum colligat orbem*, Juvenal 4.132). Though the craftsman to make this giant dish is called Prometheus (Juvenal 4.133), the ghost of Romulus, ancient builder of the wall that marked Rome out as Rome, hovers here too.

The vision of consumption satirized here is different from Archestratus' aristocratic pleasure seekers and from Ennius' geography of conquest and pacification. Juvenal's big-bellied courtier Montanus has the same kind of expertise that Archestratus specialized in, for he can recognize the distinctive tastes of oysters from various places (Juvenal 4.140–3):

> For he [Montanus] had the know-how to detect right from the first bite
> whether oysters came from Circeii or the rocks of the Lucrine Lake,
> or from a bed in Richborough harbor,
> and he used to say what shore a sea-urchin came from after just a glance.

But, crucially, unlike Archestratus and Ennius, Montanus does not himself go to those far-flung places to buy the oysters, they are brought to him via the imperial infrastructure. Consumption of this satiric seafood is centralized, just as power is centralized in the imperial household.

Rome's destiny is served up as dinner in each satiric scene of divine deliberations. No longer Ennius' idealizing representative of Roman excellence, Lucilius' satiric Romulus is a Roman peasant, hungry for turnips. The Ennian council at which the grave matter of Romulus' fate was decided by the gods is reworked by Lucilius as a meeting of the gods-as-senators to decide the fishy fate of greedy Lupus. As the title *Apocolocyntosis* ("Gourdification," known from Dio 60.35.2ff.) implies, empty-headed Claudius misses his chance for turnips with Romulus and himself becomes the dry rattling gourd.[49] And Juvenal makes Rome itself the meal gobbled by the insatiable emperor when the treatment of the Roman world under the control of Domitian is equated

---

[49] Eden (1984) 1–4.

to the treatment of the big fish: *cum iam semianimum laceraret Flavius orbem | ultimus*, ("When the last Flavian was tearing the half-dead world to pieces," Juvenal 4.37–8).

Epic poetry explains how the world order came to be; satire gives a particular slice of the here and now. In epic, Rome is the sum total of its history; in satire, the decadent and decayed residue of it. Sharing the basic metrical structure of epic, the dactylic hexameter, satire can swallow epic elements whole and reconfigure epic's cosmos-ordering world views as glimpses of Rome's everyday chaos. Satirists claim social authority for themselves – and their audiences – in their mastery of the epic tradition, treasure house of Rome's ancestral values, the *mos maiorum*. But because epic poetry explains how the world came to be the way that it is, allusions to epic also have the potential to comment on the political situation of the satirist who makes them. Lucilius and Juvenal use allusions to epic like a trumpet to make their anger big and public. Horace and Persius use epic allusions to shape the private space in which they speak: Horace uses the epic voice in ironic self-deprecation to show how unimportant he is, how separate he can be from Octavian's new world; Persius uses it like an urgent whisper, just loud enough to tell what he cannot say in Nero's Rome. From Romulus' turnips to Domitian's turbot, allusions to epic help satire tell its versions of Rome's history.

Further reading

Many scholars have discussed satiric poets' parodic allusions to traditional myths and their uses of elements of epic poetry or high and lofty style more generally. Gratwick (1982) and Coffey (1989) offer useful overviews of Lucilius' satiric techniques. Rudd (1966) remarks on the interplay of high and low styles in Horace: see 54–85 (on *Sermones* 1.5 and 1.9) and 224–42 (on 2.5); Anderson (1956) analyzes the use of epic parody in Horace, *Sermones* 1.9; Henderson (1999) 202–27 considers the public dimensions of the poet's picture of his private life in 1.9. Playful allusion to epic had been a hallmark of Alexandrian poetry; Zetzel (2002) demonstrates Horace's engagement with this Alexandrian tradition in the first book of his satires; on allusions to various aspects of the Callimachean poetic program see also Clauss (1985) and Scodel (1987). In Italian, Cucchiarelli (2001) offers an excellent detailed reading of *Sermones* 1.5; he focuses especially on the ways in which Horace defines his literary, social, and political identity through contrasts with Lucilius, some of which involve depicting Lucilius as a kind of epic figure (who rides a horse) as opposed to "pedestrian" Horace. The commentary of Barr and Lee (1987) on Persius is attentive to Persius' use of phrases drawn from (or which can be paralleled in) epic. Sullivan (1985) 74–114 detects allusion to Nero's poetic treatments of exotic epic and mythological themes in Persius' critique of contemporary poetry in satire 1. Anderson (1957) addresses epic parody in a comprehensive discussion of Juvenal 1–5. Bramble (1974) 164–73 emphasizes contrasts between the expansive "grand style" of Juvenal and what he calls "the self-consciously unpretentious form of Lucilius, Horace and Persius." Henderson (1995) makes the case for parody of Valerius Flaccus' *Argonautica* in Juvenal 1; on Juvenal 3 see Motto and Clark (1965), Staley (2000). Braund (1996b) includes comprehensive discussion of Juvenal's use of mock epic elements in satires 1–5.

Gowers (1993a), Davidson (1997), Olson and Sens (2000), and Wilkins (2000) each offer detailed – and entertaining – studies of the cultural significance of literary representations of food.

8

ROLAND MAYER

Sleeping with the enemy: satire and philosophy

The Roman satirist approached philosophy warily, first because it was Greek, and secondly because it seemed to set itself up as a rival to the native moral tradition. Satire is basically conservative in outlook, and Roman satire upholds Roman values: change is bad, the foreign is suspect. It is for this reason that Lucilius makes fun, through a persona, of a Roman Hellenomaniac, Albucius (fr. 87–93 W), that Persius depicts a centurion bidding a clipped coin for a passel of cheap Greeks (5.189–91), and that Juvenal (again through a persona) expresses loathing of a Hellenized Rome (3.60–1) and of starveling Greeks generally (3.78).

More specifically, philosophy was so quintessentially Greek an activity that its Roman adherents in the ruling élite were open to censure or ridicule.[1] Native hostility could be exploited even by the philosopher-friendly Cicero: in two trial speeches, the *Pro Murena* (§§60–6) and the *In Pisonem*,[2] he mocked the ethical paradoxes of the younger Cato's rigorous Stoicism[3] and scathingly attacked the Epicureanism of L. Calpurnius Piso because he knew he would be sympathetically heard by a Roman jury. This antipathy is parodied by Petronius, *Satyricon* 71.12: the plutocratic vulgarian, Trimalchio, insists that his epitaph will record that he took no heed of philosophers.

The native mistrust of philosophy in due course took on a political aspect: under the principate the disaffected might seek refuge in philosophy, as did the friend of Persius, Thrasea Paetus, a senator of Stoic leaning who ostentatiously retired from public life to the annoyance of Nero.[4] The ruling class's wariness of philosophy under the principate is well documented in

---

[1] See Jocelyn (1977a), esp. the conclusion on p. 366. This is an essay of fundamental importance.

[2] For the *In Pisonem* – a 'pretend' speech – see Powell (1995) 25.

[3] He later admitted that he was then playing to the gallery (*De finibus* 4.74); he made amends by composing towards the end of his life the *Paradoxa Stoicorum*, which will be mentioned again below.

[4] See in this volume Cucchiarelli for more on this element in Persius' make up.

the education of Agricola, whose mother deterred him from its study lest he might prove "more enthusiastic for philosophy than was acceptable in a Roman and a Senator," according to his son-in-law, Tacitus (*Agricola* 4.3).[5] The emperor Domitian later expelled philosophers from Rome, and it is significant of those times (in which Juvenal himself lived) that prominent "new men" in the ruling élite, Pliny the Younger and Tacitus, showed no great interest in philosophy.[6]

Changes in the attitude to philosophy have just been hinted at, and at this stage, before proceeding much further with our analysis, caution is necessary. Some two hundred and fifty years separate Lucilius from Juvenal. Within this considerable span we should hardly expect a uniform response to Greek philosophy, given the profound changes in the social and above all in the political life of Rome. As Powell (1995) 15–16 suggests, an earnest engagement with philosophy for spiritual guidance may only have developed long after Lucilius' time during the moral turmoil of prolonged civil conflicts in the first century BCE. We need also to reckon with change in the shapes of Greek philosophy itself. It was still a dynamic intellectual activity, and its dynamism was given a boost when it transplanted itself to Rome (in fact, there were arguably two "transplants," one in 88–87 BCE after the Mithridatic wars,[7] the other in 30 BCE after Octavian's defeat of Cleopatra in Alexandria). Over time philosophical discourse established itself as a primary activity, within the equestrian élite at any rate (Seneca the Younger is a case in point). But philosophy had also to adapt itself in order to take root in Latian soil. When we speak of Greek philosophy at Rome, we must be ready to see the impact that Roman reception had upon philosophical discourse. During this period there was much more borrowing of ideas and blurring of distinctions between the rival sects (again, something we see in Seneca, who prided himself on appropriating Epicurean maxims within a Stoic framework). All of this needs to be taken carefully into account, if we are to seek a just estimate of the influence of philosophical discourse upon the individual satirists.

The satirists themselves show considerable differences in their engagement with philosophy, and that too owes much to their different backgrounds and to the times in which they lived. Lucilius was an educated equestrian, whose aristocratic friend, P. Scipio Aemilianus, included in his circle the Stoic

---

[5] Nero's mother, Agrippina, was not keen that he should imbibe philosophy (Suetonius, *Nero* 52).

[6] See Jocelyn (1977a) 362 for the continuity of the Roman ruling class's antipathy to philosophy.

[7] See Rawson (1985) 7–9 and Powell (1995) 17.

Panaetius. He was himself known to the Academic philosopher Clitomachus, who dedicated a book (one of his 400!) to him.[8] Horace, on the other hand, came from an altogether less privileged background, and yet he is the only satirist known to have visited Athens to study in the Academy rhetoric and, as he stresses in his own case, philosophy (*Epistles* 2.2.43–5). His enthusiasm may well have been fueled by the recent evangelization of Epicureanism by Lucretius, and above all by the encyclopedic campaign of Cicero to create a Latin library of philosophical texts (Cicero's son Marcus was also studying philosophy at Athens when Horace was there). Persius, as we have noted, moved in Stoic circles in Nero's Rome, but as an equestrian (like Lucilius and Horace), his philosophical interest posed no political threat, and he could indulge it in safety. Juvenal is perhaps the odd man out (he was not equestrian, apparently), in that nothing in his work suggests philosophical training or interest, apart from the sort of knowledge that any moderately educated person of the day would be expected to possess.

One of the objections to philosophical ethics referred to at the outset was that Rome had its own moral tradition, handed from father to son, which we now call *mos maiorum*, and it needed no supplement, from a conservative point of view. Horace illustrates the attitude at *Sermones* 1.4.115–19, where he describes his father's admonishing him to cleave to the ancestral moral practices of Rome, practices which the philosopher can corroborate, but not replace. Juvenal adopted a somewhat similar attitude: while admitting the claims of philosophy, he finds that life teaches us how to put up with our reverses (13.19–22: *uita magistra*); later in the same satire (13.120–3), when he turns to console his friend (probably ironically) for the loss of a large sum of money, he disclaims theoretical knowledge of Stoicism, Cynicism, or Epicureanism, and takes the "plain man's" approach to advice. This "take-it-or-leave-it" attitude goes right back to Lucilius, who had noted that for all practical purposes a philosopher, *sapiens*, is not as much use as a good raincoat, horse, or slave (fr. 507–8W). A balanced assessment is provided by von Albrecht (1997) 262: "Roman philosophy may not be separated from practical life. But even if the *satura* does not indulge in theory, it is still concerned with reflection."

What especially made the philosopher an object of satiric mockery was the impracticality of his doctrines. Banter at the Stoics' expense crops up in Horace (*Sermones* 1.3.96–7 and 124–42), where their notorious paradoxes about the equivalence of all wrongdoings and the omni-competence of the wise man provoke ridicule from the satirist, who adopts the plain man's pragmatic point of view. Horace repeats the dose at *Sermones* 2.3.43–6,

---

[8] See Rudd (1986) 164.

where a speaker in a dialogue advances the paradox that all men, save the Stoic *sapiens*, are insane. Persius depicts a centurion and his bulky mates laughing at the theoretical physics of Epicurus (3.77–87). Counter-intuitive or otherworldly doctrines were easy prey for the Roman critic.

For any number of reasons, then, a satirist, as a Roman, might well cast a cold eye upon the alien wisdom. As a poet, moreover, the satirist had what might be called a generic impulse to propel this native antipathy further. Satire was a home-grown Roman genre (the only one, arguably), and as it emerged and evolved it was always staking its claim to territory – chiefly, moral behavior – in the specific context of Rome. Satire had, in addition, to acquire its distinctive tone of voice, and, as we shall see, philosophical discourse did here offer it some help. This search for its own, distinctive tone is seen in Lucilius' mockery of tragic rodomontade (satire 6 of book 26, fr. 720–34W), which Persius echoes in his choliambic prologue, and Juvenal at the opening of his first satire. The satiric voice imposed upon philosophic doctrine is heard in Horace's account of Epicurean anthropology at *Sermones* 1.3.99–112: he there borrows from Lucretius' discussion of the origins of civilization,[9] but with a single Latin obscenity, *cunnus* (107), Horace brings the whole context down to the level of satire, realistic and sardonic.[10] In effect, satire is always defining itself against older, alternative discourses (both literary and intellectual), which it may either reject or appropriate by cannibalization. So Greek philosophy, when not openly the butt of satiric humor, has to be ingested and incorporated into the discourse of Roman satire. Generically considered, philosophy must be transformed into satire.

The catalyst which wrought this transformation was a characteristic mode of later Greek popular philosophy which nowadays goes conveniently by the name of diatribe.[11] We might also call this format of ethical doctrine a lecture or sermon or preaching (the point being that it was more oral than written). Examples of the manner are found in Lucretius' great poem, in which a satirical tone is often detected, and in the late philosophical work of Cicero, the *Paradoxa Stoicorum* and the *Tusculan Disputations*.[12] The strategies of the diatribe, which aimed at persuasion of the audience rather than argument, owed a good deal to rhetoric,[13] for example, the use of analogies

---

[9] See H. A. J. Munro's note on Lucretius 5.1029 in his commentary (Cambridge, *T. Lucreti Cari de rerum libri sex* 1886; 4th edn.).

[10] For a discussion of obscenity in satire see Adams (1982) 221–2.

[11] See *OCD s.v.* diatribe, pp. 463–4, Schmidt (1966), and von Albrecht (1997) 244–5.

[12] For Lucretius see E. J. Kenney's edition of book 3 (Cambridge, 1971) 17–20, and A. G. Lee's edition of Cicero's *Paradoxa Stoicorum* (London, 1953) xxiv–xxvii.

[13] See Pennacini (1983).

(especially relating to health), of *exempla* drawn from everyday life or history, objections put into the mouth of a "straw man," and rhetorical questions. Diatribe may be seen as contemporary philosophy's chief influence upon the satirical mode, the thing which most helped it to develop its characteristic tone. The actual doctrines of the main schools were thus less important than one of the media by which they were disseminated. Diatribe additionally recommended itself because it was conversational in diction (what Persius called *uerba togae* [5.14], the language of everyday), loose in structure, and could appeal as much to emotions as to reason, especially by deploying humor (all elements Roman satire owed to comedy as well). Popular exposition of ethical doctrine by preaching was particularly associated with the Stoics, two of whom, Crispinus and Stertinius, are parodied in Horace (*Sermones* 2.3 and 2.7), and it is Horace who undeniably owes most to the manner, as he virtually admits when he speaks of his *Bionei sermones* (*Epistles* 2.2.60).[14] Persius runs Horace close in his fondness for the diatribe manner,[15] and Juvenal, too, naturally found the rhetorical element in diatribe congenial.[16]

Satire so successfully digested what it wanted from the Greek philosophical tradition that it is often unclear how much a writer derived from any particular school or teacher. Lucilius, for instance, tried to describe the very Roman concept of *uirtus* (moral excellence), and scholars (as we will see below) divide radically in their interpretation of his definition, some regarding it as purely Roman, others as basically Greek and philosophical. It might be fairer to say that Lucilius successfully turned such philosophical interest as he had into satire. As such, it is no longer exactly philosophy, but a Roman issue for a Roman audience. Similarly, Horace in his first three satires recommended the concept of the moral mean; but he does not argue for it at all rigorously; rather he shows by counter-examples drawn from everyday Roman life that the mean between extremes is "best practice." The concept of the mean had been given philosophical authority by Aristotle, but Horace never plays the Aristotle card to take the trick. Moreover, he knew that the moral value of the mean had been acknowledged long before Aristotle, and that it was deeply embedded in much early Greek poetry. It would therefore be hard to define Horace's position as entirely philosophically based here.

---

[14] He there refers to the shadowy figure of Bion of Borysthenes, famous for his witty preaching. See Lejay's general introduction to his commentary (1911) vii–xxxvi, and for sermons generally 325–6; for the two diatribe satires 360–7. See also Coffey (1989) 92–3 and Freudenburg (1993) 8–21.

[15] See Coffey (1989) 101 on the figure of the objector in Persius, Dessen (1996) 71, and Cucchiarelli in this volume, p. 63.

[16] See Bellandi (1980) and Braund (1996a) 116.

The implied audience for satire also deserves some consideration.[17] Just as Lucilius mapped its territory, so he defined his preferred reader, not the excessively learned, but not the unlearned either, rather someone in the middle (fr. 632–4W).[18] His program is thus maximalist, and rightly so when the theme is proper behavior, a matter of universal concern (but the vices satire attacks are often only available to the well-to-do with time on their hands). The middling reader cannot be expected to be an initiate into philosophy, which after all required money (to pay foreign teachers and even for travel abroad) and leisure as well as commitment. Still, the intellectually curious occupied themselves at least superficially with philosophy (so Powell [1995] 15). Such readers could be expected to understand at least a reference to the vegetarianism of Pythagoras (mentioned by Juvenal twice, 3.229 and 15.173–4), or to his belief in the transmigration of souls (so Horace at *Sermones* 2.6.63). Horace follows Lucilian precedent, and draws attention to his ideal audience in the tenth satire of the first book, where he restricts it to his circle of friends. But many of his friends are of the equestrian order, so again the appeal is to the broad spectrum of the educated élite. Such men had time and leisure to immerse themselves in general culture, but they were Roman gentlemen first and last.

Persius, too, aims at the widest possible diffusion of his views, albeit he betrays a sense of writing to a void (cf. 1.2). But so passionately does he believe in the value of Stoicism that he aims to convert us. Most striking in his satires is the sudden irruption of the second person *plural* into the discourse (so at 3.64–8 and 5.64–5); usually the satirist addresses an individual in dialogue (another debt perhaps to philosophical format), but Persius turns occasionally to a wider audience and becomes something of a preacher himself.

After these general introductory considerations, we may now turn to a brief review of the individual satirists, to draw attention to the contexts where they seem most to close with philosophy.

First in the satiric field, Lucilius had a free hand in choice of subject matter and he introduced into his satire any topic that took his fancy. Philosophers, as we have seen, were among his acquaintances, so their profession figures in his poems.[19] In an early work, the second satire of book 28 (fr. 815–34W), a philosophers' symposium is described in which Epicurean terminology is

---

[17] See Jocelyn (1977a) 343–4.

[18] Cicero reprises this sentiment, paraphrasing a different passage from Lucilius, at the beginning of two of his philosophical treatises, *De finibus* 1.7 and *De republica* fr. 1c. Again, the desire to spread the doctrine as widely as possible requires appeal to the middling sort of reader.

[19] Cf. Muecke's discussion, pp. 43–4.

borrowed "neat" from the Greek (fr. 820W);[20] in the book's third satire (fr. 835–43W) we seem to be presented with philosophical advice in a dialogue (these are pretty speculative reconstructions). The fragmentary nature of Lucilius' work does not permit us to say much more with certainty;[21] as Rawson (1985) 282–3 warned, acquaintance with the terminology is not the same as the ability or desire to engage in philosophical debate. More characteristic is Lucilius' guying of the ideal portrait of the Stoic sage (fr. 1189–90W); the satirist latches onto the pretensions of the school because they provide him with an object of ridicule.

A longish fragment defining *uirtus* – "moral excellence" (fr. 1196–1208W) – was referred to above.[22] Since "virtue" was the highest good of the Stoics, a Stoic color is often sought in this piece,[23] and some of its terminology, too, is assumed to have a philosophical hue. For instance, in this line

> *uirtus scire homini rectum, utile, quid sit honestum*
> the virtue [of a man] is to understand what is right, useful, honorable for him

the word *honestum* in particular is taken to be a philosophical term by the *Thesaurus linguae Latinae*, following the great German editor of Lucilius' fragments, Friedrich Marx.[24] And yet it was common before Lucilius in the sense "respectable," "decent." It does not obviously require any additional philosophical connotation for the context to be intelligible. After all, the fragment can be read – minimally – as traditional Roman morality,[25] and we may say that in general Lucilius' wisdom was that of the world and not of the schools.[26]

Yet even if philosophy is there, Lucilius shows less interest in it than he clearly had for Greek literary theory, which is heavily represented in the fragments (that may, of course, be owed to the interest of later excerptors). Still,

---

[20] For Lucilius' absorption of Greek *paideia* and use of philosophical terminology "neat" see Adrian Gratwick in Kenney and Clausen (1982) 167.

[21] Warmington in his Loeb edition, p. xvi note *b*, and at 162–3 – and cf. von Albrecht (1997) 260–1 – adverts to his interest in philosophy, but the textual evidence is thin given the lack of context. Older studies, e.g. Cichorius (1908) 46–7 and Fiske (1920) 68, detected development in Lucilius' use of philosophy in his satire.

[22] See von Albrecht (1997) 257 for a literary analysis.

[23] So Fiske (1920) 72: "an exposition of virtue as accepted . . . from the lips of Panaetius," and Görler (1984) 463–8, who detects the influence, heavily romanized, of Antipater of Tarsus, for whose doctrine of values see Long (1986) 196.

[24] *TLL* VI 2.2911.5–6; it may be worth noting that the author of the later article on the word of opposite sense in that fragment, *inhonestum*, did not class it specifically as a philosophical term (indeed, such a category is not even recognized for that word).

[25] So Earl (1961) 26–7.   [26] So Sellar (1881) 237.

as the inventor of satire, Lucilius set a potential agenda for his successors, to follow up as they saw fit.

Between Lucilius and Horace there was considerable missionary activity in the steady romanization of Greek philosophy by Lucretius, Cicero, and Varro. Their success fueled the enthusiasm of their compatriots for appropriating the foreign – though now increasingly less so – discipline. Lucretius and Cicero have already been referred to,[27] so only Varro deserves a brief word now.

Marcus Terentius Varro was a pupil of Antiochus of Ascalon, and so, like Cicero, allied to the skepticism of the New Academy.[28] He wrote satire in the tradition of Menippus of Gadara, a mixture of prose and verse; in a number of these short "essays" he shows some debt to the Cynics in his mockery of more formal philosophy, in particular that perennial butt, the Stoic paradoxes,[29] but respect as usual is accorded to Socrates. This recalls something of Lucilius and Horace, who hark back to the founder of ethics, and his practice of philosophy as discourse.[30] Moral exhortation seems to have been Varro's goal.[31] Cicero acknowledged the philosophical character of his satire: *multa admixta ex intima philosophia*, "much was added from the very heart of philosophy" (*Academica* 1.8).

Horace's engagement with philosophy was a lifelong interest, reflected in all of his poetry, not just the satires. Given the special tone of satire, we should come away with a distorted assessment of what philosophy meant to him if we failed to take account of his use of it in the other genres in which he composed.[32] Anyway, one thing he prized above all else was independence, whether social, or poetic, or intellectual. He never endorsed a creed wholeheartedly or consistently, since his heart belonged wholly and forever to the Muse. Lucilius had opened up for him, however, an avenue he wanted to travel down, since philosophy had always posed questions about issues of importance (especially personal independence). Even where its answers were of uncertain value or applicability, the fact of posing the question, of raising the issue, was something valuable in itself.

In *Sermones* 1.2 Horace meditates upon our inability to strike a balance, particularly in matters sexual. At no point in the discourse does he refer to philosophical debate on the issue, nor, as we have seen, does he seek to validate his own adherence to the recommended "mean" by appealing to authority (e.g. Aristotle's). The basic morality encouraged in the poem is Roman – we note citation of the Elder Cato at line 32. And yet Horace

---

[27] Powell (1995) xiii–xvii provides a helpful résumé of Cicero's philosophical works.
[28] Cf. Powell (1995) 17.   [29] See Sigsbee (1976).   [30] See Anderson (1982) 13–49.
[31] So Coffey (1989) 160–1.   [32] See Coffey (1989) 65, 72, 87, 91.

betrays a debt to Epicurean terminology, and refers to Philodemus (in his capacity as poet) at line 121.[33] What we have here once again is the diffusion of some technical knowledge among the educated, rather than a philosophically grounded argument.

Sermones 2.2 is a homily on plain living ("the mean" as applied to eating), derived, so Horace would have us believe, from a rustic neighbor, Ofellus. Ofellus is oddly described at the outset in the phrase *abnormis sapiens*. Now *sapiens*, as we have seen, is the Latin for "philosopher," but *abnormis*, a word found nowhere else in the classical language, seems to mean that Ofellus belongs to no recognized school. His precepts, then, are amateur, founded upon experience. And yet much of the content and manner of its presentation can be traced back to philosophical texts, Epicurus' especially, but also Cicero's, and to diatribe.[34] Once again, a marriage of the pragmatic Roman and the imported Greek.

But *Sermones* 2.3 marks a new departure, more nuanced in its approach to Stoic doctrine. Horace imagines himself away from Rome during the Saturnalia. His unproductive reveries are interrupted by Damasippus, a bankrupt lately converted by the Stoic preacher Stertinius. Damasippus clumsily rehearses his sermon on the Stoic paradox that all but the wise man are mad (lines 38–295). Damasippus is clearly over the top, but his criticisms are no less pertinent for that. This is an important document because it shows Horace accommodating himself (and his readers) to philosophical doctrine in an engaging way. We are invited to reflect that philosophy has something to say to us, however uncongenial the mouthpiece. It is significant that Horace presents us with a recent convert, for notoriously they are more ardent in the expression of their convictions than those who have grown up comfortably with a doctrine. Stertinius (the philosopher who converted Damasippus) is not openly mocked; rather, it is Damasippus himself who provides the butt, so that Stoicism is somewhat held at arm's length for more judicious appraisal. Horace is prepared to see something in it (as he was not in their doctrine of the parity of faults), and we are invited to share his openness to philosophical doctrine.[35]

Sermones 2.2 and 2.3 also demonstrate what Horace owed as an artist to diatribe. Ofellus' and Damasippus' sermons recall what we encountered in Lucretius, and the manner of this popular preaching was something that Horace saw he could exploit. Contemporary popular ethics therefore offered him not just his themes, but even his literary form. *Sermones* 2.7 follows the same sermonizing strategy: Horace's own slave Davus has learnt a

---

[33] See Lejay's introduction (1911) 32–3.
[34] See Lejay (1911) 313–21, esp. 316, and Fiske (1920) 378–87.   [35] See Fiske (1920) 387–98.

homily overheard by the doorkeeper at the house of another Stoic preacher, Crispinus, which he now inflicts upon Horace. The paradox this time is that all men are slaves (not just those who were owned by someone else).

Rudd (1986) 177–8 and (1993) 66 made the point that whenever Horace named a philosopher or one of the schools his tone was good natured, but irreverent; he certainly never endorsed any formal doctrine. But in *Sermones* 2.3 and 2.7 Horace adroitly has his cake and eats it: he ridicules the hectoring manner of the street preacher, but gives the substance of his homily a fair hearing, and so eases the reader (along with the writer) into the position of audience. Once there, we may find something beneficial.

Persius, alone of the satirists, embraces the teaching of a particular philosophical sect to press home his moral criticisms. Of all the still active schools, the Stoic appealed most to the Romans, and not surprisingly its ethics came most readily to play a part in satirical discourse (not always favorable, as we have seen). Horace's successor, and adroit imitator, Persius, differs from his model in making no secret of his commitment to Stoicism (cf. 3.52–5), which determines many aspects of his satires. He names representatives of the school, Cleanthes and Chrysippus (5.64, 6.80), and he went so far as to encourage his readers generally to follow its moral program.[36] We might regard this evangelism as a reaction to the degeneracy of Nero's Rome, a society that had so far lost sight of its ancestral morality that only a strong dose of systematic ethics could put the patient on the road to recovery (Persius likes medical analogies). The appeal to Persius of Stoicism is not detected on the ethical plane alone, for even his poetic style owes a considerable debt to Stoic theory about the proper use of language.[37]

Just as we need to reckon with Cicero in our reading of Horace, so we need now to foreground the writings of Persius' older contemporary, Lucius Annaeus Seneca the Younger, who provided a much larger survey of Stoic teaching than is now apparent from what has survived of his writing (it must be remembered, however, that a good deal of Seneca's extant writing postdates the death of Persius in CE 62). It has been recently stressed by Inwood (1995) 63–76 that Seneca was a first-order Latin philosopher, not a missionary like Lucretius or Cicero, and that now for the first time Romans of the élite could reasonably consider following the philosophical life, and advertise the fact. Persius takes advantage of this situation.

---

[36] Reckford (1962) 490–8 sounds a note of caution, however, and insists that Persius is a satirist first and a Stoic second. I should class him rather with Lucretius as a poet whose philosophical conviction defines his persona. For a fuller account see Cucchiarelli in this volume, pp. 69–75.

[37] For a fuller account see Cucchiarelli's discussion in this volume, pp. 71–2.

Persius' mental growth from the age of sixteen was influenced by Annaeus Cornutus, who was a versatile scholar and writer, chiefly on philosophical matters, but also on rhetoric (from his name it is clear that he was attached to the family of Seneca the Younger, perhaps as a freedman of one of his relatives).[38] It is important to recall that Persius was an equestrian, and so not involved in governing Rome. His point of view is therefore by and large ethical, rather than political.[39]

Persius' use of dialogue form for his critique shows a debt to Stoic practice; his examples, too, are generalized after the fashion of diatribe.[40] The first satire apart, the rest may seem exercises in satirical form upon ethical themes, which are given a more or less Stoic color. Satire 2, for example, is on the subject of prayer, a philosophical commonplace, but it lacks any clear Stoic note (for which see rather Juvenal in his Satire 10). In Satire 3 a young man rallies himself for backsliding. Can he, who has the advantage over others of knowing what is right, bring himself to live by his doctrine, which he plainly identifies as Stoic (52–62)? He moves, as we have noted, to a general protreptic appeal at 66–76, advocating philosophy as a guide to right living for all of us. Satire 4 takes up the proverbial injunction "know thyself!", but nothing specially Stoic appears in it. Satire 5 illustrates Persius' own moral progress by working up one of the notorious Stoic paradoxes, already treated by Cicero (*Paradoxa Stoicorum* 33–41) and by Horace (*Sermones* 2.7.83–8), that only the *sapiens* is truly free; Persius delivers a sermon on this theme from line 91. Satire 6, against avarice, hoarding, and the failure to use the good things of life, reworks Horatian themes, and in an Horatian form, the verse epistle; it is appropriately addressed to an imitator of Horace's lyric verse, Caesius Bassus. The argument is philosophical up to a point, but hardly Stoic.

Let us now return to the fifth satire, because it is there that Persius gives his most open profession of his Stoicism and makes his most obvious attempt to convert his reader to it. The poem is addressed to his teacher Cornutus, whom Persius thanks for his training and example. He praises Cornutus for preparing his students to receive the wholesome seed of the Stoic Cleanthes (5.64), and then he unexpectedly addresses us, his readers, "young and old," urging us to "seek thence" (i.e. from Stoic teaching) a sure goal for desires. This abrupt and universal appeal recalls the earlier command at 3.66 to all of us to come and learn the causes of things (a list of moral issues then follows); but that protreptic to philosophy privileged no one school. Now

---

[38] For him see *OCD*.   [39] So Morford (1984) 11.
[40] Still useful is the discussion by Jahn (1843) lxv–lxvi.

Persius sets out to convert all of his readers to Stoicism. He is unique among the satirists for his unabashed partisanship, and for the urgency with which he evangelizes.

Juvenal's satire, at least in the first book (satires 1–5), is marked by a distinctive persona: the poet presents himself as marginalized in various ways within society. He is not a member of the élite (and that may have been true in fact), and he feels excluded even as a Roman citizen from certain aspects of civic life. Thus when he attacks homosexual men in his second satire, some of his examples are drawn from the nobility (Creticus at line 67, and Gracchus at line 117), since it is their degeneracy which rouses his indignation as much as their perversion. These are not just gays, but, as Armistead Maupin called them, "the A-gays." For our purposes, what matters in this poem is that they are also hypocrites (a frequent charge against philosophers, too), in that they decorate their libraries with the statues of philosophers, but in no way live up to the moral standard of the schools. Juvenal, however, suggests that the whole ethical tradition of Greece was perverted at its source when he reminds us that Socrates was in some traditions reckoned an active pederast (line 10). Later he openly derides the objects of his satire specifically as descendants of the Stoics (line 65 *Stoicidae*), to contrast the austerity of that sect with the self-indulgence of its Roman adherents. Juvenal seems to have had little time for philosophers at the outset of his satirical career; perhaps their expulsion from Rome by Domitian shaped (if it did not rather reflect) the popular attitude, including Juvenal's own.

One matter undeniably colored Juvenal's satire, its profound debt to rhetorical declamation.[41] We must remember that declamation, too, traded in moral commonplaces. De Decker (1913) 19 n. 20 was therefore right to argue that what seems philosophical is no more than the sort of moralism that had taken root in the declamatory repertoire. He offered a particular instance of this ([1913] 38): it had been argued that Juvenal's references to Fortuna suggested Stoic leanings, but the *locus de Fortuna* was a commonplace of the declaimers. That said, in the last two books Juvenal is nowadays reckoned to show a tendency to appeal to philosophers, as his own satire becomes less critical, more protreptic.[42]

Satire 10, for example, arguably makes more of the philosophical tradition. In particular the debt to Stoicism may well be substantial, according to Reeve (1983) 32; the phrase *per uirtutem* "through virtue" in line 364 certainly seems to set a Stoic seal upon the argument. On the other hand, Courtney (1980) 451 is prudent to demur:

---

[41] See *OCD* for this exercise.   [42] See Courtney (1980) 16, 448–51 (on satire 10).

this [selection from a variety of philosophic traditions] illustrates a problem often encountered in Roman literature. Juvenal was typical of those many Romans who had a general acquaintance with philosophy, but not an exact knowledge. Such Romans, in attempting to build up a practical guide to the conduct of life, often took elements which appealed to them from diverse creeds.

In a word, eclecticism, often of a highly personal stamp, seems to be the guiding principle. We might note in this regard that along with the reference to *uirtus* in line 364 Juvenal states that we aim at a tranquil life, which suggests to some the doctrine of Democritus (often revived in various forms).

It may well be true that Juvenal tired of hectoring and turned to a more reflective sort of satire. The difficulty is that however much one focuses on the odd detail that may be given a philosophical interpretation, the overall impression left in the mind after reading one of Juvenal's satires is the virtual absence of any intellectual content. The declamatory manner is always to the fore, draining ideas of their substance. This is not to say that the writing is anything less than dazzling. But on balance it seems a long way from rational, let alone philosophical, discourse.

There can be no tidy conclusion to an analysis of the wary relation between Greek philosophy and Roman satire. If we remember the probable etymology of *satura*, we can say no more than that philosophy is one constant ingredient in the mishmash (along with sex and literary criticism). How much of the ingredient is added depends both upon the taste of the "cook" and on the palate of his consumers, the audience of readers. They were all Romans and, as we have seen, the Romans had no uniform receptivity to philosophy during the two hundred and fifty years that classic satire was being written. The prudent "cook" therefore used the ingredient sparingly; only that master of "nouvelle cuisine," Persius, took a risk in offering *aliquid decoctius*, "something concentrated" (Stoicism) to his guests.[43] In the end, all these "cooks" knew that what they were to produce was not a refined dish of foreign philosophy but a loaded platter of Roman satire.

Further reading

Short essays with recent bibliographies on some of the authors referred to above (Cicero, Horace, Juvenal) will be found in R. Goulet, ed. *Dictionnaire des philosophes antiques* (*Babélyca d'Argos à Dyscolius*) (Paris 1994) and (*d'Eccélos à Juvénal*) (Paris 2000). Essays on particular authors and issues are to be found in Miriam Griffin and Jonathan Barnes, eds. *Philosophia Togata: Essays on Philosophy and Roman Society* (Oxford 1989). For general intellectual background see Rawson (1985) 282–97, and

---

[43] For this important concept see Cucchiarelli in this volume, pp. 68–9.

Miriam Griffin, ch. 18 "The Intellectual Developments of the Ciceronian Age" in *The Cambridge Ancient History* (Cambridge, 1994) IX 717–28. For Stoicism see Marcia L. Colish, *The Stoic Tradition from Antiquity to the Early Middle Ages* I: *Stoicism in Classical Latin Literature* (Studies in the History of Christian Thought 34) (Leiden 1985) 160–94 for Horace, 194–203 for Persius, and 204–24 for Juvenal.

More particularly, for Lucilius Christes (1972) 1232 summarizes opinion to date. For Cicero Powell (1995) is most useful. Tom Tarver's "Varro and the Antiquarianism of Philosophy," in Jonathan Barnes and Miriam Griffin, eds. *Philosophia Togata: Plato and Aristotle at Rome* (Oxford, 1997) 130–64 provides up to date discussion. For Horace recent bibliography will be found in the *Enciclopedia Oraziana* (Rome, 1997) s.v. *filosofia*, II 78–90, esp. 80; this general essay by Alain Michel is followed by five on the individual schools, as follows: Accademia 90–2, *cinismo* 92–3, *epicureismo* 93–4, *Peripato* 95–6, *stoicismo* 96–8; N. Rudd, "Horace as a Moralist" in Rudd (1993) 64–88, esp. 64–71, is excellent. G. Highet's "The Philosophy of Juvenal," *Transactions of the American Philological Association* 30 (1949) 254–70 is a sensible account, and the indexes to the commentaries of Courtney (1980) and Braund (1996b) both provide reference to the poet's engagement with philosophy.

9

VICTORIA RIMELL

The satiric maze: Petronius, satire, and the novel

Petronius' *Satyricon* has often been dubbed the most controversial and daedalic text in classical literature. The question of whether and how it should count as "satiric" has long preoccupied scholars, yet this contention is part of a broader debate about how to define a work parasitic on almost every known literary form, from the Greek romance (which it is often said to parody)[1] to epic, historiography, New Comedy, Roman erotic elegy, the Milesian tale, and Greek and Roman mime. As Zeitlin argues, the *Satyricon* "seems to have been undertaken with the deliberate intention of defeating the expectations of an audience accustomed to an organising literary form."[2] There will always be problems involved in singling out one model or frame of expectations for such a generically complex text.

The *Satyricon*, or *Satyrica* (Greek genitive or nominative plural, with the former presuming the addition of *libri*, meaning "things associated with satyrs"), is an extended first person narrative told in the voice of Encolpius, a vagabond, myopic scholar who is also a protagonist in the events he recounts. The text survives fragmented: we probably have parts of (at least) books 14 and 16 and all of book 15, which likely coincided with the famous feast of Trimalchio, yet the original length remains a mystery.[3] Scholars today generally agree that the author of the *Satyricon* was probably the Petronius whose portrait is penned by Tacitus in *Annals* 16.17ff., the Neronian courtier nicknamed "Arbiter of Elegance."[4] According to Tacitus, Petronius was forced to suicide by palace intrigues in CE 66: after posting off a missive to the *princeps* cataloguing every one of Nero's "secret" deviancies, he severed his

---

[1] On this question see e.g. Schmeling (1999), Relihan (1993) 94, Courtney (2001) 24–31.

[2] Zeitlin (1971a) 635.

[3] The surviving manuscripts, from the ninth, fifteenth and sixteenth centuries, give some book numbers, but these are not consistent. See Müller (1995) xix, Rose (1971) 2–3, Sullivan (1968) 34 and 79, Harrison (1999) xvii.

[4] Note that Tacitus' Petronius looks to be the same man mentioned in Pliny, *Naturalis Historia* 37.20, yet Pliny gives a different *praenomen* ("T. Petronius").

veins and died slowly (as if "naturally") at a banquet, drinking and reciting frivolous lyrics all the while (for readers of the *Satyricon*, this scene looks like a flashback to Trimalchio's *cena*, with all its grisly luxury, fakery, and literary parody). The cognomen "Arbiter" is attested in the manuscript tradition of the *Satyricon*, as well as in other indirect pieces of evidence, and is commonly linked to Tacitus' description. Clearly, if this is right, it fuels potential for reading the *Satyricon* as an edgy, provocative performance of Neronian literary culture. Politics (both Neronian politics and the politics of Petronius' readers) become especially crucial when it comes to thinking about who or what the *Satyricon* may be satirizing.

The narrative of the *Satyricon* as we have it is lacunose, hard to follow, and varies considerably in pace and tone. The action unfolds in a *graeca urbs*, a coastal city of Campania, and begins with an exchange outside a rhetorical school between the narrator Encolpius and a teacher, Agamemnon. The story then follows Encolpius' adventures, journeys, and scrapes with his gang of companions. The characters, especially Encolpius, who is (or sets himself up to look like) a dizzy, forgetful interpreter, live out literary and sexual fantasies, flit between epic and tragic poses, fall prey to (each others') illusions and tricks, and repeatedly lose their way or drift in circles. There are no authorial subtitles to fill us in on the "reality" behind Encolpius' reveries, to tell us whether and where we too, who view this world through Encolpius' eyes, are being led up the garden path.

Events in the *Satyricon* are often precipitated by sexual jealousy (Encolpius and fellow rogue Ascyltos vie for the attentions of pretty boy Giton, who is also easy prey for Eumolpus, the poet who enters the story at *Satyricon* 83). First they are lured into Quartilla's brothel, where Encolpius offends the goose sacred to Priapus, the god who then hounds him for the rest of the fiction (just as Poseidon plagued Odysseus), finally cursing him with impotence when he falls for a young beauty named Circe at *Satyricon* 126. It is out of that frying pan and into the fire of Trimalchio's *cena*, a spectacular carnival feast hosted by the nouveau riche freedman which leaves the guests feeling paranoid, nauseous, and trapped. After escaping this "labyrinth," and cat-fighting with Ascyltos over Giton, Encolpius wanders into a picture gallery where he encounters Eumolpus, who proceeds to recite a poem based on one of the pictures, his *Troiae Halosis*, "on the fall of Troy." After a series of mishaps provoked by Eumolpus' pursuit of Giton, the gang go undercover and board a ship captained (little do they know) by their tyrannical enemy Lichas. The badly disguised stowaways are discovered and punished, but just as Eumolpus is calming "civil war" with a Milesian tale (the tale of the widow of Ephesus), a storm brews, and the ship is wrecked. Washed up on foreign shores, the gang embark on a new voyage to Croton, a once glorious city gone to rot and now inhabited solely by legacy hunters and their prey, the heirless rich. On the way, Eumolpus hatches a plan to play act as a wealthy, childless old man (the others are to play his slaves) in a bid to tease the legacy hunters, and while they are rehearsing this mime, he gives his second epic recital, the *Bellum Civile*. Once at Croton, Encolpius falls in love with Circe, but is paralysed by impotence, only recovering his virility after submitting to the tortuous "magic" of Croton's witches. The story breaks off in the midst of a gory scene in which Eumolpus draws up a will demanding that his heirs cannibalize his corpse before they get their hands on his estate. We can only guess as to what happens next.

In the last century, opinion has generally been split between those critics who seek to package this slippery text as satire and those who prefer to categorize it, with Bakhtin, as a "novel." The term novel is entirely modern: there is no equivalent label in the ancient world, and nor do theoretical discussions of texts like the *Satyricon* survive (literary critics were not much interested in them). In using the term novel of this text, modern critics flag the notion that the *Satyricon* transgresses the law of genre (for Slater, as for Bakhtin, the novel is an "anti-genre")[5] and highlight the possible affiliation between the *Satyricon* (along with Apuleius' *Metamorphoses*) and the so-called Greek novels, written from the first to fourth century CE, which expand into lengthy narrative plots typical of Athenian New Comedy, that is, stories of thwarted love. The *Satyricon*, with its all-male love triangles and tales of lewd lust rather than chaste amour, has been seen by many to mischievously invert the idealized Greek romance. In labelling the *Satyricon* a novel, therefore, critics have both underscored its generic complexity, and privileged the background of the Greek romance, with a view to identifying Petronius as a light-hearted parodist, a writer of comedy.

Conversely, definitions of Petronius as a satirist have tended either to play down or to redirect this emphasis on comedy. Discussion of the satiric in the *Satyricon* is complicated by the fact that "satire" embraces both Roman verse satire (as written by Ennius, Lucilius, Horace, and Persius), and Menippean satire, two very distinct genres. What is more, not all critics would recognize the existence of Menippea to begin with: this is an anachronistic term which was invented in the Renaissance to account for the "mixed form" used by Petronius and most famously Seneca, in his *Apocolocyntosis*. It was inspired by the Cynic Menippus of Gadara, who lived in the third century BCE and wrote in a compound of prose and verse (*prosimetrum*), and also by the title of a work indebted to Menippus, Varro's *Saturae Menippeae* (this

---

[5] Slater (1990) 234, Bakhtin (1981).

survives only in the scrappiest of fragments, while none of Menippus' output is extant).

I will examine in detail (as far as space allows) the arguments for defining the *Satyricon* as Menippean satire below. But I first want to highlight a crucial common element in recent claims for identifying Petronius as a Roman satirist (whether Menippean or not): that is, the need to determine an implicit if not explicit moral authority in Encolpius' impenetrable first person narrative, from which an aggressive (satiric) voice of censure is so obviously absent. Highet encapsulates this formula for diagnosis when he writes: "it cannot be satire, if Petronius is not a moralist. Conversely, if Petronius is not a moralist, his work is satire."[6] For Sullivan, the "edge of conventional satire" is (merely) "blunted" by the evident lack of moral impulsion in the text.[7] Because the *Satyricon* has been, for a modern Anglo-American audience, such a disturbingly "immoral" work, the imperative to infer a strict moral voice has been intense (watching a documentary on pornography, a term that has often been used to describe the *Satyricon*, is, of course, far removed from enjoying a *real* X-rated movie). Readers must be reassured that "by satirising unnaturalness, he [Petronius] is in effect recommending naturalness,"[8] or that racy passages are just harmless fun. For example, critics have sought in the poem at *Satyricon* 132.15 a defense of depravity straight from the author's mouth: here, the narrator asks why pinched Catonian moralists overreact to a work whose only crime is a refreshing Epicurean honesty about the joy of sex.[9] Yet sex in the *Satyricon* is rarely natural, simple, or pleasurable for those involved, more theatrical, tortuous, and depressing. Reading 132.15 as a peephole into authorial intention has helped to sanitize and naturalize those elements in the text which tend to cause modern audiences the most moral discomfort, just as the O family of manuscripts seems contrived "to prevent the *Satyricon* from conveying the wrong sort of pleasures."[10] That there is a complex history of *needing* to decipher satire in the *Satyricon* accounts in part for the presence of Petronius in this volume: we have come to accept that he belongs to (albeit on the margins of) a Roman satiric tradition, whereas authors such as Martial (about whom we have not asked the same questions) tend to slip just over the edge.

---

[6] Highet (1941) 177. The following critics, with varying emphases, also view Petronius as a censuring moralist: Bacon (1958), Raith (1963), Arrowsmith (1966), Sochatoff (1962) and (1970). Also compare discussion in Walsh (1974), who fails to find in Petronius "a sufficiently solid base for the title of moralising satirist" (188), and in Zeitlin (1971a, 676) who argues, "it is idle to look in the *Satyricon* for a conventional moralist."

[7] Sullivan (1968) 258.   [8] Sandy (1969) 302.

[9] E.g. Sullivan (1968).   [10] See Connors (1998) 7.

If we can find "satire" in the *Satyricon*, then we can implicitly conjure up a missing authorial voice to validate *our* interpretation of the text. Of course, it would be far more disconcerting to read a *Satyricon* in which Encolpius rather than Petronius played the satirist, in which we were never quite sure whether to take our narrator as serious, ironic, self-deprecating, sardonic, manipulative, masochistic, canny, moronic . . . It is far safer to presume that, as Sullivan proposes, "the narrator is constantly made the unconscious butt of the author's ridicule and satire."[11] Such an approach is in line with the old-fashioned view of the Roman satiric author as a sincere, elevated moralist: recent criticism, however, has emphasized how the Roman satirist constantly ventriloquizes, shifting between hyperbolic, contradictory, and hypocritical poses which pressure the limits of reader identification. It always takes one to know one, is satire's paranoid, self-implicating maxim: "for no one is born without faults" (Horace, *Sermones* 1.3.68); the satirist's thankless job is poking holes in your complacency, just as Trimalchio's freedman howls (while also digging his own grave) "you can see the lice on others, but not the bugs on yourself" (57.7). The strategy whereby the satirist abdicates his role to an implicated narrator is already a familiar one from Roman verse satire, especially in book 2 of Horace's *Sermones*, in which the principal speaking voice is not that of the author but of a character reporting back to him:[12] Petronius could be seen to take this tactic to its furthest extreme.

The Menippean question

The question of whether the *Satyricon* should be counted as Menippean satire has troubled critics since the Renaissance, when the term Menippean was first used. The tradition of Menippean satire is one we have conceived in retrospect, and many of its reconstructed characteristics are based on inference or conjecture. Its most frequently quoted feature is the unusual concoction of prose and verse. Yet the famous *Iolaus* fragment, which was published in the early 1970s and seems to display many features in common with the *Satyricon* (e.g. a fusion of low theme and heroic allusion, the use of Sotadean verse), suggests that *prosimetrum* was also possible in the Greek novel.[13] Aside from this core feature, which seems inadequate for defining an entire genre, the criteria for qualifying a text as Menippean are necessarily nebulous. For Relihan, "Menippean satire is abnormal in all of its aspects. It is an anti-genre, insofar as it is ultimately a satire on literature itself and all its pretensions to meaning."[14] For Kirk, it is a potpourri jumble of "flagrantly

---

[11] Sullivan (1968) 258.   [12] See Beck (1982) 212.
[13] For discussion see Astbury (1977).   [14] Relihan (1993) 28.

digressive narrative," outlandish fictions about "fantastic voyages, dreams, visions, talking beasts," drafted in "unconventional diction."[15] Bakhtin, who argues in his essay "Epic and Novel" that the *Satyricon* "is good proof that Menippean satire can expand into a huge picture,"[16] is more precise in formulating the requirements of the genre.[17] He proposes that Menippean satire is the literary expression of carnival, a genre directly descended from carnivalized folklore and a less direct descendant of the Socratic dialogues, which together influenced the Dostoevskian polyphonic novel; in short, Bakhtin wants to see embodied in the Menippea the ancient ingredients of the carnivalesque tradition of prose. Ancient Menippean satire is first and foremost comic, it is claimed, and closely associated with the Saturnalia, or "with the freedom of Saturnalian laughter."[18] Five pages of *The Problems of Dostoevsky's Poetics* are devoted to the characteristics of the form, which include freedom of plot, moral/psychological experimentation, a sense of miscellany on every level (from an embracing of bilingualism, sharp contrasts and reversals of roles and styles, the incongruous juxtaposition of high and low registers, "slum naturalism" paralleled by the philosophic, fantastic and mythical), a "three-planed" construction (earth, Olympus, the underworld), and social utopia (e.g. a journey to an unknown land).

Seneca's *Apocolocyntosis* arguably comes close to fulfilling all the itemized criteria, but Petronius' fiction does not fit so neatly: in particular, we struggle to glimpse utopianism, or a vision of social utopia in the text (the action is truncated at Croton, an entrapping, dystopian cityscape far removed from Bakhtin's fantasy of liberatory carnival); there is also no tripartite structure, beyond the hellish imagery of the *Bellum Civile* and hints that Trimalchio's villa is to be imagined as an underworld. It may be countered that the *Satyricon* survives fragmented, and that Bakhtin is merely sketching an idiom: it must be taken for granted that the set of categories are descriptive rather than prescriptive, that no text will necessarily include all elements, especially as the idiom is to operate transhistorically.

Bakhtin wants to claim, straightforwardly, that the marginalized Menippea has been underestimated in the evolution of the novel. And as Connors reminds us,

---

[15] Kirk (1980) xi.

[16] Bakhtin (1981) 27. Other examples he gives of the form range from Apuleius' *Metamorphoses* ("a full-blown Menippean satire" [1984], 113) and Boethius' *De consolatione philosophiae*, to Dostoevsky's story, "Bobok," and works by various European authors including Shakespeare, Dickens, Swift, Cervantes, and Edgar Allan Poe.

[17] Bakhtin (1984) 235.   [18] Bakhtin (1984) 26.

part of the impulse to view Petronius within a Menippean framework had undoubtedly been the scarcity and fragmentation of surviving ancient Menippean texts. Counting Petronius as a Menippean satirist expands the number of ancient Menippean relatively well-preserved authors from two (Seneca and Lucian) to three.[19]

It is clear that including the *Satyricon* buttresses the case for the existence and coherency of this genre, so the impulse will always be to *make* it fit. Yet the question here must be: how useful is the category of Menippean satire for critics of Petronius, and (how) does it make a difference to the way we read the text?

The definition "Menippean" risks becoming an end in itself. Such a diagnosis can function to an extent as a placebo for readers uncomfortable with trying to jam Petronius' square peg into the round hole of literary history, whether because it really was a one-off, experimental, Neronian blast, or because the texts that might help contextualize Petronius' innovations do not survive.[20] One of the most convincing arguments for genre is simply that it is a useful critical tool that facilitates debate on the relation between literary texts. Yet we have no way of ascertaining, for example, whether Petronius is adhering to or breaking any rules, for whatever effect. Menippean satire has the advantage of being a flexible, artificial category, "as changeable as Proteus,"[21] and resistant "to coherent interpretation":[22] this allows us to evade pinning the *Satyricon* down to a single genre, yet at the same time to be consoled by a label. Its unconventionality, so construed, boomerangs any interrogation it triggers: why is the *Satyricon* longer than any other Menippean satire we have?[23] Why does Petronius' extended narrative move much more realistically through space and time than any other "Menippean" text we have? "Because it is experimenting in the very spirit of the genre . . ."

This is not to say that we can dismiss the Menippean tradition as merely a convenient construct: I would suggest, rather, that in the absence of evidence it is more reasonable to propose that Menippean satire is one of *many* forms Petronius (ab)uses. As Conte notes, if Petronius creates expectations of Menippean satire, then it also looks as if he frustrates them.[24] It is also important to realize that like "satire," "Menippean satire" has been used to

[19] Connors (1998) 16.
[20] As Relihan notes ([1993] 91), "the recently discovered papyrus fragments of Greek prosimetric fiction have been sufficient for some to claim that Menippean satire is no longer relevant to the discussion."
[21] Bakhtin (1984) 113. [22] Relihan (1993) 91.
[23] Relihan's answer is that the *Satyricon* is a picaresque novel "on which the Menippean genre has been imposed" (1993) 95.
[24] Conte (1996) 168.

tag or veil a range of interpretative positions, which often contradict each other. For Coffey, the Menippea is an "alternative convention" of satire, which retains the moralizing thrust construed as distinctive of Roman verse satire: thus [it] "mocked or censured undesirable social behaviour."[25] Kirk argues for a Menippean satire "essentially concerned with right learning or belief,"[26] but Relihan, who proposes that the *Satyricon*'s "parody of satire" has its origins in the innovations of Varro's *Menippeans*, suggests rather that the influence of Menippean satire dictates the absence of "any proper moral tone."[27] Relihan's *Satyricon* is a wry comedy which exposes its characters as moralizing hypocrites. Petronius' critique of corrupt moralizing is indirect, therefore, and he does not propose any alternative way of thinking; the text is "funny" because characters are "naïve," blind to their own moral bankruptcy and unaware that their snobbish pretensions to scholarly superiority are ensnared in such a "degenerate" fiction. What makes the *Satyricon* a Menippean satire, Relihan argues, is its critical dimension: the narrator is "a hypocrite and a fool," uniting scenes "through his wholly inadequate and comic attempts to understand them."[28]

Examples given of characters' immoral moralizing include the rhetorical school scenes at *Satyricon* 1–5, Trimalchio's pretensions of learning in the *Cena*, such as the poem at 55.6 on the evils of luxurious dining, and Eumolpus' speeches prefacing the *Troiae Halosis* and the *Bellum Civile*. Yet there is perhaps more to add to Relihan's analysis, which strives to concretize a satiric voice and dictate a single source and direction of humor in the text. It is difficult, for example, not to (also) read Trimalchio's cue for a poem at 55.5 ("for what could be better written than these lines?") as ironic bait, a move typical of the tyrant jester testing out how far his subject guests will continue to smile and applaud, through gritted teeth, even the most back-handed, ear-grating performance. (Such a reading is whetted by hints that Trimalchio may be a figure for Nero himself, and by the possibility that Petronius served as *the* Neronian arbiter of taste.)[29] So, too, it would be misleading to decree that Encolpius' critique of rhetorical education should be read as heart-felt pomposity, rather than as self-conscious or offhand impression of such rhetoric, possibly crafted to placate, or to bait (or simply to cue, in a scripted exercise) the moralizing ramblings of his teacher Agamemnon. Similarly, we might read Eumolpus' moralizing discourse in 88 as a cheap seduction (and take his line at 88.6–7, "we slander the past, and learn and

---

[25] Coffey (1989) 186. [26] Kirk (1980) xi.

[27] Relihan (1993) 96. [28] Relihan (1993) 91.

[29] See Bartsch (1994) appendix 1. Reading the *Cena* as political satire might well lead us to question Relihan's claim (1993) 92 that Trimalchio's "vices are affectionately presented."

teach nothing but vices," as the poet's sardonic hint at his own perverted pedagogy). Similarly, the journey to Croton, during which the poet lectures and recites the *Bellum Civile*, is lived as a series of sketches ("why don't we make up a farce?," 117.4): Eumolpus acts as master (complete with fictional past), and the rest of the gang as slaves: in Encolpius' narrative of dressing up and make-believe, why should the speech at 118 be read as guilelessly sincere? It is by no means obvious that Petronius' characters (and narrator) are always naïve puppets rather than shrewd (self-satirizing) actors.

For Relihan, a Menippean *Satyricon* is fundamentally apolitical. For Bakhtin, however, a hostage to Stalin and a victim of exile and censorship, it is crucial that Menippean satire is a dissident genre, a foil to the classical status quo. Bakhtin understands carnival (of which the Menippea is a literary expression) as a vibrantly political symbol for dissent and revolution, a populist arena in which hierarchies can be fuddled, fears conquered and visionary hopes resuscitated. In this conception of carnival, laughter is the expression and catalyst for such renewal, and the emphasis is therefore put on a celebratory, subversive humor: us (the people, the revelers) laughing at, and in spite of, *them*.[30] Yet the motivations behind and cultural potency of Bakhtin's construction of Menippea are precisely historically situated,[31] and thus he is not concerned with reading the *Satyricon* as a political text of its own time. Although Bakhtin sees ancient Menippean satire as a pre-Christian response of high empire to a collapse of ethical norms, clash of philosophical/religious movements and subsequent fragmentation of the self,[32] his Menippean vision does not (want to) deal with a Neronian *Satyricon* likely written by Nero's *arbiter elegantiae*, at the very heart of the imperial court, with a text that is as "classic" and institutional as it is anarchic or populist,[33] or with a text that might be read as a pessimistic satire about oppression, entrapment, and decay, whose readers become anxious, jumpy courtiers waiting for the next man to react. Hence in "Forms of time and chronotype in the novel," Bakhtin uses the widow of Ephesus tale (*Satyricon* 111–12) to illustrate the triumph of laughter and life over death and military authority, yet in order to conform to this preconceived formulation, the tale has to be edited out of its context

---

[30] Bakhtin (1984) 10–11 contrasts carnivalesque parody and travesty with "the negative and formal parody of modern times," which only denies without renewing.

[31] See Holquist's introduction to Bakhtin (1981), and Eagleton (1981), summarised in Vice (1997) 150–1: Eagleton argues (144) that Bakhtin pits against the "official, formalistic and logical authoritarianism," whose unspoken name is Stalinism, "the explosive politics of the body, the erotic, the licentious and the semiotic."

[32] See Bakhtin (1984) 119.

[33] On Bakhtin's nostalgic vision of an archaic, anarchic carnival, see Edwards (2001) and Emerson (2001).

in the *Satyricon*, which might complicate our reading or burst the utopian bubble.[34] This is a text which tropes the theatricalization of public life in Neronian Rome, probably written by an erudite Neronian courtier forced to slice his own wrists at the whisper of incrimination. How carnivalesque (in Bakhtin's terms) can such a fiction be, or risk being? Would a narrative told in the first person by an unreliable narrator, a fiction which thematizes dissimulation on every level, whose every position is potentially self-satirizing, be the *only* means of composing satire under these circumstances? The *Satyricon* is only satire if you want it to be: Petronius, the distant and silent author, the discreet and savvy Arbiter, can always keep his hands clean.

Ingredients from verse satire

Many scholars have suggested that the title of Petronius' work, *Satyrica* or *Satyricon*, leads us to expect ingredients from Roman verse satire, and this may be another angle from which we might view the text as "satiric." That is, it is thought that the title puns both on satyrs and on *satura*, the Latin word for satire, meaning literally a bubble and squeak mishmash (an image which also suits this polyphonic title and text). Satyrs were in any case connected with satire: Horace is an impotent satyr in *Sermones* 2.1, where satire is spelt *satira* (v. 1), and the satyric Priapus becomes satire's semicivilized mascot in the manicured gardens of *Sermones* 1.8.[35] Although Courtney reasons that the adjective *satiricus* only came to mean both satirical in the modern sense and "pertaining to a satyr" in late antiquity, and that therefore the Roman reader "would have known" not to connect the title with *satura*, this logic seems to presume that puns, and reader imaginations, are activated only by correct etymologies.[36] Van Rooy, meanwhile, rejects the pun on *satura* on the grounds that Petronius' text lacks the moral function of Varro's Menippean satires, a potentially circular argument which, as we have seen, requires much unpacking.[37]

---

[34] For discussion of the tale in context, see Rimell (2002) ch. 8. Similarly, if the *Cena* is a Saturnalian feast, it is one which explores the extent to which carnival role-reversals and liberties may be illusory, paper thin, a licence to operate above the law (especially for the tyrant Trimalchio). The literary Saturnalia, in the *Satyricon* and Horace's *Sermones*, is a zone where freedom is contested as much as feted – not a discourse possible within Bakhtin's conception of carnival.

[35] Although there was no direct connection between satire and satyr plays, Gowers suggests (1993a) 116 that the two forms share the element of the burlesque, and that "it could have been the confusion of the two words *satura* and *satyrus* that made satire develop along mocking and in our sense satirical lines."

[36] Courtney (2001) 13–14.   [37] Van Rooy (1966) 155.

The question to which we keep returning is: how artificial, restrictive, or misleading is it to trawl the *Satyricon* for features belonging to a single genre, even (or especially) if, in the case of satire, we bear in mind that the genre itself is continually being reinvented? Our answers might partly depend on how significant a role verse satire can be seen to play, and on these terms, there is a lot to go on. Satiric landscapes, character-types and images abound in the *Satyricon*, from drinking dens, brothels, dining rooms and steam baths, street brawls and legacy hunting, literary theory and slangish banter, to misogynistic sketches of drunken, nymphomaniac women, grotesque human and gastronomic bodies spied inside and out,[38] and epic heroes dumbed down and fleshed out (like *polyaenus* Encolpius, who forgets his antidote to Circe's poison at *Satyricon* 128, or puny Giton, falling straight into Polyphemus' clutches at 98). Roman satire's ithyphallic mascot, Priapus, becomes Petronius' avenging deity, standing in for Poseidon in his epic wrath, while in the *Cena*, the *Satyricon*'s Saturnalian interlude and possibly most "satiric" passage, the guests are served Priapic cakes (*Satyricon* 60), spiteful little pastries which spurt acrid liquor into salivating mouths (thus the territorial host gets his satiric retaliation in first).

Reminiscences of tones, patterns, tactics, and quips from Roman satire are also much in evidence: for instance, at *Satyricon* 5, Agamemnon composes a poem which he suggests is inspired by Lucilian improvisation (*schedium Lucilianae humilitatis*: "a rough and ready piece of Lucilian modesty"),[39] and switches from scazons to hexameters in a move which matches Persius' shift between his prologue and first satire. Eumolpus also plays on the naturalizing *sermo* (conversation) mode of Roman satire at *Satyricon* 83, posing himself a question ("'Why are you so badly dressed then?' you ask") so that the ensuing poem at 83.10 can appear to be incorporated into the dialogue with Encolpius. Eumolpus' "here's one I prepared earlier" recitation, the *Troiae Halosis*, which is applauded with a hail of stones at *Satyricon* 90, is just the kind of epic performance slandered in Persius' and Juvenal's opening satires. Eumolpus' longest verse set-piece, the *Bellum Civile*, is written in hexameters, and could easily be construed as owing as much to satire as to (Virgilian, Ovidian, and Lucanian) epic: the poem concerns the moral decay of Rome, imagined as sewn in the grotesque bodies of its torpid, binge-eating citizens, while in the "moralizing" speech that precedes the

---

[38] On the role of grotesque bodies in Roman satire, see Braund and Gold (1998). On the metaphorics of food in Roman satire, see Gowers (1993a).

[39] Lucilius called his poetry a *schedium* (Paul. Fest. 335, 335M); cf. Apuleius, *De Deo Socratis* Pr. 1. See Sullivan (1968) 191–2 on ways in which Petronius may be alluding to or parodying Lucilian style here.

poem (118), Eumolpus echoes Horace, *Sermones* 1.4.40ff. in claiming that true poetry is not simply a matter of shaping thoughts into meter, but is the product of musical genius: yet unlike Horace, who claims (unconvincingly) to be writing harmless prose that just happens to scan, Eumolpus casts himself (whether sincerely or self-mockingly) as the talented bard heaven-sent to expose Horatian amateurs.

Much of Roman satire is concerned with, or set against, bungled, fantastical, and metaphorical feasts. We can tease out many parallel influences in Trimalchio's *Cena*, from mime and New Comedy to Plato's *Symposium*, as well as Varro's Menippean banquets, Lucian's *Convivium*, or Menippus' lost *Symposium*. Yet vestiges of Horace's *cena Nasidieni* also do much to mark the *Satyricon*'s relationship to Roman verse satire, while the sadistic host of the dinner party in Juvenal, *Satire* 5, who dines on peacock and foie gras while his client guests are fed putrefying scraps, might be also read as a tyrant in the Trimalchian mould. (In both dinners, the guests' freedom is a sham: Petronius' overstuffed guts and Juvenal's starved bellies are two sides of the same coin.)

Horace's *Sermones* 2.8, the final poem in his collection, reunites many of Horace's star satiric characters at a remake of satire's favourite metaliterary event. The satire is written in the voice of Horace's poet friend Fundanius, who reports back on the evening. He tells of the dishes served, the seating plan, the host's accompanying lectures, and describes how the ceiling collapsed on the prize main course in a dramatic "accident," whereupon Nasidienus was forced to salvage the show with inspired "improvisation." Yet the guests fled without tasting any of the newly fashioned dishes, "as if the banquet had been blighted by Canidia, whose breath is more deadly than an African snake's" (v. 95).[40] Petronius' *Cena* trumps Horace's mean, bad-breathed finale with a swollen culinary extravaganza in which the host pulls trick after trick for hours on end. Trimalchio has often been compared to the pretentious control-freak Nasidienus; Bodel suggests that we might also imagine Agamemnon playing the role of Maecenas, the cultivated guest, Encolpius and Ascyltos acting as uninvited shadows Vibidius and Servilius Balatro, and the freedman Homeros as Horace's Nomentanus. Encolpius, as narrator and participant, is a version of Fundanius, while Petronius, like Horace, is one step removed from his own satiric banquet.[41] Trimalchio's *Cena* also prompts more detailed flashbacks to *Sermones* 2.8: the calculated collapse of Nasidienus' awning, followed by an "austere" contemplation of fortune, is paralleled by *Satyricon* 47, the *coup de théâtre* in which a slave boy "falls" against Trimalchio, who pretends to be injured, and pleads for

---

[40] See Gowers (1993a) 161–79 on *Sat.* 2.8.   [41] Bodel (1999) 39.

his life: the audience await the outcome with bated breath, but Trimalchio declares the boy liberated and composes an epigram on *fortuna* to mark the occasion (echoing the beginning of Balatro's snooty speech at *Sermones* 2.8: "this is the law that governs life," v. 65). At *Satyricon* 52.4, a servant drops a cup, inspiring a mini-drama in which the audience of guests pleads for the symposiarch's leniency, whereas the trauma surrounding a smashed dish is only *imagined* by Balatro in Horace, *Sermones* 2.8.72. And at the end of Petronius' dinner, Encolpius, Ascyltos, and Giton flee, just as in Horace (*fugimus* S. 2.8.93, cf. *Satyricon* 78.8), but now they are running for their lives, having stuffed themselves to bursting point with the food Horace's guests have only sniffed (however noxious one whiff might be).[42]

Petronius' overt reference to the staged accident and recovery of Horace, *Sermones* 2.8 has the effect of spotlighting the artifice of Trimalchio's dramatics, which menace and enthrall his guests in equal measure. Yet in this politically loaded, Neronian text, such fictions of chance are replayed over and over,[43] and take on a specially provocative bite. In *Annals* 14, Tacitus hams up what he documents as Nero's packaging of sinister plots as tricks of fate, culminating in the scheme to murder his mother Agrippina by sending her out in a collapsible boat: *nihil tam capax fortuitum quam mare*, "nothing is so full of accidents as the sea," he is said to have sneered (*Annales* 14.3). When she survives, Agrippina pointedly reassures Nero that she has escaped death *eius fortuna*, "by his good luck" (*Annales* 14.6). Petronius himself is said to have staged his suicide to look accidental (*mors fortuitae similis*, *Annales* 16.19). Readers of the *Satyricon*, then, have every reason to suspect that (some? all?) "naïve" statements made by characters in the text are manipulative, convenient, or even satirizing postures, that Petronius' frivolous, loosely bound episodes may be artfully designed to give just the right *impression* of aimlessness. As Connors suggests, Petronius himself acts as Fortuna spinning out his fortuitous fictions.[44] The satiric author apes, rivals (and unmasks) the tyrant who leaves nothing to chance.

The issue of Petronius' engagement with satire is complex, therefore, not only because this fiction is an embroidered patchwork of influences, or because its first person narrator is frustratingly opaque, but also because "satire" itself has embodied so many colliding and often unexamined readings of the text. The *Satyricon* is a discomforting fiction to try to work out: it cannot be said to yield an unequivocal message, moral or otherwise, and challenges

---

[42] See Bodel (1999), Courtney (2001) 103, and Sullivan (1968) 125 for further exploration of allusions to Horace, S. 2.8 in the *Cena Trimalchionis*.

[43] For further discussion see Rimell (2002) ch. 11.   [44] Connors (1998) 82–3.

the security of precisely those literary categories it is said to juggle. The debates surrounding Petronius and/as satire have tended to strive for clarity by transforming what are fascinating questions into answers: I have tried not to do this, as it seems to me the fastest way to close down what will always be exciting and insoluble problems of reading. Clearly we can conclude that the concept of Menippean satire provides one possible frame for reading Petronius' innovations, and we have seen that elements recognizable from Roman verse satire feature throughout the text. But we might also add that Roman satire has already exploited (and tutored us in) the trickiness of first person narration, of which the *Satyricon* is a colossal, Neronian specimen. The delegation of *all* authority to the dubious adolescent Encolpius (a tactic perhaps inspired by Horace, as disengaged puppeteer in *Sermones* book 2) fuels scope for an extended experiment in Neronian doublespeak, and spikes this text with all the *potential*, at least, for a venomous satiric feast.

Further reading

To get a sense of how debate on the "Petronius and satire" question has taken shape in post-war criticism, read Sandy (1969), Sullivan (1968) 115–57, Walsh (1974), and Beck (1982), or consult overviews in Schmeling (1999) 28–32, and Connors (1998) 6–8, 10–12. On Menippean satire, and the possible definition of Petronius as Menippean, see Relihan (1993), Conte (1996) 140–70, Kirk's introduction and summary of criticism (1980) ch. 13, and Dronke (1994) ch. 1. Those interested in Bakhtin's conception of Menippea should read Bakhtin (1981, 1984), or see the convenient summaries of both books in Kirk (1980) 226–7. Vice (1997) is one of the best introductions to Bakhtin, with clear, critical explication of major elements in Bakhtinian thought, including carnival and dialogism. Branham (2001) is also recommended. Recent critical works proposing to read the *Satyricon* as a provocatively Neronian text include Connors (1998) and Rimell (2002).

II

SATIRE AS SOCIAL DISCOURSE

10

THOMAS HABINEK

Satire as aristocratic play

Roman satire describes itself as play more often than it describes itself as satire. Its playfulness consists in part of its relationship to other, ostensibly more serious, literary genres (e.g. epic, oratory, history). But in several instances Roman authors link satire with play of a non-literary sort. Thus we may regard the ancient representation of satire as play as an invitation to consider satire as a social practice as well as a literary genre. Satire, like all ancient literary genres, belongs to the history of practices as well as to the history of texts: this would be clear even without references to play. But play – its meaning, variants, and social functions – provides us with a useful means of situating satire among the practices that can be reconstructed from the largely textual remains of ancient Roman culture. Such an endeavor is valuable both as an interpretation of textual references to play (i.e. as an aspect of the so-called "literary" study of satire) and as part of the related enterprise of cultural history, which requires consideration of embodied practices, as well as of more readily accessible texts.[1]

The Roman concept of play, as expressed by the noun *ludus* and the verb *ludere*, encompasses a large and diverse array of activities, including but not limited to gladiatorial combat, dance, non-reproductive sex, children's games, the composition and performance of certain kinds of poetry, and

---

[1] For satire as *ludus* see Lucilius frs. 1039–40W (*ludus* and *sermones* of his own poetry, following the interpretation of Mariotti [1960] 17); Horace, *Sermones* 1.10.37 (of his own satires); Horace, *Epistles* 1.1.3, 1.1.10, 1.14.32 (of his earlier poetry, including satires); Persius 1.117 (of Horace); Pers. 3.20 (of himself); Cicero, *De oratore* 3.171 and 3.172 (of Lucilius). On Roman literature as practice in the narrow sense of oral performance there is a large and growing bibliography; e.g. Quinn (1982), Markus (2000), Gamel (1998). On the co-existence of reading, writing, and performance see Cavallo (1989), Wachter (1998), Wiseman (1998), Johnson (2000). On the importance of textual and bodily practices as the subject matter of historical study, Connerton (1989) is critical.

school.[2] Two characteristics construct an activity as play. First, it can be seen as preparation or substitution for an activity regarded as real, or serious. Gladiatorial combat substitutes and prepares for the contests of honor that characterize the life of the aristocrat. Dance substitutes and prepares for (at least sometimes) military activity. Children's games and school prepare for the real world of adult activity, in its various forms. Non-reproductive sex substitutes and, at least in the case of free citizens, prepares for the serious business of reproducing Roman society. Indeed, the word "play" is frequently placed in expressed or implied contrast with words referring to seriousness or reality or business.[3] At the same time, play is regularly construed by the Romans as constituting an activity of the body that entails submission to externally imposed patterns or standards of action. This aspect of play is self-evident for highly stylized activities such as gladiatorial combat, dance, and school and for activities, such as children's games, that involve acceptance of rules. But acquiescence in externally imposed patterns of action characterizes literary and sexual play as well. In the case of sexual play it is the presence of a partner that limits and facilitates specific bodily actions. In the case of literary play, the Romans regularly associate such activity either with literary challenge matches, in which the moves of one player set the pattern for the other, or with metrical and formal experimentation, that is, the acquiescence in externally imposed structures and patterns.[4] Indeed, among Roman writers, concepts of play and song are often construed as being in complementary distribution, with play, once relinquished, enabling the emergence of the authoritative voice of the true singer. Whereas contemporary references to play (casual, psychological, and cultural historical) tend to emphasize its relative freedom in contrast to the constraints of the real world, the Romans seem never to lose sight of the constrained and dependent aspects of play, even when celebrating it as an alternative to all that is serious and real. Within the realm of play, to be sure, there is license (*licentia*, from *licet*, it is permitted), i.e. forms of thought, speech, and action that are acceptable by the rules of play that might not be acceptable by the rules of the

---

[2] The discussion of *ludus* presented here is a compressed version of Habinek (2005) ch. 5. In that project I seek to revise the still influential analyses of Huizinga (1955) and Wagenvoort (1956). Basic works on the significance of *ludus* in Roman culture include Yon (1940) and Dupont (1985).

[3] E.g. Plautus, *Asinaria* 730; Cicero, *De republica* 6.4; Virgil, *Eclogues* 7.17; Seneca, *Epistulae Morales* 48.5, 111.4; Pliny, *Epistles* 5.3.5.

[4] On play and challenge matches: Catullus 50; Virgil, *Eclogues* 7.5–18; Horace, *Carmina* 2.12.17–19. On play and metrical/ formal experimentation or acquiescence in pattern: Virgil, *Ecl.* 6.28, Horace, *Epist.* 2.2.141–2; Ovid, *Amores* 3.1.27f., *Fasti* 2.6, *Ciris* 19f.; Petronius, *Satyricon* 73.5; Sil. *Pun.* 3. 349.

everyday; but *libertas*, i.e. the authoritative exercise of autonomy, belongs to reality. The license of play is a substitute and preparation for the *libertas* of the élite Roman male.

The Roman concept of play informs and structures Livy's famous (and controversial) account of the evolving history of dance, music, *satura*, and comedy at Rome (*Ab urbe condita* 7.2.1–13). While Livy's contribution to a positivist history of Roman culture has been grossly undervalued by interpreters who are determined to ascribe all real and imagined Aristotelian parallels to Livian imitation, our concern here is not to reconstruct a historical narrative or to redeem Livy's reputation, but instead to elucidate the meaning of play and the relationship between play and satire taken for granted by Livy's account.[5] Livy explains that what he is describing is the beginning (*principia*) of *ludi scaenici*, or games involving theatrical performances, which he differentiates from the older *ludi circenses*, or games involving physical competition. We notice immediately that even though the term *ludi* in the expressions *ludi scaenici* and *ludi circenses* refers to what we might regard as a political and religious institution, nonetheless it also describes activities that stand in contrast to the everyday and entail the submission of bodies to external constraints, either rules of competition as in *ludi circenses* or patterns for imitation, as in theatrical *ludi*.

According to Livy, the *ludi scaenici* were introduced in 364 BCE as part of a series of efforts to restore relations between the Romans and their gods (*pax deum*), the disruption of which had led to pestilence. What happened first is that players, or *ludiones*, were imported from Etruria. They performed without song (and so) without embodiment of the story told in song, but danced to the measures of the flute-player, and in so doing presented not unattractive movements in the Tuscan manner.[6] Livy writes in an era when pantomime dance, that is, the use of dance to communicate through gesture some well-known story, has become increasingly popular.[7] But he takes pains to make clear that this is not the kind of dance the Etruscans performed. It is not imitation of an action or a story that makes their movements *ludus*, i.e. entitles them to be called *ludiones*. Rather it is their acquiescence in the measures set by the flutist that constitutes them as players. The Roman youth in turn, according to Livy, imitated the Etruscan dancers, at the same time making jokes among themselves in rough and ready verses. While Livy does

---

[5] For Livy's alleged dependence on Aristotle the key arguments are presented by Hendrickson (1894). More useful as analyses of the passage from Livy are Morel (1970), Szilágyi (1981), Schmidt (1989), and Dupont (1993).

[6] Livy 7.2.4: *Sine carmine ullo, sine imitandorum carminum actu ludiones ex Etruria acciti, ad tibicinis modos saltantes, haud indecoros motus more Tusco dabant.*

[7] Jory (1996).

not say so explicitly, it would seem that the Roman youth have themselves become players, both as imitators of the dance movements of Etruscans and as performers of some kind of jocular challenge match (*inter se iocularia fundentes*, 7.2.5). In a further development, slave craftsmen are called upon to replace the rough and ready alternating insults of the youth (*temere/ rudem/ alternis*, 7.2.7) and instead "perform satires crammed with meters, now that the song and the movement had been aligned with the flute-player."[8] Interestingly, Livy tells us explicitly that these craftsmen received the title *histriones* because that was the Etruscan word for players (*ludiones*). Indeed, the identification of the slave-craftsmen as players would seem to be overdetermined: they dance and sing (i.e. "they were performing," *peragebant*) to the playing of the flute and they do so in a variety of meters.

As time progressed, according to Livy, Livius Andronicus substituted plotted story for the medleys, but continued, like the earlier slaves, to dance and sing simultaneously, until his voice got tired and he hit upon the innovation of having a slave do the singing while he did the dancing with increased vigor. According to Livy, this development accounts for the current performance style of comedies, which has passed from "laughter and random joking" by the collective youth (*ab risu ac soluto ioco*, 7.2.11) to specialized virtuosity (*in artem paulatim verterat*, 7.2.11), with the acting of plays left to *histriones*, and the free youth continuing their play (*genus ludorum*, 7.2.12) of competitive insults. So comedy got the plot and performance by professionals; the contest of insults continued as the play of the free youth; and *satura*, it would seem, remained available as a medley filled with measures. Whether Livy's account accurately describes how these practices evolved is less important than the fact that Livy takes for granted the co-existence of comedy and insult-contest in his own day and age, and that his understanding of *satura* does not contradict at least one of the forms familiar to him and his contemporaries, namely the metrical medley of Menippean satire. At the same time, by exemplifying various different ways that an activity can come to be understood as *ludus*, Livy in effect explains what makes Lucilian satire and its successors (Horace, Persius, Juvenal) *ludus* as well: its imitation, not of multiple meters, but of multiple situations, voices, styles, etc. – in other words, its parasitical or parodic quality. The evolved literary genre of satire is playful in its relationship to other genres and practices just as the

---

[8] Livy 7.2.6–8:

> *Vernaculis artificibus, quia ister Tusco uerbo ludio uocabatur, nomen histrionibus inditum; qui non, sicut ante, Fescennino uersu similem incompositum temere ac rudem alternis iacebant, sed impletas modis saturas descripto iam ad tibicinem cantu motuque congruenti peragebant.*

Etruscan dancers are playful in relationship to the measure of the flute-player, the Roman youth are playful in relation to each other, the slave *histriones* are playful in relation (again) to the meters of the flute-player, and Livius Andronicus is playful in relation to the stories that he is imitating through first song-and-dance and then dance alone. The *ludi scaenici* come to assume a particular, specialized form, as Livy is sorry to have to report. But that fact does not in any way invalidate the ludic character of other related activities, including *satura*.

In his survey of approaches to satire, Dustin Griffin notes that "very little has been written about the playfulness of satire."[9] Those scholars who have discussed the ludic quality of Roman satire tend to stress its relationship to the formation of élite male identity. Thus John Henderson writes of Juvenal (although the point is applicable to other satirists as well) "his texts rehearse *the* Roman activity of activities, namely oratorical sermonising, the practice of culture which constituted the civilised elite, the school where Romans learned to become Ro*men*."[10] And Kirk Freudenburg reads the history of Roman satire as "staging and agonizing over a crisis in Roman identity,"[11] one that specifically concerns the (alleged) loss of *libertas* from the glory days of the classical republic, during which Lucilius wrote, to the heyday of the empire, when, we might note, the expansion of everybody else's *libertas* was construed by élite Roman males as a reduction or loss of their own. For both Henderson and Freudenburg, the playfulness of satire would seem to consist in its self-aware substitution of satiric performance for the more "real" or "serious" activities of the élite male. Satire becomes play through its submission to the protocols of élite male speech; and its emphasis on the body, much discussed in recent scholarship, articulates its playfulness as well, since play is always either overtly or metaphorically corporeal.[12] Satire's playful rehearsal of élite identity is also manifest in its choice of setting, for it presses into the very spaces in which real maleness is expressing itself: the *conuiuium* or drinking party, the forum, the city street, the recitation hall, even the high council of the emperor.

Yet the pervasiveness of play in Roman culture poses a set of interrelated problems for satire itself and for any analysis that would focus exclusively on satire's relationship to normative masculinity. As the satirist moves about the city he inevitably encounters rivals for the authority of the élite male who are engaged in their own game of ludic substitution. These rivals must be ridiculed into silence lest they threaten the security of élite male identity

---

[9] Griffin (1994) 84.   [10] Henderson (1989) 65.   [11] Freudenburg (2001) 4.
[12] On satire and the body see for example the essays collected in *Arethusa*, vol. 31 (1998); and Gunderson, in this volume.

as well as the privileged status of the satirist as the premier player thereof. But the ridicule that the satirist directs against his, and all élite males', rivals – women, *scurrae*, philosophers, mime-dancers, foreigners, and so on – is of a peculiar sort, one that puts us in mind of the Roman youth in their relationship to the Etruscan *ludiones*. For the satirist mimes his opponents even as he ridicules them. He lets them speak and act through his text and his performance thereof. He thus re-creates what he professes to despise. Herein lies the paradox of satire as a playful construction of élite male identity. As play, satire constitutes a kind of boundary work that permits the satiric ego to establish itself in relationship to an external reality.[13] That is, it entails construction both of the satiric self and of all those who are not the satiric self. In so doing, it cannot avoid acknowledging the reality of all those outside the satiric self. For all that it seeks to disdain them, to silence them, to stain them, as one line of analysis puts it, satire ends up staging them as subjects as well. In Livy's narrative the home-born slave artificers, creators of *satura*, preserve the memory of the Etruscan dancers in their assumption of the Etruscan title *histriones*. We might regard this moment of simultaneous absorption and preservation as emblematic of satire's relationship to its targets. Even as it seeks to prepare the élite Roman male, it substitutes for his perfomance mimesis of a much more complex and diverse array of alternative selves. Indeed, satire's need, as part of its playful construction of identity, to stage alterity may help to explain another striking aspect of the history of satire: that it never succeeds. Unlike direct invective in the political sphere or legal action, which from time to time manage to silence their opponents, depriving them of their *libertas*,[14] in the Roman world and beyond, satire, as Griffin succinctly puts it, "has little power to disturb the political order."[15] Satire needs its playmates too much to destroy them.

Let us consider two examples of satire's paradoxical relationship to its targets/rivals, the first consisting of a generic type, the second of a specific, named performer. Especially in the poetry of Lucilius and Horace, the satirist frequently refers to the figure of the *scurra*, at least in part to differentiate himself from a character whose resemblance to the satirist is too close

---

[13] For this analysis of the concept of play, see Winnicott (1971).

[14] For example, at the conclusion of his invective masterpiece, the *In Pisonem*, Cicero proclaims:

> I never sought your blood; I never sought capital punishment for you. I simply wanted to see you abject, hated, despised by everybody, deprived of hope and self-reliance, looking warily at everything, fearing any little noise, anxious for your affairs, without voice, without liberty, without authority, without the appearance befitting your rank, shuddering, trembling, flattering everybody. And that's what I saw.

[15] Griffin (1994) 153.

for comfort. The *scurra*, familiar from a variety of sources and genres, is sometimes mistakenly assimilated to the comic stock-figure of the parasite. In fact, his role is somewhat different, although it may well involve sponging food and drink. As Philip Corbett has indicated, the term *scurra* at times refers to a professional entertainer, in other instances to a person whose non-professional social performance is of the same type.[16] In both instances the *scurra* is associated with the city (Corbett calls him a "Townie") and he seems to specialize in upbraiding those he perceives as falling short of community standards. His wit may earn him a place at the table of those who are better off; but his sharp tongue causes unease among his potential targets. Cicero refers to a *scurra* who is in financial straits as having "nothing left but his *libertas*" (*Pro Quinctio* 11 and 55): that is to say he is reduced to the condition that is the *sine qua non* of the élite identity constituted by satire.

The *scurra* is thus the close counterpart of the satirist, especially the convivial satirist, and so the satirist must devise strategies to differentiate himself from this rival and to protect himself from the hostility stirred up by the *scurra*. In Horace's case the repudiation of the *scurra* entails dismissing him on social grounds. Horace, unlike the *scurra*, identifies with the current élite he parodies and defends; he thus lays claim, ingenuously or not, to authentic powers of discretion. In *Sermones* 1.5, Horace introduces the *scurra* Sarmentus as a not-yet-freed *scriba*, or scribe: in essence, a lower status version of himself. Sarmentus' patrimony (*quo patre natus*, 1.5.53) cannot be identified, because his mistress (owner) is still alive (*domina extat*, 1.5.55). But the implication seems to be that, like many slaves, Sarmentus might be freed at his mistress's death. Hence the *scurra* Sarmentus is a figurative predecessor of Horace, Horace at an earlier stage of development, since Horace elsewhere presents himself as son of a freedman.[17] Moreover, Sarmentus is a *scriba* (1.5.66) as is Horace, and a runaway, at least in jest (*fugisset*, 1.5.68), somewhat as Horace was a runaway in the aftermath of Philippi. Even Sarmentus' physical appearance, the fact that he is *gracilis* and *pusillus* ("slender and boyish") anticipates Damasippus' description of Horace (*Sermones* 2.3.308–11), and may even put us in mind of Augustus'

---

[16] Corbett (1986), esp. chs. 2 and 3.

[17] Oliensis (1998a) 30 shies away from a reading that would take Sarmentus as a counterpart to Horace on the grounds that some of the associations linking the two (scribal status, small stature) "are not yet in place for those readers who meet Horace for the first time when they read *S.1*." But other characteristics (son of a freedman, concern about paternity, differentiation from a *rusticus*) are indeed familiar in book 1; and Horace's position as scribe is a matter of public record, nor would his small stature necessarily be arcane information. Indeed, a fragment of Varro preserved by Aulus Gellius (6.14.6) speaks of Lucilius' *gracilitas*, the adjective *gracilis* being applied to Sarmentus at Horace, *Serm.* 1.5.69. See Mariotti (1960) 10–12.

use of the "affectionate" diminutive in describing Horace as *purissimus penis* ("just the neatest dick") and *homuncio lepidissimus* ("adorable midget").

Anxiety about the *scurra* haunts other passages of Horace's satires. In 1.8 the *scurra* Pantolabus and wastrel Nomentanus (or is it "descendant" Nomentanus? The word *nepos* has both meanings) are buried in a common tomb with other members of the wretched plebs, a tomb inscribed with the declaration that it "is not to descend to heirs" (*heredes monumentum ne sequeretur*, 1.8.13). This end of the line for the *scurra* is a figurative disavowal on Horace's part of the performance tradition and social practice he represents, as well as an explanation of the class- or status-based motivation for that disavowal. Pantolabus, like Sarmentus, like the *scurra* attacked in Cicero's *Pro Quinctio*, is no match for the free, well-endowed friend of Maecenas. And yet he reappears, in Trebatius' legalistic analysis of Horace's verse (*Sermones* 2.1.22); and Davus of 2.7, a kind of personification of the satirist's guilty conscience, twice compares Horace unfavorably to *scurrae* (2.7.15 and 2.7.36).[18]

One might argue that the figure of the *scurra* is of special concern to Horace because of his own uncertain social status. Yet *scurrae* appear already in suggestive contexts in the poetry of Lucilius. Consider for example the following fragment, probably from a satire concerning a journey beyond Rome:

> Coelius conlusor Galloni scurra, trigonum
> cum ludet scius ludet et eludet
>
> (211–12W)
>
> Scurra Coelius, playing with Gallonius, when he plays trigonum
> plays knowingly and even outplays

Trigonum, to be sure, is a specific game, yet the quadruple repetition of *lud-/lus-* in connection with the skillful *scurra* reminds us of the other skillful player of satire, the satirist himself. Indeed, it is interesting to note that Horace depicts himself as playing *trigonum*, in a likely allusion to the Lucilian *scurra*, in the very satire in which he most forcefully seeks to differentiate himself from "the parasitic social climber."[19]

Another passage of Lucilius describes an episode in which either Cornelius Scipio upbraids (*intorquet*) a *scurra*, or a *scurra* upbraids him (255W). In any event, the speaker, probably Lucilius, describes himself as joining others in accompanying him (either Scipio or the *scurra*) home: *ibat forte domum; sequimur multi atque frequentes* (258W). On one reading, Scipio turns the

---

[18] The guilt trip continues in the epistles: see *Epist.* 1.17.19, 1.18.1–4.
[19] Oliensis (1998a) 35.

tables on the *scurra*, chastising him as we might expect a *scurra* to chastise Scipio.[20] Alternatively, the passage may simply describe the abuse to which Scipio was regularly subject – and indeed the accusations of unconventional sexual behavior recur throughout Scipio-lore. In either case – as an obnoxious castigator insulting Scipio, or an obnoxious castigator hoist by his own petard – the *scurra* is isolated from the more genial "we" that seems to include the poet. Here, as in Horace, the *scurra* and the satirist share the same space (the street) and the same social role (evaluation of élite behavior). Much as later satirists differentiate themselves from expert lecturers, particularly philosophers, while at the same time parodying their performances, Lucilius possibly and Horace surely differentiate themselves from the *scurra* while at the same time acknowledging, publicizing, indeed re-performing the power of the *scurra*.

The double game of differentiation and identification characterizes a very different sort of satire, one in which Juvenal permits the target of his abuse to speak for himself.[21] In Satire 9, Naevolus, an aging gigolo, is introduced by his unnamed interlocutor as a figure resembling Marsyas – an allusion to Socrates, perhaps,[22] but inevitably a political reference as well. The statue of Marsyas in the Roman Forum was a rallying point for the Roman plebs, a celebration (perhaps) of the end of *nexum*, or debt bondage,[23] reinterpreted by some in later generations as a symbol of élite dominance, of the victory of the aristocratic Apollo over the upstart satyr. Indeed, the episode of Marsyas in Ovid's *Metamorphoses*, with which Juvenal and his audience were no doubt familiar, was part of the process of aristocratic re-interpretation of the myth, with special emphasis now placed on Marsyas as defeated singer who joins the ranks of those who, like the Pierides or Arachne, have unwisely challenged the gods in creative endeavors.[24] As a satyr, Marsyas is also a symbol of sexual potency – appropriately enough in a satire whose main character makes his living with his *legitimus penis* (9.43–4) but of a potency

---

[20] This would seem to be the interpretation Marx has in mind in his defense of the manuscript reading of the passage. See Marx (1904–1905) 2.361.

[21] For a subtle discussion of the characterization of Naevolus, which he describes as Juvenal's "supreme creation and challenge," see Henderson (1989) 69–70 (quotation at 70). Bellandi (1974) attempts to take Naevolus seriously by de-emphasizing his sexual status and assimilating him to other Juvenalian clients, such as Umbricius of Juvenal 3. I agree that Naevolus is a *cliens*, but see no point in overlooking the fact that he is also a Roman *vir*.

[22] Henderson (1989) 65.

[23] Braund (1988) 146. Braund also emphasizes Marsyas' rusticity, a possible characteristic which does not, however, seem to be activated in Juvenal's poem.

[24] Throughout my discussion of Marsyas I am indebted to Peter Schertz, who has shared with me ideas from his dissertation in progress on visual representations of Marsyas in the Roman world. See also Wiseman (1988).

with limits, since Marsyas, in at least one version of the myth, loses his musical challenge because Apollo bribes the judge.

Now Naevolus, who is likened by the speaker to Marsyas, is frequently described in critical writings as a "homosexual," but of course he is nothing of the sort. He is, in fact, a Roman *vir*, the possessor of the phallus, and he uses it indiscriminately on women as well as men.[25] The interlocutor of Satire 9 notices that a change has come over Naevolus, that he no longer, as he used to,

plays

the home-grown knight, witty convivialist with a biting sense of humor
always ready with an urbane wisecrack

agebas

uernam equitem, conuiua ioco mordente facetus
et salibus uehemens intra pomeria natis   (Juvenal 9.9–11)

Braund, in discussing other parts of Satire 9, suggests that Naevolus resembles "the archetypal satirist," specifically because he has a secret he is afraid to expose.[26] But already here, in the poem's proem, we can see that Naevolus calls to mind not just the archetypal satirist, but also the archetypal Roman the satirist seeks to entertain, to constitute, to be. Who of the satirists – and who of their audience – does not in some sense "play the home-grown knight," that is act as though they were rich and truly Roman (when of course few were "home grown" or born into equestrian rank)? Who does not aspire to be the perfectly urbane dinner guest? Indeed, this is the satirist's ultimate claim to legitimacy, that he is neither a *scurra*, nor a scolding preacher, nor – God forbid! – a woman like Canidia or Laronia, and that through him the audience can avoid miming the same critics/constructors of masculine identity.

But now, the interlocutor notes, Naevolus has changed: as Braund observes, he looks something like a Cynic with his messy hair and emaciated physique, and indeed his long monologue consistently breaks the "unwritten rules of polite discourse."[27] The more closely we examine Naevolus, the more familiar he looks. Once he played (*agebas*) the *verna eques* or home-grown knight (notice that the term *agebas* is the technical term for dramatic

---

[25] For the meaning of *vir* see Walters (1997a).

[26] Braund (1988) 170. Freudenburg *per litteras* notes the similarity between Naevolus as *verna eques* and Juvenal's own social status.

[27] Braund (1988) 140; see also 151. It is interesting to note how often critics of satire internalize the class bias of the satiric poet. This problem also affects Corbett's otherwise superb study of the figure of the *scurra*.

mimesis, as in the slave artificers' "playing" of medleys in Livy's account); now he hopes for in capital the 20,000 sesterces a real knight earns in interest per annum.[28] Formerly a successful convivialist, he still laments the passing of the lifestyle:[29]

> dum bibimus, dum serta, unguenta, puellas
> poscimus, obrepit non intellecta senectus
>   while we drink, while we call for garlands, unguents, girls
> old age, unperceived, creeps up on us.   (Juvenal 9.128–9)

Naevolus is well educated, being able to allude to Homer, Plato, Virgil, and Ovid, although as more than one commentator notes, the elegance of the allusions contrasts with the sordidness of his own situation. He acknowledges the demand for secrecy among friends (*quodque taces*, line 26) even as he exposes Virro's secrets to the unnamed interlocutor. He is Corydon of the *Eclogues* (102) in that he laments the failure of his erotic ambitions, and yet he is not pastoral Corydon, the human analogue of Polyphemus, any more than Virro is Alexis, the darling of his master (indeed, Virro is the master of his house). Naevolus' complaint calls to mind Alcibiades' complaint against Socrates in Plato's *Symposium*;[30] yet the terms are somehow misapplied, as it is Alcibiades, if anyone, who "tots and wiggles" (*computat et ceuet*, used of Virro at line 40), not Socrates. Even Naevolus' application of sexual terminology to himself and Virro is unstable as it is clear that Virro, the receptive partner, is the one who exercises control over Naevolus: "for the very sight of a cinaedus draws a man on" (*autos gar ephelketai andra kinaidos*, 9.37, a parody of two verses in Homer's *Odyssey*).

Naevolus is, in sum, the élite male Roman in a state of flux, even disintegration – a figure of ridicule, but a serious figure as well. Juvenal's parody pushes his representation to extremes, exaggerates the moves of boastfulness, allusion, defensiveness, and not-too-ostentatious greed. But such parody, far from trivializing or banishing such practices, articulates, clarifies, and problematizes them. The character of Naevolus is prophylaxis, a display of élite male phallic sexuality taken to its absurd extreme. But the satire as a whole, in which he is subtly mocked by the interlocutor, yet given the final word, rehearses a process of differentiation and identification that seems to have constituted deeply serious play for Juvenal and his audience.

---

[28] Here I follow the interpretation of Green (1998) 180–1, who cites R. Saller (1983) *Proceedings of the Cambridge Philology Society* 29: 72–6.

[29] The parallels to earlier convivial poetry and contexts are too numerous to mention. For some examples see Courtney (1980) on these lines.

[30] Braund (1988) 146–8.

Satire's self-identification as play calls our attention to all those instances in which the satirist submits himself to externally imposed strictures, when he succumbs to the demands of external reality in an effort to craft and maintain a secure identity for himself and for those in his audience who accept the invitation to identify with him. At the same time satire's self-identification as play acknowledges the satirist's role in the creation of the reality beyond his ego. He needs his audience to believe that the world is populated with figures like Sarmentus and Laronia and Naevolus, not to mention all the characters treated with greater or lesser degrees of savagery, in order for his game of identity construction to succeed. How to define his relationship with the defining others of his play is a topic that has divided critics and readers and no doubt will continue to do so. For many, satire involves the abuse of others as compensation for the relative weakness of the self. It stains the targets of its invective.[31] It "defines the common identity of all those who are parties to it."[32] "The primal satiric act bonds the group against some reviled other."[33] It acts as a sort of "safety valve" to release or "vent" pent-up hostilities.[34]

But perhaps all of this is to take satiric play too seriously, or at least to misconstrue the seriousness of satiric play. In a study of satire not much read any longer, R. C. Elliott discusses the relationship between magic and satire. He cites a passage in D. H. Lawrence's novel *Women in Love* in which Ursula Brangwen's vituperation of Birkin, her association of him with offal, death, obscenity, and perversion, precedes and prepares for their sexual union. In Elliott's words, "the outburst acts as though it were an apotropaic spell; it drives out the hesitations, knocks flat the barriers and defenses that have stood in the way of the natural sexual union."[35] We, of course, have no way of knowing in any real sense how the satirist or his targets felt about each other. But implicit in the Roman sense of play is, as was suggested at the outset of this essay, the notion that play is both substitute and preparation for something more serious. The play of the child enables him to act like an adult. The play of a dancer develops skills of use in defending the community. The play of non-reproductive, juvenile sex prepares for the reproduction of Roman society. From observing the play itself, we cannot tell what its aim or

---

[31] Richlin (1992).   [32] Justman (1999) 7.

[33] Justman (1999) 125.   [34] Griffin (1994) 156, 158.

[35] Elliott (1960) 283. Cf. the related insights of Snyder (1991) 101, to the effect that satirists love what they deplore; their despair is formal, rhetorical, gestural. . . . In satire there are no built-in, absolute outcomes such as victory, loss, and stalemate in tragedy; no wondrous singularity of outcome as there is in comedy: and no sure teleology such as that prescribed by the novel.

outcome might be. But in calling their practice *ludus* the Roman satirists left themselves open to the possibility that it could be something constructive and humane, as well as oppressive and cruel.

Perhaps it is best to end with an image. Figure 1 is a part of a series of Etruscan visual images dating to the fifth century BCE and analyzed in relationship to early Roman cultural practices by Szilagyi.[36] This particular image depicts on the right an armed figure in a pose characteristic of a pyrrhic dancer. His dance is parodied by a larger figure on the left who wears a distinctive cap and perhaps a mask and artificial beard. This image perfectly encapsulates the complex relationship between reality and imitation, élite and professional, ridicule and respect that is at the heart of the Roman concept of play, and, we might suggest by extension, of satire as well. The smaller figure, as a pyrrhic dancer, is already participating in an activity that prepares for and rehearses the "reality" of war.[37] Like the marchers in the parade described by Dionysius of Halicarnassus, like the Salian priests, like the youth in the *lusus Troiae*, the small dancer may well be a member of the *iuventus*: the organized free-born men of military age.[38] The larger figure, if indeed he wears cap and beard and mask, has the accoutrements of professionalization, whatever his extra-ludic status. And he in turn calls attention to the artificiality, the staginess, of the pyrrhicist's performance through his own distorted imitation. His shield is held upside down and at an awkward angle; his long rod, useless as a weapon of war, is tilted rather than held straight; his arm is crooked improperly, his legs apart rather than tensely crossed. His dance is parody or play, not necessarily ridicule, but a dance alongside, a critique (both praise and blame) via indirection, a submission of his own bodily practice, however clumsily, to the pattern set by the other dancer. The pyrrhicist on his own can be said to play, to rehearse warfare, to enter the realm of *ludus*. But his play invites and is intensified by the play-alongside of the parodic dancer. This parodist, like parodists more generally, articulates the distinguishing characteristics as well as the vulnerabilities of the object of parody. Indeed, far from diminishing its object, this kind of playful imitation calls attention to and enhances its object's importance. The pyrrhic dancer is worth the wasted energy of the professional who performs alongside.

---

[36] Szilágyi (1981), endorsed by Wiseman (1988). On the prevalence of parody in early Rome and Etruria see also Cèbe (1966).

[37] Camporeale (1987), Ceccarelli (1998) 141–58.

[38] Ceccarelli (1998) 148–9. On *salii* as *iuvenes* see Dionysius of Halicarnassus, *Antiquitates Romanae* 2.70. For *lusus Troiae* see Virgil, *Aeneid* 5.545–603.

Figure 1 Etruscan vase, fifth century BCE (Badisches Landesmuseum Karlsruhe, inv. 71/37).

The image on the Karlsruhe vase cannot be said to illustrate the story from Livy with which this paper opened. If nothing else the relationship between youth and professional is the reverse of the encounter between the *ludiones* and the *iuventus* there described. But the image does testify to the antiquity – and corporeality – of the concept of play in the Roman world. That it survives on a vase strictly designated as Etruscan strengthens rather than contradicts our argument, in fact helps us understand why mimetic play, perhaps especially the play of satire, becomes central to Roman culture. In a sense, there is no Rome without an incorporated other. Rome comes to be over and against Etruscan, Greek, Sabine, and other cultures.[39] Rome is always both an agrarian community looking to an idyllic and isolated past and a city among cities, a center of trade and commerce, interconnected with Latium, Etruria, Italy, and the whole of the Mediterranean basin. In the latter context, the construction of Roman identity becomes a project not just of shoring up the frail masculine ego of an embattled élite, but also a project of continuing incorporation of the new, the threatening, the alien. Roman identity must be made secure, but it is an identity that is itself constantly evolving. As preparation and substitution for the performance of Roman-ness, play thus becomes a constant necessity. It performs throughout the ages the work of establishing psychic and social boundaries between inside and outside. Satire is the textualized trace of this widespread and essential practice, one that enacts both exclusion and assimilation, that compensates for loss and insecurity by celebrating difference, but also by seeking, however recklessly, to destroy the obstacles to love.

Further reading

Readers who wish to follow up on specific aspects of this paper would do well to pursue the leads given in the notes. In general, my approach to play has been most deeply influenced by the writings of D. W. Winnicott, especially his work *Playing and Reality* (1971). Winnicott focuses on the function of play in the emergence and maintenance of the individual ego, but his line of argument is easily extended to the analysis of cultural products and practices, as I have tried to do here. Important for understanding the relationship between texts and practices is Paul Connerton, *How Societies Remember* (1989). Connerton rightly notes the scholarly tendency to focus on texts as a path of lesser resistance. In viewing satiric play as something besides phallic aggression, I have been influenced in particular by Eric Lott's discussion of the "contradictory impulses" at work in American blackface minstrelsy, as examined in his study, *Love and Theft* (1993). Finally, I hope that remaining incoherencies in the present argument will be cleared up in my forthcoming book, *The World of Roman Song: From Ritualized Speech to Social Order*, which includes a more detailed discussion of the Roman concept of *ludus*.

[39] See, for example, the eloquent discussion of Grandazzi (1997).

II

FRITZ GRAF

Satire in a ritual context

Satire is about blame and about masks. Performance, ritual or other, is not far away. Already the (one-sided) dialogue which the persona in Roman satire develops, from Lucilius onwards, invites staging, most urgently perhaps in Persius' sophisticated satirical mimes.[1] This has called for evolutionary models long before Tylor and Frazer made evolutionism a tool of cultural analysis, and it was always performance that commanded most of the scholarly attention. When situating his satirical poetry in the tradition of free speech, Horace derived satire – however playfully – from Athenian ancient comedy, naming *Eupolis atque Cratinus Aristophanesque poetae* among his poetical ancestors.[2] The historian Livy, on the other hand, stuck to Italy and thought rather of dramas performed by indigenous actors (*vernaculi artifices*) who, following an Etruscan model, "performed satires in many varying metres, singing to the tune of a flute-player and moving in a fitting rhythm."[3] Modern evolutionists preferred more up-to-date paradigms: Robert Elliott pursued satire – understood rather broadly as blame and curse poetry – back to a Frazerian magical satirist whose power of words was enough to damage any enemy;[4] Michael Seidel followed René Girard's model of rerouted and covered-up violence as the basis of ritual action and focused on the satirist's verbal violence which the ethical concerns thinly disguised as what they were – early man's destructive emotions against fellow human beings.[5] The

---

[1] *Quis leget haec? min tu istud ais? nemo hercule, nemo!* Persius 1.2, according to the scholion taken over from Lucilius' first (book, presumably, not verse) (*de Lucili primo transtulit*), hence Lucilius, fr. 2 Krenkel (but not Marx and Warmington who followed a different manuscript tradition).

[2] *Sermones* 1.4.1, in "an absurd over-simplification," Rudd (1966) 89.

[3] Livy 7.2.6f. – see the contribution of Thomas Habinek in this volume.

[4] Elliott (1960).

[5] Seidel (1979). He refers back to Jane Ellen Harrison and Sigmund Freud; Frazer's ghost, however, looms large and had, after all, been a formative influence on both.

historian of religion and ritual cannot repress a smile (*difficile est* . . . , with just a whiff of the satirist's arrogance) when he sees how familiar paradigms made an unexpected impact in literary theory at a time when his own field was busily rejecting them. Girard's take on violence, or rather its rerouting and suppression through social institutions, seems as much anthropological fiction – "if I were a horse" anthropology, as E. E. Evans-Pritchard memorably dubbed it[6] – as Frazer's concept that magic was a wrong way of thinking about nature: both belong to an anthropology that highlights one human (intellectual/emotional) characteristic, and then constructs an early humanity which did not use it in the correct way – our way – but which also over time realized how wrong it was, and therefore developed and invented institutions to correct and better human ways. In its basic approach, this differs not very much from Cicero's theory that an eminent individual (*magnus videlicet vir et sapiens*) invented rhetoric in order to shape his fellow humans into social beings, or from any other such Greek or Roman construction.[7] The longevity of the approach demonstrates its basic attractiveness rather than its correctness.

This view also lumps together all possible uses of aggressive language in Roman society, from playful lampooning to serious cursing as the last resort against wrongdoing, as if these were exactly the same. Romans saw things differently: public (or not so public) bad words belong to an entire spectrum of social practices that the indigenous actors differentiated carefully.

Roman social practice

Cursing (dirae, imprecationes, devotiones)

Cursing, in Rome as elsewhere, excludes an individual from the social group and delivers him or her into the hands of superhuman powers: the person turns *sacer*, and thus loses any protection from the law: "To kill a *homo sacer* is lawful," as Macrobius tells us, not without some surprise at this use of *sacer*.[8] Such a "sacralization" (*sacratio*, in Macrobius' language) might result from perjury and thus was built into the oath formula,[9] from a specific crime which the authorities punished in this way ("let him be accursed,"

---

[6] Evans-Pritchard (1965).

[7] Cicero, *Inv. rhet.* 1.2; see already Lovejoy and Boas (1935).

[8] *Sat.* 3.7.5 *hominem sacrum ius fuerit occidi*; Macrobius' surprise is justified by the Digest where *sacer* is used for things and places only. For Roman cursing, see Speyer (1969) 1160–28 and Watson (1991).

[9] Lovisi (1997) 175–84.

sacer esto),[10] or from a private ritual act against an adversary. In all cases, it was a last instance when other means of defense had been exhausted, or were not available at all: curses promote justice, and they are enforced by the divinity, be it "the unsleeping eye of Justice"[11] or simply the "ire of the gods" (*deorum ira*) as the grammarians etymologize *dirae*, "curses."[12] Language was vital for the function of the curse: "to curse" is *precari*, *male precari* or *imprecari*, "to utter a (evil) prayer," or, in a more specific form, *devovere*, "to vow to those down below." The actual words could be quite spectacular – at least in the imagination of Plutarch's source on the curses which the tribune Ateius directed against his political enemy Crassus. When Crassus marched out at the head of his army against the Parthians, Ateius "uttered dire and terrible curses, calling up against them by their very names some terrible and outlandish deities." He must have felt rather bad, one assumes, when the curses worked so well as to destroy an entire army and its general in the battle of Carrhae.[13] Language was vital for the functioning of curses: "These words," Plutarch writes on Ateius' curse, "have such a power, according to Roman belief, that no one who falls a victim to them can escape." Lesser humans, using less spectacular methods, wrote their spoken *imprecationes* on a piece of lead and then hid it in a grave or any other underground place: as long as the text stayed written and thus froze the spoken word into eternal duration, the curse was efficient; it needed the destruction of the lead – the annihilation of the efficient word – to stop it from doing harm.[14]

Public shaming (flagitare, occentare, convicium facere)

Cursing is only the strongest and most extreme way of using the destructive force of language against fellow humans. The curse appeals, in the opinion of the natives, to the gods who will step in and restore the justice that the cursing human thought crushed. Or it will help him against a rival and enemy. At the same time, however, the curse either excludes an individual

[10] Twelve Tables 8.21, *patronus si clienti fraudem faxit, sacer esto* – a matter of *fides* which is social capital, not otherwise sanctioned by Roman law.

[11] Ammianus Marcellinus 29.2.19f. *inconivus Iustitiae oculus, arbiter et vindex perpetuus rerum, vigilavit attente: namque caesorum ultimae dirae perpetuum numen . . . Bellonae accenderant faces.*

[12] Festus, *Gloss. Lat. s.v. dirus* (61.1 L.); Nonius 30 M.; Isidore, *Etymologiae* 10.75.

[13] Plutarch, *Crassus* 16, 5–6. The same story, with some other details, in Velleius Paterculus 2,46,3; Cassius Dio 39, 39, 5–7; Appian, *Bellum Civile* 2.66; Florus 1.46.3, whereas Cicero, contemporary to the event, does not know it (*Div.* 1.29).

[14] See Graf (1997), esp. 167–9; see for the destruction e.g. a Greek text from Pannonia, *Tyche* 5 (1990) 13–16 (first or second century CE). For the most recent overviews (not always up to date), see Jordan (1985) 161–97 for Greek, and Solin (1968).

from his community (when a public curse turns an individual into a *homo sacer*), or it attaches a blemish to him and gives the community a matrix in which to read any misfortune that might happen to him. Crassus' defeat and death could as well be read in a different matrix from the one Ateius offered with his public action: their contemporary Cicero, who does not mention the curses of Ateius (for whatever reason), tells us that Crassus disregarded, in his eagerness to set out against the Parthians, all the opposing omens; Crassus thus was guilty of disobeying the gods' well-meant advice.[15] And when misfortune hit someone after he had taken an oath, this could be read as the result either of perjury at the very moment of oath-taking, or of a later action that broke away from what he had sworn.

Besides cursing, there is public abuse in ritual form, addressed to someone whom public shaming should reform and bring back in line. Terminology is important in order to understand the social facts. There are several Latin terms; the principal words are *flagitium*, *convicium*, and the verb *occentare*. Terminology changed over time. According to Festus, "the ancients said *occentassint* for what we now say *convicium fecerint*"; in our written record, *occentare* dies out after Plautus.[16] Another word, *flagitium*, only changed its meaning over time, as Hermann Usener showed long ago.[17] In its older attestations, *flagitium* does not mean "disgrace," as in its classical attestations, but "a public demonstration of disapproval outside one person's house," as the *OLD* defines it. This meaning is receding already in Plautus and fully disappears after him. The social institution of public remonstration outside one's house, however, lived on: one of Quintilian's (if they are indeed his) declamations starts from the situation that "a poor man used to shout abuse [*conviciari*] at night in front of a rich man's house"; this protest took a rather bad turn.[18] *Flagitium* seems to have been used especially for dealing with a reluctant debtor (hence *flagitare*, "to demand loudly"): the creditor would accost the debtor in the marketplace and demand back his money in no unclear terms, audible for everybody around – to the embarrassment of the debtor and often, one would think, with some repercussions for his credit ranking. Misuse, however, was excluded neither in this case nor in other cases. The elder Cato tells the story of someone whose wife brought a large dowry into the marriage and later came into considerably more money; this she did not formally hand over to her husband, but she gave it to him as

---

[15] See note 13.

[16] On *convicium*, see Hendrickson (1926) 114–19; on all these words, Usener (1901) 1–29; see also Kelly (1966) 21–3.

[17] Usener (1901) 1–29.

[18] Quintilian, *Declamationes* 364 *pauper ad divitis domum nocte conviciari solet*. See Shackleton Bailey (1989) 367–404.

a loan. "But after she became angry at him, she sent a slave to chase and harass [*flagitare*] the man"[19] – not in their common house presumably, but at the marketplace where everybody could hear it; it added insult to embarrassment that she did not come in person but sent a cheap slave. A funnier instance is the transposition of such a public harassment (*flagitatio*) in Catullus' iambic poetry: the poet sends his *iambi* to chase and harass (*persequamur et reflagitemus*) the courtesan who stole the poet's tablets. "Stand round her and demand them back: 'Dirty drab, give back the tablets, give back the tablets, dirty drab!'"[20] The *versiculi* act as a gang of street urchins hired by the poet to publicly shame his enemy. The final twist – "give back the tablets, chaste and honorable woman!" – makes perfect sense when imagined in a public setting: it effectively undercuts and threatens to ruin a reputation which could not have been based on chastity.

In two rare instances, the vocabulary used for such a public harassment is different. One of the laws in the Twelve Tables makes provisions for a peculiar way of forcing a reluctant witness to stand up in court: "Whoever is in need of evidence, he shall go every third day to raise a clamor in front of the house" (of the reluctant witness).[21] In another case, the same action serves to get property back: in Plautus' *Aulularia*, the cook Congrio threatens to raise hell in front of the angry old man's house: "If you don't give me back my pots, I'll raise a hullabaloo in front of your house to make you known!" In both cases, the rare Latin words (*pipulum* in Plautus,[22] *obvagulatum* in the Twelve Tables) insist more on the disagreeable noise than on any clear and discernible words: the noise was social message enough, neighborly rumor supplied more detailed information.

In all these instances, public abuse tries to right a wrong, real or imaginary. Other occasions were less clear cut than these; they nevertheless provoked abuse chanted or sung against someone, often in front of a house, sometimes at night. The early Latin term, in these cases, is *occentare*, "to sing or chant towards/against someone." Technically speaking, *occentare*, a compound of *cantare*, was "to abuse someone, when it was done loud and resoundingly, so that it could be heard from afar." Festus, who gives this definition, adds:

---

[19] Cato, or. fr. 158 Malc. (Aulus Gellius, *Noctes Atticae* 17.6.1) *principio nobis mulier magnam dotem attulit; tum magnam pecuniam recipit, quam in viri potestatem non committit, eam pecuniam viro mutuam dat; postea, ubi irata facta est, servum recepticium sectari atque flagitare uirum iubet.*

[20] Catullus 42 (the translation is John Gould's, in his Loeb edition): *circumsistite eam et reflagitate: "moecha putrida redde codicillos, redde, putida moecha, codicillos!"*

[21] Tab. 2.3, *Cui testimonium defuerit, is tertiis diebus ob portum obvagulatum ito*; Festus, *Gloss. Lat.* 262.19 L. cites the law because of *portus* in the sense of *domus*.

[22] *Aulularia* 445f. *nisi reddi mihi vasa iubes, pipulo te hic differam ante aedis.*

"It was thought to cause infamy: people assumed it must have been done with some reason:"[23] no smoke without fire, as popular wisdom has it. No wonder that already the earliest Roman laws wanted to curb it.

Occasions for such songs varied and must partly be reconstructed from troubled sources. In Plautine comedy, *occentare* means simply "to serenade," the Latin equivalent of a Greek erotic *komos*[24] – often with some some violence involved, and blatantly with the expectation of attaining the sexual goal aimed at. In the *Persa*, the prospect of nightly serenades and a burning door is a sales point when trying to sell a slave girl to a pimp, although the prospective buyer is reluctant to jump for it; the serenade thus advertises the high desirability of the girl in question.[25] The *Mercator* inverts this situation: when old Demipho tries to dissuade his son from bringing a beautiful slave girl into their house as the lady's personal attendant, he goes to some lengths to develop the negative public attention (*flagitium*) the *matrona* and her girl will get when they set out for the city: in the streets and in the market, men will "see her, watch her, signal, wink, whistle, pinch, call, be a pain; they will serenade the house, scribble my door full with erotic graffiti." What amounts to a recommendation when a woman's sole virtue is the very absence of virtue turns into defamation when the virtue of a *matrona* and her maid are publicly questioned.[26]

Even with a Greek background behind Plautus' descriptions,[27] there must have been a Roman custom of nightly singing in front of one's house, although rather more serious than the erotic serenading of Roman comedy. Indeed, Roman society viewed it as so serious that already the Twelve Tables severely sanctioned *occentare*; this cannot be the comic serenade. Cicero, excerpted by Augustine, gives all the information we possess. In the *Republic*, Scipio talks about the limits of free speech and introduces as a bad example the public defamation of outstanding citizens on the Athenian comic stage. He disapproves of the fact that in Athens poets arrogated to themselves what in Rome would be the censor's task. With some approval, he then cites

---

[23] Festus, s.v. *occentare*, 191.10 L. *occentare dicebant pro convicium facere, cum id clare et cum quodam canore fieret, ut procul exaudiri potuisset; quod turpe habetur, quia non sine causa fieri putatur.*

[24] Stressed, long ago, by Copley (1942) 96–107; but the terminology is Latin, and it has a longer prehistory than Copley was willing to accept.

[25] *Persa* 569: *at enim illi noctu occentabunt ostium, exurent fores* – just get an iron door to be safe! See also *Curculio* 145 among the possibilities of courting a courtesan.

[26] *Mercator* 405: *quia illa forma matrem familias flagitium sit sei sequatur; quando incedat per vias, contemplent, conspician omnes, nutent, nictent, sibilent, vellicent, vocent, molesti sint; occentent ostium; impleantur elegeorum meae fores carbonibus.*

[27] Fraenkel (1960) 394: "Il contenuto e i costumi qui presupposti sono schiettamente attici."

the law that punishes this with capital punishment *si quis occentavisset sive carmen condidisset quod infamiam faceret flagitiumve alteri.*[28] The law thus deals with two different forms of public shaming, *occentare*, that is "serenading" in front of a house, and the distribution of a pasquil, a political defamatory song, such as, in literary form, Catullus' epigram on Caesar (C. 81), but also several other verses against Caesar and other prominent politicians that are preserved in our record, needless to say all anonymous.[29] Both "serenading" and singing defamatory verses damaged the public standing of a prominent citizen, his *honor* and his *fides* (especially, one assumes, of a *nobilis*), and they were regarded by the law-makers as causing personal *iniuria*, "contumelious wrong."[30]

As a weapon of political warfare, both survived in some forms at least into Cicero's epoch.[31] Immediately after Cicero's return from his exile, Clodius made use of public unrest and fears about the corn supply to defame his arch-enemy again: "Did you not," asks Cicero, "instigate that gang rally at night that shouted out for grain from me?"[32] Although Cicero does not say so, such a rally would have been most effective in front of his house: being situated on the slope of the Palatine on the Via Sacra, the house must have been highly visible from the Forum. Clodius in turn made his own experiences with public shame, as Cicero is happy to report a few months after this incident. This time, Clodius went out against Pompey and made him responsible for the grain shortage; this resulted in a riot in which one could hear "all sorts of defamations and finally highly obscene verses against

[28] Augustine, *De civitate dei* 2.9, after Cicero, *De republica* 4.12, citing *Twelve Tablets* 8.1. See Bruns (1887) 27f. for all the attestations and the differentiation between *occentare* in 1b Bruns (1a Warmington), "to utter public abuse (*carmen famosum*)" and *incantare* in the direct fragment 1a Bruns (1b Warmington), "to direct a spell (*carmen malum*, what we would call magical)"; one might add *excantare* in 8.8a, "to remove (a harvest) by a spell." The debate about what Cicero and the law meant has been settled in two reviews, one by Eduard Fraenkel, *Gnomon* 1 (1925) 185–9, the other one by Arnoldo Momigliani, in his review of Laura Robinson, "Freedom of Speech in the Roman Republic," (dissertation Johns Hopkins University, 1940), *Journal of Roman Studies* 32 (1942) 120–3; for an overview of the rather complex debate see Smith (1951) 169–79, here 169. On the power of words implied here, see already Pliny, *Naturalis Historia* 28.10–17; Bäumer (1984) 84–99, and my "The Power of the Word in the Graeco-Roman World," in Beta (2004) 79–100.

[29] Suetonius, *Iulius* 80.1.3; see also the septenarii against Ventidius Bassus, Aulus Gellius, *NA* 15.4.3, and the poems against Augustus, Suetonius, *Augustus* 70.

[30] An important step in understanding this law was done by Arnaldo Momigliano (see n. 28 above); see also Lepointe (1955) 287ff.

[31] The culture of honor and shame survived much longer: in J. E. Lendon's seductive reading (1997), governing the empire would have been impossible without it.

[32] Cicero, *De domo sua* 14, *operarum illa concursatio nocturna non a te ipso instituta me frumentum flagitabat?*

Clodius and Clodia";[33] Cicero need not tell us what these verses were about. The above-mentioned pasquils against Caesar and others belong to the same world of Roman manipulation of public opinion.

The change of terminology (from *occentare* to *convicium facere*) and semantics (*flagitium*), however, is momentous and should not be overlooked: it might indicate and conceal a change of social practice. The early practice seems to have been a public shaming as a means of self-help in some specific circumstances; as most often in Roman law, the initiative for this rested with an individual. The public stage for these performances seems to have been either the marketplace (especially in the case of recalcitrant debtors), or in front of a private house (especially in the cases of reluctance to serve as a witness, or the restitution of possession); confrontation in the marketplace took place during the day, when the place was crowded. Shouting in front of the house happened at night. Quintilian seems still to remember such a distinction: when questioning the reason of the nightly *convicium*, he has his lawyer ask why the poor man had kept his quiet during the day, "why did he not abuse him in the marketplace?" And he has only one answer: because the entire serenade was a trap, and the singer was hiding his companions in the dark.[34] Quintilian implies that his *pauper* used plain (although aggressive) language; the Twelve Tablets rather suggest either an inarticulate noise (*obvagulatum*) or aggressive verses (*carmina*). Incidentally, Quintilian also assumes that the serenader was not alone but that he came with a band of helpers – as Catullus attacked with a band of *versiculi*, and Clodius sent his street gangs against Cicero.

At least some parts of this scenario look familiar to any historian. Bands of males, assembling during the night in front of a house and either making inarticulate but all the more disgusting noise or singing defamatory verses are well known from early modern Europe.[35] In late medieval France, they performed the *charivari*, in German cities, they were singing *Katzenmusik*. They were recruited from the neighborhoods, and they attacked members of the community whose bad behavior set them apart – excessive avarice, but especially sexual and marital deviations such as unsuitable marriages (old men marrying very young girls, rich widows marrying beyond their station)

---

[33] Cicero, *Epistulae ad Quintum Fratrem* 2.3.2 (February 12, 56) *omnia maledicta, versus denique obscenissimi in Clodium et Clodiam.*

[34] Quintilian, *Decl.* 364 *quare enim die tacuit? quare in foro non maledixit? Apparet enim illum noctem exspectasse quo facilius comites absconderet.*

[35] See, for a first orientation, the elegant essay by Meuli (1953) 231–41 = *Gesammelte Schriften*, ed. Thomas Gelzer (Basel 1975) 471–84 (who cites Usener's paper for early Rome, 473 n. 1) and esp. Le Goff and Schmitt (1981); an interesting case study from a period when neighborhood justice clashed with the state's intervention in Davis (1984) 42–56.

or wives beating their husbands. Roman *convicium* was thought to derive from *vicus*, the "neighborhood" (*convicium a vicis, in quibus prius habitatum est*, says Festus),[36] and if this should be a *Volksetymologie*, it would be all the more significant. Its participants sometimes seem to be a group of males, and if the Plautine use of *occentare* to designate the erotic *komos* is a guide to the participants, in Rome, too, those who acted up were the unmarried males (the destruction of house doors as the main borderline between the outside community and the inside refuge of the house appears regularly in early modern Europe).[37] They have the same basic aim, to correct unsocial behavior and misdemeanors against the community, but the details differ considerably: where the early modern reports focus especially on sexual and marital deviations, in Rome the focus is on public matters – failure to pay one's debts, keeping unlawful possessions, refusing to stand as a witness. This might reflect a difference in focus among our sources, which are scant anyway, or a difference between the social priorities of early Republican Rome and those of early modern Europe. But sexual and marital problems, at any rate, will loom large in Juvenal's satire. And as in early Europe, these means of communal justice were running against the establishment of a more centralized judicial system: the French *charivari* in the villages was suppressed once city and Church established their jurisdiction even in outlying villages, and over details of sexual behavior and marital life as well; the Roman *occentare* was prohibited by the law of the Twelve Tablets when it damaged the social existence of Rome's citizens, and it remained acceptable only in a few cases.

Versus Fescennini *and lampooning*

Charivari and *Katzenmusik* had not only their actors that often were loosely organized in young men's associations (German *Burschenschaften*, comparable to the Roman *iuvenes*); their ritual structure inscribes them among carnivalesque rituals. None of this is visible in the scant material on Roman *convicium*. The comparison of some of its manifestations to animal or baby sounds as expressed in the terminology of *pipulum facere* (connected with *pipare*, "to chirp") and *obvagulatum ire* (connected with *vagire*, "to wail," of babies and young animals) tempts one to see the vestiges of carnivalesque reversal, but it is scarcely enough to vouchsafe such a structure.

---

[36] Festus *s.v. convicium*, 36.27 L.; he also proposes a derivation from *convocare* which is favored by contemporary etymologists: *convicium* has a short "i," *vicus* a long one.

[37] See Karl Meuli (1975) vol. I, 459, 475f.

But worth considering here are the *versus Fescennini*. These improvised poems have loomed large in the pre-history of Roman satire, and their carnivalesque associations are obvious. They were blame poetry, usually tied to highly ritualized occasions. Horace talks about the *opprobria rustica* that early Latin farmers exchanged (*versibus alternis*) in their Fescennine verses when relaxing from hard work,[38] and Livy comes close to this in his first, rough, and rustic stage of Roman drama:[39] in the indigenous prehistory of satire, both the exchange of improvised blame poetry (*Fescennini*) and the highly ritualized occasion are stressed. In the late Republic, it seems, these verses had moved away from ritual: Augustus at least made use of them whenever he felt inclined to lampoon one of his contemporaries (or then Augustus did not care about ritual restrictions, as he did not in his passion for playing dice).[40] Were the victims of his barbed wit as adept in survival skills as Asinius Pollio, they refrained from an answer when the power was as unequally distributed as here.[41] Which also means that under less one-sided circumstances a counter-lampoon was what society still expected, well after the age of Horace's agricultural entertainment. Horace, incidentally, can preserve earthy language and agricultural imagery when it helps to evoke the Roman tradition: witness the exchange between Rupilius Rex and the *Graeculus* Persius in satire 1.7.[42]

In late Republican Rome, the one ritual occasion left for Fescennine verses was the wedding. Festus firmly connects the *versus Fescennini* with the wedding ritual.[43] Catullus' *Carmen nuptiale* (C. 61) confirms this, as do Claudian's verses on the marriage of the emperor Honorius to Stilicho's daughter in 398, although the late antique court ceremonial transferred them from blame poetry into imperial praise. In Catullus, witty aggression is still present, but it is directed not only at the groom but also at his minion

[38] Horace, *Epist.* 2.1.145 *Fescennina per hunc inventa licentia morem | versibus alternis opprobria rustica fudit. | libertasque recurrentes accepta per annos | lusit amabiliter.*

[39] Livy 7.2.6f.

> *vernaculis artificibus, quia ister Tusco verbo ludio vocabatur, nomen histrionibus inditum; qui non, sicut ante, Fescennino versu similem incompositum temere ac rudem alternis iacebant, sed impletas modis saturas descripto iam ad tibicinem cantu motuque congruenti peragebant.*

[40] Suetonius, *Augustus* 71.1.

[41] See Macrobius, *Sat.* 2.4.21 for the anecdote about the Fescennini of Octavian against Asinius Pollio, and his measured reaction: *At ego taceo, non est enim facile in eum scribere qui potest proscribere.*

[42] Some of it was pointed out already in Fraenkel (1957) 120f.

[43] Festus s.v. *Fescennini versus*, 76.6 L. *Fescennini versus qui canebantur in nuptiis, ex urbe Fescennina dicuntur allati, sive ideo dicti quia fascinum putabantur arcere* (an early precursor of Frazer's idea that obscenity is apotropaic).

(*concubinus*) whose time is now over. *Carmen* 61 was an actual wedding song and preserves alive what Festus handed over as a factoid.[44] The transition of the wedding ritual is a standard place for carnivalesque inversion, after groom and bride have arrived, leaving their former social position, but before the final reintegration into their new status as a married couple.

But there were other ritual occasions for public lampooning, especially the triumph and the aristocratic funeral. Triumphal jokes were antiphonal (*alternis versibus*).[45] It is unnecessary to underline that the ritual jesting took place at the same transitional moment in both rituals: both take place during the "procession" (*pompa*) that led the victorious general into the town and the body of the deceased out.[46] Both cases focus on male aristocrats; in both, the construction of the aristocratic male personality contains a normative element that measures the individual against the background of expected values and behavior, sexual,[47] familial,[48] or social.[49] The funeral even used masked actors to represent the deceased in "his bearings and the details of his individual appearance."[50] Although it is only from Vespasian's funeral that we actually hear of jokes performed by an actor, we have reason to generalize this for any aristocrat's burial.[51]

The place of satire

The scant testimonies from Republican Rome help to sketch the outlines of the society in which Lucilius invented satire as a literary genre. To really

[44] Catullus 61.119–43, see esp. Thomsen (1992).

[45] Pliny, *HN* 19.144, on Caesar's triumph.

[46] Main passage Dionysius of Halicarnassus, *Antiquitates Romanae* 7.72:

> To those who introduce the victors it is permitted to satirize and mock the most outstanding citizens together with the generals, as it is in Athens to those who participate in the wagon processions who in former times jested in rough language but today sing improvised verses. And even at the funerals of distinguished men (and especially at the funerals of the rich), I have seen, together with the rest of the procession, choruses of satyr dancers preceding the bier, dancing the sikinnis.

On the triumph, still seminal is Versnel (1970); on Roman funerary rituals, see Flower (1996), esp. 105f.

[47] See the triumphal jokes on Caesar, Suetonius, *Iulius* 49. 51.

[48] See the triumphal joke on Antonius and Lepidus, Velleius Paterculus 6.67.3.

[49] Caesar's (unusual) parsimony during the siege of Dyrrhachium, Pliny, *HN* 19.144; Vespasian's avarice in the jokes at his burial, Suetonius, *Vespasianus* 19.

[50] Diod. Sic. 31.25.2.

[51] Suetonius, *Vesp.* 19.2. Suetonius insists that this is custom (*ut est mos*), and the "satyrical dancers" (*satyrístai*) of Dionysius of Halicarnassus, *Ant. Rom.* 7.72 find their easiest explanation in this way; the passage would have to be added to the small corpus of texts that combine satyrs and satire.

cover all social practice, one would have to add formal rhetorical invective to the material analyzed above.[52] It shared with the more ritualized forms the occasion of public display, and it shared with it the main purpose, to confront a member of the Roman élite with the value system that Roman society adopted. Invective, however, was much more exclusive and served not to reinforce values but to destroy the personal credit and standing of an opponent in court or in the assembly. But it is less urgent for my purpose to discuss it here: rhetorical invective surfaces only with Cicero, and although public speaking must have been part of running the *res publica* at least from the time of the Elder Brutus, it would be rather otiose to speculate on the presence and function of invective in the early or middle Republican epochs, without a written record of public speeches.

The information we have scanned depicts a society in which public and ritualized blame was an instrument of social control and enforcement of social values. This became visible already in the Laws of the Twelve Tablets, written down, according to tradition, in the middle of the fifth century. During most of the Republican epoch, communal self-justice in the form that is known in early modern Europe as *charivari* was on the way out, driven back by a judiciary system that was slowly enlarging its grip on society, and by Romans presumably mainly of the upper classes who began to resent it when they were brought into line with overarching community values by public shaming in the Forum or in front of their ever more magnificent houses. It cannot be a coincidence that the respective vocabulary is dying out after Plautus. The slow modernization of Roman society in the fourth and third centuries (with the cities of Greece as the standard of modernity) helped to remove all-too-painful, indigenous instruments of social control. The traditional forms had a better chance of survival when they were protected by the tradition of other rituals: in the wedding ritual,[53] the triumph, and the burial rites. Here, ritual blame was more strongly formalized, often in the shape of a more or less improvised exchange of mocking verses, and it retained its carnivalesque character of social inversion, ritual suspension of hierarchies, and enhanced communal feeling (Victor Turner's *communitas*, see n. 54): it was not an instrument that was used to enforce community values in very circumscribed but blatant transgressions; it rather bridged the large social gap between an outstanding individual and his group – the triumphing general and his army, the groom and his unmarried pals, the powerful ancestor and his surviving community. Rather than rejecting these rituals, as they had

---

[52] For invective, see most conveniently Corbeill (1996).

[53] It might be worth notice that French *charivari* was transformed in the southern and mid-western states of the US into shivaree, a noisy mock serenade for newlyweds.

done with the rituals of the *charivari* type, the aristocratic élite used them to construct their own social values. The deviations from the ideal that were highlighted in these latter rituals were not used to bring an individual back into line (or, failing that, to exclude him for good from the group). They rather were the foil for the ideal from which a margin of deviation was granted to any outstanding individual.

In this respect, the *Fescennini* and their homologues in triumph and burial rites belong to what Mikhael Bakhtin called carnival laughter. This he described in terms that often came close to Victor Turner's description of *communitas*.[54] The satirist's laughter, in Bakhtin's view, is quite distinct from this: the satirist "places himself above the object of his mockery, he is opposed to it."[55] If we were to accept this distinction, the satirist would become the successor of those who used public blame as an instrument for coercing individual group members: Lucilius thus would appear shortly after the last *Katzenmusik* in mid-Republican Rome had embarrassed a Roman. This sounds neat. But maybe it is too neat, for several reasons. For one, Bakhtin's characterization of the satirist is too uniform: it might fit the earlier masks in Juvenal's satires, but it sits uneasily on Lucilius, and even more so on Horace. Furthermore, the nature of our sources for Roman *charivari* might distort the facts: what we know about this form of popular justice in early modern Europe inscribes its humor more into the carnivalesque than the satirical form. And finally, carnivalesque laughter has a wider range of possibilities than Bakhtin might be willing to concede: at least Seneca's *Apocolocyntosis*, the one text from Rome whose recitation during the Saturnalia of CE 54 makes it a carnival text, is far from being sympathetic to its object.[56]

This raises the question what role, if any, the Saturnalia, Bakhtin's favored ritual, played in all this. The Roman Saturnalia was an end-of-year festival with many traits that are characteristic of the reversal and the *communitas* so common to New Year festivals in many cultures: masters dine with their slaves or even serve them, games of chance, forbidden the year over, are now allowed. Rome's institutions come to a halt; no wars are declared, no trials are held, the senate does not meet, and free Romans shed their toga and

---

[54] Bakhtin (1968) 5–12; Turner (1969). Turner himself became later interested in spectacle and performance; see Turner (1982) and (1984) 19–41.

[55] Bakhtin (1968) 12.

[56] For *Apocolocyntosis*, Saturnalia and carnival see Versnel (1993a) 99–122; the idea that *Apocolocyntosis* was recited during the Saturnalia of CE 54 goes back to Henri Furneaux, see Eden (1984) 5.

dress informally and don a freedman's cap.[57] Rules and boundaries of regular social life are suspended for the duration of the festival. Lampooning or even satirical criticism of those higher up, however, is only marginally attested to. Poems dedicating presents given during the Saturnalia could sometimes bear lampooning inscriptions – "poems whose composition does no [sc. legal] damage," as Ovid remarks.[58] Martial preserves a collection of them in his *apophoreta* (book XIV), although only a few would qualify as satirical. Perhaps more relevantly, Horace makes his Davus use the traditional *libertas Decembri* to ask his master some uncomfortable questions (*Sermones* 2.7): it is, however, not easy to tell whether this was really a traditional freedom or whether Horace simply let it grow out of the overall structure of the festival. Any hierarchical society can develop some freedom of speech during the time hierarchy is ritually suspended without necessarily turning this into a ritualized custom. The Saturnalia, that is, never gave rise to a literary or oral genre of lampoons, unlike some European carnivalistic traditions whose *Schnitzelbänke*, highly formalized poems, still can delight an entire city and sometimes even damage a public career.[59] The *Apocolocyntosis* is the result of extraordinary circumstances, and Macrobius' *Saturnalia* belongs to another genre that makes no claims to being funny.

Thus, as in the beginning, things get blurred again towards the end. What is clear is how Roman satire is embedded in a culture in which public shaming had a long tradition as an instrument of social control. This is what we would expect in a society where honor was a central value, at least for its ruling élite, but presumably well beyond that. In this respect, Roman satire appears as the literarization of fundamental social concerns and ways of behavior. Livy and Horace were both aware of this when they tried to develop a neat and linear model of evolution. They deserve full credit for this – not for more, but neither for less. Modern followers were tempted by such a neat derivation to go well beyond where we can safely tread: it is not this ritual or that, but a general social inclination that was responsible for satire.

Further readings

Ancient and modern scholars have debated at length on the origins of satire; for some more recent accounts, see the respective chapters in Van Rooy (1966); Knoche

---

[57] See Versnel (1993a).

[58] *Tristia* 2.491f. *talia luduntur fumoso mense Decembri, quae damno nulli composuisse fuit.*

[59] See, for an example that still goes strong, Gelzer (1992) 29–61, and the excellent comparison between the ritual background of Attic Old Comedy and the carnival in Basel.

(1975); Coffey (1989). My approach, however, is different from most earlier ones, and there does not exist much scholarly work on social rituals in Rome besides what I cite in my footnotes: no one has returned to the interest which nineteenth-century German scholars, especially Hermann Usener, Albrecht Dieterich, and their more recent relative Karl Meuli, had in these matters, although the books of Lendon (1997) and Flower (1996) and, to some extent, Corbeill (1996) help to return to these topics in a broader form.

12

ALESSANDRO BARCHIESI AND ANDREA CUCCHIARELLI

Satire and the poet: the body as self-referential symbol

The satiric gaze: the physician, the body, and the mirror

Roman satirists are experts at reading the body's signs. The satirist's eye, like that of a physician or an expert in physiognomy, is keen at detecting indications of sickness or health, virtue or vice.[1] That the satirist is able to "read past" the body for the condition of the soul is an idea solidly attested already in Lucilius at fr. 678W: "we see that one who is mentally ill gives an indication of this through his body."

The principal object of the satirist's gaze is the world of contemporary social experiences: he catalogues his society's distortions, sometimes aggressively, sometimes with an ironic smile, but always respecting the body's symbolic potentials as an index of moral values and internal states. This cognitive tension, by analogy, intrudes upon language by literalizing images or metaphors and reducing abstract concepts to their real or corporeal referents, thereby extracting from them a moral significance. An illuminating example is Lucilius fr. 904–5W, where through a process of steady intensification, the satirist underscores the hard, physical aspects of flattery: "when that man sees me he fawns all over me, he pats me down lightly, scratches my head and picks out the lice."

But what happens when the satirist turns that same, deeply seeing eye towards poetry itself? When his ability to see things doubly, the soul through the body's signs, becomes metarepresentational and thus aware of its own poetic identity? That is to say, what happens when the poet describes, and thereby reflects on, himself, and his body, in satire?[2]

---

[1] See Bramble (1974) 35–8. For the body in satire, see esp. Braund and Gold (1998). For further observations on Roman "corporeal" culture, see Moreau (2002).

[2] Satire shares this "reflective" character especially with New Comedy. For comedy as a *speculum uitae* ("mirror of life") in ancient thought, see Brink (1982) 211, on Horace, *Epistles* 2.2.168.

By its own admission, satire is a "marginal" genre, to be ranked among Roman poetry's "minor" works. Reckoning his efforts more akin to prose than to poetry (*Musa pedestris*, "a walking muse") Horace leaves the impression that he arrived late on the literary scene, and that he thus chose to write satire only because all of the other, "better" genres had been taken by others (Horace, *Sermones* 1.10, esp. 46–8). But, in addition to these gestures of self-deprecation, satire allows us to label it as marginal because it does not present itself as a fixed and separate literary form. Rather, it thrives on producing analogies with other literary forms, such as with the grand texts of epic and tragedy. As if positioned alongside those texts, satire works "in the margins" like a set of scholarly notes or a commentary. From this particular position satire enjoys ample freedom of movement. It can mimic the text it stands alongside, or parody it. Or, in some cases, it can put to it direct questions of literary criticism, as Lucilius once did and, to a lesser degree, Horace. The possession of such an "external" view, detached and critical, produces among its effects a distinct urge for the satirist to define his work in poetic as well as social terms. For just as he needs to give proof of his moral integrity in criticizing the moral vices of others, the satirist must demonstrate his authority as a poet, even in those styles that he judges critically. It is as a result of this dynamic that Persius cannot commence his praise of Cornutus, a dear teacher and friend, without first distancing himself from the epic-encomiastic commonplace of the "hundred mouths" at Persius 5.1: "inspired poets have the habit of demanding one hundred voices" (*Vatibus hic mos est, centum sibi poscere uoces*). Once set apart from that commonplace, Persius can proceed to redeploy it in a varied form: "here I myself would dare ask for throats by the hundreds" (verse 26, with *fauces* replacing *uoces* in verse 1, both at the verse end, and *poscere* made more emphatic in *deposcere*). It seems that the satirist is precluded from delivering the commonplace without first establishing a critical distance from it. To use it, and thereby to avail himself of epic's elevated tone, he must first regard it with a commentator's eye, noting: "the trope is typical of epic, panegyric, and other 'inspired' forms." Conversely, if he wishes to parody epic, he need only go straight at it by showing that he has the competence to do it well.

When the satirist's external, "critical" view of poetry is conflated with a "clinical" view of the body, the full analogical experience of X (bodily sign) referring to Y (mental state), and thus also to Z (larger poetic/social values), is short-circuited, so that the satirist cannot avoid conflating his own moral nature with that of his body and his poetry. The comic principle stipulating a direct correspondence between what a poet is and what he writes is well known from as far back as Aristotle's "ethical" description of the history of Greek literature, where he argues that the most serious writers, because they involve themselves with noble persons and activities, compose noble works, such as hymns and encomia, while those who are less serious mix with worthless persons, and therefore write lampoons (*Poetics* 4.1448b24–7).[3] This principle is a tremendous resource for satiric invention. For in availing themselves of it satirists are free to run back and forth along the line that connects poetry to poet. With it they detect in the poet, and in his body, the "signs" of his poetry, and vice versa.[4] Through a process that we will call "circulation," a larger literary significance is shifted onto the various entities and parts that were thought to make up the poetic text: topic, vocabulary, and poet (*res, uerba, poeta*) according to a distinction well worn already in Horace's day.

The poet's physical appearance, like that of the philosopher, historian, or of any grand political figure in antiquity, played an important role in figuring and expressing the moral and literary character of his work. Busts of not only Menander, Homer, and Epicurus, but also of Latin poets such as Accius and Ennius, adorned the private and public spaces of the city, the villa, and the Roman house. In his *Imagines*, Varro portrayed images of famous Greeks and Romans, attaching to each image its own biographical sketch and epigram. As far as we can tell, this was the first illustrated book in Latin literature. It taught that bodily characteristics could evidence moral greatness. The face of Socrates may have played an exemplary role here, with the philosopher's satyr-like visage being taken as the visible symbol of his tireless, and often paradoxical, dialectical research.[5] Hellenistic literary learning, by availing itself of an already ancient comic tradition (via Old Comedy and iambic poetry), found a cause for scholarly diversion in this: one recalls, for example, scholarly tales told of the archaic iambic poet, Hipponax, whose physical appearance was as disgraceful as his poems were rough (and who is said to have inveighed against the sculptors Bupalus and Athenis for producing an unflattering likeness of him [Test. 7–9 Degani]). Similarly the Alexandrian writer Philitas of Cos is said to have suffered from a flesh-consuming disease that was the perfect counterpart to, and expression of, his consuming passion for philological research.[6]

There is, then, a well-defined ancient context for thinking of the satirist's body as a literary expression. Taking this into consideration puts us in a position to respond to the question we have posed: it is actually *through*

---

[3] For the actual functioning of these concepts in ancient literary theory, see Cucchiarelli (2001), esp. 9–13.

[4] One sees the comic outcome of this procedure at Horace, *S.* 2.5.40–1, where the hack poet Furius is said to be "distended with fat tripe," and to "splutter" (*conspuet*) snow onto the Alps.

[5] See Zanker (1995).   [6] See testimonies 1–16 collected in Sbardella (2000) 77–9.

his own body that the satirist finds a complete and economical means for expressing his poetic consciousness. His body, besides functioning as a social instrument, is thus an intertextual device, useful for making comparisons with other poets and texts. Already Horace shows that he is aware of this peculiar property of the poet's body when he observes how imitation can be extended past matters of style to the precise physical acts and characteristics of the poet-model in question: "but if I should happen to turn pale, they [my hack imitators] would drink cumin to drain their blood" (*Epistles* 1.19.17–18).

Lucilius: fragments of a tireless body

It is likely due to the fragmentary state of his *Satires* that we do not possess a full and detailed image of the "body" of Lucilius. Such a hypothesis suits the available evidence, since the preserved fragments, however scarce, do provide explicit assertions about the poet's regard for his bodily concerns, such as for food, sex, and other basic needs. Lucilius' eye, we have already seen, knows how to isolate "physiognomic" particulars, and to note their comic potential, for example, by making stunning associations with the world of animals: "Broncus Bovillanus, with his tooth sticking straight out, he's a regular rhinoceros" (fr. 109–10W).[7] Such references to the body are often scrutinized by Lucilius in medical terms. Diseases, physicians, and body parts are particularly prominent in a satire of book 26 (fr. 676–88W). This book is the original context of fr. 678W (quoted on p. 207 above). But it also contains another more general reference to the connection of body to mind: "first, all physicians say that a human being consists of soul and body" (fr. 676–7W). In Lucilius, the satirist's role as healer was apparently prominent enough to leave the lasting impression that his moral discourse was conceived in the manner of a medical cure. For it is this aspect of Lucilius' work that Horace seems to seize on when he defines Lucilius' moral and political discourse as a kind of caustic, but beneficial, "salt rub": "But that same man is praised on the very same page for scrubbing the city with abundant salt" (*Sermones* 1.10.3–4).[8]

The fragmentary state of Lucilius' *Satires* prevents us from asserting too much. Most importantly, we cannot be certain that fragments spoken in the first person are to be taken as "Lucilius'" voice. But our general sense is that

---

[7] The bodily aspects and habits of animals are comically applied to humans elsewhere at Lucilius, frs. 273–4, 605–6, 1079–80, 1184W. For bibliography see Classen (1996).

[8] Ancient medical literature contains numerous prescriptions for "rubbings" (*defricationes*) of various kinds, e.g. with saliva, salt, oil, etc. Salt rubs are attested also in veterinary prescriptions, e.g. Columella, *De re rustica* 6.2.7 and 6.33.1.

he often lurks in their shadow. In his poetry Lucilius started from his day-to-day experience, as Archilochus and Hipponax once did. As an imitator of their works, it is very likely that Lucilius knew how to disclose that same "realistic" view, of which so many testimonies remain, concerning himself and his own body. As, possibly, in fr. 688W: "when I had sweated my body dry in the stadium, in the gymnasium, and in the game of double ball," where the poet seems to call attention to his athletic skills.[9]

Lucilius takes his most decisive stance towards literary matters, and questions of satire, in the same book (26, likely his earliest book of satires, despite the late numbering). This book must be treated as an important locus of satiric self-representation, for the existing fragments allow us to intuit how Lucilius chose his audience, and how he expressed himself on the limits of anger and on the freedom of speech. But also under review in this book are the physiological aspects of poetic inspiration – all questions with clear relevance to a writer of satire, as Horace, *Sermones* 2.1, directly recalling this book, will later make clear.[10] But, despite the suggestiveness of these fragments, in reality we have come to know Lucilius, the expansive poet, able to write in diverse meters on questions of love, and on rhetorical and literary matters, and so much more, for a total of thirty books, chiefly through the image that Horace has left of him. For Horace, Lucilius is a kind of noble and lumbering giant of the old Republic. He is not without stylistic faults because he belongs to a past stage of Latin literary history. Yet he is incomparable in the energy and free-wheeling openness of his poetry. When Horace calls himself "inferior to Lucilius in fortune and talent," he tinges his comments with irony. But in this act of inventing the genre's *inuentor* as his richer, and elder, superior, he tells a substantial truth.[11] Certain characteristics that have come to identify Lucilius as a poet of satire, since they are by no means the compelling or necessary sum of his fragments, are perhaps best understood as points of contrast with Horace, based squarely in the story he tells.

Horace and the physiopathology of an inadequate satirist

In his *Odes* (his mature lyric poems composed in a variety of meters and traditions) Horace does not hesitate to figure himself in the role of a poet divinely inspired, and thus able to write verses that cannot be diminished by

---

[9] It is not clear that the "I" of these lines refers to the poet himself.

[10] The first "physiological" description of poetic inspiration in Roman satire is that of Ennius, *Saturae* 6–7V: "Greetings, poet Ennius, you who offer to mortals draughts of verse burning deep in the marrow."

[11] In the same way, Callimachus "invents" the Hipponax of his *Iambs*. For the invention of poetic *inuentores*, see Cucchiarelli (2001) 172–4.

the passage of time. If in his *Sermones* he comports himself in a very different, unassuming manner, this is not simply a matter of his being a younger poet, and thus naturally insecure. His *Epodes*, of roughly the same date as book 2 of his *Sermones* (ca. 30 BCE), prove that he has no difficulty addressing himself boldly to an entire community of citizens, taking the role of their spiritual guide – a surprising turnabout for a son of a freed slave (1.6.6), one that cannot be explained merely by reference to Roman political and juridical customs.[12]

The law of satire conspires with social necessity in this case, urging the poet to choose irony as his way of proceeding in satire. The author of the *Sermones* is not ensconced in the psychic trappings and enthusiasms of his other poetic worlds (especially those of his *Odes*, where he is often a civic spokesman and inspired bard). Rather, he is a citizen of Rome who measures himself against a complex web of powers and customs to achieve a difficult balance between his sense of belonging to a privileged group (he is a friend of the powerful Maecenas) and the attendant risk of self-pride (*superbia*) that brings public censure and dislike (*inuidia*). And yet, whereas epic poets can write about heroes and gods without having to declare Homer their unreachable exemplar, because epic does not require poets to account for themselves personally, the poet of satire, who is located in that reflective, "marginal" space alongside poetry, and apart from it, is naturally given to reflect on the problem of the genre's *inuentor*. Horace is generically constrained to tell us why he is not like Lucilius (fully three satires are dedicated to this question). And that series of explanations is shot through with social and political ramifications. For, as we have seen, it is not only his "talent" (*ingenium*) that separates Horace from his predecessor, but his "financial status" (*census*), and therefore this concerns his social standing and power. Intertextual engagement with Lucilius assumes that this social comparison is both evident and antagonistic.

This split perspective, at once both social and literary, conditions *Sermones* 1.4 and 1.5, the diptych that closes the first half of book 1. In *Sermones* 1.4 the comparison with Lucilius is explicit, announced in the high critical tones of a modern poet endowed with refined sensibilities: "The poets Eupolis, Cratinus, and Aristophanes . . . ," he intones. But later in the poem Horace thinks back on his own family background. In clear contrast to Lucilius'

---

[12] See Fraenkel (1957) 42–7. It is true that the poet of the *Epodes* cannot achieve his Archilochean aspirations – the collection closes with a palinode to Canidia; see Barchiesi (1994). Even in his *Odes* Horace is not a "true" Alcaeus. And again in his *Epistles* he breaks free from the expected, stereotypical perspective of a recent convert to philosophy (*Epist.* 1.1.14 "I am bound to swear by the words of no master").

descent from Old Comedy's highest nobility, Horace finishes the poem with a contrasting portrait of his father. Whereas Lucilius took his habits of free speech (*multa cum libertate notabant*, 5) from his Old Comic ancestors, the young Horace took his (*liberius/iocosius*) from his freed-slave father (103–6). Clearly social differences, as well as literary, are ironically underscored by this passage.[13]

In *Sermones* 1.5, however, the comparison with Lucilius is expressed intertextually. His predecessor is never explicitly named, but memories of Lucilius' famous *Iter Siculum* ("trip to Sicily") are encountered at every turn of Horace's parallel *Iter Brundisinum* ("trip to Brindisi"). And they are all the more prominent in coming directly after a satire dedicated to an explicit comparison with Lucilius. To underscore the comparison, Horace has chosen a theme in which a writer of satire must necessarily be seen in terms of his own experience. Like a data-gathering probe, the traveling satirist observes, registers, and selects. His satire is the result of his observation, and of his own subjectivity in relation to a specific social reality. We do not know much of Lucilius' *Iter Siculum*. But certain facts are sufficiently clear: Lucilius, a rich landowner, undertakes that long and demanding journey presumably to visit his holdings in Sicily. The journey is conducted both on land and sea, and during those long days of travel Lucilius experiences a series of different mishaps and adventures. His fragments of the poem regale us with lively descriptions and comic scenes. The impression they leave is that Lucilius, as a traveler, lived out the very qualities of freewheeling vitality that characterize his poetry – the *Iter* seems to have occupied the entire third book of the collection. Typically forceful and down to earth is fr. 102–5 W: "But everything there was fun and games. All was easy-does-it, I tell you, peachy and sweet. But when we reached Setia's border, that was tough going. Goat-clambering mountains, every one of them an Aetna, sheer as Athos."

But what most separates Horace as a traveler from Lucilius is his lack of social wherewithal. Horace does not undertake to visit his own holdings. He has no holdings to visit. With no particular goal of his own, he travels as a "companion" (*comes*) in the train of important political figures. Under the surface of Horace's poem there is the dark threat of the renewal of civil war, but what we view on the surface are the journey's incidental details. That is what Horace provides us with. He moves slowly. He plods, and "crawls" and gets stuck in the mud.[14]

---

[13] See Freudenburg (2001) 44–51.

[14] For the satirist's plodding pace in S. 1.5, see Gowers (1993b), and Cucchiarelli (2001) 15–55, 57–66.

Contrast Lucilius, a knight (*eques*) of old and illustrious lineage. He was famous for his fiery political combativeness – Horace would have us think of this at the beginning of *Sermones* 1.4. Whereas Lucilius's journey to Sicily was the expression of his private experience, letting us see another "relaxed" side of a famously political and well-connected man, Horace's journey to Brindisi represents his coming out into the public sphere and showing himself in the enviable role of one of Maecenas' closest friends. It seems, then, that in moving from Lucilius to Horace, along with a change in literary tastes, we experience a significant change in the social role of the satirist.

Horace wishes to express this difference, from one satirist to the next, as a difference in persons, employing his own body as a privileged instrument of satire. When his patron arrives in *Sermones* 1.5, at the point in the satire where, for the first time, he informs us of the "big issues" which are the cause of the journey, Horace describes himself applying ointment to his swollen eyes to soothe the symptoms of inflammation (*lippitudo*).[15] And in another moment of private relaxation with his patron, that same *lippitudo* prevents Horace from playing ball: "Maecenas goes off to play, Virgil and I to sleep. Yes, playing ball is nasty for those with bad eyes and upset stomachs" (48–9). Later in *Sermones* 2.1 the reader will learn that Lucilius, for his part, had no trouble in passing time in games and play with his friends, Scipio and Laelius (72–4), after leveling attacks against "the foremost citizens and the people, tribe by tribe" (69).

Just as Scipio and his friends relaxed with Lucilius, Maecenas was wont to unwind in the company of Horace and his other friends. But one gets the sense that the relationship of Horace to Maecenas is not on even terms. In *Sermones* 1.5 Horace is just one member of a larger "retinue" (*comitatus*), so one does not think that his absence from the group will spoil the fun. With Horace, the poet is no longer deeply in the know about grand political issues. Instead, Maecenas stands out as "patron" in order to show the literary specificity of his poet-friend, Horace. The poet's body thus becomes emblematic of his inferiority to his predecessor, a difference that only irony can defuse or, to some extent, redeem. From fr. 688W (cited above) it seems that Lucilius did not hold back from physical effort, including a good "draining" game of ball. Not only in 1.5, but also near the end of 1.6, Horace shows himself only moderately engaged in sport (125–6). The two diverse physical natures of the poets match their diverse manners of writing satire. Lucilius, Horace says (1.4.9–10), knew how to write 200 verses in an hour while standing on one foot, while he himself wrote rarely, and with painstaking attention

---

[15] *S.* 1.5.27–33. For *lippitudo* as the professional malady of poets and writers, associated also with humble crafts, see Cucchiarelli (2001), esp. 66–70.

to detail (1.4.18). Clearly in Lucilius Horace saw certain qualities of robust physical health. His nose was "wiped clean," Horace says at *Sermones* 1.4.8, referring to the sharpness of his wit (cf. Pliny, *Nat.* praef. 7 "Lucilius, who first established the nose [i.e. sharp wit] of style").[16] But in reference to his defects Horace draws images of excess and overflow (e.g. *Sermones* 1.4.11).

In *Sermones* 1.6, as in 1.5 and later in 1.9, we are treated to the world of Horace's daily routine as he moves from one place to the next, exploring and taking notes. We step into his shoes as he visits his usual haunts. But it is in *Sermones* 2.1 that the connection between the poet's own physical body and his verse fully rises to the surface. There Horace tells us that he writes because he suffers from insomnia (7). And one understands that Trebatius' prescription for him (intense physical activity and wine) is not what suits him. Later he gives us details about his *natura*, describing his origins in south Italy (34) that require him to write defensive poetry, just as a wolf must bare its teeth, and a bull must wield its horns (52–6).

Through his body Horace expresses his refusal to think big political thoughts, and to take an aggressive, and haughtily authoritarian (Lucilian), stance. Yet, in refusing aggression and censure, the *Sermones* also step away, more generally, from Lucilius' "healing" satiric regime. Already in his first satire Horace shows that he is comfortable with referring to medicine (80–3). And the body, especially in its comic, sexual aspects, plays a large role in *Sermones* 1.2, on the theme of adultery. In 1.3 the satirist's eye becomes more penetrating and attentive to scanning the bodies and minds of others for defects (especially 38–48, 73–4). And yet, he does this only on the way to refusing any too-rigid moral view. Rather, the real priority, he says, is friendship (*amicitia*), a companionable spirit that does not peer too deeply into the faults of others when these are minor in nature: "while you look at your own faults with swollen eyes daubed with ointment, why do you peer so keenly into the vices of your friends like an eagle or the snake of Epidaurus?" (1.3.25–7). The reader will soon discover, in 1.5, that the poet who writes these words is himself blear-eyed (*lippus*) and constrained to use ointment on his eyes. He himself necessarily lacks the sharp critical eye of the censor.

The inept teachers of *Sermones* book 2 subscribe wholeheartedly to various medical-dietetic regimes. This is perhaps most pronounced in the case

---

[16] For the nose as expressive of sharp wit, see *OLD s.v. nasus* 2. Clearly built into Horace's descriptions of his freed-slave father, esp. in *S.* 1.6, and of his poetical "father," Lucilius (as a means of contrast), in 1.4, are memories of the father of Bion of Borysthenes, as described at Bion fr. 1 Kindstrand: "a freed slave, one who wiped his nose clean with his sleeve." Horace names Bion as a model for *sermo* at *Epist.* 2.2.60.

of the farmer Ofellus (especially 2.2.70–88) and Damasippus, who regurgitates the hard Stoic teachings of a certain blowhard, Stertinius, on the theme "all men are fools" (especially 2.3.142–55, 288–95, with Horace responding back to him in strictly medical terms at 306–7, "just give me the complete details: what is the mental disease that you think I'm suffering from?").[17] In *Sermones* 2.4 and 2.8 medicine is prescribed in a more subtle form: Catius and Nasidienus are two gurus who teach their truths in gastronomic terms, theorizing about physiological costs and benefits as they go.[18] Here again, through alimentary references to the body, Horace delineates his own literary and moral values as a poet of satire. When the host's incessant nattering on the "causes" and "natures" of his feast incite Nasidienus' guests to flee, the *Sermones* end. This ending is, by implication, a way of commenting ironically upon some of the same, stereotypical habits of the satirist's own moral/physiological discourse.

The Stoic physician, Persius

Much of the referential play that takes place between Lucilius and Horace is lost to us and cannot be restored. But Persius' allusions to Horace are constant, and can be tracked from poem to poem. As we move through the satiric tradition and include Persius in it, we see the poet's referential work becoming more involved, and his references more intense (for the same process of intensification in later English satire, see Hooley in this volume). Persius thinks back on Horace, but also on Lucilius. And he thinks back on Horace's reflections on Lucilius (or, if you prefer, on Horace's Lucilius).

Persius' first "programmatic" satire is the best place to investigate the poet's referential practices and views.[19] Towards the end of that poem the poet turns toward satire's inventor, Lucilius, in whom he recognizes the great castigator of vice as drawn by Horace in *Sermones* 2.1: "Lucilius slashed the city [sc. with his whip]: you, Lupus, and you, Mucius. Those are the ones he cracked his tooth on" (Persius 1.114–15, recalling Horace, *Sermones* 2.1.62–70). But whereas Horace proceeded in his telling of the tale to describe Lucilius as a trusted *amicus* of Scipio, and of Scipio's friends

---

[17] This satire (2.3) can be interpreted as Damasippus' "therapy" for a lethargic Horace, who suffers from severe writer's block (1–2).

[18] For Catius' medical language, see esp. S. 2.4.21–29, 55–62.

[19] Despite the many problems that surround the disposition of his poems, published shortly after the poet's death, it is clear that Persius considered his first hexameter poem programmatic.

(*Sermones* 2.1.71–8), Persius puts Horace in the Lucilian role of a powerful man's intimate friend: "Flaccus touches on his laughing friend's every vice, and once let in he plays near the heart, an old hand at dangling the people from his nose" (Persius 1.116–18). But this is to develop an idea implied by the Horatian model itself: "whatever I am, though no match for Lucilius in fortune and talent, still Envy will have to admit that I have lived among great men all along" (*Sermones* 2.1.74–7). Slightly farther on in his first poem, Persius completes his list of literary ancestors by naming the canonical authors of Greek Old Comedy, and this again reads as a reference to Horace, who at the beginning of *Sermones* 1.4 drew a direct line of influence from Old Comedy to Lucilius (and thus to satire).[20]

In certain other respects Persius' relationship to Horace is less sanguine. His Augustan predecessor kept direct attack, in the manner of iambic poetry, out of his satiric "conversations." For Horace, satire in hexameter verse is a prose-like means of cataloguing and commenting on his social experience. Clearly, his is a softened generic scheme that excludes iambic raging in the manner of Archilochus (or Lucilius). This is not the right mode for a freed slave's son who has been admitted into the circle of Maecenas. In his *Epodes*, however, in a generic register more formalized and marked clearly as "poetry," the reader finds verbal violence in ample measure, and the strong, expressionistic tones of aggression, of death, of sex, and magic. It is precisely this "epodic" side of Horace that interests the Stoic satirist Persius. He wants to reintroduce into satire the Lucilian mode of aggression that Horace understood quite well, but had relegated to a different generic space.

This difference between the two poets can once again be expressed through the poet's body, thus reconfirming the body as an instrument of literary self-awareness. This is a lesson that Persius learned in minute detail from Horace.[21] For example, in his *Epodes* Horace describes a wild fig tree (*caprificus*) in connection with one of the witch-hag Canidia's magical rites. There the weedy "cursed" tree is noted for its ability to crack apart tombs with its roots (*Epodes* 5.17). It is precisely this tomb-cracking quality of the wild fig that Persius uses to symbolize the poetaster's "bursting" bodily urge to compose bad poetry. The fool interjects: "but what was the point of my studying so hard if this yeasty stuff, and this wild fig, once it has

---

[20] The importance of Greek Old Comedy is by no means limited to the explicit theorizing of *S.* 1.4. See Cucchiarelli (2001), esp. 21–55, 199–203.

[21] For corporeal imagery in Persius, fundamental studies are Reckford (1962), Bramble (1974), Bellandi (1996).

started to grow inside, should not break its way out of my liver into the open?" (Persius 1.24–5).[22] By reference to an organ of the body, the liver, specifically figured as epodic/Horatian (esp. via *Epodes* 5.37–40), Persius degrades the Lucilian idea of the satirist's unchecked spontaneity: "when I myself bring forth a verse straight from my heart" (Lucilius, fr. 670–1W).[23] In a procedure typical of Persius, in which multiple satiric voices intersect to produce a layered effect, confusing to the reader, yet, at the same time, demanding the reader's attention, the idea of poetry as a physical impulse is assigned to a hack poet who proudly vaunts that he has a wild fig "bursting" from his liver. His putting the tradition to this mistaken use is a satirically effective means for describing a kind of poetic inspiration that is, in Persius' day, itself unattainable and irrevocably compromised.

At times Persius assimilates his body to that of his predecessor, inheriting from him the specific marks that Horace had used to typify his inadequacy. If one characteristic that identifies Horace as an inadequate satirist is, as we have seen, a pair of sore and bleary eyes that he must constantly daub with salve, Persius claims to have learned to smear oil on his eyes as a schoolboy in order to avoid performing from memory the last "great words" of Cato in the throes of death (Persius 3.44–7). One is left to assume that he was precociously afflicted by *lippitudo* which, he says, he could feign as needed. But we know that this is exactly how Horace reacted to the arrival of Maecenas and Cocceius on the way to Brindisi (see above), and it is how he escaped having to play a game of ball.[24] In the case of both poets, *lippitudo* functions as a kind of poetic *recusatio*, and as a handy means of recusing the poet from certain big expectations.

Lucilius' idea of the satirist as a physician is given its most thorough and literal application by Persius, who resorts to dietary and curative imagery more often than any other satirist.[25] Often this finds him

---

[22] Already in v. 12 Persius speaks of satirizing as a physiological necessity: "my spleen is unruly, so I break out in laughter;" cf. 3.8–9, 4.6, 5.144. Perhaps following the satirist's own physiological clues, the biographers of Persius blame his premature death on a digestive ailment (*uitio stomachi, Vita Persi* 1.50) that perfectly suits an angry writer of satire (Latin *stomachosus* = "irritable").

[23] For Horace the "outer heart" (*praecordia*) was the seat of venomous iambic rage: "what is this venom that rages in my chest [*in praecordiis*]?" (*Epod.* 3.5); cf. Persius 1.116 (cited above) describing Horace's seasoned skills at "playing near the heart" (*circum praecordia*).

[24] In the biographical tradition, where biographical information accumulates with time and is therefore open to contamination, similarities between Persius and Horace extend to other details, often quite minute. For example, the sluggishness that characterizes Persius' rate of composition (*Vita Persi* 1.41, *scriptitauit et raro et tarde*) recalls the description of Horace in *S.* 2.3.1 (*sic raro scribis*).

[25] For specific occurrences, see Migliorini (1990).

literalizing and intensifying certain metaphorical notions ironically suggested by Horace. But for Persius, the body, and certain gross physical qualities, are not things ironically toyed with. They are obsessed over and scrutinized with a demanding, analytical eye that searches out ulcers that hide under an attractive surface (Persius 4.43–5).[26] One can easily see how Persius turns a physician's eye on poetry itself by exploiting the physiological connection between the poet and his verse.[27] Again this takes us to his first satire. There Persius uncovers the remote origins of his "diagnostic" procedure in Greek Old Comedy, by re-adapting that scene of Aristophanes' *Thesmophoriazusai* where the playwright Agathon's effeminate verses effect the sexual arousal of his listeners. To conclude his performance Agathon tells his audience: "it is necessary that what one writes should resemble what one is" (167, see above, n. 3). Agathon's counterpart in Persius 1, all primped and speaking softly, brings his audience of Roman citizens to a high state of sexual arousal (Persius 1.15–21). But for Persius the body of his "victim" (or "patient"), which this satire picks out for special study, functions as symbol and symptom of a much larger moral condition. The act of chiding physical defects, though funny in a superficial way, is never an end in itself for Persius. It has no programmatic relevance, as he himself says at the conclusion of his first satire, where he writes off for failing to appreciate his work the person who is quick to make fun of somebody's Greek shoes, or the one who can say "hey, one-eye" to a one-eyed man (127–8).[28]

Juvenal. Or, how the satirist's body finally faded from view

After Persius, with Juvenal, we come upon a significant break in Rome's satiric tradition. It is as if the last of Rome's verse satirists wished to step aside from his role as epigone and respecter of a continuous tradition. Regarding Horace's light and ironic "conversations" Juvenal has nothing specific to say – a silence that sometimes seems hostile (Juvenal uses language rather harsh against Horace the "parasite" of Maecenas). It is clear that Juvenal

---

[26] Similarly Persius at 1.9–10 describes himself as "visually" inspired in his urge to write satire. His urge to laugh aloud first came "when I turned my gaze [*aspexi*] toward our old-timers and their hard and frugal ways."

[27] Already in his choliambic prologue Persius describes poetic inspiration by means of bodily figures, through images of lips washed, bellies fed, etc. Likewise, the figurative language of Persius 5.5–6 is strictly alimentary. In using the topos of the hundred mouths the inspired poet is said to "ingest huge chunks of song."

[28] Persius' revision of satire turns the satirist's critical focus from public, "superficial" matters to internal matters of the soul; see Freudenburg (2001) 188.

conceives of satire as a "high" literary enterprise, a form sustained at the level of rhetorical invective or declamation (see Victoria Rimell and Catherine Connors in this volume). He regards Lucilius, his favored model, as a kind of epic charioteer who races at a reckless pace across the plains of his native Suessa Aurunca (*Satires* 1.19–21). It will come as no surprise, then, that his satires often come into much closer contact with Horace's *Epodes* than they do with his *Sermones*. But in withdrawing from satire's more recent traditional register, Juvenal also avoids providing autobiographical specifics about his life and his physical condition. The two phenomena go hand in hand.

If Juvenal eliminates from his *Satires* all detailed references to his body and to his personal biography, this relegation is actually an effect of his embracing the impersonal, "objective" voice that he knew from the epic tradition. It is as if the satirist's personal details, so important to all satirists who preceded him, are no longer of interest to this satirist or to his readers. Rather, what counts for Juvenal is the gusto of high invective and of moral sermonizing, a tone of speech that actually becomes much softer in his later satires. In the opening attack of his first satire we hear the poet's ranting as a voice out of the blue, all on its own, without any helpful lead in or further specification: "am I always to be just a listener!?" (1.1). And it is this reactionary stance that defines the poet for who he is. For he tells us that his best means for reacting against the bad, long-winded, and meaningless poems to which he has been subjected for so much of his life is to write satire. This explanation reads like a paradoxical reprise of Horace, *Sermones* 1.10.40–9, where Horace described how he came to "choose" to write satire by determining that all the other genres had already been taken (both poets provide fairly extensive lists of the possibilities that they have ruled out). Only Juvenal takes a different tack, by depersonalizing the genre, and figuring it as a kind of "epic" rant. His satiric voice is thus completely absorbed by the generic practices that he sets out to emulate. And like Persius, but in a much different way, Juvenal too seems to want to reintroduce into satire a mode of criticism that Horace had relegated to his *Epodes*: by claiming to be fired by "indignation/resentment" (*indignatio*) he taps into the force that energized the iambic poet at Horace, *Epodes* 4.10.

There seems to be one instance in his first satire where Juvenal treats us to a biographical detail. But the reference is more generic than specific. He says at 1.25: "when I was a young man, my beard rasped heavily under the barber's razor." That is it. What we learn from this is that Juvenal, upon reaching manhood, went to the barber for his first shave, like so many other of his fellow Roman citizens. But the verse perhaps concedes something rather more satiric than epic, in a pun upon the poet's name (*iuueni mihi* = *Iuuenali mihi*).[29]

Here in Juvenal, the poet's bodily expression (in this case, the pronounced absence of his bodily self) collaborates with his choice of satiric register. For Juvenal, satire's "rediscovered" register is in the depersonalizing ambit of epic, or in a tragic mode that tends towards generalization. And it is precisely this complete break with the satirist's traditional openness in providing us with specific details (rather than generic references to the life of any old indignant Roman citizen) that informs those rare and teasing references that he gives us to the life that he presumably led. As if to toy with our expectations, he says at 11.56–9:

> today, Persicus, you will find out whether I've been leading you on with pretty words in reference to my life, my habits, and my wealth; whether, while praising pea soup, I'm secretly a glutton; whether in front of the crowd I call for porridge, while whispering "cakes" in the waiter's ear.[30]

From his own unique perspective, Juvenal makes full use of the fundamental tools of satiric language. Physical specimens, bodily functions, and diseases he often subjects to his satirist's expert medical eye.[31] And the concept of the body as an instrument for reading the mind he makes explicit at 9.18–20, recalling similar sentiments in Lucilius and Persius: "in a sick body you can detect the soul's hidden pains, and its pleasures. The face takes both expressions from there." Thus even the epic satirist feels the need to reaffirm one of satire's most basic and powerful assumptions. In Satire 7 Juvenal focuses on the topic of poetry and poets in order to re-engage with the topic of his first satire. And like that poem's precursors in Persius' *Choliambs* and Persius 1, and Horace's *Sermones* 2.1, Juvenal's seventh poem is another "first" satire because it introduces book 3. Here again the poet's bodily aspects are drawn in detail, with the poet's vocation described as a matter of "chewing on bay [leaves]" (*laurumque momordit*, 19), an alimentary

---

[29] Another possible teasing reference to the poet's biography is *Sat.* 3.319, where Umbricius' casual reference to "your Aquinum" has been taken by many commentators to imply that Juvenal was born there.

[30] Cf. *Sat.* 4.106: "more shameless than a sodomite writing satire."

[31] For example, at *Sat.* 3.232–6, 13.124–5, 208–16. The notion of wrath as a corporeal necessity is developed in full by Juvenal: "my dry liver blazes with anger" (1.45), "blazing with seething guts" (13.14–15), and so on. His satire's alimentary associations are best known from the two outlandish feasts of satires 4 and 5 of book 1. *Sat.* 15 draws connections between anger, the specific motivating force of the poet's early works, and cannibalism. For useful observations on Juvenal's physiological language, see Weilen (1996).

variation on Persius *Chol.* 1 "I never rinsed my lips in the nag's spring." He then draws a picture of his ideal poet who is far detached from reality and utterly free from quotidian worries: "but the outstanding poet, a man of no common mettle . . . this poet, though he is the sort I cannot point to, but can only intuit, he is the product of a mind free from worry" (7.53–7). This freedom from everyday concerns, he says, renders the poet's mind "just the right sort to drink from the Muses' spring" (58–9). But in studying the bodily conditions of poets, Juvenal sarcastically congratulates the skinflint patron for choosing to keep a pet lion instead of a poet: "for of course everyone knows that beasts are cheaper to feed, and that it takes more to fill a poet's guts" (77–8). Again at vv. 96–7 the poet's digestive apparatus is a product of satiric invention, as are the stereotypical "bodily" means he uses to attain a state of high inspiration: "then [sc. in the days of great patrons long past] rewards were equal to talent. In those days plenty of poets found that it paid to turn pale and abstain from wine for the whole month of December."

Even in this satire, a poem especially attentive to the physical states of poets, Juvenal does not offer his own body as a specimen of study. Instead, he has us consider the genre's previously open-handed habits of bodily self-expression in the exemplary image of a satirist who told us much about himself, in all of his works, and who fully exploited the literary significance of his own body: "Horace is punch-drunk [*satur*] when he says 'hooray!'" (62) – where the idea of satiric fullness/inebriation contrasts ironically with the shout of bacchic/lyric drunkenness and high poetic inspiration (*euhoe*!). Here, one last time, we observe not only the impersonal distance that the epic satirist Juvenal maintains, but we also have an instance of his employing that "clinical eye-view" that typifies the satirist's way of looking at the world since the time of Lucilius.[32]

It is through their bodies, each possessing its own peculiar set of strengths and inadequacies, that the poets of Roman satire configure their satiric principles. Through these bodily expressions, each satirist establishes his relation to his predecessors. And with them, each satirist provides a means for the genre's further configuration.

Further reading

On the corporeal figuring of satiric poetry in Rome, the pioneering study of Bramble (1974) remains fundamental. To this Labate (1992) provides insights that are both

---

[32] This does not imply that Juvenal may not occasionally make indirect references to his own body. It is likely that he does this in *Sat.* 11 where, in the process of inviting a friend to dinner, the poet describes his own *uictus simplex*; cf. esp. 56–9 (cited above). In verse 203 he tells of having "wrinkled skin," a detail that may well have been true since he was quite old when he wrote the poem.

valuable and complementary. For the redeployment of the literary-critical "body language" of comedy and iambic poetry in satire, see Cucchiarelli (2001). Zanker (1995) addresses the physical-iconographic portrayal of intellectuals in antiquity. On the biographies of ancient poets, still a reliable guide, with full bibliographical documentation, is M. Lefkowitz, *The Lives of the Greek Poets* (London 1981). For Latin authors a good starting point is J. Farrell, *Greek Lives and Roman Careers in the Classical Vita Tradition*, in P. Cheney and F. A. de Armas, eds. *European Literary Careers: the Author from Antiquity to the Renaissance* (Toronto 2002) 24–46. Required tools for the study of literary criticism in antiquity are D. A. Russell and M. Winterbottom, eds. *Ancient Literary Criticism: the Principal Texts in New Translations* (Oxford 1972) (a source-book) and D. A. Russell, *Criticism in Antiquity* (London 1981).

13

ERIK GUNDERSON

The libidinal rhetoric of satire

What makes for a good companion? What makes for a good companion to satire? The present volume offers a variety of versions of companionship, of course. I expect to be a sort of short-term companion, a companion met briefly and fortuitously, a companion who whispers a dirty little secret in your ear and then walks off leaving you to decide what to do with this information. The image is not, of course, casually chosen, for I am here to talk about the production, reproduction, and public dissemination in and by satire of a dangerous dirty little Roman secret. Better still, there is a crisis: bad sex has gone public. Satire upbraids. But I want to talk about the desire to talk about desire, and the perverted pleasures of reproaching perverts.

I plan to neglect the question of the persona of the narrator of the satire. There are a variety of accounts of this character. But I do hope that an investigation of the structure of the satirical narrative of desire will be complete in and of itself. And I hope as well that readers will themselves take these conclusions and apply them to the broader question of the "masks of satire."[1] I am not after a biography such as Highet (1954). Nor do I even offer a reading that aims for the man behind the mask as frequently found in Winkler (1983). Furthermore, I am not even looking to decide whether or not the satirist "is serious" or if he "means what he says" even though an essay like Gold (1994) makes it clear that it is hard to claim that Juvenal offers a mere parody of moralism that self-destructs amidst its own vitriol.[2] Instead, this is a reading for a key satirical proposition about the relationship between the putting into discourse of the body as a locus of libido and the psychic life of this satirical libido.

---

[1] See also Rimell's piece in this volume: Juvenal's various masks shift in appearance when seen from the variety of imposed perspective.

[2] Henderson (1989) is emphatic: satire participates profoundly and inevitably in the discourse of gender at Rome. Even as Juvenal's poetry ironically flags itself as declamation, it cannot avoid offering up a Self, and there are consequences for any who would listen even to an evacuated persona: (1989) 65–6.

The libidinal rhetoric of satire, then, will be twofold. First there is satiric retelling of libidinal histories that satire claims are others' stories. We might consider this the manifest rhetoric of the text. Next there is the libidinal economy governing the drive to talk about perverted drives. Let us think of this as the latent rhetoric of satire, the system of implicit metaphors and metonymies that subtends the explicit tropology of the poetry.

In order to find our way to the sordid underbelly of the desire to talk of sordid underbellies, I will pursue the following course. First, I offer a brief review of the state of the question. Next I take a look at the rhetorical staging of a few perverted bodies. Then I pose a follow-up question to satire: "What does a pervert know?" This leads us to the further question of the pleasure of repudiation. And the last stop on our journey will be a few musings on the proposition that every witticism has its psychic community and some speculation on the true costs of real estate in the said community.[3]

Versions of the present essay have already been written more than once. The focus, though, has been more on the bodily rhetoric of satire. And here one finds the bodily grotesque from satire sensibly catalogued and redisplayed for our edification. The emphasis, I would say, is more on the "what" than on the "why."[4] These are, of course, important and necessary studies: it is essential to figure out the structural logic of the obscene body from satire.[5] Specifically, it is vital to note that the grotesque body is not exuberant and fertile, as might be the case in the ludic Saturnalian play of Bakhtinian carnival, but instead this body is sterile and fruitless.[6] These bad bodies misbehaving are furthermore counterpoised to an everywhere implicit yet strikingly never

---

[3] Johnson (1996) has one of the most psychoanalytic accounts of satire. It is, though, a bit of a tease: Freud and Jung are there in a more generic than specific sense, as named figures and not cited authors. Lacan enters by way of allusions to a recurring but also unnamed Althusser.

[4] Walters (1998) has offered some of the most explicit arguments of "why" satire likes these bodies, but I read them more as provocative invitations to further analysis than as fully elaborated theses. My own arguments will frequently converge with his conclusions, but I hope to have offered a clearer analysis of the modality of satiric inverted pleasures. And observations like Winkler (1983) 213 as to "a Freudian inferiority complex that leads the male to fear and hatred of the female" are interesting enough, but a bit too ready-made for present purposes.

[5] Gold (1998) 369 observes that Juvenal is especially interested in "focalizing bodies." Moreover she investigates the way in which gender is mobilized as a "fictive construction that supports various regimes of power" ([1998] 370) along the lines spelled out by Judith Butler. Her methodology is here closely related to my own. Gold, though, ends more in the mode of reaffirming the notion of a reified "gender code" (Gold [1998] 380–3) than reading for the "psychic life of power." Such a shift, then, puts Gold closer to the objectivist reifications of sociology and anthropology than it does to the Foucauldian and psychoanalytic dimensions of Butler's performativity.

[6] See Miller (1998).

present idealized male figure: the hegemonic male, the good man, the sexual penetrator who is not himself penetrated.[7] In Bakhtinian terms – and Bakhtin has played an axial role in the shaping of this question within classical scholarship – there is a distinctive monologism within satire seemingly thwarting the true dialogic imagination. It would appear that the coordinating figure of this ideal man and ideal body remains too central to the project to allow for the radicalization of the many voices of satire.[8] Instead they remain duly subordinate to the man who has always been on top and is so once again.[9]

Accordingly one notes that satire provides a valorization of the normative by way of its appeals to implicit "community standards" and concomitant valorization of certain "protocols" of masculinity.[10] While acknowledging the importance within ancient thought of the "unpenetrated penetrator" model of masculine sexual behavior, I would caution that this is a "model of reality" being strategically propagated within antiquity, and that, accordingly, it is important to steer clear of accepting the "reality of the model" by hypostatizing it and "understanding" ancient sexuality by way of the structural oppositions offered by some of our native informants. Such objectifications of the social field are always also themselves players in the same field.[11] Rather than finding in satire a Saturnalia of playful inversions we discover instead an indictment of such play and a lamentation that the holiday revelry has turned into year-round fare at the expense of all that is good and proper.

---

[7] For example, see Braund and James (1998) on the "ideology" of Claudius as grotesque.

[8] Reckford (1998) offers a portrait of the poet Persius' frail body as at the base of a certain split self within his poetry. And the poetry becomes a way of putting together an ideal body that was never there. Though perhaps a bit too attached to biography, Reckford's notion of the ideal as a specifically literary production provides a valuable insight. Johnson (1996) notes that it is actually hard to find ideal men in satire and that their absence is a vital structural feature of the satiric project. Gold (1998) 271 makes the same observation.

[9] Habinek's essay in this volume emphasizes the aristocratic genealogy of satire and hence helps to explain the gravitational pull exerted by this more conservative tendency within satire.

[10] See Walters (1998) 361 and 362. The question of protocols of masculine sexual behavior has been much elaborated by Walters himself (1997a, 1997b) and especially by the strongly structuralist reading of Parker (1997). Both are heavily indebted to the pioneering work of Amy Richlin on Roman sexuality and to studies like Richlin (1992) and Richlin (1993). The most sustained version of this line of thinking is provided by Williams (1998). See also Braund (1996b) 168–72, which directly applies these lines of thought to Juvenal's second satire.

[11] See, then, Bourdieu (1990) 23–51 and especially 37. Indeed, we are presently interested in the stakes of such satirical propositions about the reality of certain satirical sexual models. See also my remarks at the opening of the fifth chapter of Gunderson (2003).

If immoralists are a problem in the narrative universe of satire, then immoralist moralizers deserve special reproach. Juvenal's second satire attacks seeming old-school philosophers who turn out to have a most scandalous *philosophie dans le boudoir*. If you cannot trust a man's face (*frontis nulla fides*, 2.8) you can at least trust the irrefutable truth of his hemorrhoid-wracked anus (2.12–13). His doctor is laughing while he applies the knife. In a humorous genre we are presumably invited to see here a focalizer, a guide to our own mirth. Dr. Satire is on the case, he finds that while the face and public anatomy may lie, the private parts speak volumes. Indeed, they are made to speak the volumes of his own poetry. That is, the narrator narrates the true tale that has gone unspoken, that would go unspoken without him. You cannot trust men talking of morals, you can only trust immoral bodies that speak against them. Only the speech of the proctologist can be trusted. Whole, with a chaste eye, he looks upon the bodily truth and offers his diagnosis.

But this perverted proposition speaks against the second satire and its own talk of morals. This satire itself requires the immoral body as the *fons et origo* of its own speech. And one wonders about the back side of this text, about the inverted pleasures of decrying perversion. The specious moralist is, we are told, a stern fellow. But he also speaks rarely (*rarus sermo*, 2.14), indeed, he has a "lust for silence" (*libido tacendi*, 2.14). And here we have a clear rift between the philosophy of the speaker and the sensualist philosophers he decries. There is nothing rare or rarefied about the narrator's speech. And his pleasure lies precisely in telling the tale of the anus. He is, then, a most lewd ventriloquist, but we are not supposed to leave him liable for his lust for talking of lust. The false moralists loved not talking about sex while simultaneously having a good time, but the narrator loves to recount while apparently refusing the doing itself. Accordingly the narrator resembles – but at a key distance – none so much as the very effeminates he lambasts at 2.110, men whose language is unchaste (*hic nullus verbis pudor*). And so, too, does the narrator revel in his license to speak (*libertas loquendi*, 2.111–12), differing only from the deviant inasmuch as he does not do so with a "broken voice" (*fracta voce*). Here brokenness is equivalent to womanishness. And there is an obvious implicit proposition: the hale and whole is the (properly) manly. Somehow the jagged rhetoric of satire hopes to put Humpty Dumpty back together again. Salvation lies in voluble repudiation.

We are asked to trust only the bodily eloquence of the pervert and the derived eloquence upon the theme of bodily perversion offered by the narrator. Vile bodies speak against their owners, they perform the truth of their own histories even as the sensualist speaks out in the name of propriety. The narrator takes no particular pleasure in talking about Peribomius, the man who confesses his sensualism: their madness excuses such cases (2.18–19). But when the speech of a man clashes with his true desires, the tone of the narrator grows harsh: he hates the man who shakes his ass while talking about the virtue of Hercules. Indeed, he turns to him and asks the indignant question, "Am I to stand in awe of you as you wriggle, Sextus?" (*ego te ceuentem, Sexte, uerebor?* 2.21). We find two words for posterior pleasures in a single line, *clunem* and *ceuentem*. We see in this satire an anal dialogue. The "true speech" of the depraved body is the ideal interlocutor for the philosophy of satire. And much like the most passive of the Socratic interlocutors, the body here can either only assent to the force of the satirical arguments made against it or else provide the satirist with yet more grist for his mill.

This version of rhetoric of the body as it encounters the satirical persona is then pseudo-dialogic. Smutty volumes are legible on the body's surface, and the narrator reads them to us. The body from satire presents corporeality as betraying the truths of the bearer inexorably, provided one knows how to decipher the flesh. The proposition necessary to the satirical rhetoric itself, then, is the authenticity of bodily rhetoric. The foundation for satire's own arguments about decorum accordingly rests on a bodily bedrock. You can believe satire because the body does not lie. And yet how can one be confident in a building erected upon the quicksand of fleshy depravity? For it is precisely the proposition that bodies are betraying their owners that allows for the staging of the satirical persona as the non-fooled voice of authority. Authority launches its attacks and takes up its reactionary defense from the vantage afforded by this position seized from within the enemy's own camp. And yet the viability of such a position requires the permanence of the rival as thing-to-be-overcome.[12] The rival body is a tombstone (*sōma*) upon which to inscribe the living word of outrage. The rival body is likewise a signifier (*sēma*) become a signified within the truth-regime staged by the satiric voice.

The narrator requires us to accept the (rhetorical) proposition that "bodily style is the man."[13] It is this rhetorical sleight of hand that allows the narrator to posit himself as in contact with a lost version of Rome where men are good and so are their bodies. The recovery of the ideal is also simultaneously the grounding of the position from which that norm is sought out. The finding of the position of the narrator is also the refinding of it.[14] *Avant moi, le déluge.*

---

[12] See Habinek's essay in this volume.

[13] Compare, then, Seneca, *Epistulae Morales* 114.1, where the subject of style is introduced by a proverb that "Men's lives were as their oratory" (*talis hominibus fuit oratio qualis vita*).

[14] This formulation is meant to evoke Freud (1962) 88 where all object relations are the rediscovery of the primary object relation. But see Lacan (1994) 53 for the important consequences of the idea that what is refound is never just what was lost. The image of the object

Implicit, then, in the coherence of the narrator's own rhetorical position is the soundness of his own bodily and sexual economies. Apparently, if we were to read his desire, the coherence of the narrator's position would not be betrayed. His longing is only for that lost whole.

Vile, castrated bodies are the prerequisite for the satirical nostalgia for wholeness. Thus when the narrator of the first satire offers his programmatic "it's hard not to write satire" (*difficile est saturam non scribere*, 1.30), we should note that the first of the long list of things that imposes upon him his genre is the marriage of a eunuch (1.22).[15] There is an important echo of this monstrous and barren union in Gracchus' male–male marriage of the second satire (2.117–21). The impossibility of children from such a union does not, though, keep the satirist from comparing the prodigy of the event itself to a woman giving birth to a calf or to a cow delivering a lamb (2.123). And one should recall as well the portrait of the aborted fetus of Julia that recalls her uncle in appearance (2.33). Only depravity seems to have any fecundity in these texts. Better yet, only depravity and the fertile possibilities for its denunciation seem to bear any fruits.

The narrator of the first satire, though, is further provoked to writing satire by the woman who fights with bare breast as an Amazonian gladiator. And here, too, there is an important parallel in the second satire: Gracchus the fallen aristocrat fights as a net-gladiator baring the naked shame of his debased status for the pleasure of all (2.143). The putative bodily soundness and integrity of the good man, the *vir bonus*, has been lost, and thus the genres that properly present and represent those men are now themselves hard to write. Instead the narrator implies that there is a new sort of writing that comes in the wake of a new sort of body. Thus even as the first satire opens with the literary complaint that it is time for the poet himself to speak forth after hearing so much garbage, his response cannot be to simply write the good epic that Cordus did not write, or to offer good elegies or good historical dramas in Roman dress (*fabulae togatae*). Instead, if he writes an epic, it is a saga of the un-founding of Rome; if an elegy, it is a plaintive love-song for a long-lost body that kept itself clean; if a play in Roman dress, it is the tale of the sullying of the toga that dramatizes past luminaries of vice.

The bulk of the second satire excoriates effeminate men. The transition to the major theme is effected by one Laronia who gets tired of hearing

---

as mediated by the meaning of the object within the universe of meaning can never add up to primary enjoyment. Instead the object is always already structured by its relationship to loss and privation.

[15] Women loving eunuchs reappears in 6.366 as well.

about the sad state of marriage and shoots back that no matter how bad women are, it is men who sleep with men that constitute the real problem. The narrator brackets her reproach by depicting her as providing an obvious and true song (*vera ac manifesta canentem*, 2.64). Given that the word for singing has strong resonances with specifically poetic song, we see in her an ironic double of the narrator himself.[16] Indeed, the narrator challenges us to find anything amiss: "Did Laronia say anything untrue?" (*quid enim falsi Laronia*, 2.65). And then he launches into his catalogue of perversions. The closing sentiment reveals the depravity at the core of Rome and of the Roman core: the manly men we conquered come to Rome and learn effeminacy. Defeat at the hands of the Romans entails a scandalous sexual Romanization as well. "Behold the fruits of commerce" (*aspice quid faciant commercia*, 2.166).[17]

Did the narrator say anything untrue? Of course not: a poem, especially a satiric one, cannot be caught out in falsity. And yet we need to reflect on the conditions of veracity that have been constructed within the satiric discourse. From where does the voice of reasonable outrage emerge? And whither would it invite us to travel if we were to join it in refusing the bodily perverse? If the rectum has been posited as a grave, then surely we are invited to enjoy light and life through satire?

And yet let us consider the stance of Satire 6, the invective against women. A man is about to wed. The narrator advises against it. A eunuch takes a wife: disgusting, see Satire 1. A man takes a man-bride: disgusting again, see Satire 2. And here in the sixth satire a seemingly sensible man decides to take a wife: madness. There is little or no space left for desire. The traffic in bodies, in coupling, and in pleasure keeps on producing visions of catastrophe. After the poem's pre-history wherein Chastity and Justice flee the earth in tandem, the life of man as "we" know it has seen constant outrages against propriety.[18] Why marry when you could hang yourself (6.30)? Why marry when you could pitch yourself out of a top-floor window (6.31)? Why marry when there is nearby a nice bridge from which to jump (6.32)? The drive to marry is, then, nothing but a disavowed death drive. Why go for the substitute when you could have the real thing? The vagina, too, then, is a species of grave.[19]

---

[16] See Freudenburg (2001) 252–3 on Laronia and the narrator.

[17] See also Habinek (1997) for a careful evaluation of the sexual politics of this scene.

[18] See again Johnson (1996). Johnson argues that the satire traces out a failure of men in their manliness. Men are no longer manly enough. Women are made to foot the bill by way of the "dreamwork" of the text.

[19] Compare Gold (1998) 375 on the sterility of female genitals in Juvenal.

If death is not your cup of tea, an alternative is presented: how about a little lad (*pusio*, 6.34)? The advantages are, apparently, numerous. He will sleep with you. He will not argue all night. This seems benign enough: we are offered some peace. But the next two points refine the issue. The boy will not demand that you "do him a little favor" (*munuscula*, 6.36). Context and precedents make it clear what the favor is: the boy will not initiate sex. Sex is at your discretion. Better still, when you do want to have sex and decide to go at it, if you do not give it your all (*lateri parcas*) and if you do not quite huff and puff as much as he might ask you (*nec quantum iussit anheles*), you will not get any complaints from the boy (6.36–7).

These are telling revelations, and ones that ought to shape any reading of the whole. The advantage that the boy uniquely provides is his docility. Specifically the boy lacks autonomy as a desiring subject. The boy is thus not just a *pusio*, but so also a *puer* where the latter word is not only from the same stem as *pusio*, but it occupies two semantic fields as it means both boy and slave. A boy submits. He does not complain. Male sexuality is happy only where it is a sort of lordship. "Give me mastery or give me death," says the narrator. Either one is a sovereign – and this ultimately implies as well self-control – or one falls into the grave of desire where passivity reigns and all conceptions are maculate.[20]

Women are apparently out because they do not recognize virile lordship, because they will not spare a man if a man spares himself in the sack.[21] With them the play is all work, and still they cheat. Note, then, in the passage where the narrator imagines a good woman filled with every virtue, the famous Cornelia, he ranks her second to the common whore if she is going to be too proud (6.164–9). Perfect sexual submission trumps perfect virtue if the woman is determined to remind the man that he is not all he is cracked up to be.

And here we find the critical conundrum of the satirical rhetoric of libido. The narrator insists that we worry about the other's desire. We are somehow caught up in an unhappy meditation upon what the other wants. Satirical desire watches the desire of others. Satire desires that this desire be a

---

[20] For the stakes, compare Derrida (1986). Is the narrator Hegel? Is he Genet? Is he unwriting sensualism? Is he unwriting the philosophy of phallic presence?

[21] Compare the wife-as-tyrant passage running from 6.200–42. Contrast sparing one's sexual effort with a boy (*lateri parcas*) with the version of "sparing" in the declaration, "You'll find no woman who spares the one who loves her" (*nullam invenies quae parcat amanti*, 6.208). See also the image of a (tyrannical) Sicilian palace at 6.484. And another monster who hits closer to home for a figure like our narrator is the woman who knows her books better than her husband, and shows him that his literary culture is also not all it pretends to be (6.434–56).

species of perfect submission, a recognition of sovereignty.[22] The moral valuation of the other's desire is a function of the other's relationship to the subject: does the woman or the boy recognize the man as self-mastering master?

And yet in this passage reproaches are flying. What these others want is not "us." On the one hand they get their pleasures elsewhere, and on the other hand, it seems entirely likely that we do not have what it takes to satisfy them in any case. "Our" outrage at "them" is specifically grounded in their failure to desire us as good men, in their failure to recognize our goodness and to react accordingly.

So let us consider for a while the mechanism of perverted desires. And next let us consider the paranoid logic via which perversion is staged in satire. The pervert challenges the moralist by proposing that he knows where to find *jouissance*.[23] The obscure object of desire is seen with complete clarity by the deviant. The pervert first takes satisfaction as the object of his drive, and next refuses to admit that the normative means to the end of satisfaction interest him in the least.[24] Indeed, he is happy to refute the Socratic notion that nobody does bad willingly by suggesting that the voice of conscience is not itself to be trusted. For the pervert the voice of conscience offered by the superego is nothing but the harsh barking of a vicious tyrant. This tyrant is likewise sadistically invested in his conception of morality: the law as prohibition is nothing other than a blind and punishing imperative.[25] Perversion insists, though, that true happiness is already to hand: one need not get off by taking the detour of enjoying refusal.[26]

And so we arrive at the following rhetorical proposition in the discourse on libido from satire: "What would it mean to let oneself get fucked?" In the specifically sexual image there are other related questions: would giving up my role as active penetrator allow me more pleasures, new pleasures, true success? And, lastly, would it bring me into closer relations with the principle of hegemony itself? Here, then, is my own obscene suggestion. First and familiarly, satire decries passive men, castrated men, and women as one and all "perverts," as happy in their surrender, as delighting in the unlivable condition of passivity. And a host of sins follow in the wake: they

[22] This is the porno version of Hegel's celebrated take on lordship and bondage. See Hegel (1977) 111–19 and the review of the later theoretical elaboration of Hegel in Butler (1999).

[23] See Miller (1996a) and (1996b), and the resumption of the same basic thread in Žižek (1999) 247–73. It should be noted that Žižek is a key participant in the discussion headed by Miller (1996a).

[24] See Miller (1996b) 313.   [25] See Miller (1996a) 225–6 and Miller (1996b) 318–19.

[26] See Butler (1997) 181–2 for how one can view the melancholy of normativity as constructed by way of a set of constitutive refusals.

elaborate; they play baroque fugues upon their sleazy theme. Next, though, the satirist is himself a pervert. His pleasure consists precisely in decrying the pleasures of others. Pleasing the tyranny of the sadistic superego means making it offerings of outrage. Angry at the immediate pleasures of others, he makes a gift of anger itself to propriety. And this is a pleasurable act.

The satirical voice of these poems emerges from a space where all women are sex maniacs and where the world is in a shambles. But this same voice itself makes a bid for recognition by the authority everyone else outrages. The satirist wants the absolute Other to smile in approbation. Individuals may not recognize the desirableness of the good man who refuses pleasure, but the sublime should. Even as the satirist says "The sovereign principle of masculinity is dead," he says as well "Long live the King." Satire also offers an invitation to forge an entire community taking pleasure in the refusal of pleasure. Satire proposes that homoerotic bonds of sublime literary pleasure felt between (male) author and (male) reader could serve as legitimate and legitimating substitutes for concretely sexual pleasures.[27] They both enjoy their cake precisely for having not eaten it. And they enjoy as well smirking at the folly of those who ate their cake and thus no longer have it.

The cultured world of the literary élite is specifically the sublimated realm of legitimate pleasure. It is pleasure in and as sublimation. This holds good for much of Latin literature.[28] The scandal of satire, however, is specifically its reinvestment in the scandalous. Compare the sublime artistry of Virgil, for example, as an aesthetic from which carnal lust has been largely written out. Think of the "overcoming Dido" problem, a problem that is not, of course, simply resolved. And we likewise "enjoy" (aesthetically) the complex non-resolution. Conversely, satire reinvests in the body in such a manner that it cannot reach the sublime without passing through the ridicule of the body. Even as the body is presented as a dead weight, as the weight of the death of potency itself, the body nevertheless can never be jettisoned. The moral community of outrage needs the outrageous body in order to sow the seed of its own satisfaction.

Literary culture here acts the part of a rival lover, jealous that the body should so powerfully attract the attention of good and sensible Romans. Indeed, culture is outraged that the body should have the power to please them at all. "What does the body have that I don't have?" "The body is such a slut: surely you are not interested in *that*?" And so forth. Meanwhile, the

---

[27] Walters (1998) 365 similarly dismantles the illusion of satirical chastity.
[28] See, for example, Gunderson (2000) 187–222 on Ciceronian dialogue. Gunderson (1997) makes similar observations about Catullus and Pliny.

proper seems unable to stage a version of good pleasure except by way of these fantasies of impropriety.

"Voyeurism involves trying to see a woman as devoted to the jouissance of her own body and making her realize that, even when she is alone, she is being watched by another."[29] There is something naughty about peeking. The naughtiness consists in proposing that the eye of the peeper is a substitute for the absolute eye of the Other, a substitute for the eye of the unmoved mover of all meaning and for the eye to which meaning itself is referred. The pleasure consists in adopting a position, in miming a function, that of the absolute gaze. The look of the satirical eye mimics this gaze and therewith pretends that the world and its meaning is its to survey and to judge.

And yet the satirical eye is forever and only looking in on perversion. Satire stages for itself a peep-show consisting of representations (*Darstellungen*) of travesties of the very absolute authority whose position satire seeks to represent politically (*vertreten*). Hence satire postulates a "politics of representation" that usefully elides the slide between the optical and political registers. The object of visual/literary representation loses its political standing in the same gesture as the narrator who constructed that representation becomes the legitimate political stand-in displacing and replacing the illegitimate libidinal subject. Moreover, as it peeps with revulsion from the locus of the authoritative gaze, satire simultaneously makes a present of itself to that same position of authority: it stages for the gaze of authority an ostentatious show of itself watching with horror. It is vital, then, that satire be "caught looking": this *Selbstdarstellung* is itself a bid at becoming a *Vertreter*, and the author becomes the author of his own authorization in being seen by authority adopting an authoritative position.

My staging of the satirical staging is complex and involuted. And yet this very complexity is itself usefully confusing when deployed by the satirical narrator. Furthermore, this critical re-evaluation of narrative poses allows us to recognize that the proposition that the other is vile and castrated is a trick of optics that does double duty as a rhetorical trope.[30] The look of the satirical eye, then, even as it decries perversion is necessarily itself thoroughly perverted: it cannot possibly see what is "really" there, for it is only by seeing libidinal monstrosities that it can satisfy via repudiation its own desire for recognition. In such a manner the viewpoint and the vanishing point of satirical representation converge. And thus my own punch-line is little

[29] Miller (1996b) 318.

[30] Compare Silverman (1996) 172: "The male look at the female genitals is emblematic of that exteriorizing displacement through which the male subject repeatedly situates his lack at the site of the female body, and naturalizes it as essentially [i.e. anatomically] 'other.'"

different from that of Lyotard's reading of Duchamp as cited by Silverman: "*Con celui qui voit*. He who sees is a cunt."[31] That is, the libidinal rhetoric of satire only "works" if that which must not be true is simultaneously also true. Objects are vile, but the satirical eye has to make an object of itself seeing in order to get off on the pleasure of being recognized *qua* seer.

A return to the text will help to support some of these indecent propositions of mine. Let us take another peek at satire looking in at the ladies. We will find that the optics of the female look are staged in such a manner as to emphasize inversion and passivity. Juvenal's sixth satire time and again watches women watching. They look, and they lust. The two verbs coincide. And yet not only is it true here that *con celui qui voit*, but so too is the thing seen decidedly not the phallus. What the women orgasmically delight in seeing are passive men and men pretending to be women. Thus the repressed male homoerotic phantasy of the satires themselves becomes a portrait of the super-sexy passive male, of a man being desired by a woman and yet mis-desired by her as well. And so, too, does the male homoerotic phantasy also become a portrait of female homoeroticism.

We take a trip to the shows. Forget that they were staged by hegemonic males, by Roman magistrates, and for an audience of "the people" who will have been mostly men. Instead note that both spectacle and spectator are immoral and embody the subversion of the very order that made possible the show in the first place. The soft Bathyllus dances the part of Leda: Tuccia wets herself; Apula moans;[32] Thymele pays close attention: the country-girl is learning city ways (6.64–6). An effeminate man plays at being a woman. The women get hot and bothered. Bathyllus, though, is specifically playing a woman who gets raped by the king of the gods, Jupiter. "What would it be like to get fucked by the king of the gods?" The myth itself encodes a split vision reproduced both on the stage and by the satire: the god is also a beast, the highest is also the lowest, the sublime is ridiculous – Jove, hung like a swan. Still, the satire insists that if you ask Bathyllus and the ladies, then they would answer unambiguously that this is all hot, hot, hot. And then all of their alleged passion is converted into a corresponding dose of moral revulsion, of satirical outrage, of, that is, rhetorically displaced libido.

Bathyllus is but the first of a string of examples of actors playing women whom the women desire. The list ends with an indignant question: "Did you think that they'd love Quintilian?" (*an expectas ut Quintilianus ametur?*

---

[31] Also at Silverman (1996) 172.

[32] The verb is *gannit*. The primary association is with the sounds made by dogs. The dictionary encourages "snarl" or "whimper" as translations. But there is a great deal of space between those two. Let us be satisfied with a sound of raw animality, of, for example, a bitch in heat.

6.75). Instead of the man who teaches manly comportment and offers instructions on how legitimately to offer legitimate speech in the public space, the women want the man who plays the woman. The spectacle of authority fails to provoke their desire, instead they desire passivity. Does not, though, the narrator expect *us* to love Quintilian and his manly men?[33] But perhaps the only way we can enjoy the sensual aspect of our love for Quintilian is by way of hating the lust for actors. And as should be abundantly clear by now, Juvenal's "we" can only mean "us men."[34] Conversely, the female reader is everywhere represented as the misreader. The space for the reception for this lusty material is itself pre-mapped according to satire's own programmatic libidinal topography. Reappropriations of satire are thus sentenced in advance to a struggle against accusations of being so many depraved, female/effeminate perversions.

If the masculine mystique consists of the aura of authority, of the disavowed sexiness of power itself, then our next woman has made a terrible mistake. Eppia leaves her senator husband to follow a gladiator to Egypt and other points foul (6.82–113). She swaps the sexiness of station for the sexiness of the performer. She sees on the gladiator's scarred and ugly face the marks of beauty. She has mis-libidinized power. The set of metonymous relations that should eroticize legitimate male hegemony for her becomes instead a set of substitutions whereby the explicit spectacle of male violence displaces the showy grandeur of a noble house and an important husband. Eppia's folly, then, lies precisely in her inability to know how to look at a man and to desire him. And yet the person to whom such a logic of desire matters most is the hegemonic male. For it is his burning question that Eppia mis-answers, not her own: she is happy enough. No, it is the man who needs to know how to look at a senator and to feel reverence for him. It is the man who needs to keep from getting hot and bothered by the dancer and the gladiator. The man needs to refuse to identify with the abject performer and with the desire such performers elicit. Instead he needs to imagine himself as the chaste spectator of proper manliness as well as to imagine himself as the noble object of the spectacle of aristocracy.[35] He needs, then, to sustain his own theory of optics by arguing for the thesis *Phallus celui qui voit.*

---

[33] The woman's only use for Quintilian is the Quintilian of (specious) declamatory rhetoric. This Quintilian supplies her with a declamatory "spin" (*color*) when she is caught *in flagrante* with a slave (6.280).

[34] For a detailed account, see Henderson (1989).

[35] And so the woman who trains as a gladiator offers a variation on the same phantasmatic theme where active and passive swap (6.251.64). And she specifically subverts masculine logic by "not wanting to become a man" (*vir nollet fieri*, 6.254) even though "she loves violence" (*vires amat*, 6.253). The narrator asks that we accept as a "legitimate" pun

Perhaps, then, we are finally in a position to step away from Juvenal and to consider instead Persius and one of the most obstinate images in the satiric corpus, the orgasming eye (*patranti ocello*), an *oeil* whose *histoire* has resisted easy retelling.[36] Persius' programmatic first satire begins with an account of literary production and consumption. Like Juvenal's first poem, so too is Persius' version of literature swiftly sexualized. Set against the narrator who writes for "Nobody" or maybe two Almost-Nobodies (1.2–3) and who has a dirty little secret about asses' ears that he refuses to whisper in anyone's ear (1.8 and 1.121),[37] we find a world of seedy public performance. Can one write poetry in this world without being implicated in the scandal? Can an author perform the refusal of such writing without nevertheless being caught in the sticky mess of libido? Is even the performance of revulsion itself implicitly revolting?

While the refusal of carnality is clear enough, the events antecedent to the sensual crime are not themselves obviously scandalous. Instead, it is the very sharing of literature as a performance by men and for men that suddenly comes to seem sicker than anything Bathyllus ever danced for a Tuccia. In short, Persius is much more manifestly worried about the libidinal implications of literature in general and hence of satire's potential guilt by association. Lines 13–21 depict literary composition, performance, and reception. First, "We write closed off" (*scribimus inclusi*, 1.13). Even if we readers ultimately conclude that this passage as a whole is a critique of others, before we know it as such, it begins with "us." This we, whom we hope will turn out not to be me, unexpectedly shifts to "you" in line 17: "From your lofty chair you will offer a reading . . ." How? Like "a fairy with an ejaculating eye" (*patranti fractus ocello*, 1.18). The womanish, broken voice from Juvenal is here a broken man, a man broken by his obscene eye. This little eye comes as a punch-line: it is put off to the end of its line, an unexpected subject and object of Persius' rhetorical climax.

We write. You read. They watch. Or, rather, you read your verse aloud, and once you read "then you would see" (*tunc . . . videas*, 1.19). You would see, that is, with your perverse eye Tituses being penetrated down into their loins by your poetry (*carmina lumbum intrant*, 1.20). They are tickled by your tremulous verse (*tremulo scalpuntur ubi intima versu*, 1.21). The position of *versu* at the end of the verse about versification parallels the position of

---

vir = *vires*, man = violence, and to see this woman as having parodically mistaken the sense of this strategic slippage by having taken to gladiatorial training.

[36] Freudenburg (2001) 151–72 offers a much more learned and agreeably lewd account than I could possibly provide.

[37] For the former line as a prelude to the latter, see Freudenburg (2001) 158.

ocello. Your eye sees you giving them a "verse-job." Your orgasming organ of sight looks into their trembling loins and beholds with pleasure their pleasure. Your oral gratification of their bodies becomes your own undoing: you break, and sperm shoots from your eye. The pleasure moves in both directions. Of course the eye comes: there is the pleasure of seeing and the pleasure of being seen; there is the pleasure of seeing oneself give pleasure, and there is the pleasure of being the object of other's look of pleasure. The pervert's question: why should not the organ of this pleasure likewise climax rather than deferring to the penis?

Monstrous! Of course. Impossible! Of course not: the perverse eye feels pleasure immediately. None of this makes sense, though, until we have articulated a theory of the libidinal rhetoric of satire: only such a rhetoric allows you to connect the dots and to see the scandal of seeing. Moreover this rhetoric lets "us" readers "see" the catastrophic implications of "us" in Persius' poem. "We write," he says. "We" are about to get ourselves implicated in something, no? But "we" don't perform, "we" never get in trouble. Instead things shift into the second person. Suddenly "you" are performing. "I" never read "my" poem: you were the pervert. We wrote, but only you read it aloud. And when you read, look what they did, they got aroused as they watched you lustily watching their pleasure.

The narrator and the reader are disowning these pleasures even as they find themselves grammatically and structurally implicated in them.[38] This is bad poetry "we" are talking about. This is bad production and consumption. Our nobody or two would never do that. If Persius whispered a dirty joke in your ear, that would be OK, would it not? Or would it? Can one see arousal without being aroused? Can one speak sex without affecting sexually the listener? Does assuming the position of masterful onlooker and of the authoritative gaze always also break a man? Does he feel therewith a pleasure that he ought not and yet necessarily does feel as he is seen seeing? Is the eye of the proctologist always also in danger of ejaculating as it looks upon a well-fucked ass and makes a smirking report to a third party?

All discussions of humor run the risk of tedium. They tend to be distinctly unfunny. Worse still, they often fall flat. Did the author really get the joke? Or, worse still, did the author not understand that the satirist was joking? But one should take seriously Johnson's analogy of the satire to Freud's dreamwork.[39] We can go further by pointing out Freud's own insistence that the work of wit is one and the same as that of the

---

[38] See also Reckford (1998) on the split self in Persius.   [39] Johnson (1996) 178.

dream.[40] And one needs specifically to entertain the notion that the manifest content of the dream or of the witticism is in fact an elaboration of a latent content by means of condensation and substitute formation. The notions lying at the base of the satirework on the body seem to have the following form: what is the proper relationship between good men? In order to address the desire of the other (man), must I behave in a manner that is in fact abhorrent to me as a good man? Can I indirectly and thus safely satisfy this desire by offering a satiric witticism as a gift instead?

This set of questions can help us to elaborate the significance of the observation that there are no good men in satire. They are missing objects. And yet they should be taken both as the objects of desire and as the subjects to whom desire is addressed. They are metonymously present through the satirework, present in their absence, present as a structuring lack that generates the community of the witticism.[41] The refinding of the lost object "the good man" mobilizes the energy of the satiric structure. It is this structure *qua* structure that makes for the pleasure of the witticism whose goal is specifically the acquisition of pleasure by way of substitutions and condensations.[42] The witticism machine, though, is not a device producing random pleasures. On the contrary, satire is manifestly (if not latently) opposed to any old joy. Instead, the joke is addressed to an Other. It is addressed to an Other who sanctions and gives meaning to the joke.[43] The always absent phallic Other is the one whose desire and sanction is sought. And yet one cannot simply "seduce" this phallic Other: only perverts do that. Instead he is approached by way of a series of identifications with his hegemony, with his authoritative position, and with his critical gaze. And to him is offered

---

[40] Freud (1993) 30–2 and 249–87. And Lacan begins his seminar entitled "Les formations de l'inconscient" not with a discussion of the dream, but with a reading of Freud on wit (Lacan [1998]).

[41] See first Freud (1993) 223 on the community of the witticism. See next Lacan's summary of the object of desire from his fourth seminar as paving the way for his fifth seminar:

> [J]'ai voulu vous montrer qu'il n'y a pas d'objet, sinon métonymique, l'objet du désir étant l'objet du désir de l'Autre, et le désir toujours désire d'Autre chose, très précisément de ce qui manque, a, l'objet perdu primordialement, en tant que Freud nous le montre comme étant toujours à retrouver.   (Lacan [1998] 13)

[42] See Freud (1993) 287.   [43] Lacan (1998) 45:

> C'est l'Autre que donne à la création signifiante valeur de signifiant en elle-même, valeur de signifiant par rapport au phénomène de la création signifiante. C'est la sanction de l'Autre qui distingue le trait d'esprit du pur et simple phénomène de symptôme par exemple.

the gift of the joke, a gift of love that cannot speak its name. But it has a thousand names for the loves of others, and they are all most filthy indeed.

Further reading

A special volume of the journal *Arethusa* entitled *Vile Bodies: Roman Satire and Corporeal Discourse* appeared in 1998. The essays offered a progressive take on the relationship between work on the body and satire. The volume encapsulates the kind of conclusions entailed in the approach of scholars who had been working on histories of the ancient body. These pieces and their bibliography are a natural next stop for present readers. It should not be one's only stop, though: Henderson (1989) and Oliensis (1991) are not to be missed. Parker (1997) and Williams (1998) codify the consensus on how one approaches same-sex relations at Rome. The strongest single non-classical influence in the above bibliography would be the antiquity-oriented volumes of Foucault's *History of Sexuality*. Bakhtin's readings of Rabelais have also shaped the discussion. Readers who are interested in Lacan, Derrida, or even a post-Foucauldian like Butler will find less to read: theoretical polyglossia has generally eluded the field.

III

BEYOND ROME: SATIRE IN ENGLISH LETTERS

14

COLIN BURROW

Roman satire in the sixteenth century

Literary understanding is often a matter of creating spaces. You read a poem and align it with another, and think about the aspects of each which are not there in the other. Literary genres often work in a similar way: they develop as writers work out and give shape to the space between themselves and their predecessors. This space might be chronological, geographical, temperamental, cultural, or linguistic; it might be narrowed by personal affinities, admiration, and cultural allegiance, or widened by differences in the forms of social relations experienced by each writer. But it is always there, even in those rare literary relationships when a writer seems to be consciously attempting to catch the flavor of a predecessor exactly. And it is by feeling what is *not* there in one poem or poet that you come to know what *is* there in another. The habitual mannerisms or recurrent points of unease of one writer are much more obvious when you read the work of another person who does not have them. This is why comparative literature matters, and this is why this volume not only contains but needs to contain chapters on the afterlife of Roman satire. Gaining a full understanding of Roman satire entails also understanding what it is not like, or not quite like, and imagining how it would look if some of its central concerns were altered or nudged slightly off center.

The relationship of Elizabethan to classical satire is one of defining differentiation, as we shall see. But relationships between individual satirists in the Roman tradition of satire are also to a profound degree determined by this law of literary unlikeness. When Quintilian claimed that "satire at least is completely ours" (10.1.93) he meant both that satire is a Roman phenomenon, rather than a Greek, and that "we" Romans have a collective and distinctive sense of what satire is. The satirists themselves are not so sure. They are certain that they are akin to their predecessors, but they are equally sure that they are unlike them. Horace parades his debt to the "innovator" Lucilius (1.10.48) while also suggesting that there is something unsophisticated in his predecessor, insinuating in the process that satire is as much Horace's own as generically "ours." In a similar way the tirades of Juvenal are evidently rooted in the urban landscapes explored by Horace, but they also repeatedly insist that times have changed. One of Juvenal's favorite rhetorical ploys is to describe a past period and then to imply a "but now" after it, which differentiates the present from the past. Earlier critics often presented this as a straightforward manifestation of literary and cultural decline: Juvenal's Latin is "silver"; his Rome is a Rome of decline and fall. His relation to earlier satire is far more complex than this, however: a decline in the customs of the present guarantees that Juvenal will be unlike all satirists who have gone before. So the more Rome is seen as at once aging and founded on new customs, the more Juvenal can transform the genre. In this respect Juvenal establishes the main dynamic force in the genre of verse satire: the satirist is someone who makes his authority by creating an environment of change and decline. If his age is more decadent and more deplorable than the last, then this will guarantee his distinction.

But the history of satire is not simply a matter of the satirist establishing his presence within a new, corrupt present which he can deplore in ways which are necessarily new. The genre is also marked by the tendency of each of its contributors to create a void in an area which a predecessor had made a defining feature of his own writing. The relationship between Juvenal and Horace illustrates this aspect of the genre, too, since Juvenal is eager to show that in his age forces on which Horace could rely have become unstable and unsettling. So, what appears to be straightforwardly the "character" of Horace is partly built from a complex of relationships to patronage and the law. This relationship changes in the course of his career, but it is almost always relatively equable. When Horace writes of his first meeting with his patron Maecenas that "I said what I was" (1.6.60), he does not actually say what he was; rather he says "I said what I was" in order to mean "I was frank with this great man, and the fact that I can be frank with him is the main thing you need to know about me and about him." The identity which Horace presents in the satires is, to a great extent, that of a frankness which comes of having a secure patron whose tastes shape those of the satirist's audience.[1] Satire 1.9, for example, when Horace is beset by the bore, shows how vital the relationship between the satirist and his patron, and between the satirist and the law, is for Horace's persona. The bore wants to know him because he knows Maecenas; and the poet's superiority to his victim derives from the fact that the poem is a *sermo* which is imagined as performed before an audience including Horace's patron, for whom the attempts of the bore to win access to him through Horace would seem laughable. At the end of that

---

[1] Cf. the more hostile account in Henderson (1999) 184–5.

poem, too, Horace escapes from the bore not by finally demolishing him by wit; instead Horace's companion is whisked off by a creditor to a trial. The law is not a pronounced force in Horatian satire, but Horace is confident enough that he is safe from legal assault to be able to write satires which can acknowledge the power of the law without abasing himself before it. The conversation with the lawyer Trebatius in satire 2.1, for example, is founded on a jocular unease about the relation of satire to libel: the *mala carmina* (2.1.82) proscribed by the Twelve Tables of Roman Law are probably spells or curses, rather than libels or poems. Horace knows this, and compounds the joke by turning the law in question into one against "badly written verses."[2] Since his satires are not curses and are not badly written, and since they do not risk giving a name to individual objects of attack, they can enjoy a wary freedom to jest with the language of the law.

Juvenalian satire is not just *not* Horatian satire. It is satire in which Juvenal has blasted the shaping nodes of Horatian satire out of the form, and in which he blames history for having done so. Historical changes in Rome do play their part in this process of transformation, to be sure, but the demands of literary history accelerate and exaggerate the actual decline in patronage in first-century Rome which Juvenal depicts.[3] In an age where there are no Maecenases (*quis tibi Maecenas?*, 7.94), patronage becomes not a life-defining relationship with a single man, but a matter of waiting hungrily for *sportulae* (the dole), or, in satire 5, taking the worst seat in the lowest couch at a feast and being served the worst wine by snobby waiters, while the lordly patron eats the best food and drinks Falernian wine (in these details as in so much else Juvenal owes a massive debt to Martial). The relationship of the satirist to constituted authority also, and consequentially, becomes far more uneasy than that represented by Horace: Juvenal's silence over contemporary politics is matched by his eager criticism of past rulers such as Domitian, whose obsessive desire for giant turbot in satire 4 clearly implies that a desire for turbot is not all that was excessive about him, or about his Flavian successors. The shape and concerns and cultural *modus operandi* of Juvenalian satire is unlike Horatian satire; but Juvenalian satire also defines the primary impulses of Horatian satire by ruthlessly departing from them. And it also makes its own claims for novelty by doing so.

And yet, as Quintilian said, "satire at least is completely ours," and, as Horace said, Lucilius is the "innovator" of satire. What unites Horace, Juvenal, and Persius as part of the same project is the fact that they are all insistently, obtrusively *Roman*. "Rome" in satire is a different thing from "Rome" in epic: it is a place of arguments, dinners, adulteries, smells,

---

[2] See Cloud (1989).   [3] Rudd (1986) 160–1.

diseases, and of bodies which strain to eat and have sex, while critical voices deplore and sometimes succumb to these distracting and destructive forces. One task of the satirist is to present such a fascinatingly repellent description of customs at home that they seem strange and unnatural to the analytical eye of the satirist and his reader. Satire is the most Roman of literary kinds in the ancient world because the customs of Rome, the smells, the tastes, the hybrid origins of the slang and street-life of the city, all are deliberately held up as objects for attention and bemusement. New generations bring with them strange new customs; a new satirist will make satire new by representing those new customs and exaggerating their novelty. This is the principal reason why it is extremely dangerous to regard satire as a straightforward source of evidence about Roman life. The satirist has a stake in accelerating the cultural decline of the city, because the more the customs of his culture become alien from those of its past, the more the satirist will stand out from those who have gone before.

This raises both an immediate problem for post-classical imitators of Roman satire and an immediate benefit. The benefit is that satire is necessarily at its most lively in periods which feel themselves to be decadent, and so those who *feel* post-classical are in a good position to write satire. The problem is that if Roman satire is so very Roman, what would "Roman" verse satire mean outside, say, a 200-mile geographical radius from the city, or outside a chronological boundary of more than a few years from the death of the customs it describes? One of the major developments in responses to the satirical tradition in the sixteenth century was an awareness of the fact that satire is a genre of strangeness, which creates an exaggerated gap between present and past by insisting on the topicality of the abuses it attacks. Montaigne's essay "Of Ancient Customs" illustrates this association of satire with the curiosity of custom: in that essay Montaigne lays aside his usual favorite sources of Lucretius, Virgil, and Plutarch, in favor of Horace, Persius, and Martial, who illustrate the eating practices, the modes of bathing, the sexual proclivities, the ways of paying boatmen, and the methods of wiping bottoms in ancient Rome.[4] Satire makes the present appear odd, and the past appear odder.

The fact that Roman satire is so very Roman is one reason why Horace, Juvenal, Martial, and Persius had relatively little influence before the sixteenth century, not just in English, but in European poetry: their potential imitators in the late middle ages and early Renaissance were not particularly interested in either recuperating or exaggerating the differences in *mores* between themselves and their Roman sources. *Sententiae*, such as Juvenal's

---

[4] Montaigne (1993) 333.

maxim that virtue is true nobility (8.20), could and did have an immediate value for writers in the chivalric tradition, for whom that maxim became a cliché;[5] Horace's ideal of *aurea mediocritas* ("golden mean") from the *Odes* could be rolled out to suit an occasion where a poet needed to sound priestly, poised, and authoritative. But the Roman-ness of Roman satire – its reek of the city in the nostrils, its fascination with barbarous and bizarre customs within the city – leaves relatively little imprint on European writing before the sixteenth century. *Orazio satiro* gets a bow from Dante in the *Commedia* (*Inferno*, 4.89). Glancing references to Juvenal in Chaucer's *Troilus and Criseyde* (4.197) and the *Wife of Bath's Tale* (1.192) do not imply any detailed familiarity with his work. Juvenal is briefly mentioned as a precursor for biting satire by Skelton, *The Garland of Laurel* (line 95) in the first years of the sixteenth century. It is not until the 1520s and 1530s that European poets start thinking about how their own customs might be as strange as those of the Rome depicted in Roman satires, and about how their circumstances and voice could be made to chime with those of Juvenal or Horace.

Roman satire is what might be called an anthropological form: it looks at its own culture and sees it linguistically and ethically odd, accelerating and exaggerating emergent tendencies of a culture. The stance of the estranged observer who knows he is reluctantly a part of what he is observing is central to the mode, as is an effort on the part of the satirist to create an ethical (and often also a geographical) distance from what he is describing. In the early sixteenth century several courtly writers had reason to need this stance, and to combine it with a Horatian intimacy with a small audience of patrons and friends. These men – chief among them were Ludovico Ariosto (1474–1533), Luigi Alamanni (1495–1556), and Sir Thomas Wyatt (ca. 1503–42) – were all courtiers, and had as a result of a mixture of professional and political reasons experienced exile from their homes. Alamanni was exiled from Florence for plotting against the Medici in 1522; the Ferrarese Ariosto refused to accompany his patron, Ippolito d'Este, to Hungary in 1517, and in 1522 was made commissioner of the brigand-ridden province of Garfagnana;[6] Wyatt had spent most of the years 1537–40 as ambassador to the imperial court in Spain.[7] These men had an urgent need to adopt the mode of Horatian epistolary satire: they wrote to friends in a "Horatian" vein from places which were physically removed from centers of authority, and their addresses to carefully targeted groups of like-minded men sought to develop a moral stance from which they could criticize the court (in Alamanni's case from an

---

[5] See Vogt (1925).   [6] Details are in Ariosto (1976).

[7] See further Burrow (1993). On Ariosto see Marsh (1975).

explicitly republican perspective). These writers are evidently Horatian, and think of themselves as Horatian; yet they are not at all urban. Juvenal has an influence on Alamanni, whose tenth satire is close to Juvenal's third, but his spluttering heat is damped in the majority of early sixteenth-century satire by a desire to create a Horatian persona who could stand firm against the corruption of courts, rather than of cities. Ariosto and Wyatt write Horatian satire *rather than* "Roman" satire (in the sense of poems rooted in the city), and they do so because they had a particular need to give themselves a moral authority which would enable them to present themselves as geographically and morally separate from the court, in Wyatt's case at home "in Kent and Christendom."

A lively tradition of vernacular complaint and satire runs through the early Tudor period,[8] but it is not until the 1560s that this converges in England with the classical tradition. The first signs of this convergence occur in the work of Thomas Drant, who translated Horace's *Satires* as a "medicinable moral" for the times, and united them with a version of the lamentations of Jeremiah in 1566.[9] By the 1570s cheap editions of all three Latin satirists were beginning to appear in London.[10] Although these volumes tended to subordinate Juvenal and Persius to Horace, pithy characterizations of the three satirists (such as Scaliger's *Iuvenalis ardet, instat aperte, iugulat. Persius insultat. Horatius irridet* "Juvenal burns, openly confronts, and goes for the jugular; Persius insults; Horace smiles")[11] gave readers a clear sense that Roman satire did not speak with one voice. The massive expansion of London in the later sixteenth century created an urban environment which could build on these bookish developments. The prose satirists Thomas Lodge and Thomas Nashe produced a heady blend of Juvenal and the Greek prose satirist Lucian in their attacks on London life in the 1590s. And they gave fuel to a group of young verse satirists, many of whom had connections with the theater and the Inns of Court, who began around the mid-1590s to feel like Juvenal; isolated from a political culture with which they could not identify, fascinatedly oppressed by the sprawling corruptions of late Elizabethan London, they repeatedly echo Juvenal's cry that *difficile est saturam non scribere* ("It's difficult *not* to write satire," 1.30). They rapidly became a target for parody. The spoof on literary fashions of the 1590s, *The Return from Parnassus* (performed ca. 1601), opens with Ingenioso coming on stage with a copy of Juvenal in his hand. He quotes *difficile est saturam non scribere* and bellows

---

[8] See Peter (1956), esp. 104–56.   [9] See Mukherjee (2000).

[10] Horatius Flaccus (1578); signed sequentially with an edition of Juvenal and Persius, as was Horatius Flaccus (1592). On Renaissance editions of the satirists, see Wheeler (1992) 23–5.

[11] Scaliger (1561) 149.

out "Ay, Juvenal: thy jerking hand is good" (anon. (1606), sig. A4ʳ). The anger of the satirists often leads them to produce writing which seems anything but "classical," if "classical" is taken to mean "valuing form, decorum, and moderation." John Marston insists that "Rude limping lines fits this lewd halting age,"[12] and his fellow satirists share his opinion that their roughness reflects the customs of their time. Like Juvenal, they invent a corrupted cityscape in order to deplore it.

As Alvin Kernan has shown, many of the English satirists of this period – chief among whom were John Marston (?1575–1634), Joseph Hall (1574–1656), Everard Guilpin (*floruit* 1598), William Rankins (*floruit* 1587), and "T. M." (probably Thomas Middleton) – were attracted to the irate abrasiveness and obscurity of Juvenal and Persius, rather than to the modulated tones of Horace. He argues that they deliberately adopted the personae of "Satyrs," the aggressive and wild woodland creatures from whom they believed the name of the genre to derive.[13] George Puttenham's account of the origins of satire is typical of many in the period, and had an undoubted influence on its practitioners: "to make their admonitions and reproofs seem graver and of more efficacy they made wise as if the gods of the woods, whom they called *Satyrs* or *Silvans*, should appear and recite those verses of rebuke."[14] Elizabethan satire, certainly when practiced by Marston, can adopt this persona so fully that it seems to choke on its own spleen, as its exponents seek to transform Juvenalian rage into a bubbling stream of invective which is unbounded by any decorum:

> I cannot hold, I cannot I, endure
> To view a big-wombed foggy cloud immure
> The radiant tresses of the quick'ning sun.
> Let custards quake; my rage must freely run.
> Preach not the Stoic's patience to me:
> I hate no man, but men's impiety.
> My soul is vexed, what power will'th desist,
> Or dares to stop a sharp-fanged satirist?[15]

Marston was much mocked for those eminently mockable quaking custards, but they testify to the main rule of Elizabethan satire: that rage has its own clotted, implosive style. Late Elizabethan satire was angry, anxious about its own status as literature, aggressively innovative in its language,

---

[12] *The Scourge of Villany* (1598) 5.18. Quotations modernized from Marston (1961).

[13] Kernan (1959); but see the critique in McCabe (1982) 34–42.

[14] Quotation modernized from Smith (1904) II 32.

[15] *The Scourge of Villainy*, 2.1–8. Ben Jonson parodied these lines in *Poetaster*, 5.3.513 and *Volpone*, prol. 21.

and insistently topical in its subject matter. It sprayed its hostility widely: fellow poets ("His windows strewed with sonnets, and the glass | Drawn full of love-knots"),[16] fellow satirists, courtiers, usurers, transvestite whores, women who used make-up, those who wished their children to become members of the gentry – all are spluttered and spat at with venomous enthusiasm. Joseph Hall went as far as to derive the name of the genre from "sat irae" (full of anger).[17] William Rankins is the most explicitly satyr-like of the satirists, declaring in the "Induction" to his *Seven Satires* (1598) that:

> My shaggy Satyrs do forsake the woods,
> Their beds of moss, their unfrequented floods,
> Their marble cells, their quiet forest life,
> To view the manner of this human strife.
> Whose skin is touched, and will in gall revert,
> My Satyrs vow to gall them at the heart.[18]

Kernan's influential account of Elizabethan satire, though, overstates the savagery and the uniformity of Elizabethan satire. It also does not fully explain *why* at this moment and this place this group of writers turned to Juvenal and Persius rather than to Horace, or *why* they cultivated a style so thickly clotted and obscure. And in neglecting these questions, as we shall see, Kernan understates the sophistication of this ostentatiously unsophisticated form.

Scaliger insisted that a good man should abstain from reading Juvenal,[19] which must partly explain why so many young men read him with such zeal in this period. But Elizabethan satirists had a view of literary history which made Juvenal and Persius, with their exaggeratedly post-classical and non "literary" manner, the ideal models for them. Sir Philip Sidney in the 1570s and 1580s, and Edmund Spenser in the 1590s, had provided what very rapidly was perceived to have been a brief "classical" period of perfection, which left those born in the 1570s feeling prematurely decadent and post-classical. Like Juvenal, Joseph Hall presents himself as a late-comer in the feast of literature, who deplores the corruptions of his fellow writers, as they be-whore the Muses:

> Now is *Parnassus* turnèd to the stews [brothels],
> And on bay-stocks the wanton myrtle grows,
> *Cythêron* hill's become a brothel-bed,

[16] Marston, *Certaine Satires* (1598) 3.61–2.
[17] *De suis Satyris*, line 1. Quotations modernized from Hall (1969).
[18] "Induction," lines 3–8. Quotations modernized from Rankins (1948).
[19] Scaliger (1561) 149.

And *Pyrene* sweet, turned to a poisoned head
Of coal-black puddle, whose infectuous stain
Corrupteth all the lowly fruitful plain.[20]

The willful obscurity of Elizabethan satire is the result of its exponents'
belief that they belong to a new phase of literary history. Satirists from this
period saw the difficulty of Juvenal and Persius as not just linguistic, but the
consequence of the strangeness of Roman customs. As Marston put it:

> *Persius* is crabby, because ancient, and his jerks, (being particularly given to
> private customs of his time) dusky. *Juvenal* (upon the like occasion) seems to
> our judgement gloomy . . . But had we then lived, the understanding of them
> had been nothing hard.[21]

Their own obscurity was aimed to create a similar effect: Hall, Marston,
and Guilpin were attempting to make late-sixteenth-century London appear
as thick with "private customs" of their time as ancient Rome: "*Tiber*,
the famous sink of Christendom | Turn thou to Thames, and Thames run
towards Rome."[22] By adopting Juvenal's post-classical horror at his times,
Hall, Marston, and Guilpin aimed to make themselves and their times have
the fascinating corruption of their Roman originals.

But the main reason why Elizabethan satirists needed Juvenal was that
he was so consciously not Horace, and showed that it was possible to write
satire even if you did not have a patron or a Sabine farm. They lacked many of
the points of support which Juvenal had so pointedly excluded from his form
of satire. In particular they had no patrons. None of their printed volumes
has dedications (which makes the genre unique in this period). Indeed, they
are typically introduced by a "Defiance to Envy" rather than an appeal for
protection to a powerful courtier. Marston even went so far as to dedicate
the second edition of *The Scourge of Villainy* (1599) "To his most esteemed,
and best beloved Self." Juvenal also mattered to Elizabethan satirists because
they could not match the equability of Horace's relationship to the law. In
the 1590s the law of libel was bewildering: a massive increase in prosecutions
had led to the introduction of a rule, known as the *mitior sensus* rule, to ease
pressure on the courts.[23] According to this, potential defamations should be
interpreted in the mildest possible sense: so an accusation that "thou hast
stolen by the highway side" was not libellous, since it could be taken to
mean that "thou hast stolen along by the side of the highway." Political
satire which impugned the monarch or the common law, however, could be
punished severely under statute law by the loss of one or more ears. And

---

[20] *Virgidemiae*, 1.2.17–22. On Hall's satires, see McCabe (1982) 2450, 29–72.
[21] Marston (1961) 100.   [22] Hall, *Virgidemiae*, 4.1.134–5.   [23] Milsom (1981) 386.

these statutes resonated with poets: when Pope in 1733 sought an analogue to the prohibition on *mala carmina* in the Twelve Tables about which Horace jests, he turned to Tudor statutes ("Consult the Statute: *quart.* I think it is, | *Edwardi Sext.* or *prim. & quint, Eliz:* | See *Libels, Satires* – here you have it – read").[24] Elizabethan satirists trod a particularly delicate line among these statutes: they might attack types of vice, but assaults on social and political abuses were hazardous. As a result of these legal pressures they tend to mask attacks on general ills, such as the depopulation of the countryside through enclosure, as attacks on types, such as crooked lawyers or legalistic poets.

Unease about the relationship between satire and libel also led late-sixteenth-century satirists to worry about the relationship between what they wrote and the interpretation of their words by their readers. And it is here that they show far more sophistication than one would expect from the creatures presented by Kernan as rustic satyrs. A premiss of their writing is that if satire appears to attack identifiable individuals, it is the fault of malicious or guilty readers rather than of the author. As Marston put it in his defensive note "To him that hath perused me" "what lesser favour canst thou grant than not to abuse me with unjust application?"[25] That word "application" (which means "willfully turning a general satire into a specific libel") was repeatedly used to blame the warped or guilty minds of readers for moments when the satirist appeared to be assailing the mighty. And this concern with the responsibility for meaning also extends into a concern with the question of who owns the satirist's words. This interest derives largely from Martial, who was regarded as a central figure in classical satire in this period (epigram and satire are instinctively linked by Elizabethan writers), and who worries about plagiarism more frequently than any other Roman poet. And the very term "plagiary" enters English from Latin in the satire of the 1590s. It occurs in Joseph Hall's *Virgidemiae*, when Lollio pays for his son to go to the Inns of Court (training-grounds for barristers, who comprised an influential element of the market for literary texts in this period). Lollio wants his son to become a gentleman. He succeeds so well that his son has nightmares about being reminded of his contact with home:

> May be some russet-coat parochian
> Shall call thee cousin, friend, or countryman,
> And for thy hopèd fist crossing the street,
> Shall in thy father's name his God-son greet;

---

[24] "The First Satire of the Second Book of Horace Paraphrased," 147–9. Quotation from Pope (1963). On the law, see Clegg (1997) 27. 1 Eliz. c. 5 renewed Mary's law punishing verbal treason. 1 & 2 Phil. & Mar. c. 3, on malicious rumors, was renewed as 1 Eliz. c. 6.

[25] Marston (1961) 176.

Could never man work thee a worser shame
Then once to minge [mention] thy father's odious name,
Whose mention were alike to thee as leeve ["lief"; welcome]
As catchpoll's [debt-collector's] fist unto a bankrupt's sleeve;
Or an *Hos ego* ["I wrote those lines"] from old Petrarch's sprite
Unto a plagiary sonnet-wright.[26]

This is a quintessence of the environment of Elizabethan satire: at night in London, with teeming corruptions around him, Lollio's son is haunted by debts to his father, which are figured as literary debts. Plagiaristic writers of sonnets are haunted by the ghost of Petrarch just as the son is haunted by Lollio for abandoning his cultural origins. This web of concerns brings with it a use of the word "plagiary" which pre-dates the first citation in the *Oxford English Dictionary* (from another satirical work, Jonson's *Poetaster*) by about three years. The shaggy satyr's voice adopted by Hall is working through a sophisticated set of anxieties about how the assimilation of an old form into a new cultural landscape relates to the creation of poetry and to the poet's claim to originate and own his writing. And the more completely Hall himself can adapt Roman satire to the customs of London, the more fully he can claim literary ownership over the landscape he creates.

These "shaggy satires," for all their sophisticated analyses of literary property and of the ways readers interpret general attacks on the time, had a short life and all but no afterlife. The savagery of their attacks on contemporary abuses, from corruptions in the law to the decline of hospitality in the countryside, led to the whole genre's being banned in June 1599 by the archbishop of Canterbury and the bishop of London in the most categorical of terms: they ordered "That no Satires or Epigrams be printed hereafter."[27] This was only two years after Hall had boasted in *Virgidemiae* of being the first English satirist. The bishops' ban consigned printed works by John Marston, Everard Guilpin, William Rankins, and "T.M." to the flames. Hall's *Virgidemiae* escaped incineration, but copies of his work were none the less recalled. John Weever (who had translated one satire of Persius in 1600) and others leapt to whip satire when it was down with pamphlets which at least have memorable titles: Weever's *The Whipping of the Satyre* (1601) sadistically relishes its collaboration with the bishops' ban on the genre, and Guilpin trotted out *The Whipper of the Satyre his Penance* in response.[28] A few satires on classical

---

[26] Hall, *Virgidemiae*, 4.2.75–84.

[27] Arber (1875–94) II 677–8. On the political reasons for the ban, see McCabe (1981); Clegg (1997) 198–217 relates the ban closely to Essex's campaign in Ireland in 1599.

[28] See Breton and Guilpin (1951).

models emerged after the ban, but they tend, understandably enough, to keep the word "satire" from their title-pages. Richard Brathwaite's *Strappado for the Devil* (1615) is a typical example of this transparent means of avoiding censorship, although his *Natures Embassie: Or the Wilde-Mans Measures: Danced naked by twelve Satyres* (1621) risks a picture of twelve satyrs dancing on its title-page. Nicholas Breton used the mouthpiece of Pasquil the Plain to conceal that he was writing satires, and he, like the other main Jacobean satirist George Wither, rarely alluded to classical satire.

We have seen that it is reductive to regard Elizabethan satirists simply as "shaggy satyrs." But the greatest objection to Kernan's view that Elizabethan satire is dominated by the "satyr" persona is that it fails to fit the two most influential and successful contributors to the genre in this period. Both John Donne and Ben Jonson wrote satires on classical models, but neither shows any tendency to identify the speakers of their satires with satyrs. And both of them have been remembered while Rankins, Hall, Marston, and Guilpin have sunk into ashy oblivion. Donne was accorded the status of a metrically rough originator of English satire by Dryden, and Pope's "Fourth Satire of Dr. John Donne, Dean of St. Paul's Versified" gives him the dubious accolade of playing the rugged Lucilius to Pope's polished Horace.

The greatest difference between Jonson and Donne and the other Elizabethan satirists is that when they write satires they adopt a persona derived from Horace rather than Juvenal, although as we shall see their "Horace" is very different from the Horace presented in critical and historical accounts today. Jonson certainly knew Juvenal well: he imitates satire 10 for the description of the death of Sejanus,[29] and makes more than one Juvenalian attack on the customs of his times (notably in *Underwood* 15 and *Underwood* 84). He was also familiar enough with Persius to give a copy of Casaubon's edition to his friend Sir John Roe in 1605 and to write a Latin epigram for his friend Thomas Farnaby's edition in 1612. But, early and late, Jonson's poetry grounds itself on Horace; he is not just fat, but "As Horace fat" (*Underwood* 42.2),[30] as though without a literary prototype he would have eaten less; he adapts the manner of a Horatian *sermo* to the new customs and concerns of London in his "Speech According to Horace" (*Underwood* 44), and captures the reflective mode of Horatian epistles in "To Sir Robert Wroth" (*Forest* 3). The depiction of the Stoic sage as *teres atque rotundus* ("smooth and round", 2.7.86), centered in himself, and resistant to the hostility of the masses, repeatedly informs Jonson's self-presentations (e.g. *Underwood* 47.60).

---

[29] *Sejanus*, 5.763–842.   [30] Quotations from Jonson (1975).

His early play *Poetaster* (1601), however, marks the start of his career as a Roman satirist, and presents a rougher, more street-wise Horace than that which dominates his later verse. It also shows that Jonson's Horace shared many concerns with the Juvenalian satirists of the 1590s. *Poetaster* is set in Augustan Rome, and is peopled by Roman poetasters with lesser-known or unknown figures mentioned in Horace's satires (these transparently represent Jonson's enemies John Marston and Thomas Dekker), and by Ovid, Horace, and Virgil. This play aspires to be both about and by Horace: 3.1–3 re-enacts Horace's attempts to escape the bore on the Appian way in satire 1.9, and ends, like its original, with the poetaster Crispinus being carried away from Horace by a creditor. But even this highly Horatian play shares with Marston and Hall a distinct pattern of differences from Horace's satires. Jonson's Horace writes poems which are maliciously taken to be specific attacks on the Emperor Augustus by Crispinus and Demetrius. Horace insists that if readers interpret his poems maliciously, then that is their fault not his, and he is backed in this claim by the ultimate figure of authority, Virgil:

> 'Tis not the wholesome sharp morality,
> Or modest anger of a satiric spirit,
> That hurts, or wounds the body of a state;
> But the sinister application
> Of the malicious ignorant and base
> Interpreter, who will distort and strain
> The general scope and purpose of an author,
> To his particular and private spleen.
>
> (5.3.132–9)[31]

Jonson has clearly learnt here from Marston how to insist that satire only appears to attack individuals or the state because of the warped minds of its readers. It is often suggested that his insistence that the author cannot be blamed for his readers' misinterpretations shows a distinctively Jonsonian concern with his own authority. It does not: it derives from his close reading of earlier satirists. And, despite Jonson's defense against libellous intent, there runs through the play a seam of anxiety about the relationship between satire and libel, which roots Jonson's Horace in the Juvenalian satire of his immediate predecessors more deeply than he would wish to admit, or his critics have recognized. *Poetaster* 3.5 recreates a scene (which was added to the folio of 1616) between Horace and the lawyer Trebatius in which they discuss the relationship between satirical attacks and the law

---

[31] Quotations from Jonson (1995).

of libel. The majority of the dialogue is a free translation of satire 2.1. As we have seen, this discussion in Horace depends on a relatively light-hearted misinterpretation of what *mala carmina* are (satires? bad poems? curses?), a misinterpretation carefully glossed by Jonson's friend John Bond in his edition of Horace in 1606.[32] In Jonson's play, however, which was composed while the ban on satire in 1599 was still ringing in the poet's ears,[33] and which contains scenes in which malicious readers have a manifest power to corrupt the words of a poet, the conversation becomes an urgent discussion about how a poet can make a general attack on vice and retain control over how that general attack is interpreted. Jonson's Horace insists "I will write satires still, in spite of fear" (3.5.100), and the origins of that "fear," imported by Jonson into his original, begin to emerge when the English Trebatius warns against the danger not just of *mala carmina*, but specifically of libel:

> There's justice, and great action may be sued
> 'Gainst such as wrong men's fame with verses lewd.
> (3.5.128–9)

To which Jonson's Horace does not wryly respond with *Esto, si quis mala* ("Fine; if they're *bad*"), but with "Ay, with lewd verses, such as libels be," and goes on to conclude the scene by giving a far fuller defense against the charge of composing libellous verses than his original, professing his aim (like Martial, who was to Jonson as to his contemporaries the fourth Roman satirist) to "spare men's persons, but tax their crimes" (3.5.134, translating Martial 10.38.10). Jonson needs to insist here, since his play *is* transparently a libel on his rival playwrights Marston and Dekker (at the end of the play Crispinus is made to vomit out a stream of Marstonisms, including his notorious quaking custards). Jonson wants to tap the security offered by Horace and Horatian satire, but his imitation is overshadowed by unease. His Horace is shaped by the uncertain relations between satire and libel and between satire and the law which had run through the work of the earlier Elizabethan satyrs/satirists, as well as being profoundly influenced by the ban which had so abruptly terminated their literary experiments. The result is that his Horace does not appear "Augustan"; rather he seems to be a poet who survives in an atmosphere akin to the imperial court as represented by Tacitus, in which power and misinterpretation continually press threateningly down on the words of the courtier.[34] He is a distinctly post-classical Horace.

---

[32] Horatius Flaccus (1606) 199.
[33] See Loewenstein (1999).   [34] Cf. Freudenburg (2001) 219–21, 236.

The other Elizabethan satirist to have been remembered by literary history is Jonson's friend John Donne, who composed five satires in the early 1590s. The quick-fire dialogues embedded in these poems, and their dense enfolding of image within image, make them hard to read fast, but they are nonetheless the finest product of late-sixteenth-century reading of classical satire. Like Jonson, Donne follows a Horatian path (although he evidently knew Persius and Juvenal, too) when he adapts classical originals.[35] He is also conscious, as a Catholic or a recent convert to Protestantism, that satire can be the product of a sinner whose language is as fallen as the objects of his attack.[36] Donne's satires circulated in manuscript from about 1593, and so predate the main efflorescence of the genre in print: he, rather than Hall, has claims to be the first English classically inspired satirist. Jonson composed a poem to accompany a manuscript copy of Donne's satires which was presented to Lucy, countess of Bedford. By 1598 they were well enough known for Everard Guilpin to imitate them in print. Although the satires were only printed in the posthumous edition of Donne's works in 1633, and even then in a version which prudently excises criticisms of kings and favorites, Donne still claimed in the early seventeenth century that "to my satyrs there belongs some fear."[37] And that fear is the most powerful force which differentiates Donne's satires from those of Horace. Donne's Horace, like that of his friend Jonson, differs from Horace's Horace as a result of many of the concerns which drew his contemporary satirists to imitate Juvenal. The shaggy satyrs' uneasy suspicion that writing might be a disease, and their anxiety about plagiarism and literary property, punctuate Donne's satires:

> . . . they who write to Lords, rewards to get,
> Are they not like singers at doors for meat?
> And they who write because all write, have still
> That excuse for writing, and for writing ill.
> But he is worst, who (beggarly) doth chaw [chew]
> Others' wit's fruits, and in his ravenous maw
> Rankly digested, doth those things out-spew
> As his own things; and they are his own, 'tis true:
> For if one eat my meat, though it be known
> The meat was mine, th'excrement is his own.[38]

---

[35] See Wheeler (1992) 118–19.

[36] Baumlin (1991) 73. Hester (1982) 15 argues that "Donne has replaced the spokesman of Horace, Juvenal, and Persius with a speaker of Christian zeal."

[37] Donne (1967b) 111.

[38] Donne, "Satyre 2," 21–30. Quotations modernized from Donne (1967a).

Here, though, Donne puts clear water between himself and Hall's attacks on plagiaristic sonneteers. He presents himself as the provider of nourishment; it is his plagiarizers who, in a grisly transformation of the metaphor of digestion often invoked in descriptions of literary imitation (after Seneca's 84th Epistle), turn his poems into "excrement." Donne presents a rich feast of words – a *satura* – for his imitators to plunder and half-digest; he knows, however, that "The meat was mine."

But Donne does not and cannot simply recreate the points of security on which Horace had relied. His imitations of Horace are conscious at all times of that awkward relation between the satirist and the law which had been so dominant in the satire of the 1590s; and he, like Juvenal, notably lacks the reassuring presence of a Maecenas to nourish his poetic authority.[39] His two extended imitations of Horace's encounter with the bore in 1.9 show very clearly that he can try to imitate Horace, but that he cannot invent a patron for himself or cast Horatian urbanity over his uneasy attitude to the law. In satire 1 the satirist is drawn from his study by a "fondling motley humorist" (1.1). This version of the bore, though, does not wish to use Donne as a high road to Maecenas; and, indeed, the principal weakness of this very early poem is that Donne has no explanation as to why the "humorist" seeks the satirist's company, or why the satirist goes out with him, beyond their shared love of change. At the end of the poem, when in Horace the creditor drags the bore off to court, Donne again leaves a gap where Horace had introduced a powerful external force. It is not the law which assists Donne's escape: the bore is "Violently ravished to his lechery" (1.108), and goes off to see his whore, driven again by his own desire for change. And when he has been beaten and thrown out of her house, he comes back. The satire seems locked in an endless cycle of wandering, and it is locked in that cycle because the forces of patronage and the law are not available to Donne in quite the same way that they were to Horace.

Donne returns almost compulsively to 1.9 in satire 4, in which the Via Sacra becomes the English court; the bore is turned into a courtier who scuttles up to the poet with the arbitrary punitive power of God ("God! | How have I sinned, that thy wrath's furious rod, | This fellow chooseth me?", 4.49–50). The desire of the bore for the patronage of Maecenas is again almost audibly absent from this poem: the "court" of Maecenas is replaced by the English court, a place of teeming gossip, in which the only motive for human conduct is desire for gain or worse. And the poet shortly encounters another swallowing gulf as he listens to the courtier's gossip:

[39] See further Erskine-Hill (1972).

Who wastes in meat, in clothes, in horse, he notes;
Who loves whores, who boys, and who goats.
I, more amazed than Circe's prisoners when
They felt themselves turn beasts, felt myself then
Becoming traitor, and methought I saw
One of our giant Statutes ope his jaw
To suck me in . . .[40]

The law here is not the force which finally delivers Horace from the bore in
1.9. It is a gaping maw which threatens to engulf the satirist. The courtier's
gossip makes the poet nervously remember that the penalty for repeating
"News, Rumours or Tales to the Slander and reproach of" the monarch was
the loss of one ear, while the penalty for originating such slanders was the loss
of both ears.[41] This satirist is not grounded by a relationship with Maecenas;
he ducks temporarily into his home, and then is magnetically drawn back
to court again, enchanted by the mystery of power and corruption, despite
being in imminent danger of being swallowed up by the malicious gossip
which swirls around him. Even as he imitates Horace, Donne replaces the
framework of cultural and legal supports which his original possessed with
potentially consuming voids. This makes him a very different writer from
Horace. But it also illustrates why no reading of classical satire is complete
without a reading of its imitations. These works cannot reproduce the shape
and animating concerns of their originals because times, patrons, and laws
have changed. But what they do show is the guiding principle of the genre of
verse satire: that new satirists need new customs and new forms of corruption
to give authority to their new poems.

Further reading

Gransden (1970) presents a well-selected volume of primary texts with a good introduction. The most venerable critical study of Elizabethan satire is Kernan (1959),
but as I suggest here, his snarling satyrs now seem a little long in the tooth. His study
is usefully supplemented by Wheeler (1992), which gives a very full account of the
sources and motifs of sixteenth- and seventeenth-century satire, but is not primarily
intended to offer critical insight, and Peter (1956), which traces the emergence of
"Renaissance" satire from the tradition of complaint. The now elderly Alden (1899)
finds more classical echoes in early modern satire than most readers will hear. Burrow
(1993) discusses the Horatian background to Ariosto, Alamanni, and Wyatt, while
Wiggins's edition of Ariosto's *Satires* (Ariosto [1976], esp. xvii–xxiv) is sound on both
biographical context and classical allusions. There are good introductory accounts
of English sixteenth-century verse satire in Baumlin (1986) and Prescott (2000). The
remainder of the material covered by this chapter has to be pieced together from

---

[40] Donne, "Satyre 4," 127–33.   [41] Under the statute 1&2 Phil. & Mar. c. 3.

Davenport's excellent editions of Marston (1961), Hall (1969), and Rankins (1948), and from Carroll's edition of Guilpin (1974), all of which offer valuable guidance on classical sources, although they necessarily provide little comment on how or why those sources are transformed. Still very valuable on Donne is Erskine-Hill (1972), which gives a sharper account of satire 4 and its relation to Horace than Hester (1982), the standard work on Donne's satires. Baumlin (1986), too, is conscientious and thoughtful on Donne's satires. Remarkably there is no monograph on Jonson's Horace; Martindale (1993) is the best guide to the relationship (more penetrating than Pierce (1981)), and Peterson (1981) is excellent on Jonson's imitative practice in general. Steggle (1999) gives a valuable account of the battle for Horace and Jonson's part in the "War of the Theatres."

15

DAN HOOLEY

Alluding to satire: Rochester, Dryden, and others

Histories of English literature tell us that the defining terms of Restoration (1660) poetry were established by John Dryden (1631–1700). Samuel Johnson (1709–1784), in his not entirely uncritical *Life*, makes Dryden's transformation of English poetry analogous to Augustus' Rome: "he found it brick, and he left it marble." He is the seminal poet of his age. So too the masterworks of Restoration satire are Dryden's *Mac Flecknoe* and *Absalom and Achitophel*, and his later *Discourse concerning the Original and Progress of Satire* set out the ways in which the Roman satirists were to be read and adapted right through the eighteenth century. Pope's (1688–1744) and Johnson's conceptions of Horace and Juvenal derive directly from a typology that Dryden popularizes, if not invents. This should, then, be an essay on Dryden. But it is not; for the brilliance of Dryden's work has tended to leave us a distorted picture of what satire, or indeed Horace and Juvenal, might have meant to a Restoration reader; we look back at the Restoration and see Dryden; a contemporary reader of satire would have seen Dryden and others experimenting with classical satire's legacy, sorting out its manners and place in the hotly contested literary and social politics of the Restoration. That said, I cannot offer a significantly less inflected version of Restoration satire here; merely another view from its slightly seamier underside, and here too Dryden plays a role . . .

John Wilmot, the earl of Rochester (1648–1680), cultivated, violent, impetuous, promiscuous, by turns carefree and tormented, spent most of his life as a member of Charles' court, dancing attendance on the king in a role that became increasingly tiresome to him.[1] At his best, he wrote lyrics of poignant brilliance; at his other (satiric) best, he could be painfully crude, though his obscenity is often colored by a *jouissance* that makes Rochester's language something other than the merely low abuse roughly the same words effect in

---

[1] Developed nicely in Germaine Greer's superb short book (2000).

other hands. Even apart from the major satiric works "Timon," "Artemiza to Chloe," and the "Satyr against Reason and Mankind," the minor (obscene) pieces like "A Ramble in St. James Park," "Tunbridge Wells," "To the Postboy," "Signior Dildo" and the explicit satire on King Charles II whom, or whose penis, he calls "the proudest peremptoriest Prick alive" are compounded of qualities that make this Restoration satire a good deal more than the sum of its vulgar parts. The neat balance of impertinent guying and incisive analysis of the associations of power and sexuality come through in the often-quoted squib on Charles:

> Nor was his high desire above his Strength:
> His Scepter and his Prick were of a length,
> And she may sway the one who plays with t'other
> Which makes him little wiser than his Brother.
> For Princes Pricks like to Buffoons at Court
> Doe governe Us, because they make Us Sport.
>
> (85–6)[2]

Particularly these last lines with their mention of failed or inverted governance, not only point to real political problems in the early–mid 1670s when confidence in Charles II's ability to govern was low and Rochester's resentment of the monarchy high ("Monarchs I hate and the thrones they sit on / From the Hector of France to the Cully of Britton"),[3] they widen the scope of what "power" and "politics" mean. Rochester's take on the exercise of that power, who is wielding it, and who are its victims, as well as its frequent failures (impotence is a major theme, both Rochester's own and that of the targets of his satire), and the haunting darkness of his vision make his perhaps the most intriguing meditations on the dynamics of language and authority in the Restoration.

Around about 1675 Rochester composed for private circulation his "Allusion to Horace," an imitation of Horace's satire 1.10,[4] a poem written

---

[2] The text of Rochester is that of Love (2000), the most recent and authoritative edition. In the case of the present squib, ill-advisedly presented to the king himself in 1673, the manuscript versions are several, none having clear authority. I quote from Love's "Group-A" text.

[3] Rochester's patron and friend Buckingham had recently declared his opposition to "the king's pro-French policies" (Love (2000) 420, who refers us to David Ogg's discussion of the climate of political discontent in his *England in the Reign of Charles II* (2nd edn. Oxford 1956), ii.526).

[4] Johnson credits Rochester and Oldham with initiating the practice of imitation in English, though there had been prior to Rochester's work closer and freer translations of classical texts, and Boileau preceded him in free adaptation while adding in heaps of contemporary references to make the poem's application current. See Griffin (1973) 246–51; Hammond (1995) 166: "If Rochester was not quite the first English poet to press a Roman satire into the service of

ostensibly as a self-defense against charges that Horace had not been sufficiently gracious in an earlier satire (1.4) to Lucilius, his aristocratic predecessor in the genre. Horace had said there (1.4.11ff.) that Lucilius was "a
witty fellow with a keen nose, but harsh when it came to versification . . .
He was a muddy river with a lot of stuff that should have been removed."[5]
In 1.10 Horace goes on to itemize ways in which Lucilius' great satiric temper needed to be moderated and polished, leading to an account of his own
theory of satire: what it should be about and how it should be made. Conventionally read, Horace is credited with importing the new Hellenistic literary
value of exact craftsmanship into the rougher and readier satire inherited
from Lucilius.[6] Rochester imitates this work, taking onto himself the role of
Horace and substituting for Lucilius, as critical target, his older contemporary Dryden, who was still in the relatively early part of his long career. The
hostility in this treatment often comes as a surprise to readers. Rochester
was Dryden's patron for a time until the latter turned for financial help
to Rochester's enemy (John Sheffield, duke of), Mulgrave. Little evidence of
the relationship remains: a flattering letter from Dryden to Rochester written
before the break; the old, probably false story of Rochester's instigation of
the Rose Alley beating of Dryden. It may merely be that Rochester, enviously,
saw in Dryden a great poet in the making as well as signs of social and literary overreaching.[7] The poem affords few clues on the score of motive, but,
beyond savaging the ambitious poet/dramatist of 1675, does raise interesting
generic issues.

First, like Ben Jonson before him, Rochester seems to assume the mask and
authority of Horace (over against Dryden's Lucilius) for his own purposes.[8]
The parallel is important; Jonson, the major classicizing poet of the early
seventeenth century, identified himself from relatively early years with the

---

his own times, he was the first to appreciate that this could be done systematically over the
length of an entire poem . . ." On literary imitation in English, see Weinbrot (1969) 1–58 and
(1988) esp. note 1 for bibliography; Stack (1985) with regard to Pope in particular, 18–26.
Others, worthwhile, on "The Allusion": Weinbrot (1988); Thormählen (1993); Hammond
(1995); Rogers (1982); Hewison (1987).

[5] Quoting, throughout, Niall Rudd's translation of Horace (1973).

[6] That convention may well be wrong; see, for instance, Freudenburg (2001) 44.

[7] Hammond (1995) 167 mentions the different political allegiances; Dryden in the York camp,
Rochester a partisan of Buckingham. We know too little of the personal relationship between
the two writers. Dryden had dedicated *Marriage A-la-Mode* to Rochester, and, as Combe
(1995) points out "chose as an epigraph to his play a passage from Horace (Satire 2.1.74–79)
that both invokes the name of Lucilius and compliments Rochester by placing the earl in the
position of Maecenas to Dryden's Horace . . . Rochester ruefully explodes Dryden's fancy
with his use of Horace's Satire 1.10 in *Allusion to Horace*" (145).

[8] See the discussion of Jonson by Colin Burrow in this volume.

verse and character of Horace, an identity that came to be yet more deeply felt later in life in the face of controversy, the failure of his dramatic work, and disappointments with courtly allies and patrons. But the aristocratic Rochester – not, like Jonson, the stepson of a bricklayer – was in a different literary as well as social position. An amateur courtier-poet, he had no need of the same sorts of patronage, did not require the mask of the adept who had won a position of influence by dint of native genius, as had both Horace and Jonson. In one important sense, then, the idea of a Horatian Rochester is a paradox. A paradox whose implications may be seen on a broad scale throughout the poem, beginning with the most crucial word in Rochester's title; "allusion" in one's title is overkill – or misdirection. Allusion, as commonly understood, whether the classical "Alexandrian footnote" or a trope of memory or *aemulatio*,[9] is an intertextual relationship intended to be perceived by the "full-knowing reader," in Drayton's phrase.[10] Drayton clearly uses the word in the sense of "a covert, implied, or indirect reference" (*Oxford English Dictionary* 4): "The verse oft, with allusion, as supposing a full knowing reader, lets slip." Rochester on one level does not let slip; rather he lays out explicit and systematic correspondence, which *could* be what Rochester meant by the word, but the overkill in the title should incline us to look further at the rather interesting dynamics of reference. In 1673 Dryden had published his comedy *The Assignation: or Love in a Nunnery* whose dedication was written to Rochester's courtly friend Sedley; here he defends himself against the charge that he had criticized Ben Jonson by referring to Horace's respectfully critical treatment of Lucilius in 1.4 and 1.10. Two years later, Rochester – surely taking the idea from Dryden himself – puts Dryden in precisely the same Lucilian position.[11] There are complicated literary controversies implicit in this reversal having to do with incipient Tory/Whig politics and the struggle for Jonsonian authority between Dryden and Shadwell.[12] Rochester's "allusion," then, is multi-referential: alluding to

---

[9] The best general summary of this nexus of related conceptions of influence is Hinds (1998). See too Weinbrot (1988) 69–70.

[10] The phrase comes from Drayton's *Polyolbion* (1622) and is used by Joseph Pucci for his very good book on the general subject (1998). For a fuller discussion of "allusion" in its seventeenth-century context see Weinbrot (1988) 69–70.

[11] Hammond (1995) neatly sets this out for us (167–8). Combe (1995), in his helpful article on the literary rivalry of Dryden, Shadwell, and Rochester, points out that Dryden had also used 1.10 against Shadwell in his "Defence of the Epilogue; or, An Essay on the Dramatique Poetry of the Last Age" (1672) and that Rochester used this tactic against Dryden himself in the "Allusion."

[12] See Hammond (1995) and Combe (1995) on this.

Horace, alluding to Dryden's allusion to Horace, or alluding to Dryden's self-defensive gesture in alluding to Horace – then bringing it home by making Dryden effectively his own target. There is almost cruelty in the wit. And it may extend further, to Jonson himself, who had, as we have said, in both specific and general terms over the course of long years taken on a Horatian identity. Rochester takes up the Horatian mask in an altogether different mood, playfully, like a courtier got up in costume at a masked ball, and so twists the literary exercise into a kind of sham ventriloquism – speaking "through" a character or literary model *transparently*, that is, in such a way as not to hide the very different bearings, character, situation of the author. Rochester, not needing to "become" Horace in the way that Jonson did, could use the literary dislocation to generate diachronic tensions and complications.

This kind of engagement can take place on a number of levels; among them, intertextual reading/writing. Rochester's "Allusion" is close enough in points of contact with its model for the latter to be traced fairly clearly in the imitation. Here, we note only a few. The opening shows a clear analogue: Horace, *Sermones* 2.1.1–4 corresponds to Rochester 1–7. Horace:

> True, I did say that Lucilius' verses lurched
> awkwardly along. Which of his admirers is so perverse
> as not to admit it? But he is also praised on the same page
> for scouring the city with caustic wit. While granting this,
> however, I cannot allow the rest as well, for then
> I should have to admire the mimes of Laberius for their poetic beauty.

While Rochester begins this way:

> Well Sir, 'tis granted, I said Dryden's Rhymes,
> Were stollen, unequal, nay dull many times.
> What foolish Patron, is there found of his,
> So blindly partial, to deny me this?
> But that his Plays, Embroider'd up and down,
> With witt, and learning, justly please'd the Towne,
> In the same paper, I as freely own.
> Yet having this allow'd, the heavy masse,
> That stuffs up his loose Volumns must not pass;
>
> (Love, 71)

Horace "explains" his earlier criticism of Lucilius while maintaining that he never meant to deny his predecessor's greatness, particularly in "scouring the city with caustic wit." Rochester uses Horace's gambit to say something quite different: first, while Lucilius scours, Dryden pleases the whole town: the backhanded compliment emphasizes the selling out of Lucilian honesty. Rochester further claims that he "said" Dryden's rhymes were "stollen, unequal, nay dull many times" when, so far as anyone can tell, he had not – he says that here (as Dryden and others read it) for the first time, perhaps as an extra twist of malice. Some conclude that Rochester is merely following Horace in this (Horace wrote, "I said Lucilius' lines ran haltingly"), but surely the point is the opposite: in seeming to follow Horace Rochester is pointing out how his criticism is not merely an echo of Horace on Lucilius. Rochester misleadingly "follows" Horace again with a reference to "what foolish patron," a translation of Horace's *quis tam Lucili fautor inepte est*, but that word "patron," for *fautor*,[13] is a direct dig at Dryden's new patron and Rochester's rival, Mulgrave, and again difference leaps out, difference that is not merely "topical" reference but the generated point of the satire.

Rather less clear, or less direct, is another intertext, at Horace's line 50, "But I did say he was a muddy river, and that in what he brought down / there was more to be removed than retained." That muddy river is of course metapoetic, a literary critical metaphor, contrasted in and after Callimachus with a more refined style enfigured as a pure spring from the Muses' mountain, Helicon. When Horace uses the metaphor it is meant to invoke an entire school of modern poetry. Rochester dodges this line; he does not translate it. But I think it is present in the constipation metaphor that seems to lurk here (8–15):

> Yet having this allow'd, the heavy masse,
> That stuffs up his loose volumes must not pass:
> For by that Rule, I might as well admitt,
> Crownes tedious Scenes for Poetry, and Witt.
>   'Tis therefore not enough, when your false sence
> Hitts the false Judgment of an Audience
> Of clapping-fools, assembling a vast Crowd
> Till the throng'd Playhouse, crack with the dull load.
>
> (Love, 71)

Ostensibly this also draws on a Horatian model where Horace claims that poetry lies in more than pleasing the crowd (7–11):

---

[13] Kirk Freudenburg suggests, *per litteras*, that Horace may be using the multi-valent word, usually taken as "supporter" or "fan" in the context of appreciators of (long-dead) Lucilius, in a politically loaded way, thus drawing in lost potentials of the Latin word, recovered to some extent here by Rochester. I owe our editor, too, the observation, a bit above, on Rochester's characterization of Dryden's "pleasing" as opposed to "scouring" verse.

So it's not enough to make your listener bare his teeth in
a grin – though there's some virtue even in that. You need
terseness, to let the thought run freely on without
becoming entangled in a mass of verbiage that will hang heavy
on the ear.

"Thought running freely along" becomes a stopped up mass, an image that
melds into concerns about overproduction and crowd pleasing: the muddy
flow of a literary digestive system, clogged up (or checked by right criticism)
until, transformed into the playhouse thronged with clapping fools (wrong
criticism), it cracks (open) under its load. But in transforming this neat little
Callimachean lesson into a metaphor that looks to Horace's muddy river,
Rochester raises the satiric stakes, for once again a layered or misdirected
allusion – to "Lucilius" – is involved. In lines 81–6, Rochester makes the
point:

> But does not Dryden finde even Johnson dull?
> Fletcher, and Beaumont, uncorrect, and full
> Of Lewd lines (as he calls 'em), Shakespear's style
> Stiff, and Affected; to his owne the while
> Allowing all the Justness that his Pride,
> So Arrogantly, had to these deny'd?   (Love, 73)

Dryden had written in his "Epilogue to the Second Part of Granada" (1671)
this:

> They who have succeeded on the stage
> Have still conformed their genius to the age.
> Thus Jonson did Mechanique humour show,
> When men were dull, and conversation low. . . .
> Fame then was cheap, and the first comer sped;
> And they have kept it since, by being dead.

And in his "Prologue to *The Tempest*" (1667), Dryden, praising Shakespeare,
cut Jonson neatly:

> Shakespeare, who (taught by none) did first impart
> To Fletcher wit, to labouring Jonson art;
> He monarch-like gave those his subjects law,
> And is that Nature which they paint and draw.
> Fletcher reached that which on his heights did grow,
> Whilst Jonson crept and gathered all below.

Yet Fletcher, and Shakespeare too, had been censured in his "Defence of the
Epilogue" (1672) and *Of Dramatick Poesie* (1668): "[Shakespeare] is many

times flat, insipid, his Comick wit degenerating into clenches, his serious swelling into Bombast."[14] Dryden's consistent line in this criticism is almost exactly that of Horace concerning the "primitive" aesthetics of Lucilius: respect for their genius and achievement despite the frequently uneven execution.[15] There is arrogance in this, as Rochester directly points out. But the indirect, allusive satire makes the point devastating, for Rochester, in using Horace in precisely this way, placing his enemy in the role of Lucilius, makes Dryden, again, his own target. Two can play the Horace v. Lucilius game, and Rochester, in this instance, holds trump.

At lines 77–80, Rochester gives a fairly close rendering of Horace, who had been explaining why satire was his chosen genre. History, tragedy, epic – these were taken by others; only in satire remained the opportunity for making his mark. The Horatian original reads (*Sermones* 1.10.46–9):

> This form had been tried by Varro of Atax and others
> without success and was therefore one which I could perhaps
> develop – though always inferior to its inventor. I wouldn't presume
> to snatch from his head the crown which he wears with such distinction.

In adapting this, Rochester focuses on that crown (77–80):

> But to be just, 'twill to his praise be found,
> His Excellencys, more than faults abound.
> Nor dare I from his sacred Temples tear
> That Lawrell which he best deserves to wear.
>
> (Love, 73)

Lucilius' crown is that of the genre's inventor: Horace will not presume to usurp that honor despite his expressed reservations about the founder's art. Dryden's crown (having nothing *per se* to do with satire), on the other hand, is "that Lawrell," the poet-laureateship Charles had awarded Dryden in 1668. A nice non-parallel, as Rochester realizes: the laureateship is his to keep; the "crown" of satire rests elsewhere. This is fair enough; Dryden's reputation still rested on his plays, and he had not yet written his great satires. But Rochester's oblique self-assertion as satirist, in this satire alluding to, and on, satire, conditions, too, a frequently noted passage of satiric defamation. Referring in lines 61ff. to the "songs and verses, mannerly Obscene / That can stir Nature up, by springs unseen, / and without forcing blushes, warme the Queen," Rochester continues in lines 71–6:

> Dryden, in vaine, tryd this nice way of Witt
> For he to be a tearing Blade thought fitt,

[14] Walker (1984) 289.   [15] Thormählen (1993) 321.

But when he would be sharp, he still was blunt,
To friske his frollique fancy, hee'd cry Cunt:
Wou'd give the Ladyes a drye Bawdy bobb,
And thus he gott the name of Poet Squobb.

(Love, 73)

This does not translate Horace, so Rochester again has for a moment taken off that mask. What he is saying is that Dryden had tried on the manner of the courtly libertine and failed – possibly a mark of distinction in a more salubrious environment than Charles' court (indeed, Johnson's characterization of Dryden's even temper and slowness off the mark in verbal repartee might confirm this). But Rochester is not interested in the larger canvas – nor could he be for his satire to function, understanding as he does that satire is always built of some smaller rhetorical world whose infrastructure of priority and "value" is as conspicuous as it is deceptive, and within which target-denizens struggle against a world perversely and precisely *made against them*. In *this* little world, reflecting elements of the larger, the metaphor of "tearing blade" reflects both the wit that cuts potential rivals and sexual prowess, where again sex is an index of power. In both these respects Dryden is caricatured as "blunt." Dryden here presents not a whetted blade but a "dry Bawdy bobb," perhaps combining the senses of "a blow that does not break the skin" and Eton slang denoting "dry" sport, contrasting the rower's wet blade (*Oxford English Dictionary*); editors point out the sexual reference.[16] If Dryden is capable of but a dry bob, Rochester touches home with artful point. And touches, too, something crucial about his conception of satire. Dryden is "used" in this poem by Rochester, just as Horace and Jonson were earlier, in this case to claim, in the oddly ambivalent way noted above, Horatian status for himself. And further oddly, because Rochester is clearly the most Lucilian of the lot. Yet the Horatian claim is necessary to him. Horace had persuasively made the case in 1.4 and 1.10 (as well as indirectly in 1.1 and 1.3) that satire was more than rough abuse, that it was an odd mix of literary registers that invoked both a kind of Aristotelian serious-ness and broad comedy. Eschewing open lampoon and invective, Horace proposed a pliant discourse that ranged across human behavior: its ambi-tions, its failures, its delusions. As a consequence his satires are challengingly complex, and somewhat strange, literary documents, even while remain-ing deeply embedded in the life and politics of their time. Rochester builds directly on the obvious, radical Horatian message: style and satiric idiom matter (24ff.):

---

[16] See Vieth (1968) and Walker (1984) on this passage. Weinbrot (1988) 75, n. 26, points out another contemporary dig at Dryden's alleged sexual inadequacy.

Here be your Language lofty, there more light,
Your Rhetorique with your Poetry, unite.
For Ellegance sake, sometimes allay the force
Of Epethets, 'twill soften the Discourse;
A Jest in Scorn, poynts out, and hitts the thing,
More home than the morosest Satyrs sting.
Shakespear and Johnson did herein excell,
And might in this be imitated well.

(Love, 71)

The mention of Shakespeare and Jonson (standing for masters of Old Comedy in the original) is a direct rebuke to Dryden, of course, for reasons we have already seen. And it seems straightforward enough Horatianism: middle register, elegance, concision, balance. But we may fairly ask if any of this describes the verse principles of the man (Rochester) who can write of Mulgrave that he "rears a little when his feeble tarse [is presented with] a straight well-sphinctered arse" or of his mistress as a "passive pot for fools to spend in"? Now Rochester's lyrics are famously "ellegant," but his satire characteristically makes it a point to sink to registers well beneath Horace at his crudest. In fact, Rochester's invention and effervescent wit never fall neatly into Horatian stylistic descriptors. But the paradox of this focus on the poetics of style and apparent disingenuousness is, as well, at the heart of the perplexing mystery of *Horatian* satire: Horace is the first and perhaps the only satirist whose fussy talk about the idiom of his and Lucilius' satire generates a rather complicated self-reflexive frame of discourse whereby the metapoetic assertion of literary value becomes the mechanism of a kind of self-indictment. Horatian satire takes in Horace. Under a Lucilian aegis, the satirist would mince no words, stake his claim; with Horace we have a shambling, by turns abashed and chest-thumping, evasive, apologizing apologia. William Anderson has called the early persona employed by Horace *doctor ineptus*, a neat paradox capturing much of the problem.[17] But Horace's damaged satiric speaker, behind all that (only apparent) self-irony, disorients the entire project, so that satirist, satirized, and the larger game itself are all pulled into the target zone of the satire. As in some instances in Swift, and famously Defoe for different reasons, we are almost never sure of the point of Horace's satire; it is a house of mirrors, and the reader is right there inside with our satirist *ineptus*. Its greatness and its challenge emerge from this elusiveness – I do not mean irony – and satire's critical reception has not been up to it. Most Restoration and eighteenth-century theorizing of satire, Dryden conspicuously, look to style and tenor only, finding Horace

---

[17] Anderson (1982 [1963]) 41–9; see also Freudenburg (1993) 3–43.

polished and subtle and ironic, with Juvenal's ferocious rhetoric more suited
to the big job of making one's enemies feel the pain. Which is too easy to
be true.

In Rochester's world this Horatian quality, call it disabled satire, assumes
particular importance. Living in the strange microclimate of the court where
reputation and the manners of self-presentation were all, Rochester knew it
was not a nice place to be. His poems are rife with that knowledge, with disgust, disillusionment, contempt, self-loathing.[18] In the face of which, moral-
istic regard or indignant invective – there was plenty around from conservative elements of the aristocracy and clergy, as well as the unlucky losers after
the Restoration – could merely deplore or rant. The lesson that Rochester
takes from Horace is that satire can inhabit the small artificial world it both
creates and satirizes; rather than rant or deplore from without, it twists its
targets from within, catching them in the web of their own language and
style. Horace had claimed that the language of Lucilius would no longer do
the job, not because Horace wanted simply to be up to date, but because
the job had suddenly got far more complex. Horace needed a language that
would loop itself back into the satire so that the enframing, satiric perspectives become "involved." And this seems precisely true of Rochester as well.
Take that dissection of "courtly" Dryden in 71–6; when pressed to find
the "mannerly obscene," all he can manage "to frisk his frolick fancy" is
to cry "cunt" (Shadwell's notorious lampoon of Dryden, "The Medal of
John Bayes," instances similar desperate stabs at wit).[19] For all the cruel
caricature, it is effective satire because it takes the known writer, perhaps
uneasy in Rochester's society, and gets him up, mis-performing, on the stage
of courtly antics in the costume of the comic fop, so common to Dryden's
own Restoration stage. The absurdity of the type arises from the dissonance
between the fop himself and what he imagines himself to be within courtly
society – and then between that courtly world, its strangely artificial codes
of priority and authority, and the larger construction of values that the audience lives in and with and calls home. Or audiences: in this case Rochester's
readership consists of a "knowing" inner circle of aristocratic amateurs, but

---

[18] How much Rochester's thinking was influenced by neo-Epicurean ideas in circulation is an
open question; for general orientation see Kroll (1991).

[19]
                Thy Mirth by foolish Bawdry is exprest;
                And so debauch'd, so fulsome, and so odd,
                As–
                Let's Bugger one another now by G–d.
                (When aske'd how they should spend the Afternoon)
                This was the smart reply of the Heroick Clown.

Shadwell's satire-in-rebuttal rather confirms Dryden's point(s) in *Mac Flecknoe*.

the imitation of Horace casts, perforce, a wider net, invoking a wider range of audience perspectives. Rochester's satire catches both "Dryden" and the courtly values that indict him within the frame of his satire, and in doing that he of course catches himself and his readers. Which is simply to say that while this satiric costume play works in wounding Dryden, the falseness of both costume and play stand revealed as well.

Like Horace, Rochester cannot escape the transparently vulgar self-positioning, the pettiness of the court, though his protests were at times almost as heroic as they were jejune; like Horace, he knows it and expresses his restiveness – not as Horace does, with an almost pathological elusiveness and rhetorical instability that creates an entirely new mode of discourse, but with a comprehensive ferocity that lets no part of his world, least of all himself, off the hook. If Horace employs a "damaged" and unreliable persona disillusioning his social world from *within*, with minute turns of rhetoric and nuance, Rochester takes that idea to an extreme. Satire, as Horace and Rochester seem to have seen, works within a given or invented discourse, always metapoetically focused on that discourse as much as it is on its ostensible targets. Satire is self-regarding, watching itself watch the world, and therefore caught in a generically inescapable *mise en abîme*; Horace writes as a diminished moralist, thus both satirist and satirized; Rochester as perhaps the most diminished of possible moralists. His satire, in general, is best described as a searing indictment of failure, itself implicated by failure, hence always, in some fashion, working against itself – and against its readers, for they, or their surrogate selves, become denizens of this same strange place he writes.

Rochester's is only one example of what satire might be, fairly limited in terms of pages of text, in a period that was rife with satiric writing of a variety of sorts: squibs, lampoons, invectives, songs, letters.[20] The court of Charles II offered both provoking occasion and hospitable climate for these kinds of literary exercises. Though laws against seditious and treasonous publication, notably the Treason Act and Licensing Act of 1662, were occasionally enforced, Charles was himself notably relaxed about satire directed against him. He even sought at one point to cultivate Marvell, whose opposition to the Stuart court never relented. All the same, the naval disasters against the Dutch of the middle 1660s (provoking Marvell's several *Instructions to a Painter*), the sometimes riotous and licentious doings at court, founded and unfounded fears of popery, the prorogations of Parliament and

---

[20] Lord (1987) points out that "over 3000 satirical pieces from this period [1660–1714] survive in print" (107).

secret entente with France of the 1670s, all generated an atmosphere in which satire became an important tool in contesting the fate of the nation.[21] Dryden himself was no little involved, taking the part of the king with an increasingly prepossessing satiric muse. His *Absalom and Achitophel*, born of the exclusion crisis that peaked in 1681, gave satire an overtly political and public voice and offered a reading of national crisis and its resolution so extraordinary as to assume, momentarily, a controlling hand on the issues. Classical and post-classical satire had never been so openly ambitious, never so directly and effectively a player in matters of national moment. On the smaller stage of literary rivalry, *Mac Flecknoe* demolished Shadwell with a relish and decisiveness that puts into shadow Rochester's ingenious but less focused treatment of Dryden. *Flecknoe*, of course, leads in direct descent to Pope's *Dunciad*, and Dryden's satiric achievement as a whole inaugurates the great English age of the genre, the eighteenth century of Swift, Pope, Gay, Churchill, and Johnson. Yet writing in 1692–3 Dryden himself made note of the generic slippage in this, categorizing his great satires with the mixed mode satires of Varro rather than with the hexameter satires of Horace, Persius, or Juvenal. *Flecknoe* relies prominently on the manners of mock heroic and *Absalom* can probably only be called satire by way of convenient shorthand; it is a composite, problematic generic formulation.[22] Swift and Pope will take their leads from this.

But Dryden's restless mind would not lose touch with his old masters, and when he turned to translation late in his career, he looked to Persius and Juvenal. The translations are variously interesting (much of the Juvenal is not his, but was, according to Pope, probably revised by his hand); the more abidingly important contribution of the project being his long introduction, the *Discourse of Satire* (1693),[23] in which he treats at some length the "original and progress" of the genre through its major Roman exemplars. While impressively learned, the *Discourse* leans hard on the scholarship of Dacier and Casaubon in particular and repeats the history of satire largely from their point of view.[24] Beyond (surprisingly persistent) reductionist *dicta* about "correct" satire (a poem must focus on a single vice, that is have a unity of subject, must exhort "one precept" of moral virtue and caution against one vice), competing etymologies (*satyros/satur*) are discussed, as are Greek versus Roman origins, relations to drama, generic development, and salient

---

[21] Lord (1987) covers all of these points in some detail, 107–44.

[22] See Maurer (1997). Miner (1967) concludes that the poem is not a satire (41).

[23] Quotations come from the California Dryden: Swedenberg (1974).

[24] See Hammond and Hopkins (2000) 304–6 for a concise survey of the scholarly dialogue involving Scaliger, Casaubon, Heinsius, Rigault, Dacier, and others that Dryden ventures into.

characteristics of each of the major verse satirists. This last issue becomes in Dryden's treatment, following an old seventeenth-century game of preferences, a rather strange Judgment of Paris, and after relegating Persius to a meritorious third place, he dithers for pages between Juvenal and Horace. Juvenal, who gives him "as much Pleasure as [he] can bear," wins out in the end, a verdict that is not as important to us as the characterization of the two satirists Dryden offers in deliberation. Dryden's formulation would influence the reception and treatment of Horace and Juvenal for the next century and beyond. Horace, the "better instructor," censures folly rather than vice, is the superior philosopher, subtler, more courtly, delicate, of "pedestrian" stylistic register, though witty and elegant; Juvenal, a "more vigorous and Masculine Wit," denounces vice rather than folly, thunders indignation in a higher rhetorical register, and offers more pleasure. In a sententious preliminary summation, Dryden adumbrates eighteenth-century reception:

> The Meat of Horace is more nourishing; but the Cookery of Juvenal more exquisite; so that, granting Horace to be the more general Philosopher; we cannot deny, that Juvenal was the greater Poet, I mean in Satire. His Thoughts are sharper, his Indignation against Vice is more vehement; his Spirit has more of the Commonwealth Genius; he treats Tyranny, and all the Vices attending it, as they deserve, with the utmost rigour: And consequently, a Noble Soul is better pleas'd with a Zealous Vindicator of Roman Liberty; than with a Temporizing Poet, a well Manner'd Court Slave, and a Man who is often afraid of Laughing in the right place: Who is ever decent, because he is naturally servile. (65)

Niall Rudd has pointedly discussed the misperceptions here ("Dryden's essay is wrong or misleading on almost every major point"),[25] but in the history of reception misprision has not mattered: the contentious, politically engaged satirists of the early eighteenth century, even the conspicuously "Horatian" Pope (living under a Hanoverian king and an overweening first minister) would find in Horace something of this spineless courtier, friend of kings, and in Juvenal something more vigorous and principled, more capable of noble expression. Johnson's Juvenal is the natural outcome.

But Dryden's essay also includes, by the by, this little digression on servile Horace, who is seen to have been a little too complicit in Rome's nastiness:

> [Horace] was not the proper man to arraign great Vices, at least if the Stories which we hear of him are true, that he Practis'd some, which I will not here mention, out of honour to him. It was not for a Clodius to accuse Adulterers, especially when Augustus was of that number . . . our Poet was not fit to

---

[25] Rudd (1966) 273.

represent [vices] in an odious Character, because himself was dipt in the same Actions. (69)

However unreliable these (probably Suetonian) "stories," Dryden's comment makes an interesting point – remembering roguish Rochester having taken on that Horatian mask to satirize Dryden himself. If one vision of satire, conveniently self-gratifying, is that of the paragon laying out the snarling dogs of vice, another is of the fallen man writing of his and his world's condition. And just how does the fallen man write? Reacting to Barton Holiday's claim that "A perpetual Grinn, like that of Horace, rather angers than amends a Man," Dryden, in defense, takes another line:

> I cannot give him up the Manner of Horace in low Satire so easily: Let the Chastisements of Juvenal be never so necessary for his new kind of Satire; let him declaim as wittily and sharply as he pleases, yet still the nicest and most delicate touches of Satire consist in fine Raillery. (70)

"Low satire" at least has this, for Dryden, supreme virtue ("this way of Horace was the best, for amending Manners, as it is the most difficult"), though precisely how it comes about he cannot say:

> This, my Lord [the earl of Dorset, Rochester's Buckhurst], is your particular Talent, to which even Juvenal could not arrive. 'Tis not Reading, 'tis not imitation of an Author, which can produce this fineness: It must be inborn, it must proceed from a Genius, and particular way of thinking, which is not to be taught; and therefore not to be imitated by him who has it not from Nature: So easie it is to call Rogue and Villain, and that wittily! But how hard to make a Man appear a Fool, a Blockhead, or Knave, without using any of those opprobrious terms! (70)

In part, Dryden seems to mean here merely a kind of subtlety: "there is still a vast difference betwixt the slovenly Butchering of a Man, and the fineness of a stroak that separates the Head from the Body, and leaves it standing in its place" (71). The axis of the satire is still *ad hominem*, as he goes on to show in respect of his own work:

> I wish I cou'd apply it to my self, if the Reader wou'd be kind enough to think it belongs to me. The Character of Zimri in my *Absalom*, is, in my Opinion, worth the whole Poem. (71)

In fact, Zimri, George Villiers, duke of Buckingham, old literary enemy, gets anything but subtle treatment in *Absalom*: "Stiff in Opinions, always in the wrong; / Was everything by starts, and nothing long; / but, in the course of one revolving Moon, / was Chymist, Fiddler, States-man, and Buffoon . . ." (547ff.). Indeed, much of the satiric rhetoric in *Absalom* draws on the rough matter of personal lampoon and the strident political pamphleteering of the day, where tit-for-tat abuse was the standard idiom. But Dryden is surely correct in observing a difference between such invective all about him and the artful thing he has done with his Buckingham and others.[26] The biblical episode from second Samuel wherein King David is confronted with the rebellion of his son Absalom neatly fits, as others had noted, the situation of Charles, his illegitimate son Monmouth, and the conspiring Whig Shaftesbury, but Dryden so constructs the narrative of this "heroic satire" as to control individual characterizations in tight balance between biblical "type" and determined political role in this particular crisis. Buckingham, for all his wit, and Shaftesbury, for all his principle, are trapped by their own prominence in a satiric construction so consummately framed and decorated that their real-world qualities scarcely matter. Dryden's Horatian "fine Raillery" suggests, then, more than delicate banter. In execution it entails the creation of a literary landscape that displaces mockery or renders it otiose, that makes possible for the reader a degree of involvement in the sorting out of things ("to make a man appear . . ."). In *Absalom*, a little like Rochester, but more elaborately, publicly, and successfully, he fashioned a satiric space between the poles of biblical authority, public spectacle, and opinion, and personal vision wherein satirized characters live through their scripted, necessary failures.

Yet Dryden knew that his was not to be the last word, that his victims and their proxies would return the gesture, as they did, in vigorous attack, always destabilizing the earlier "position." So the game would go on, these shifting, succeeding screens of imaginative vision, characterizations of self and enemy and public enemy playing first this role, then that. Self-justificatory scripts are heroic, but disabled by their own interests; the plotless plots of pamphlet and invective likewise self-indicting. Satire, only for the nonce, holds author and his targets in balance, sketches out a temporary relation of things as they might be, this day, in this light, in the eyes of this satirized maker of satire.

England's taste for satire continued at high water through mid-century before yielding to the rising popularity of prose fiction and the verse of early Romanticism. Grub Street polemic, lampoon, prose essay, and fiction, squib, satiric

---

[26] See Bruce King's (1969) analysis (65–83) of the "imaginative patterns" of the poem and his assertion that *Absalom* is "almost Elizabethan in its correspondences between the microcosm and the macrocosm, the particular and the individual" (83). See also Elkin (1973) 15–19, for the distinction, observed throughout the seventeenth and eighteenth centuries, between "raillery" (or "rallery") and the harsher, personal abuse, variously characterized, sometimes by "railing."

theater, verse imitation of Horace and Juvenal, and satire of satire itself, all swirled around more ambitious fusions of art and politics in Drydenesque mode. In that idiom, Dryden's politically implicated "Varronian" satires – in preference to the earlier examples of Donne, Marston, Hall, and Oldham – became benchmarks of artistic value. In theoretical terms the recursion to classical sources and authority, an approach popularized by Dryden, became a standard reflex. Satirists thought and wrote in terms Dryden taught them. But carried on in their own ways too. By way of double sphragis to this chapter, then, I want to glance (scandalously) briefly at just two later specimens, by Pope and Johnson respectively, resuming some of the ideas raised in the context of Rochester and Dryden.

Alexander Pope's precocious rise to prominence took place during Anne's reign, and, as a Catholic Tory who suffered considerable persecution from Whig circles, he was devastated by the political turn that Hanoverian succession represented. Consequently, having retired from the city to the country, he published in 1733 a denunciation of George II's court ("such a varnished race / of hollow gewgaws, only dress and face!") in his *Fourth Satire of Dr. John Donne, Versified*, which might almost be read as Dryden's revenge on Rochester. The type of the Rochesterian courtier may be seen too in Sporus, a character in Pope's *Epistle to Dr. Arbuthnot* modeled on Lord Hervey: outwardly fair but inside a "child of dirt that stinks and stings," a "cherub's face, a reptile all the rest."[27] The split between Pope's country party and the court of the king and his first minister Walpole, who effectively ran the government for the frequently absent monarch, was so dramatic, the literary enmities so virulent, that legal and even physical threats were not uncommon. Pope had at times good reason to fear for his safety. In this context in which the public role of the satirist was an issue of genuine moment, Pope early in 1733 undertook his imitation of Horace's satire 2.1, whose staged conversation between the poet and the lawyer Trebatius raises precisely the

---

[27] After writing this chapter, I received Julian Ferraro's informative "Pope, Rochester, and Horace" (2000). Ferraro investigates, chiefly, the ways in which Pope was influenced both in poetic language and "attitude" by Rochester (and even Scroope's attacks on Rochester). The argument is convincing in almost all respects and should be read by anyone interested in the relationship of these two poets. Ferraro notes that the "stance" Pope takes in "Arbuthnot" "owes a great deal to Rochester's aristocratic filtering of Horace and Boileau" (125), and points out how the imagery used in description of Sporus/Hervey derives from Rochester and Scroope (127). See, too, Ferraro's discussion of the coterie of friends mustered by Pope in "Arbuthnot" 135–44, corresponding both to the close Horace's in satire 1.10 and Rochester's "Allusion"; he points out that while echoing the "rhetorical strategy of Rochester's attack on Dryden, he revises, and in some respects reverses, the political, personal and aesthetic allegiances of his model – put simply, Pope's allegiances are with Dryden's party and against Rochester's" (130).

issue.[28] Horace declares that some people are upset with his satires; what does the lawyer advise? He suggests leaving off satire and writing verse that flatters Caesar instead. Horace counters that he needs to write, that vice and folly cry out for critique; finally, after Trebatius cites the laws of libel, Horace asks what the case would be if *Augustus* approved the verse: well, then, that would be all right – your case would be thrown out of court! There is no opportunity here to go through either poem, but I want to look just at the opening and close. Horace had written:

> Some people think I'm too sharp in my satire and stretch
> the form beyond its legitimate limits; the rest maintain
> that whatever I write is slack and that a thousand verses like mine
> could be wound off every day. Please advise me, Trebatius:
> What am I to do?
> > Take a rest.

Pope makes this of it – speaking to his lawyer-friend, Fortescue:

> There are (I scarce can think it, but am told)
> There are to whom my satire seems too bold,
> Scarce to wise Peter complaisant enough,
> And something said of Chartres much too rough.
> The lines are weak, another's pleased to say,
> Lord Fanny spins a thousand such a day.
> Tim'rous by nature, of the rich in awe,
> I come to council learned in the law.
> You'll give me, like a friend both sage and free,
> Advice; and (as you use) without a fee.
> *Fortescue*: I'd write no more.

Noting that Pope names names here (Peter, Chartres, Fanny [Fannius = Pope's Hervey]) while Horace does not, that Pope's irony is heavy, and that Pope goes on in the remainder of the poem to defend "virtue" with "Juvenalian" ferocity, it is sometimes said that Pope's intention is to supersede Dryden's supine Horace, even to quarrel with him in showing what satire must be in the dark new world of the Hanoverian eighteenth century.[29] I think this may be only partially true. And the reason goes back to Rochester's Horace, who gave to that courtier the model of satire's inscape,

---

[28] See Weinbrot (1988) 77, who contends that the imitation presumes "an historic community of thought" wherein the recognized parallels would play a positive role in Pope's political critique.

[29] Weinbrot (1988) 128–43.

the idea that satire does its work not merely by open abuse or attack – like the infamous invective of Dennis on Pope – but works within a given discourse and metapoetically focused on that discourse as much as its ostensible targets. Just as had Rochester, Pope in this poem assumes the role of virtue's champion, brandishing rhetorical threats, an all-too-easy parody of a misread and misunderstood Horace, all the while, with his eye simultaneously on the mode of expression, this inherited genre of satire, tweaking this discourse world so as to create insiders who know and outsiders who do not. So when he renders Horace's closing lines, substituting Walpole for the approving Caesar, there is anything but literal sense in the solution:

> P. *Libels* and *Satires*! lawless things indeed!
> But grave *Epistles*, bringing vice to light,
> Such as a king might read, a bishop write,
> Such as Sir Robert would approve –
> F. Indeed?
> The case is altered – you may then proceed;
> In such a cause the plaintiff will be hissed,
> My lords the judges laugh, and you're dismissed.

Pope writes no grave epistles such as a bishop would write; his king is notoriously a non-reader; Walpole could never approve.[30] Only in this fantasy counterfactual realm will Pope be "dismissed." The fantasy and counterfact are important. Rather than an assertion of real probability, it is an imaginative refraction through Horatian satire, where such an assertion is "possible"; that is the point of imitation after all, which consciously shifts the frame of literary formulation away from literalist bearings into a politically contingent space where Pope and Horace and Walpole and Augustus all bump into one another in odd ways. And when they do, each opens the others to question. Sometimes with simple irony – you're no Augustus, Mr. Walpole – sometimes with a trickier juxtaposition of kinds and orders

---

[30] See Stack (1985) 56. Stack examines the poem as it should be done, in the context of the facing-page Latin of the original publication, and thereby brings Pope's imitation to life in ways not seen elsewhere. He summarizes near the end of his chapter:

> The whole poem as a poetry of imitation is a reflection of this: the relationship between the texts is perpetually fluid, weaving back and forth along the edge of paradox – it is all from Horace, and it is all different. This is the result of the extreme freedom implicit in the whole idea of imitation, which Pope here exploits to the full. Far from tying Pope to a single vision imitation seems profoundly liberating. The relationship between the texts changes moment by moment and line by line; and Pope's relationship with himself is just as fluid, just as momentary. (58)

of authority, always with a generic "enlargement" wherein the play of fantasy, desire, personal assertion, and invention compound and qualify the polemics of politics and abuse. All this, and the fact that Pope's conclusion escapes both ludicrous wish-fulfillment and a dreary compact with political reality, derives directly from his writing through and about the consciously "satiric" prism of Horace, alluding to the larger medium of his expression, the constructed discourse world that is his satire, whose "laws" may be as compelling in their way as those of state.

In the 1946 Michael Innes thriller *From London Far*, the unlikely hero, tweedy, Juvenal scholar Richard Meredith, stumbles, impossibly, into a murderous art-smuggling ring that takes him to the further reaches of Scotland, "from London far." The quotation, like many others in this old fashioned, posh-talking crime novel, comes from Johnson's *London*, upon which Meredith distractedly muses, "not really a good poem . . . you could never have guessed on the strength of it that he would write so great a thing as *The Vanity of Human Wishes*. For a moment his mind went off down the resounding corridors of the later composition . . ." It is a verdict close to scholarly consensus.[31] *London*, Johnson's imitation of Juvenal's third satire and his first poetic success, published in 1738, is seen as rather (too?) deeply involved with opposition politics and topical issues; the *Vanity* composed ten years later, modeling itself on Juvenal 10, is held to be, with its wider ethical application, sententious moral gravity, and those "resounding" rhetorical corridors, the more accomplished poem. It is not my intention here to revise that view, or to look at either of the great poems in detail, though certainly the *Vanity*, with its grand, Christian resolution, marks a change from *London* and betrays a moral tenor quite unlike the earlier poem or anything in Juvenal. In this there is loss as well as gain. On the other hand, *London* and the imitations of Pope are cut from the same ideological cloth. Pope himself, having read it, inquired of its author, and upon learning that he was "some obscure man" declared "he will soon be déterré."[32] Both wrote out of a personal involvement in opposition, anti-Whig politics, both attacked the administration of Walpole and the Hanoverian court, both subscribed to Bolingbroke's political dichotomy of court and country, taking the part of country, and of course both used literary imitation to formulate all this.[33] Johnson's tendentious reading of Juvenal is evident from the first:

---

[31] For example, Weinbrot (1969) 191: "the poem is nevertheless not as successful a formal verse satire as *The Vanity of Human Wishes*." Innes was the literary scholar J. I. M. Stewart.

[32] Venturo (1999) 57. Venturo is helpful on the political content of the satire.

[33] Venturo (1999) 58–64.

> Though grief and fondness in my breast rebel,
> When injured Thales bids the town farewell,
> Yet still my calmer thoughts his choice commend,
> I praise the hermit, but regret the friend,
> Resolved at length, from vice and London far,
> To breathe in distant fields a purer air.
> And, fixed on Cambria's solitary shore,
> Give to St. David one true Briton more.

Juvenal's Umbricius, "shadow-man" or "shade" of some imagined *Romanitas*, becomes Thales here, with altogether more salubrious philosophical tincture. His suitably reasoned preference is for country(side) and church and true patriotism. Juvenal's symbolically loaded Cumae, setting for his diatribe, becomes the politically loaded Greenwich:

> Struck with the seat that gave Eliza birth,
> We kneel and kiss the consecrated earth;
> In pleasing dreams the blissful age renew,
> And call Britannia's glories back to view.
>
> (23–16)

Against this idealized past of fierce independence and national power ("Ah! what avails it, that, from slavery far, / I drew breath of life in English air; / Was early taught a Briton's right to prize, / And lisp the tale of Henry's victories" [117–20]), Johnson deplores Walpole's accommodations to the Spanish, the insidious influence and social presence of the French, a foreign king, and the domestic intrigues fostered by a corrupt court.

Though the barbs were sharp and had immediate effect, *London*'s jingoism does not any longer travel well. Juvenal's rather more complex satiric formulation of urban society as seen by a flawed, envious, decidedly self-interested speaker is reduced to a more limited set of political targets without, it is usually seen, a sense of irony.[34] Venturo summarizes reservations about the narrow politicization:

> Paradoxically, the partisan, political fervor that gives the poem its remarkable energy limits the moral perspective of its main speaker, Thales. Consequently, while *London* brilliantly reflects Bolingbroke's "Country" ideology, the analysis of city life offered by Johnson's Thales lacks the more complicated and subtle perspective of Johnson's model, Juvenal's Third Satire.[35]

This is in one sense perfectly true, and it would be wrong to insist that somehow Johnson did not really mean to satirize Walpole et al. in the direct

---

[34] Lascelles (1959) 41, on which perspective, in criticism, Weinbrot (1988) 164–71.

[35] Venturo (1999) 65.

and reductive manner seen here, where literary imitation becomes a quick and dirty means of registering satiric point.

And yet . . . Juvenal 3 is a fantastic *farrago* of satiric energy; compounded of literary intertexts that function as source, counterpoint, cliché, convention, and reflection; of these he has built a generic funhouse where middle-class Roman paranoias and resentments and fears loom in hugely exaggerated form; his Umbricius is the shadow of a Roman in part because what he sees has drained him of substance; wanting out of the urban funhouse, he retreats (or *says* he is retreating) to a pastoralism that is itself a bookish image of the thing on a par with the other images of fear and loathing that haunt this literary dream ("Shady" Umbricius because the projected shadow of his own fears?). In any case, he is part of the mix; no disinterested observer of "real" Roman life.[36]

And Johnson, no dull reader, has taken up the very poem. Is "Thales" just a little rich? Is Thales' own image of rural retreat a little too complacently comfortable ("Couldst thou resign the park and play content, / For the fair banks of Severn or of Trent; / there might'st thou find some elegant retreat, / Some hireling senator's deserted seat")? People *have* noticed – beyond the partisan fervor – the shifting ground, the hypocrisy, the meanness, narrowness, and prejudice.[37] Is this contamination from the source? Some of the incongruity of the satire surely does stem from Johnson's substitutions of satiric targets in a script whose outlines are necessarily dictated by Juvenal. So while the political gibes take center stage in *London*, secondary targets may seem incommensurate or only loosely connected to the imitation's major theme: the diatribe against the wheedling, sycophantic, maddeningly successful French ("No gainful trade their industry can 'scape, / They sing, they dance, clean shoes, or cure a clap" [113–14]) is Johnson's substitution for "Juvenal's" bigoted screed against Greeks; the fire that sweeps one's "little ALL" – while only Orgilio's obscenely grand palace is lamented – is likewise scripted from the original; as are the murderous night attacks ("Prepare for death, if here at night you roam, / And sign your will before you sup from home . . ." 224ff.). But the game of imitation suggests more. If Johnson wanted to make a point for the opposition,[38] he clearly did not want to do *only* that; his criticism is part and parcel of a rhetoric that overpitches, that

[36] See Braund (1989).

[37] Weinbrot (1969) 191: "[U]nlike the character of Juvenal's Umbricius, the character of Johnson's Thales is marred by contradictions, suggestions of insincerity, self-pity, self-righteousness, and arrogance: it is hard for us to believe in a person who exhorts us both to retreat to the country and to declare war on Spain." Umbricius is not so unflawed, but Weinbrot's analysis of Thales is on the mark.

[38] See Venturo (1999) on Johnson's lack of confidence in the real-world efficacy of satire.

slips into ludicrous caricature, that views the city through a glass dark to the point of obfuscation, twisting it toward Juvenalian fantasy. This is a rhetoric that necessarily betrays itself, though I do not think that it bespeaks a partisanship mired too deeply in its own hidebound framing of right and wrong as might be true of Juvenal's Umbricius. Rather, the act of imitation offers the converse: emotional distance. Johnson can lacerate his king and Walpole in the context of other indictments that derive from a mode of discourse whose bearings are more self-referential than otherwise; in imitating, Johnson, too, "alludes" to satire, as discourse, in the very act of satiric indictment. And does so within a conspicuous diachronic frame – motions of time and context are foregrounded and also placed in problematic relativity. Satire fixes the satirized in a web of indicting words, yet the web itself, its verbal constructions, are themselves destabilized by historical relativity. Satire names its targets, allusions to satire name satire in gestures that undo as well as bind up. Which is *not* to say, decidedly, that the fact of literary imitation defuses the attack Johnson wants to make, or that because he has consciously called what he is doing "an imitation of satire" he admits that this is only what satire does and is not to be taken seriously; rather it is to say that this is a discourse whose very identity is *about* its own problematic relation to reality, always asking "what is true in this partial and tendentious formulation of things?" Couched in the rhetoric of fallibility, as Rochester and Pope knew, satire is a performative speech act, requiring from the conscientious reader negotiation and "placement" of what it formulates, while remaining as resistant to definitive resolution as it is insistent in its provocations.

Further reading

Books and articles of relatively recent vintage on Rochester are fairly thick on the ground. For a refreshing literary-biographical orientation see Greer (2000); Thormählen (1993) offers substantial insight into the poetry, as do, on smaller scales, Combe (1995), Hammond (1995), Hewison (1987), Rogers (1982), and Weinbrot (1988). Ballaster (1998) has written an excellent introductory article and Fisher (2000) gives us a good set of recent essays. Love (2000) will be the preferred original-spelling text(s), but both Vieth (1968) and Walker (1984) provide valuable commentary in their editions.

Dryden, Pope, and Johnson have drawn vast critical attention and I could not hope to summarize fairly here. *Faute de mieux*, then, and for the general reader and emphasizing focus on the satirical work and Roman connections, I can recommend (*still* recommend, in some cases) Brower (1959), Ferraro (2000), Gordon (1976 [1993]), Hammond (1999), Kupersmith (1985), Lord (1987), Maurer (1997), Stack (1985), Venturo (1999), Weinbrot (1969 and 1988), Winn (1997), and Zwicker (1998). Kroll (1991) presents a useful materialist context for the period.

16

CHARLES MARTINDALE

The Horatian and the Juvenalesque in English letters

It is a time of trouble in California. Deaths from AIDS are everywhere. Nor is the wider political scene much brighter. In Reagan's America the poor queue up for private charity. Thom Gunn writes to his brother from San Francisco to invite him to come and share dinner, walks, talk, community. The tone – intimate, conversational, relaxed, jokey, detached – darkens as Gunn turns to current discontents:

> By then you will have noticed those
> Who make up Reagan's proletariat:
>   The hungry in their long lines that
> Gangling around two sides of city block
>   Are fully formed by ten o'clock
> For meals the good Franciscan fathers feed
>   Without demur to all who need.
> You'll watch the jobless side by side with whores
>   Setting a home up out of doors.
> And every day more crazies who debate
>   With phantom enemies on the street.
> I did see one with bright belligerent eye
>   Gaze from a doorstep at the sky
> And give the finger, with both hands, to God:
>   But understand, he was not odd
> Among the circumstances.
>   Well, I think
> After all that, we'll need a drink.[1]

The struggles of the poor are seen from a relatively comfortable Horatian outside, and the middle-class punch-line about needing a drink moderates any undue *saeva indignatio*. The greater part of the poem depicts the two brothers enjoying middle-aged pleasures: observing the neighbors, taking a

---

[1] Gunn (1992) 7 ("An Invitation").

trip on the ferry, climbing the hills, and preparing their dinner, with some elision of the political. This, we may say, is "Horatian" *sermo*, from 1992.

A century earlier Dickens surveyed, with radically disenchanted eye, the oppressive opulence and human emptiness of a dinner party among the newly arrived Veneerings. "She treats me like a piece of furniture," we like to say. In Dickens' nightmare world one taken-for-granted guest becomes a piece of furniture. The unwary reader may even be briefly deceived:

> There was an innocent piece of dinner-furniture that went upon easy castors and was kept over a livery stable-yard in Duke Street, Saint James's, when not in use, to whom the Veneerings were a source of blind confusion. The name of this article was Twemlow. Being first cousin to Lord Snigsworth, he was in frequent requisition, and at many houses might be said to represent the dining-table in its normal state. Mr and Mrs Veneering, for example, arranging a dinner, habitually started with Twemlow, and then put leaves in him, or added guests to him. Sometimes, the table consisted of Twemlow and half a dozen leaves; sometimes, of Twemlow and a dozen leaves; sometimes, Twemlow was pulled out to his utmost extent of twenty-leaves.[2]

At this table objects and appearances assume an energy that the conversation or the inner life of individuals lacks (something similar happens in Juvenal's fifth satire):

> The great looking-glass above the sideboard reflects the table and the company. Reflects the new Veneering crest, in gold and eke in silver, frosted and also thawed, a camel of all work. The Heralds' College found out a Crusading ancestor for Veneering who bore a camel on his shield (or might have done if he had thought of it), and a caravan of camels take charge of the fruits and flowers and candles, and kneel down to be loaded with the salt.

In this coruscating second chapter of *Our Mutual Friend*, his version of the satiric dinner-party (*cena*),[3] Dickens is writing within a well-established tradition but one that, in terms of style at any rate, owes little or nothing to Horace. The exaggeration and "caricature" (as we say, self-flatteringly); the garish light cast over the objects of the attack; the vividly observed "realistic" detail that topples into the surreal or hyper-real ("perhaps it is enhanced by a certain yellow play in Lady Tippins's throat, like the legs of scratching

---

[2] Dickens (1971) 48; subsequent quotations from 52 and 54. The passages could also be said to have "Ovidian" qualities (paradox and metamorphosis).

[3] The dinner party is where we learn/are forced to learn, through imitation, a site of symbolic violence ripe for satire; it is also where we learn satire, by imitation. Other obvious examples are Horace *S.* 2. 8 and Petronius' *cena Trimalchionis*.

poultry"); the dazzling leaps between literal and metaphorical – all bespeak a mode that we might term the "Juvenalesque."[4]

Of course the classical presences here are mediated (as classical presences always are). Dickens, notoriously, was self-educated, and may never have read Juvenal even in translation. But he had a gift, exceeded only by Shakespeare, of assimilating or intuiting kinds of discourse – as a result, like Shakespeare, he could be "influenced" by writers he had never read. Gunn is approaching Horace by way of his much-loved Ben Jonson; indeed, the poem can be regarded as an imitation of Jonson's 101st epigram "Inviting a Friend to Supper," itself an amalgam of Horace and Martial in "Horatian" vein. Such are the workings of the classical tradition.

From the sixteenth to the eighteenth centuries – what may be called the neoclassical phase of our literature – Roman verse satire was regularly translated and imitated. During this period views of Horace and Juvenal were central to the definition of satire, the question of its proper character, and its justification. Satiric invective raised problems both ethical and religious for its practitioners; the standard defense was that satire served for the promotion of virtue and the reformation of vice.[5] Elizabethans and Jacobeans generally favored a more dyspeptic satire modeled on Persius and Juvenal, but by the end of the Augustan period there was a preference for better-mannered approaches. "Fine raillery" became the preferred gentlemanly mode.[6] For Pope *The Rape of the Lock* was "a sort of writing very like tickling,"[7] and one may say to that degree "Horatian." Even the irate Swift preferred, or claimed to prefer, humor to lashing, "which gives Horace the preference to Juvenal."[8] The adjectives associated with Juvenalian satire – "furious," "tart," "nipping," "choleric," "austere," "bitter" *et al.* – might suggest a personality insufficiently amiable. Disputations about the etymology of satire could be brought tactically into play: if derived from *satura*, the word might suggest a relaxed "Horatian" medley; if from *satyr*, something altogether more scabrous and wanton.[9] Even the contrast between a stern Jonson and a more genial and capacious Shakespeare could be drawn into the debate.[10]

---

[4] Cf. Jenkyns (1982) 204–5. His is one of the best accounts of the stylistic merits of Juvenal's writing. In the early modern period characterizations are often rather two-dimensional, stressing only the sneering, scoffing character of Juvenal.

[5] For the material in this paragraph see in particular Elkin (1973); also Weinbrot (1982).

[6] So Dryden observes that "there is a vast difference betwixt the slovenly butchering of a man, and the fineness of a stroke that separates the head from the body and leaves it standing in its place." On those grounds he particularly relished his portrait of "Zimri" (the Duke of Buckingham) in *Absalom and Achitophel* (Hammond and Hopkins [2000] 423–4).

[7] Elkin (1973) 150.   [8] Elkin (1973) 159.

[9] See further Burrow in this volume.   [10] Elkin (1973) 65.

Of course, there were voices on the other side: an outspoken Juvenal could be linked favorably to a tradition of English freedoms (as he was, if perhaps with some irony, by Dryden, who implied that he was "a zealous vindicator of Roman liberty").[11] But in general by the end of the Augustan period Horace (or "Horace") had emerged largely victorious. That victory, however, was destined to be short lived, as Romanticism brought new literary priorities and new classical favorites. Nonetheless, it could be argued that "Horace" helped to mediate the transition from the revolutionary crises of the seventeenth century to an Addisonian mode of gentlemanly consensus in the eighteenth.

At all events the names of Horace and Juvenal were by 1700 constantly linked in a mutually defining pair. A *synkrisis* was a set-piece rhetorical exercise with its roots in antiquity, for example the comparison of Caesar and Cato as the two greatest men of the time in Sallust's *Catiline*, 54.[12] The predominant trope in such writing was antithesis. Comparisons of poets and writers in this mode were common in the early modern period: Virgil and Homer, Virgil and Ovid, Virgil and Lucan, Jonson and Shakespeare. In such binaries one element is defined in terms of its perceived other; such categories seem needed "to think with," as the structuralists liked to tell us. The danger is the forcing out of middle terms.[13] The common opposition between Horace and Juvenal was both constructed out of, and contributed towards, a particular "take" on either author (sometimes there is also a triangulation with Persius).[14] Dryden in his "Discourse Concerning Satire" works, for the most part, in a relaxed and exploratory way with many of the traditional antitheses from previous scholarly discussions – instruction and pleasure, satire comical and tragical, vice and folly – to give a subtle and personal account of the two poets, which also legitimates his own satiric writing. If a poet is to be of use to his successors, there is a need for such images, without which constructive engagement may be difficult. These images, though, are best regarded as constructions, always open for renegotiation, always based on privileging certain elements over others, on selecting particular works as characteristic.[15] In the case of Horace's *Sermones* traditional favorites

---

[11] Hammond and Hopkins (2000) 415. So, too, Gibbon thought that, unlike Horace, "Juvenal alone never prostitutes his muse" (Weinbrot [1982] 39).

[12] Compare Horace's comparison of himself as "lover of the countryside" with Fuscus, "lover of the city," in *Epist.* 1.10.

[13] See e.g. Hartog (1988) 212–59. Hooley's chapter in this volume shows how, *in practice*, the redeployment of Horatian and Juvenalian modes does not necessarily result in a strongly antithetical image of this poet or that.

[14] Quintilian (10.1.93–5) compares Lucilius, Horace, and Persius.

[15] For a fuller version of this argument see the introduction to Martindale and Hopkins (1993).

have been 1.9 and 2.6; poems judged less favorably are often dismissed as "immature" or "untypical" (like most of the *Epodes*). But it would be possible to construct a more Juvenalian Horace – or should that be "Juvenalian" and "Horace"? – from, say, 1.2 and 1.8, and 2.5; just as satires 9, 11 and 14 could be used to construct a more Horatian Juvenal (with, or without, the scare-quotes).

In such binaries either name is closely implicated with the other. One can go further and argue that the opposition is always already inscribed within the original texts (from the perspective of reception). In *Sermones* 2.1, a defense or mock-defense or mock-mock-defense, of his satiric writing, Horace says there are some to whom he seems too sharp (*acer*), while to others he lacks spunk (*sine nervis*), foreshadowing, or helping to create, the terms of later comparisons. In his first satire Juvenal places himself in relation to a tradition that includes Horace, wishing to replicate his predecessors (writing things worthy of Horace, *Venusina digna lucerna*, 51) but unable to do so because of his belatedness (a trope indeed appropriated from Horace).

Horace has been fully naturalized in English poetry (as, indeed, an element of "Englishness"). For this purpose, as in Thomas Wyatt's Horatian imitations in the sixteenth century, the satires blend seamlessly into the less caustic *Epistles* (did not Horace himself call both *sermones*?), and indeed into the entire œuvre. This English Horace is ironic and urbane, lover of the countryside, devoted to friendship and quietude (both political and philosophical), with the Sabine "farm" (aka a small villa-estate with eight tenant farmers) as the appropriate symbol of his moral preferences. For a textbook instance of such a Horace we can turn to the version of the end of *Sermones* 2.6, the tale of two mice, first published in 1663 by Abraham Cowley, one aspirant to the title of "The English Horace" (others include Ben Jonson and Alexander Pope).[16] Reading Horace through Cowley we encounter an amused but sympathetic treatment of both denizens of a mousey world, whose opposed lifestyles enable us to reflect on the difficult balance to be achieved by any searcher after the good life. Cowley gives to the "Epicurean mind" of the town mouse a speech that is no mere parody but recalls sentiments that animate some of Horace's most moving poems:

> Why should a soul so virtuous and so great
> Lose itself thus in an obscure retreat?
> Let savage beasts lodge in a country den;
> You should see towns, and manners know, and men,
> And taste the generous luxury of the Court,

[16] For a fine analysis of this neglected poem see David Hopkins, "Cowley's Horatian Mice" in Martindale and Hopkins (1993) 103–26.

Where all the mice of quality resort,
Where thousand beauteous shes about you move,
And by high fare are pliant made to love.
We all ere long must render up our breath;
No cave or hole can shelter us from death.
Since life is so uncertain and so short,
Let's spend it all in feasting and in sport;
Come, worthy sir, come with me and partake
All the great things that mortals happy make.

(34–47)

"You should see towns, and manners know, and men" looks back to the opening of the *Odyssey* by way of Horace's imitation in *Epistle* 1.2.19–20, not without help from another English Horatian, Ben Jonson ("Roe (and my joy to name) thou'art now to go/Countries and climes, manners and men, to know": *Epigrams* 128.1–2). There is humor in attributing sentiments so lofty to a mouse, but also a persuasive nobility of expression. As with Pope's treatment of the diminutive sylphs in *The Rape of the Lock*, Cowley's mock-heroic mode holds in balance both the tininess of a murine world and our own analogous insignificance if seen from some larger perspective. At their country feast the *pièce de résistance* is "a large chestnut, the delicious meat| Which Jove himself (were he a mouse) would eat" (16–17): the mention of Jove introduces a measure which reduces humans as much as mice.

Perhaps Cowley is a touch too comfortable with his own Horatianism.[17] Indeed, in general the English are often quick – over-quick? – to identify with the figure of an ingratiating Horace. In *Sermones* 1.9 most readers appear to associate themselves with the poet, not his interlocutor – the "bore" or "pest" as he is sometimes called (though to Ben Jonson, who turned this poem into a scene in his play *Poetaster*, he was both a bad poet and a bad man).[18] Such identification may serve only to reinforce our own complacencies: moreover is the "Horace" of this poem so different, in his actions and aspirations in relation to Maecenas and the court, from his unwelcome companion – unwelcome perhaps as raising precisely such

---

[17] An edition of Horace edited by Alexander Broome (1666) contains a composite translation of the whole of *Sermones* 2.6, with Cowley's mice preceded by the first half in a version by his friend Thomas Sprat, which gives the poem a contemporary setting and wittily makes Horace's Cervius into Cowley himself. Perhaps Sprat is twitting his friend on his over-earnest Horatianism.

[18] *Poetaster* III.i.4. A later scene (III.v) dramatizes Horace, *Sermones* 2.1, defending satires "That spare men's persons, but tax their crimes" (134). In v.i.94 Horace is commended by Augustus for his "free and wholesome sharpness." The epilogue is a defense of satire, deploying classical arguments.

questions?[19] Horace by contrast, it has been argued, continually tests the extent to which he is "a true Horatian."[20] As his slave points out, the supposed enthusiast for the countryside is quick enough to rush back to town the moment Maecenas beckons, a parasite of parasites (*Sermones* 2.7.28–34). In that respect Pope's engagement with Horace is a more probing one than Cowley's. Dr. Johnson complained of the *Imitations of Horace* (where the Latin text was printed parallel with Pope's version) that: "Between Roman images and English manners there will be an irreconcileable dissimilitude, and the work will be generally uncouth and party-coloured; neither original nor translated, neither ancient nor modern."[21] But the play of likeness and difference may be the animating point of the procedure, one in which each text reads the other, and at times resists the other. Walter Benjamin in "The Task of the Translator" argued for the truth-revealing qualities of such interlinearity: truth for Benjamin lying not so much *in* texts as *between* texts. This is the basis of one defining characteristic of great poetry: its *translatability*, by which we should understand not that any great poem has been successfully translated but that it *demands* such translation:

> For to some degree all great texts contain their potential translation between the lines; this is true to the highest degree of sacred writings. The interlinear version of the Scriptures is the prototype or ideal of all translation.[22]

In the case of the *Imitations* the interlinear version allows for the truth about both Horace and Pope.[23] In the words of T. S. Eliot, Pope can be seen as "giving the original through himself, and finding himself through the original."[24]

Identification with Juvenal is perhaps a rarer phenomenon. For example, where in Juvenal's version of the satiric dinner, satire 5, should the reader position herself? With the overweening host or the guest complicit with his own humiliation? Maybe for this reason, or because of the long-time preoccupation with him as primarily a moralist, Juvenal has resisted successful naturalization in English. His seventeenth-century translators and imitators, with the exception of Dryden, seem to bring little but a generalized sense of nipping choler to the task. One can point to (or construct?) isolated instances of the Juvenalesque, as I have done with the passages from

---

[19] The most suggestive treatment of this poem is Henderson (1999) 202–27.

[20] See Colin Burrow in Martindale and Hopkins (1993) 27–31. There is a *mise en abîme* here: by testing whether he is a true Horatian Horace becomes a true Horatian.

[21] Johnson (1905) II 247. Johnson's remarks may reflect his dissatisfaction with his own imitations of Juvenal.

[22] Benjamin (1970) 82.   [23] For an excellent reading along these lines see Stack (1985).

[24] Eliot (1933) introduction xiv.

Dickens. (E. J. Kenney writes of Juvenal's "simple inability to see beyond the end of his nose," but qualified this criticism thus: "up to that point his vision has hardly ever been equalled except by a few such as Hogarth and Dickens."[25] Significantly the way the sentence is troped could itself be termed Juvenalian.) Ben Jonson seemed inhibited by a sense of classical decorum, when in his play *Sejanus* he directly imitated Juvenal's description of the fall of the Tiberian favorite. Juvenal's lines describing the melting down of a statue of Sejanus, which fairly crackle with life (10. 61–4),[26] are drained of energy and particularity to become the relatively colorless:

> Now
> The furnace and the bellows shall to work,
> The great Sejanus crack, and piece by piece
> Drop in the founder's pit.   (v. 773–6)

As H. A. Mason has it, Jonson's rendering "represents only the *surface* of Juvenal. It is an abstraction from the text. What is absent from Jonson is Juvenal's *wit*."[27] And, one might add, his descriptive vividness achieved in part by the inclusion of "low" words, which would have been inadmissible in a tragedy. But Juvenal seeps more deeply into Jonson's consciousness elsewhere, for example in his grotesquely physical depictions of old age in *Volpone*. The Fox is feigning illness and age to gull gifts from legacy-hunters (a stock topic of Roman satire), and Juvenal, if more submerged than in *Sejanus*, becomes evident in the writing with its hyperboles, grotesquerie, similes, descriptive precision (though with less pathos):

> Mosca
>   Would you once close
> Those filthy eyes of yours, that flow with slime,
> Like two frog-pits; and those same hanging cheeks,
> Covered with hide, instead of skin (nay, help, sir)
> That look like frozen dish-clouts, set on end.
> Corvino
> Or like an old smoked wall on which the rain
> Ran down in streaks.
> Mosca
>   Excellent, sir, speak out;
> You may be louder yet; a culvering
> Discharged in his ear would hardly bore it.
>   (1.v.56–64)

---

[25] Quoted by Jenkyns (1982) 220.

[26] *[I]am strident ignes, iam follibus atque caminis/ardet adoratum populo caput et crepat ingens/Seianus, deinde ex facie toto orbe secunda/fiunt urceoli, pelues, sartago, matellae.*

[27] H. A. Mason, "Is Juvenal a Classic?" in Sullivan (1963) 111.

Dryden comes closest to achieving a consistently compelling English Juvenal in his translations. What is missing from the *Sejanus* passage is shown by Dryden's freer rendering, from his Juvenal translations of 1692:

> The smith prepares his hammer for the stroke
> While the lunged bellows hissing fire provoke;
> Sejanus, almost first of Roman names,
> The great Sejanus crackles in the flames;
> Formed in the forge, the pliant brass is laid
> On anvils, and of head and limbs are made
> Pans, cans and pisspots, a whole kitchen trade.
>
> (91–7)

The last line gets some of the climactic, or anti-climactic, effect of Juvenal's final stab, *matellae* (64), while the phrase "a whole kitchen trade" sharply evokes an entire personal existence in a Juvenalian way. Dr. Johnson thought Dryden's translation wanted "the dignity of the original"; in his view "the peculiarity of Juvenal is a mixture of gaiety and stateliness, of pointed sentences and declamatory grandeur."[28] Certainly his own imitation of satire 10, the celebrated "Vanity of Human Wishes," has dignity, but its unremitting stylistic seriousness and moral sanity have seemed to many readers to miss Juvenal's "peculiarity" a great deal more than Dryden (whether it was designed to represent Johnson's sense of Juvenal, or rather to correct what was morally and stylistically undesirable in the original is unclear). Juvenal ends his declamation against Hannibal with an acknowledgment (perhaps imbued with self-loathing as well as a sense that everything has been said) of its hackneyed character:

> i, demens, et saevas curre per Alpes,
> ut pueris placeas et declamatio fias.
>
> (10.166–7)

In his imitation Johnson allows both himself and Charles of Sweden (his equivalent for Hannibal) their measure of uncompromised grandeur:

> He left the name, at which the world grew pale,
> To point a moral, or adorn a tale.   (221–2)

Dryden (who admittedly omits the contemptuous mention of the Subura, perhaps misled by the commentators, and has "corrosive juices" for Juvenal's blunt "vinegar") gives:

---

[28] Johnson (1905) II 447.

Go, climb the ragged Alps, ambitious fool,
To please the boys, and be a theme at school!
(271–2)

In general Dryden's Juvenal is witty, but not merely opportunistically so, and combines "pathos, surreal fancy, studied observation, or delicately imagined beauty,"[29] reflecting Dryden's enthusiasm for a writer who "gives me as much pleasure as I can bear" (the sexual connotations of the language are evident, and indeed traditional in satire):[30]

> He fully satisfies my expectation, he treats his subject home; his spleen is raised, and he raises mine . . . he drives his reader along with him, and when he is at the end of his way, I willingly stop with him. If he went another stage, it would be too far; it would make a journey of a progress, and turn delight into fatigue.[31]

Imitation, of course, can combine different models (scholars call this *contaminatio*). The great French satirist Boileau was praised for "uniting the style of Juvenal and Persius with that of Horace."[32] Howard Weinbrot argues that Pope eclectically combined ancient models, rather as Shakespeare blended tragedy and comedy, to produce a mixed mode.[33] Horace may often have been the declared model, but Pope, it has been argued, found Horatian equanimity difficult of achievement and was in some respects temperamentally closer to "Juvenal." For example, the *Epistle to Arbuthnot* starts in relaxed colloquial vein, and employs an autobiographical mode to present an apologia for Pope's life and works; but the range of tones goes way beyond the *sermo pedestris*. Thus the line about the dunce in his garret (42) – "Lulled by soft zephyrs through the broken pane" – lovingly uses the grand style only to undercut it with demeaning detail to produce an effect that could be called Juvenalian.[34] The blending of tones, grave and gay, owes much to Horace, but the range is greater. When Pope turns on the hated Lord Hervey, the seesaw of the endstopped couplets perfectly combines with the barrage of metaphors (including Pope's favorite insect imagery and references to *Paradise Lost*) to anatomize his victim's slippery and satanic androgyny. Only with Dante, perhaps, has anger been such a spur to poetic creativity:

---

[29] Hopkins (1995) 52 (part of an excellent account of Dryden's translation of Juvenal 10).
[30] E.g. Persius 1.   [31] Hammond and Hopkins (2000) 412.
[32] Elkin (1973) 43 (quoting William Shenstone, 1764).   [33] Weinbrot (1982) 276–364.
[34] For an account of the poem as enacting the failure of a good-humored "Horatian" satiric mode to give an adequate response to contemporary abuses see Weinbrot (1982) 240–75.

Let Sporus tremble – 'What? That thing of silk,
Sporus, that mere white curd of ass's milk?
Satire, or sense alas! can Sporus feel?
Who breaks a butterfly upon a wheel?'
Yet let me flap this bug with gilded wings,
This painted child of dirt that stinks and stings;
Whose buzz the witty and the fair annoys,
Yet wit ne'er tastes, and beauty ne'er enjoys;
So well-bred spaniels civilly delight
In mumbling of the game they dare not bite.
Eternal smiles his emptiness betray,
As shallow streams run dimpling all the way.
Whether in florid impotence he speaks,
And – as the prompter breathes – the puppet squeaks;
Or at the ear of Eve, familiar toad,
Half froth half venom, spits himself abroad,
In puns or politics or tales or lies
Or spite or smut or rhymes or blasphemies,
His wit all see-saw between 'that' and 'this',
Now high, now low, now master up, now miss,
And he himself one vile antithesis.
Amphibious thing! that acting either part,
The trifling head or the corrupted heart,
Fop at the toilet, flatterer at the board,
Now trips a lady, and now struts a lord.
Eve's tempter thus the rabbins have expressed,
A cherub face, a reptile all the rest;
Beauty that shocks you, parts that none will trust,
Wit that can creep, and pride that licks the dust.

(305–33)

No wonder the upright Johnson felt discomfort with the passage.[35]

The modern phase of aesthetics, for which Kant's *Critique of Judgement* is the key text, has tended to separate the artistic sphere from the ethical. Kant himself was concerned only to distinguish different kinds of judgment (the judgment that "X is beautiful" from the judgment that "X is (morally) good"). But subsequently, particularly with the development of versions of aestheticism like art for art's sake, art became a separate realm of human activity. In Swinburne's words, "To art, that is best which is most beautiful; to science, that is best which is most accurate; to morality, that is best which is most virtuous."[36] The result is that the standard moral defense of satire

[35] Johnson (1905) II 246 ("The meanest passage is the satire on Sporus").
[36] Quoted by Prettejohn (1999) 1.

left the genre looking rather exposed as non-art. Indeed, satire does not feature in Palgrave's *Golden Treasury* (1861) and hardly in *The Oxford Book of English Verse* selected by Arthur Quiller-Couch ("Q") and published in 1900, while Roman satire is omitted altogether from H. W. Garrod's *Oxford Book of Latin Verse* (1912). Today, critics are mostly uneasy with any neo-Kantian notion of aesthetic autonomy; satiric writing may be valued precisely as a carnivalesque challenge to the very idea of "art."[37] But it seems reasonable to argue that the virtue of satire *as poetry* may differ from its virtue as moral discourse, and even that the two may pull in opposite directions. One may go further and argue that satire only becomes great poetry when it reveals artistic impulses of a non-moral kind.[38] Critics have noted how irony takes on a kind of autonomous life in both Swift and Pope.[39] The chaos that Pope's satires reveal to us is not the dull chaos that ordinarily surrounds and cramps us but a kind of sharp, manic, surreal vision of a bright disorder. An example is a detail from the chapel service from the *Epistle to Burlington*:

> And now the chapel's silver bell you hear,
> That summons you to all the pride of prayer.
> Light quirks of music, broken and uneven,
> Make the soul dance upon a jig to heaven . . .
> To rest, the cushion and soft dean invite,
> Who never mentions Hell to ears polite.
>
> (141–5, 150–1)

"Pride of prayer" inverts the Christian ideal of humility before God, while the neat coupling "cushion and soft dean," with the adjective cheekily trans-ferred from the noun it more "naturally" goes with, is a typical Popean zeugma. The couplet about the music, however, belongs to a different imagi-native order. The ostensible point is incongruity (this secular-sounding music hardly suits conventional ideas of what is appropriate in divine service); but

---

[37] So e.g. White (1993) 122–59.

[38] The best of Dryden's satires can also be analysed in this way. *Mac Flecknoe* is much more than an attack on Shadwell:

> Such writing is neither heroic nor burlesque, neither for nor against, neither political nor aesthetic. This is heroic writing that despairs of itself and laughs at itself; it is satire that for the first time in English takes on not Juvenalian power nor Horatian civility but something softer and wilder and, if one wants, more English. This is satire as dream ('His rising fogs prevail upon the day', 'Thoughtless as monarch oaks that shade the plain', 'And lambent dullness played around his face') – satire as longing, as true poetry.
> (Everett [2001] 32)

[39] So e.g. Griffin (1994) 65.

nothing in the language registers disgust, and instead we are presented with a curious moment of felicity, almost a childish beatific vision, which runs imaginatively counter to the purported moral.[40] In Juvenal, too, the satiric impulse is a fluctuating one, even if he is less elusive than Pope. In satire 5 the moral point is that the host gives inferior food to his less important guests, but it is the food itself that fires Juvenal's imagination:

> aspice quam longo distinguat pectore lancem
> quae fertur domino squilla, et quibus undique saepta
> asparagis qua despiciat conuiuia cauda,
> dum uenit excelsi manibus sublata ministri.   (80–3)

look with how long a breast the lobster which is brought to the master marks out the dish, and fenced on all sides by what asparagus spears, with what a tail it looks down on the dinner party, when it comes carried on high by the hands of the attendant.

Epic diction presents us with the lobster as great man (an image worthy of the imperious host as well as of Juvenal's epicizing satiric *lanx*), borne on high ringed by a green palisade.[41]

The Romans seem to have been proud of their primacy in satire, or rather *satura*, even while acknowledging the low status of the genre (Horace pretends at least that his satires are not "real" poetry, like Ennius' *Annals*). It constituted a distinctive but in the last resort a limited achievement. Perhaps its greatest gift was its later progeny. As a verse satirist Pope combines many of the virtues of the satires of Horace and Juvenal to surpass them both in imaginative reach. At the end of the fourth book of the *Dunciad* Pope, the English Horace, produces a maimed sublime that owes something to Juvenal and more to Milton (who also wrote some extraordinarily powerful satiric passages)[42] to set forth, while at the same time resisting through this very act of writing, the ultimate apocalyptic triumph of Dullness:

> In vain, in vain, – the all-composing hour
> Resistless falls: the Muse obeys the power.
> She comes, she comes! the sable throne behold
> Of Night primeval and of Chaos old!
> Before her fancy's gilded clouds decay,
> And all its varying rainbows die away.

---

[40] For the childlike in Pope see Martindale (1983); for a brilliant account of the *Dunciad* along these lines see Jones (1968), a classic essay.

[41] See Jenkyns (1982) 218.

[42] See e.g. the speech of St. Peter in "Lycidas," or "the Paradise of Fools" (*Paradise Lost* 3.440–97).

> Wit shoots in vain its momentary fires,
> The meteor drops, and in a flash expires . . .
> Lo, thy dread empire, Chaos, is restored,
> Light dies before thy uncreating word;
> Thy hand, great Anarch, lets the curtain fall,
> And universal darkness buries all.
>
> (627–34, 653–6)

What Roman satirist ever wrote anything like that?[43]

After the eighteenth century the direct influence of Roman verse satire waned somewhat, but its traces can be tracked even in unexpected places. *The Waste Land*, for example, in whose genesis Popean satire played a significant part, can be seen as a modernist version of mock heroic, or perhaps *mock mock heroic*:[44]

> Unreal City,
> Under the brown fog of a winter dawn,
> A crowd flowed over London bridge, so many,
> I had not thought death had undone so many.
> ('The Burial of the Dead', 60–3)

(The echo of Dante's *Inferno* in this grim modern cityscape can be seen as a characteristically satiric gesture towards the stylistic grandeurs of a great tradition.) One wonders if, and how, the Horatian and Juvenalesque will continue their manifestations in the twenty-first century. The matter ought to be of some concern to all who read this volume. Will satirical verse in the twenty-first century find the need of the sharpnesses of a classical tradition to ignite itself against?[45] In a review of Elizabeth Cook's recent novelette *Achilles* (2001), Michael Silk issues this timely warning to his fellow classical scholars, a warning that the profession would do well to heed:

> The past is dead past or living past. It lives only in its current renewals, the most vital of which are artistic, even if many academic custodians of the past have difficulty grasping that point and its significance. Renewals of the classical past are for the Western world the prime instance – both of renewal and of academic incomprehension. 'A pretty poem, Mr Pope, but you must not call it Homer', said the eighteenth-century scholar, Richard Bentley, of Pope's *Iliad*:

---

43 Of course, Horace is capable of this kind of imaginative reach in the *Odes*, as is the epicist Lucretius, in diatribe or "satiric" mode. But it remains true that ancient and modern satirists work with different notions of what the genre can, or cannot, do.

44 So Rawson (1982) 60–1. Part 3 of *The Waste Land*, "The Fire Sermon," originally contained a section in heroic couplets after Pope, which Eliot deleted on the advice of Ezra Pound.

45 Classical satire seems currently out of fashion with poets; by contrast Martin Amis, though no Juvenal, has something of his brattish sharpness.

portentous and still dismally representative words . . . As Elizabeth Cook's dismally dead Achilles says to her Odysseus: 'don't you know it's sweeter to be alive . . . than lord of all these shadows?' Then, 'he strides away, leaving Odysseus unblessed.' Academic custodians beware, lest you too prove to be mere lords of shadows – in fleeting communion with the unblessed.[46]

Further reading

Currently the best basic introduction to English satiric writing and the issues it raises is Dustin Griffin, *Satire: a Critical Reintroduction* (Lexington 1994) – the material is organized thematically.

For useful collections of translations and imitations there are two Penguin volumes: *Horace in English* (1996) ed. D. S. Carne-Ross and Kenneth Haynes (with an admirable introduction by the former) and *Juvenal in English*, ed. Martin M. Winkler (Harmondsworth 1996, 2001). For the reception of Horace generally see Martindale and Hopkins (1993).

For Augustan attitudes to satire see Elkin (1973). For individual satirists see the following: on Oldham – Paul Hammond, *John Oldham and the Renewal of Classical Culture* (Cambridge 1983); on Dryden – Hopkins (1995) 31–60; on Pope – Stack (1985); Weinbrot (1982).

---

[46] Silk (2001) 24. On the whole neither ancient nor modern satire has attracted the best critical minds. Accordingly I would like to thank the members of an *ad hoc* Satire Reading Group at Bristol, who served to arouse my interest in the topic: Paul Duffus, Duncan Kennedy, Genevieve Liveley, Ellen O'Gorman. Thanks are also due to Colin Burrow, Elizabeth Prettejohn, and, above all, David Hopkins.

17

DUNCAN KENNEDY

The "presence" of Roman satire: modern receptions and their interpretative implications

It is a commonplace to say that satire is the most difficult genre to define, and always has been. "Metamorphic" and "Protean" are terms commonly applied to it, the latter perhaps suggesting that it not only has no stable form but will also continue to elude attempts to tie it down. The task of exploring what constitutes the "presence" of Roman satire in the present and recent past is thus a rather delicate one, for how can we recognize it to be "there" if we are not sure what we are looking for? If one looks hard enough, one can find James Joyce referring to *Ulysses* as "farraginous."[1] The satiric associations of this term (*nostri farrago libelli*, Juvenal 1.86) will certainly not have been lost on Joyce, but most readers could be forgiven for failing to spot the writer of Latin hexameter verse in this novel shape. Formal verse satire is still practiced, but not in a way that seems central to the œuvre of any major author or to cultural practice more generally, as it could be argued it was in the seventeenth and eighteenth centuries.[2] Although Martin Winkler in his anthology *Juvenal in English* detects some significant echoes in T. S. Eliot and W. H. Auden,[3] twentieth-century engagement with Horace and Juvenal has largely come in the form of translations, but nothing has emerged that could begin to match the response of Dryden and Johnson to Juvenal. Instances of the invocation of Roman satirical texts as clear as *Fellini's Satyricon* are very few and far between. Thus, while "satire," or perhaps rather "satiric(al)," are words we run up against constantly in analyses of contemporary culture (an issue I shall consider in what follows), the search for any defining formal characteristic that will link past to present may turn out to be more frustrating than enlightening. But would we be right to assume that, because we do not encounter it in its most familiar forms, the Roman satirical tradition is dead in the water?

---

[1] I found it in Fowler (1982) 190.   [2] Cf. Martindale in this volume.
[3] Cf. Winkler (2001) liii.

If the adjective "satirical" seems to occur more readily than the noun "satire," that suggests that we are currently more comfortable dealing with satire as a mode rather than as a genre or a form; and when it is conceived of *as* a mode, the question of antecedent kinds or models does not seem so pressing. Thus the invitation to compare, say, Juvenal and *Spitting Image* usually downplays the question of genealogical connection in favor of an appeal to tropes, subjects, or perspectives perceived as shared, as transhistorically "typical" of satire. The two to be compared are quietly lifted out of any historical context and made to stand face to face in a (timeless) "present" constructed by that invitation. But even as a timeless "feature" of satire is made present in this way, a complementary urge to historicize equips it with a genealogy (and so Juvenal can become the precursor of *Spitting Image*). So, for example, if it is asserted, as it was at the outset of this essay, that satire's problems with generic definition have been "there" all along (and here – the complementary genealogical move of which I have just spoken – we may think of Horace's attempts to codify the genre he is practicing in satire 1.4), this suggests that any process of definition is an *ad hoc* construction, and that once the preferred *modal* attributes are highlighted, and thus represented as historically transcendent, they can be "discovered" to be "there" in works from the past, whatever their form. Thus Horace "finds" the satire he is practicing not only in Lucilius but also in Greek Old Comedy; and, writing in the late 1960s, Matthew Hodgart's definition of "the impulses behind satire" as "basic to human nature"[4] allows him to trace antecedents back not only through a Greco-Roman Western tradition beyond Greek Old Comedy to the iambic invectives of Archilochus, but also transculturally to "savages"[5] and (recall that we are talking about the expression of a historically transcendent human "nature" here), in a grand universalizing gesture across time, to the "primitive" stages of human development. But why draw the line there? Hodgart's view of satire as expressing impulses of a "nature" that extends even beyond that of the human ("indeed, they probably go back beyond human nature, to the psychology of our animal forebears")[6] allows his analysis to transcend species. Satire, he says, aims to make its victims lose face, and the most effective way of humiliating them is by contemptuous laughter, because, we are told, "as is well known, horses and dogs do not like to be laughed at."[7] Represent satire *as* something as broad as Hodgart does, and you can "find" it everywhere, even in your four-legged friend asleep at your feet.

---

[4] Hodgart (1969) 10.   [5] Hodgart (1969) 17.
[6] Hodgart (1969) 10.   [7] Hodgart (1969) 11.

Hodgart's arguments are (I take it) seriously meant. Such displays of biological determinism, however, sit uncomfortably in literary criticism, and it will not be everyone whose first thought is of Petronius or Juvenal when the mutt they have affronted sinks his teeth into their leg.[8] Theory pursued so single-mindedly can lead to strange conclusions; what need have you of a dog when you are barking yourself? The point is not an entirely frivolous one. Where we find Roman satire in the "present" will depend on what are represented as the defining features of satire, and the genealogies that emerge will reflect this. Two theories of literature in the twentieth century, both ambitious, and with strong universalizing pretensions, are relevant to our argument here: those of Northrop Frye and Mikhail Bakhtin. Both seek to explore the formal features of prose fiction, and both construct genealogies that extend back to the Roman satirical tradition.

Frye's *Anatomy of Criticism* (1957) seeks to develop a fourfold scheme of types (novel, confession, anatomy, and romance) into which, singly or in combination, all works of fiction could be placed. A term such as "novel" does not readily embrace all the manifestations of prose fiction, Frye remarks, and continues:

> most people would call *Gulliver's Travels* fiction but not a novel. It must then be another form of fiction, as it certainly has a form, and we feel that we are turning from the novel to this form, whatever it is, when we turn from Rousseau's *Emile* to Voltaire's *Candide*, or from Butler's *The Way of All Flesh* to the Erewhon books, or from Huxley's *Point Counterpoint* to *Brave New World*.[9]

Even as a new transhistorical "type" is invoked, the complementary urge to historicize equips it with a genealogy: "The form thus has its own traditions, and, as the examples of Butler and Huxley show, has preserved some integrity even under the ascendancy of the novel . . . The form used by these authors is the Menippean satire." Conversely, then, one place where we might sense

---

[8] When a text (or a body of ideas) is cited in such a way as to open out a distance from the original intentions or pretensions to truth retrospectively imputed to it, we have the conditions for satire. And, having wagered on a defining feature of satire, let me now construct a genealogy: consider the use of appeals to biological determinism and the primitive in Horace, *Sermones* 1.3.99–124 or 2.1.50–3 or in Juvenal 6.1–13. Poststructuralist theory would have it that all discourse involves citation, and consequently the distance I have suggested as one of the conditions for satire; conversely, all discourse involves a recursive mimesis of tropes (more on these themes below). From this theoretical perspective, the study of satire may feel most "appropriate" when cast in a satisfyingly recursive mimesis of satirical tropes.

[9] Frye (1957) 308.

the presence of Roman satire, if we follow Frye's theory, is in certain modern prose fictions. Frye goes on to define the form thus:

> The Menippean satire deals less with people as such than with mental attitudes. Pedants, bigots, cranks, parvenus, virtuosi, enthusiasts, rapacious and incompetent professional men of all kinds, are handled in terms of their occupational approach to life as distinct from their social behavior. The Menippean satire thus resembles the confession in its ability to handle abstract ideas and theories, and differs from the novel in its characterization, which is stylized rather than naturalistic, and presents people as mouthpieces of the ideas they represent . . . A constant theme in the tradition is the ridicule of the *philosophus gloriosus* . . . The novelist sees evil and folly as social diseases, but the Menippean satirist sees them as diseases of the intellect, as a kind of maddened pedantry which the *philosophus gloriosus* at once symbolizes and defines.[10]

This move allows Frye to embrace authors from Petronius and Apuleius through Rabelais, Erasmus, Swift, Voltaire, and Sterne to the Alice books ("perfect Menippean satire") as works which rely on "the free play of intellectual fancy and the kind of humorous observation that produces caricature . . . At its most concentrated the Menippean satire presents us with a vision of the world in terms of a single intellectual pattern."[11] The Menippean satirist, we are told, "shows his exuberant attitude in intellectual ways, by piling up an enormous mass of erudition about his theme or in overwhelming his pedantic targets with an avalanche of their own jargon."[12] In satire, such citation (which can range from single words to larger formal characteristics) serves, as we have seen, to open up a distance from the source in which irony can be given play. Frye mentions Varro in this regard, but critics working in the wake of Frye have drawn attention to the way that a number of satiric writers apart from Varro are also known as scholars and antiquaries of language, rhetoric, usage, and style. Thus a received tradition embracing Lucian, Rabelais, Erasmus, and Johnson could be extended to include in the twentieth century figures as diverse as A. E. Housman, H. L. Mencken, and George Orwell. Furthermore, satiric texts can take works of scholarship as their style (e.g. Ambrose Bierce's *Devil's Dictionary*) or the ways of scholars as their theme, as in the campus novel, for example David Lodge's *Changing Places* and *Small World*, which attempt to take an ironized synoptic view of contemporary intellectual fashions. For Frye, "this creative treatment of exhaustive erudition is the organizing principle of the greatest Menippean satire in English before Swift, Burton's *Anatomy of Melancholy*," and, for all the importance he grants to Menippean satire in the definition of this type, Frye thus prefers "anatomy" as his generic title in preference to what he calls

---

[10] Frye (1957) 309.   [11] Frye (1957) 310.   [12] Frye (1957) 311.

"the cumbersome and in modern times misleading 'Menippean satire.' "[13] "Anatomy," of course, provides the title of Frye's own work and prompts the thought that scholarship, if not circumscribed by Frye's category, has affinities to it. This could raise questions about the encyclopedic pretensions of *The Anatomy of Criticism* itself and its "vision of the world in terms of a single intellectual pattern" – only insofar as scholarship can be regarded as a "work of fiction," of course, rather than a direct revelation of knowledge and truth, though this is a move feasible within a poststructuralist framework which sees all discourse, whatever its pretension to truth, as a "construct," and, through citation, amenable to ironic re-presentation.

Bakhtin's theories predate Frye's, but did not generally become available in the West until the 1960s. In *Problems of Dostoevsky's Poetics* (1929), the challenge for Bakhtin was to find a suitable formal categorization and historical genealogy for what he saw as "Dostoevsky's polyphonic use and interpretation of generic combinations."[14] Bakhtin "finds" what he is looking for in a coalition of forms encompassed by what the ancients called *spoudogeloion*, the serio-comical, and represented for him primarily by the Socratic dialogue (which tends more towards the serious) and the Menippean satire (which tends more towards the comic). Bakhtin's main concern is not with ancient texts but with the modern (i.e. Dostoevskyan) novel, and so he avoids "Menippean satire" as his generic term (attested as such first only in 1581, anyhow)[15] in favor of a coinage of his own, *menippea*. He suggests no fewer than fourteen basic characteristics of this latter genre derived from the ancient texts,[16] and the broad taxonomy that results could embrace a wide selection of twentieth-century fiction. The genre, he says, is characterized by an extraordinary freedom of plot and situation for the testing of a philosophical idea or truth, often embodied in the figure of a protagonist (reminiscent of Frye's *philosophus gloriosus*) who is the skewed seeker of this truth. It thus deals with ultimate questions, though its depictions often wander from conventional plausibility, and its style from the "free fantastic" to "slum naturalism." In this context, one might think of the novels of Flann O'Brien (e.g. *The Third Policeman* which takes "seriously" and to their logical consequences pre-Socratic theories of nature), John Barth (e.g. *Giles Goat-Boy*, a wild variation on the campus novel, with a distinctly "satyric" protagonist, which treats the culture and history of the world as if the product of a surreal university), or Thomas Pynchon (e.g. *Mason & Dixon*). These examples could also illustrate other features highlighted by Bakhtin: the abnormal psychic states of the characters, and the associated eccentricities

---

[13] Frye (1957) 312.   [14] Bakhtin (1984) 105.
[15] Relihan (1993) 12.   [16] Bakhtin (1984) 114–19.

and illogicalities of their behavior; abrupt transitions and oxymoronic contrasts, matched by a mixture of styles and tones and the juxtaposition of incongruous inserted genres. Another feature is a concern (often a very topical concern) with social utopias, or their opposite. Although neither *Animal Farm* nor *1984* corresponds very closely to the rest of Bakhtin's criteria (the former perhaps does more than the latter), they do have some affinities to his idea of the Menippean, though not as many as Terry Gilliam's movie *Brazil* (1985), which satirizes dystopic fictions as much as it does dystopic societies.

Crucially for Bakhtin, *menippea* is the literary manifestation of a concept central to his thinking: carnival. Carnival itself, he insists, is not a literary phenomenon. Whilst it is instantiated in social practices such as the Roman Saturnalia and the medieval Feast of Fools, it has "its deep roots in the primordial order and the primordial thinking of man."[17] Bakhtin is at pains to emphasize the lived experience of carnivalistic behavior (the emphases in the following extract are Bakhtin's):

> Carnival is a pageant without footlights and without a division into performers and spectators. In carnival, everyone is an active participant, everyone communes in the carnival act. Carnival is not contemplated and, strictly speaking, not even performed; its participants *live* in it, they live by its laws as long as those laws are in effect; that is, they live a *carnivalistic life*. Because carnivalistic life is life drawn out of its *usual* rut, it is to some extent 'life turned inside out,' 'the reverse side of the world' ('*monde à l'envers*'). The laws, prohibitions, and restrictions that determine the structure and order of ordinary, that is noncarnival, life are suspended during carnival: what is suspended first of all is hierarchical structure and all the forms of terror, reverence, piety, and etiquette connected with it – that is, everything resulting from socio-hierarchical inequality or any other form of inequality among people.[18]

Phenomena such as the Saturnalia are thus seen as the institutionalization of a more generalized form of cultural energy and experience. Bakhtin's presentation of carnival is on the whole positive, even indulgent. The behavior associated with it is characterized by the forgiving word "eccentricity,"[19] and the repeated use of the term "festival" suggests that, although "carnival is the festival of all-annihilating and all-renewing time,"[20] the explosive energies associated with it remain safely channeled within ritualistic contexts, legitimized but thereby also restricted and contained. Nevertheless, Bakhtin does open up the possibility that the members of society generally might come to "act" in a carnivalistic way beyond such sanctioned occasions

---

[17] Bakhtin (1984) 122. Note the appeal to the primitive, and cf. note 8 above.
[18] Bakhtin (1984) 122–3.   [19] Bakhtin (1984) 123.   [20] Bakhtin (1984) 124.

when the received "hierarchical structure and all the forms of terror, reverence, piety, and etiquette connected with it" are suspended, and the world is turned upside down. "Carnival," he says, "does not know footlights, in the sense that it does not acknowledge any distinction between actors and spectators . . . Carnival is not a spectacle seen by the people; they live in it and everyone participates . . . While carnival lasts, there is no other life outside it."[21] He is even prepared to hazard that carnival generated a key cultural period in the Western tradition: "on the basis of this carnival sense of the world, the complex forms of the Renaissance worldview came into being."[22] The carnivalistic quality of Renaissance culture, Bakhtin suggests, is indicated in the way that Menippean literature flourished then, for carnivalistic categories are not "*abstract thoughts* about equality and freedom, the interrelatedness of all things or the unity of opposites" but "concretely sensuous ritual-pageant 'thoughts' experienced and played out in the form of life itself," and this is why they were able to exercise such an immense "*formal, genre-shaping* influence on literature."[23]

Genre for Bakhtin is something dynamic rather than static. Although there are always preserved in a genre "undying elements of the archaic . . . these archaic elements are preserved in it only thanks to their constant *renewal*, which is to say, their contemporization . . . Genre is reborn and renewed at every new stage in the development of literature and in every individual work of a given genre."[24] Here is Bakhtin's rationale for the presence of the past in the present: in our every outburst of indignation, we might say, can be caught the trace of a Juvenalian voice, even if we do not immediately characterize it as such. Out of this arises the Bakhtinian concept of "genre memory," which suggests that each specific genre encodes, in its strategies and tropes and in the expectations fostered by previous examples, a distinctive way of seeing and understanding the world; in this way, we see reality "with the eyes of the genre." But the genre memory is experienced and played out "in the form of life itself." Bakhtin's view of genre involves an inversion of the conventional idea that satire is a distorting mirror held up to reflect reality.[25] Each genre, rather than being viewed as the reflection of *prior* reality, is seen as creating the conditions for the production or construction of a *consequent* reality and of a lived experience of the world. Thus lived experience, no less than literature, emerges as a recursive mimesis, as tropes are enacted and re-enacted. One particular genre can come to dominate or characterize a historical period, as, for Bakhtin, *menippea* does the Renaissance.

---

[21] Bakhtin (1968) 7.   [22] Bakhtin (1984) 130.
[23] Bakhtin (1984) 123; emphases Bakhtin's.
[24] Bakhtin (1984) 106.   [25] E.g. Highet (1962) 158.

For all that Bakhtin feels that the carnivalesque is liberating, it is for him, as he writes in the 1920s, tinged with a sense of belatedness, since he feels that "the Renaissance is the high point of carnival life. Thereafter begins its decline."[26] However, it could be argued that the "Menippean" qualities claimed for many twentieth-century novels, the characteristics of films such as Fellini's, the "relativity" of poststructuralist thought and, indeed, the enthusiastic reception of Bakhtin's very own ideas, are manifestations of a deeper (and, for some, darker) resurgence of the carnivalesque in contemporary society, in which the received "hierarchical structure and all the forms of terror, reverence, piety, and etiquette connected with it" are suspended, and the world is turned upside down. For some, another "Renaissance" perhaps (with all the positive associations that have accrued to that term), for others a helter-skelter, in which "[t]he behavior, gesture, and discourse of a person . . . freed from the authority of all hierarchical positions" become not simply "eccentric" or "inappropriate"[27] but positively dangerous. Did someone mention "the Sixties"?

For Michael André Bernstein, the experience of "the Sixties" and its aftermath is, in the title of his book, a *Bitter Carnival*.[28] He takes his cue from Bakhtin's theories of carnival and genre memory, but gives the theory's celebration of the lived experience of carnival a negative spin: "when the tropes of a Saturnalian reversal of all values spill over into daily life, they usually do so with a savagery that is the grim underside of their exuberant affirmations."[29] Bernstein sees the eruption of the carnivalesque and the Saturnalian in this period in works with an enormous capacity to disturb such as William Burroughs's *The Naked Lunch*, Hubert Selby's *Last Exit to Brooklyn* and the films of Rainer Werner Fassbinder. His own book, a critical work on the figure of the "abject hero" in Diderot, Dostoevsky, and Céline, finds consideration of these writers disconcertingly sandwiched between accounts of two iconic "cult" figures of their time, Ira Einhorn and Charles Manson, both of whom were implicated in particularly horrific murders. For Bernstein, these two men, in their self-representations and the reactions of others to them, inhabited a world in which the carnivalesque had become the norm, and was complacently regarded as positive for being so:

> The sway of a powerful literary convention is exercised as effectively in mass culture as in great art, and the entire career of someone like Ira Einhorn was possible only because he succeeded in focusing upon himself all the identificatory sympathy aroused by the character type he seemed to incarnate . . . In effect, what seduced Einhorn's admirers was less a particular individual than

---

[26] Bakhtin (1984) 130.   [27] Bakhtin (1984) 123.
[28] Bernstein (1992).   [29] Bernstein (1992) 6.

a literary/philosophical character by whom they had already been won over numerous times in the books and movies on which they had grown up, a character who could draw on all the resources of a long tradition heroicizing his defiant integrity and refusal to "conform".[30]

So too Manson: "If Charles Manson helped to 'end the sixties,' it was because he *should* have been a fictional character in some apocalyptic fantasy novel and not an actual resident of a particular place and era, sending out gangs of disciples to butcher total strangers."[31] Although he disowns the desire to indulge in "sixties bashing," Bernstein nonetheless wants to argue that

> when we celebrate the carnivalesque and speak so confidently of the utopian longing for a radically open and unfettered relationship, not just toward one another, but toward the conflicting impulses and desires whose interactions shape us, there is a cruel human risk to these idealizations. The viciousness that can be released by the carnival's dissolution of the accumulated prudential understanding of a culture needs to figure in our thinking about the rhetorical strategies and ideological assertions within which utopian theorizing is articulated. And this necessity is all the more compelling because the theorizing so often prides itself upon transcending the historical consequences of its own axioms.[32]

The "accumulated prudential understanding of a culture" is at odds with the Saturnalian desire to invert hierarchies and to question the moral authority of anyone who would speak in the name of transcendent values, who is likely to be dismissed as a charlatan or a pedant. We may recall Frye when he said that at its most concentrated Menippean satire presents us with a vision of the world in terms of a single intellectual pattern. If we look "into" a particular work of satire (from the "outside," as it were), the consequences are often self-evidently ludicrous or grotesque; but what if that vision is being acted out in the reality *within* which we live, and that single intellectual pattern is the carnivalesque itself? In that case, it will seem that, in the Derridan tag, there is no outside-text, and a frustrated gesture to "beyond" the single intellectual pattern is all that seems possible. This is a dilemma Bernstein is acutely aware of as he struggles to gesture towards absolute differences that the theory may seek to elide (ultimately, he suggests, the moral difference between murderer and victim), while he himself is self-consciously enmeshed in the assumptions of the Bakhtinian carnivalesque and is recursively miming its tropes. And one of the chief characteristics of the carnivalesque, and of its literary manifestation, satire, is a resistance to closure: "The carnival sense

---

[30] Bernstein (1992) 5, 8.   [31] Bernstein (1992) 171; emphasis Bernstein's.
[32] Bernstein (1992) 8–9.

of the world . . . knows no period, and is, in fact, hostile to any sort of *conclusive conclusion*: all endings are merely new beginnings."[33] Bernstein laments:

> And so, although I intend the argument of this book polemically, even now, at the end, I find myself unable to come down entirely on one side or the other of the debate whose changing contours I have been tracing. In spite of the discomfort that many literary critics still feel at the notion of an ethical conclusion, I have been searching for just such a closing, but find that, like my chosen texts, my formulations keep coming out in a split or, to put the matter more generously, a dialogical way.[34]

Satirists have no problem in getting started, "polemically" in a burst of indignation (*difficile est saturam non scribere*), and it is indeed the function of "anatomy" to "open up"; yet, a satirist's final word, as Harry Levin has said, is likely to be "But."[35]

Further reading

Dustin Griffin (1994) 3 remarks:

> In the last two hundred years satire in the Western tradition is most commonly found not as an independent form or parody; it is found in the novel. But what happens when satire invades the novel is a subject so vast and unwieldy that I do not attempt to treat it here.

Sadly no one else does either, though Frank Palmieri, *Satire in Narrative: Petronius, Swift, Gibbon, Melville and Pynchon* (1990) and Snyder (1991), which deals with Petronius, Cervantes, Butler, Twain, and Hasek, do essay broader perspectives. Otherwise, for an inevitably piecemeal view, one must look to studies of individual authors. Alistair Fowler's *Kinds of Literature* (Cambridge, MA 1982) offers an always interesting and entertaining account of generic definition and the difficulties satire poses to it. On the campus novel see Christian Gutleben "English Academic Satire from the Middle Ages to Postmodernism: Distinguishing the Comic from the Satiric" Brian A. Connery and Kirk Combe, eds. *Theorizing Satire* (London 1995), 133–47. On Fellini, see Peter Bondanella, *The Cinema of Federico Fellini* (Princeton 1992). For tracking the changing responses over time to the verse satirists, the anthologies *Horace in English* (eds. D. S. Carne-Ross and Kenneth Haynes, Harmondsworth 1996), *Juvenal in English* (Winkler, 2001) and *Martial in English* (eds. J. P. Sullivan and A. J. Boyle, Harmondsworth 1996), all with excellent introductions, are invaluable.

[33] Bakhtin (1984) 165; emphases Bakhtin's.   [34] Bernstein (1992) 182.
[35] Levin (1980) 14, cited in Griffin (1994) 112.

JOHN HENDERSON

The turnaround:
a volume retrospect on Roman satires

Does a Companion suit Roman Satire?

Is a Companion what Roman Satire needs?

It is easy to see a point in building a team to accompany study of the topic. Satire doesn't immediately strike us as a conformist or consensual arena, and so it's bound to be a good idea to have a line-up of experts all wanting to be our special friend and bag the attention. They are unlikely to prod us for where we are coming from; or to insist on laying out their own individual(ist) wares – exposing hopes and fears/proposing apparatus and theories. That is not how this contemporary genre of critical commentary works. Not everything, perhaps, in the present collection rides comfortably in the same carriage. But there is precious little friction between the contributions on view, and if you half-anticipated that the plainstyle writing of the textbook marketplace might meet the subject matter halfway with a dash of malice, a pound of scurrility, and a sprinkle of innuendo, you'll have to admit that you skipped or nodded – or else it passed you by. No, it's plain to see, these scholars don't mess with slang, either. Or histrionics. Or fiendish in-talk. (Martindale does grouch that work on satire isn't top notch, and Roman satire isn't so big a deal . . .) So maybe *Roman* satire is'nt what we mean by satire – what *we* think "we" mean by satire? And can you tell if there is a truce in Satireland, or is the battle raging, or is this a critical post-bellum? Which companion can you catch pissing on the ancestors' tombs? Have the jokers been weeded from the coalition pack? Wonder, would German company blend in? (It is hard to generalize. It is hard to say if today's German Latinists are fighting their way free from ingrained descriptivist *Altertums-wissenschaft*, or continuing this eternal fight as their *raison d'être*. Is there a Swiss connection? Graf.) As for the *French*? (*Etudes latines* is its own world apart: a poor traveler, it will not travel.) Does the Italian cohort bring a flavor, a special strain, to a seamlessly specious Anglo-American outfit, or is it a worldwide classics confederate? (Where satire goes, xenophobia goes too – another own goal in the multiculture of superstate Rome.) In any case, did they make your lip curl often enough? And did they come up with your answers? Who-are-you, what-kind-of-company, and why-you-are-here, for example. (More, much more, from Gunderson.)

One audience is here for satire; another, for Rome. The questions line up differently for these blocs. Reception in literary modernity (English, Anglo-American modernity) traditionally turns around to look back at historical conjunctures when writers gained or sacrificed prominence by reconceiving their productivity in a fresh, or any rate supplementary, posture against the backdrop of literary tradition. The genre of satire breeds bouts of dialectical positioning in terms of polarity between Horace and Juvenal. More specifically, however, this praxis imitates (emulates, displaces, . . . satirizes?) that of Horace, who positions himself most specifically against Lucilius; and of Juvenal, who positions his work against his predecessors, in general. On the other hand, literary modernity receives satire from classical Rome as a mode, wherein a Greco-Roman branch of writing – the "Menippean" – plays off against the verse of the "Lucilian" stemma. Satire then spreads wings and tentacles until we soar to view literature as a set of cultural modes or throttle the Icarian flightiness of generalizing criticism, and get down to the materialities of a closely inbreeding, formal sub-category of Latin poetry in variously styled, variegated, hexameters.

Roman Roman satire

Stick to Ennius the shadowy herald, Lucilius the sparky father, Horace the dodgy son, Persius the nervy nephew, Juvenal the brassy grandson. There were others: Pacuvius, Varro of Atax, a certain Turnus; but *tant pis* – that's plenty for one Companion. We have two great lost writers read until the empire fell, whom we can only profile through the murk. No, we cannot *study* Ennius' *Satires*. But, yes, their production was a significant component of the authorship of the most prolific and beatified poet of the Roman republic. Either the *Satires* were marginal to his output, but typical of Ennius' open-ended freedom to self-invent, or else they typify his work, and color the intent of the whole œuvre, and its reception as the prime paradigm for authorial authority in the new world of Roman superpower. As the Mediterranean fell into place, expansion became the greatest story that Latin could tell, and its celebration fell to Ennius' verse. He would be the Roman Homer – he fought in the war that brought Rome supremacy, and toured as an embedded reporter in campaigns across the Adriatic Gulf. His satire was a miscellany: parerga signed by a Shakespeare (Connors). Satire only moved toward a place in the sunshine with Lucilius, who wrote – did? – nothing else, or, as we might say, invented himself as the one who lived satire. In his case, satire involved turning his back on variegated miscellany, as his verse settled into the groove of exclusively hexametric form (through the last score and more of his thirty books), and he expanded his expounding of what he was doing until it became a personal praxis for real, and a literary institution was founded (Muecke). Ennius' thundering epic immortalizing imperial success was the relevant other for intertextual subversion: Lucilius' Rome would write one cavalier's thoughts into the space where Ennius' Rome had waved the flag; instead of spreading his personality across the sprawl of writing forms, he jammed and spliced all the stylistic options into the one hybrid mishmash of self-promotion. The world according to Lucilius had heroes (friends) and villains (opponents); some of both were big guns (dead or alive) – but he poured just as much energy into spelling and pronunciation, or lust and insult, as he did them. The Companion fills us in with both these extravagant harbingers of satire – for Lucilius is just a shadow for us, and a series of reflections pushed our way by the classics to come.

First, Horace. Now the classicist knows (our) Horace – the other half of Virgil's Augustan soul, between the two of them the complete map of Latin poetry at its self-proclaimed zenith. Virgil not only dethroned Ennius, his epic of Rome revised the nation's story as the myth of eternally Caesarian Roman cosmopolis. *His* exclusively hexametric œuvre plotted a tripartite rise from short to solid to monumental, aesthetic-moral-political, singing-instructing-immortalizing; and virtually never a word about the poet, the thinking, the *writing*. Horace supplies what Virgil shrugged off. His twin-barreled output tracks Virgil's obsessional monorail career from debutant through to established grandmaster status. Horace wrote lyric verse from acidic aggression through celebratory flourish to hymnal parade. Along the way, he matured from in your face ruffian to observer-participant in worlds of biorhythm, camaraderie, politicking, and literariness, before ascending to conductor of the aspirations of Romankind. In classics, this high culture poet dances a duet with the Horace of Roman satire. Both expansive personalities interplay between their every line – or stanza. As the Companion does not fail to underline, lyric Horace runs unspoken commentary through his hexameter excursions (Cucchiarelli). Horace and Horace(-and-Virgil) play off the displacement of the Roman Republic by the Augustan Principate: they write off Lucilius and Ennius and, in their range of ways, they write that they are revisiting the old scenes, for overhaul and remake. When we discuss Horatian satire, we ordinarily have in focus the eighteen poems of *Sermones*, books 1–2. This is, indeed, one major protocol that has governed the economy of this volume. But in Roman Roman satire, this target unpacks to englobe the subsequent *Epistulae*, books 1–2, and the climactic *Ars Poetica*. The pattern is youthful rough diamond maturing into multi-tasking élite operator before climbing onto Aristotle's chair and lecturing a future for poesie. The trajectory is irresistible, the reader *of Horace* gets sucked along the trail. So Latinists turn round from the completed career, to watch Horace start up with, and work away from – worm his way through – satire. The performances he put in as he poked his nose into the convulsive world about to knock government by elected magistrates out of the Roman ring for good thrust him straight into a hotseat close to the righthandman and entourage of Octavian the golden boy heir to Caesar, soon to mature, along with his poet duo, into the emperor Augustus, and eventually, the apotheosed divinity "Saint" Augustus. Where Lucilius paraded authentic selfhood, this successor feints and weaves, underacts the part. Raiding the surface meanings of these studied voicings of bluff chat is never going to survive historical contextualization. So much in the *Sermones* provokes us, every which way: it's dull, it's tosh, coughs up that it's never *poetry*; it duckbills platitudes, shies away from big guns, keeps its head down – or make that *up*, itself (cannot stop talking bodies, touchy-feely, orificial: Barchiesi and Cucchiarelli). The point just cannot be disclosure or "follow me" swagger. So must this be the rubbishing *of satire*, instead (Gowers' "anti-satire")? The Companion takes the modern line, which hardens up a critical position that's hovered around other times, other places, namely, that Horatian satire turns the tables on reading. These days, it holds the ring. Response to what is said is put under pressure by the indigestibility of its combination of "Lucilian" update with "post-Lucilian" self-disinheritance. Horace tells bad jokes, overdoes the finger-wagging, until the dish runs away with the spoon. If you enjoy watching him squirm, and then wheel on dummies, nutters, and hams, you'll know he's filling his head with hot air along with ours; but of course it's all by design, he creates triggers for response, suckers us into playing the game he's rigged. Not what's *he* up to, but what's our problem? If we have had it up to here – what exactly was it that got to us? We must've come looking for it, whatever it was, and stayed till it arrived. Our fitting companion (Gowers).

Second –? Well, that's the problem of Persius (no Anglo-petname for *him*, notice). Latin literature in most of its modern incarnations has done nicely without him. One of the precocious poetic meteorites that fizzed brief and strident down their political-artistic chorus-leader Nero's fast lane to unforgettable oblivion. Roman Persius is all tied into the scandal of "Silver" or "post-Virgilian," "post-Ovidian," imperial culture. In these parts, an accelerating snowball of critical revaluation is reclaiming one disparaged site of decadence after another. Difficulty of style may be acclaimed once attractively provided with motivation. Repressive culture under an under-aged autocrat all too keen to promote a fellowship of artists makes an excruciating draw for playing satire. Where once free-range expressivity rampaged, now a heavy-eyed student fights off the world at large, fights his bodily connectedness to that world, fights even to find a free spot in his own mind. Satire? Satire intoning caustic castigation of the self, using ideas, phrasing, images, taken to heart from Horace, only getting you down in the hole that he's in . . . (Cucchiarelli). The turnaround this time is satire eating itself. Horace's therapy inoculates the slacking learner, for weakness of will hangs up private grief for us all to empathize, and rehearse the ineffectual cramming of recipes for salvation. Six short and demonic bursts of Latin mashed into failure-fixated cacophony. Persius is an acquired taste(lessness). You'd enjoy swashbuckling satire out on Lucilius' Roman road or square? Persius makes you tell yourself you shouldn't. People, Nero's people, live inside their skin, in their skull, in their losing skiamachy between their selves; they record diaries for nobody, write secrets for remaindering, turn satire inside out, haywire, risible. Whatever reasons Horace gave for evacuating Lucilian gusto, Persius' verbal stomach-pump eviscerates the lot (Cucchiarelli). Companions have to fess up: Persius is a *modern* author: bags of annihilatory skepticism to pull the rug from beneath his own feet; but we won't get it without teasing out the opacities of his self-deleting allusivity to (anti-)Lucilian Horace; and we classicists will always be stuck muttering "philosophy, no – not philosophy, nor diatribe, either . . . – rather, the *Neronian* turn to Satire"? (And here the denial escapes aloud: Persius' failure to philosophize, to count as Philosophy, is not not – indeed, it *is* – Roman philosophy: cf. Mayer–Cucchiarelli. Satire is one good reason Romans and philosophy don't gell: it is, Persius demonstrates, a Roman critique of culture as praxis: a denunciation of ethics before the bar of morality?)

In the thick of Rome, it proves hard to triangulate the genre round our classic trio: Persius must spoil the stark binary "Horace :: Juvenal." His role was formerly scholar's favorite – reserved for those with more Latin; the whizzkid who somehow knew no lessons ever stick; the poet who scorned his public for liking it – and now his comeback is though the sedition of despair. Shoehorning these satires into "the genre" is the *taunt* they set us, so shan't the Company explain, "Neronian satire – see?"

Last in line, *the* Roman satirist, Juvenal. Miraculously unleashing a broadside of fury at "his" Rome, kerbside, forum-packed, empirewide, yet no way trapped in the politics of time of writing, this is no "Flavian satire" (the material belongs to that dynasty, before Domitian became last in his line), nor, fortunately, does it butter much bread to stamp this "Ulpian satire," for Latin literature under Trajan and Hadrian never does come together as an epoch, dynamic scene, or story-shaped drama. Rather, Juvenal joins forces with Tacitus' and Suetonius' retrospects over the first century of the Caesars, to enact a strong closural fade. Classical Latin breaks up hereabouts as a

continuous parade; ties between literature and history dissolve; this is where
we turn around, and head on back through the classical library, through
Nero to Augustus, Ennius' Republic and Hellenism back to Homer. Juvenal
knows what "we" classicists are meant to know (the full Monty of intertextual antiquity). He knows how to write (and says so). Satire is what he
does, fifteen and a half grand poems assembled through five books. It's as
if some poet took it upon himself to take off Lucilius taking off Ennius'
grandest epic writing. In fact, that's very much what Juvenal is about, in
our company (Connors: overlay a Virgil turning Horace around into epic).
He performs – he tells us he's a performer – immoderate denunciations of
Romanness, so as to make Romans of us all, as we are provoked and lured
into (dis)agreeing with the next extremist expostulation to come our way.
The game is as real as theatrical monologue gets, since the audience of readers are obliged to follow or part company with the barrage of views dinning
through these forcible hexameters. For real: too much. Just where does com-
monsense topple into distemper? Which last straw deserves the Jeremiad?
When is hyperbole self-caricature (Rimell, "Feast")?

Our Latinists insist for all they are worth that Juvenalian wrath is a color of
rhetoric. Abusing Rome for the hell of it is indeed a major option for reading:
circus of freaks, host of parodies, phobic fuss about Roman rôles and rules.
Proclaiming that the end of the world is at hand, so now, finally, it's satire's
turn, unlocks the whole Greco-Roman store of nostalgia-trip sermonizing
for inversion. And the end of history condemns the "now" culture to the
inauthenticity of empty vessels. So runs our revisionary account, but knows
it undersells the corpus. For Juvenal's vice is, in fact, that he wrote too
much too long (scale–value: see Rimell's "Feast"). For most classicists, the
first book, *Satires* 1–5, is *plenty* to study. Especially now that we won't
skip the second poem's vivid gender-bending outrage(ousness)es for anything
(Gunderson, Mayer, Rimell's "Feast"). Add in the second salvo, the book-
length satire 6, fulminating on the comradely theme "Son, Never Marry a
Woman," and we surpass satis-faction (Gunderson). The irate frothing at
social-cultural-political institutions and idioms has now been matched with
domestic-personal-emotional routines and régimes, and the sum is done:
maleness : civil :: femaleness : virile (i.e. why Romen must be losers). We know
this won't do. The rest of Juvenal is not one vast "etcetera" disappearing
over the horizon. It's embarrassing, but the Companions will just have to
whisper that we're still working on it, offer a scatter of suggestions, and (I
think) plead lack of space. Actually, "late Juvenal" is still hugely innovative
Roman satire, and I think you could enjoy a tour. On a flying visit, *this*
guide would try out for size the idea that the frenzy of Juvenal persists
through convulsive sketches where quasi-Horatian attempts to anchor the

gaze to irenic catalysts founder on our declaimer, who can't help but lapse into backsliding rodomontade to spare his ulcer; we've learned to enjoy turning on the crackpot where he oversteps our mark – now we can blow the whistle when his transparent efforts to talk sense come apart at the seams – and wither on our vine (see Rimell, "Feast," esp. on 8–9; on 9: Habinek; 10: Mayer; 15: Connors).

The question "Why not *sort* Juvenal?" is something to do with "satire." What we usually do with *Roman* satire is work close into the literary grain, texture, voicing. If you please, line by polished line. We want to enthuse over this Latinity. *And* we want to join in with these poems fighting their way out of their paperbags of Roman protocol, prejudice, axiom, face. It's a devil of a job to extrapolate from these tricky, prickly, provocations. That's half their point. But which half? Well, a Companion must hit the road, not dwell. The big picture requests the pleasure of your company. Now's not a moment too soon.

Satire (and Rome?)

"We" are up for satire. So what is it, (who) says who, and where are you taking us to take a look, and maybe find out? "Elizabethan," through "Restoration," to "Regency" Greater London (Burrow, Hooley, Martindale)? If the nineteenth and twentieth centuries did not write quasi- or para-epic verse with the expectation that readers would turn around to explore interaction with the classic Roman texts, this means it only looks like a Companion or two have gotten lost. (Martindale says Kant killed Lucilian satire; Kennedy rakes over the idea that we all know it's long gone.) Our reception chapters show us how playing displayed-model Horace off against dissembled-model Juvenal had become a resource in the English poet's armature which fed off and fed back into current interpretation and dispute over the Latin authors. The specifics of the various re-presentations of these opposed poetics always bent the projects into fresh tensions and ironies, just as ancient caricature and refiguring of Lucilius showed the way. So long as satire kept on satirizing satire and satirist(s), the sport of raiding and misrepresenting the Roman texts animated the reception of ancient and modern alike. Always, distortion went hand in hand with recycling, and the bitching continued to feature literary-critical, scholarly, odium, just the way it had in the original polemic (and its criticism: cf. Hooley's Rochester on Dryden). Satire feeds nit-picking, pedantry, ostracism; that was its stock-in-trade, *olim*. Po-face! Stickler! Bad sport! (Badmouthing licensed by Classics, Inc.)

But every bitch has her *belle époque*. Clearly "satire" lives on in our culture. (Un)healthier than ever. So the question for Roman satire must be how it compares with "ours," not as parent, but as ancestor. It needn't stump us if it turns out that there's nothing *we* would call satirical about Roman satire. Looking into what we have by tracing its origins does not in our day spell faith in genealogy at work, but a heuristic quest for structural coordinates. So let's get the Companion to *include* Roman satire within the field of satire, since that is where our stake in it is realized (Kennedy). The magic category developed for this project is "mode." Bracket the formal properties of Latin hexameter verse, together with the inter-references and other intertextual connections between the Roman writers, and see where Roman satire overlaps with "ours" – and where they part company. The "family" of apparently shared features may then supply terms for dynamic analysis. So, too, with the successive English satire(s) that mark off their territory through overlay and departure from Rome, and from each other (Burrow, Hooley, Martindale).

Now such a move replicates (and, of course, crowds – and displaces) critical analysis within ancient Rome, and indeed within the very texts of Roman satire. Puzzling and pontificating about satire is what satire did, back then, too. So did ancient "companions," in the literary history department. Asking Rome what satire is (was) delivers us various theories that tell us where "it" came (to them) from, and what manner of "it" it had turned into. To begin at the end, Roman academics maintained that Lucilian satire was one of two branches of satire. The other, known as "Menippean," was named for a Greek writer of, shall we say, skits or sketches, whose work is entirely lost, though we have a number of texts that could show us something about him. In particular, we have a large number of short fragments of Varro's "Menippean satires," once a typically massive outpouring of (short? how short?) fictional pieces from one of Rome's most prolific writers, working away through the last decades of the Republic. We are told to regard as definitive the formal property of "prosimetrum," the co-presence of verse and prose within a single work of fiction. The skit on the deification of the m-m-m-mockery of the emperor Claudius which we know as Seneca's *Apocolocyntosis* focuses on the disconcerting pungency of embedded quotation held up for self-parody: this *may* be Menippean – it may be Menippean simply because it puts prosimetrum in the window, it might be *something* like Varro's stuff, or it might be typically "Menippean" because it is a *lusus* – an unplaceably "miscellaneous" up-yours from textuality, lodged at literariness (O'Gorman. NB. This inaugurates "Neronian" literature).

Once "satire" enlarges to include "Menippean" works, the space opens for a crowd of thoughts: is there something Menippean in Lucilian verse? Is there anything "Menippean" or "Lucilian" about other texts than those which wear the labels? As the parameters go porous, does the "genre" already stultify? The very first thing Horace himself says (in his very first book, *Sermones* 1) about what he's doing by re-doing Lucilius is to put out that it all hangs on ancient Greek comedy. So was(n't) there satire before Rome, just as there is, today, without Rome? And, O Literature!, what culture does not have its satire, by whatever name? "Mode" means "cultural" form, and so we're up to here, now, in functional accounts of artistic behavior in human society. Need satire be confined to writing of any kind whatever? Rather, we shall *include* written satire within a general field of human social behavior.

Along the way, the Companion stands Roman satire on its head for you: our century reads novels more than everything else put together. Naturally we know the category of satirical novel. Current classics revels in telling anyone who will listen that Greece had novels, and Rome did, too. The biggest boom in ancient literature has up-thrust a half-dozen – at a stretch, a dozen – fictional narratives, most of them love-stories, though fantasy-travel, surreal adventure, and (as we hasten to say) picaresque-through-po'mo' parody are on offer. And we have shamelessly zipped the atrociously mangled remains of Petronius' once-gargantuan sprawl of ("Neronian") sex, filth, and drugs into this winning grab-bag: his *Satyrica* makes a Roman novel-and-a-half, and its amoralist riot of divine on the road decadence segues wondrously well into Apuleius' perfectly preserved *Golden Ass*, where a second tale of sex, filth, and magic serves up first-person thrills and spills in worlds undreamed, straight from the donkey's mouth. But Petronius also ties into shifting "Menippean" product. Snatches of (mostly murderous, suicidal) verse crop up in the text, and more, perhaps much more, once did – before the great mutilation. The Companion follows suit, and says why (Kennedy, Rimell's "Maze"). It's not that "prosimetric Latin" makes much more than a hold-all for a mess of texts of disorder – a "dummy," even "pseudo-" literary category – however crucial it may be to recognize that the dominant center-ground of classical culture is founded fair and square on just such formal criteria patrolling the gate of civil writing. Rather, there's a grand *récit* out in the wide world which has put together a universalizing configuration of "satire" according to which Rome plays big. Bigger than the legacy of Lucilius.

Scandalous texts that plow straight through the boundaries of "high culture" must always deal double-speak with forked tongue. They fold us into a literate world that mucks around with what it constitutively excludes. Maybe this is a game. Maybe it's a ritual. Playing at subversion, jazz up the funfair, and then, after the carnival, it's business as usual? Looking for energy, go for the real, and write into the fold fresh challenges for representation – whole vocabularies, hybrid stylistics, demonized perspectives, pluralizing value-systems – ripe for plowing *into* the field of literary imagination. For half a century now the name "Bakhtin" has fathered, powered, or at least authored, a massive twentieth-century crusade to revalue folk, demotic, vulgar, popular, refused, repressed, "low" cultural work. Let me be frank. Whatever variously bogus myths of reification compete for our attention in this connection, there is so much democratizing revisionary pull to this movement that the serial explosion of their vacuity pretty well makes no odds. All the scenarios where, "despite itself," hegemonic culture blinks or cracks to admit elements of "spoudogeloious" subculture may not stitch comfortably into anything more critical than a fairy story, but anyone will see that they can compare and contrast thisaway to spectacular effect. You'll have to go along with a superb con if you accept that the tag "Menippean" bosses a Roman "genre" of literature; and you'll have to squeeze a rag-tag-and-bobtail legion of cultural practices onto the same train, way beyond Lucilian verse, or prosimetric, novelistic, parodistic texts, if you mean to explore the cultural mode of (Bakhtinesque) Satire, & Co. Unltd. (Kennedy, Rimell's "Maze"). Since our classics is no more wed to cultural élitism than anyone else's subject, we are bound to play to-and-fro between the re-envisioning of antiquity and its pertinence to the renovation of our culture. Classical Rome played out mockery in a style of its own, based on its own social dynamics (Graf). Rome tacked together ham fairy stories to account for satire in its own backyard (see Habinek). So turn around, bright eyes: Lucilian satirists enact their stunts in highly crafted poems that take and give pleasure in sending up their own cultured matrix. With or without the high gloss, other Latin texts uglify, monstrify, sterilize, and castrate Rome, too – and doublethink the plotting of (perverted) desire (Gunderson). And wherever we walk on the wild side of our own cultural forms, we'll be in the bad company we need if we take a trip through Roman satires, in all (their) versions, and (our) perversions. It works – dysfunctions – every which way.

  – But.

KEY DATES FOR THE STUDY OF ROMAN SATIRE

Some dates are necessarily approximate or speculative.

BCE

650–600	Era of early Greek iambic poetry, Archilochus and Hipponax
440–405	Era of Greek Old Comedy, Eupolis, Cratinus, Aristophanes
404–321	Era of Greek Middle Comedy
364	Livy's legendary date for the introduction of *ludi scaenici* at Rome
320–250	Era of Greek New Comedy, esp. Menander
315	Bion of Borysthenes arrives in Athens, active as lecturer until 245 BCE
290	*Floruit* Menippus of Gadara
260	Callimachus, *Iambs*
205–184	Plautus writes Greek-style comedies (*fabulae palliatae*) for the Roman stage
204–169	Quintus Ennius active in Rome as playwright, writer of panegyric epic, and *Saturae*
166–159	Terence writes Greek-style comedies for the Roman stage
129–101	Lucilius writes thirty books of *Saturae*
81–67	M. Terentius Varro writes 150 books of satires in the manner of Menippus of Gadara
65	Horace born on 8 December in Venusia
42	Horace fights on the losing side at the battle of Philippi
37	Pact of Tarentum renews détente between Octavian and Antony
35	Horace publishes book 1 of his *Sermones*
31	Battle of Actium (2 September); Antony defeated
30	Horace publishes book 2 of his *Sermones*
27	Octavian named "Augustus" by the Roman senate
23	Horace publishes books 1–3 of his *Carmina*

19	Horace publishes book 1 of his *Epistles*
10	Horace publishes the *Ars Poetica*
8	Horace dies on November 27

CE

14	Death of Augustus
14–37	Reign of Tiberius
34	Persius (Aulus Persius Flaccus) born at Volterrae
37–41	Reign of Gaius (Caligula)
41–54	Reign of Claudius
54	Accession of Nero. The deification of Claudius (13 October) satirized in Seneca's *Apocolocyntosis*
62	Death of Persius, satires edited and published posthumously
64	Great fire of Rome
65–6	Suicides of Seneca, Lucan, Petronius
68	Suicide of Nero
69	Civil wars; year of four emperors
69–81	Flavian period commences: reigns of Vespasian and Titus
81–96	Reign of Domitian
85	Domitian named *censor perpetuus*
86–96	Martial in Rome, composes *Epigrams* books 1–10
95	Quintilian, *Institutio oratoria*
96	Domitian murdered in a palace coup, September 18. Accession of Nerva
98	Death of Nerva, accession of Trajan (January). Martial in Spain
100–130	Juvenal writes satires in five books
116	Tacitus publishes first book(s) of the *Annales*
117	Death of Trajan, accession of Hadrian
180	Lucian, *Dialogues of the Dead, Icaromenippus*
190	Helenius Acro writes commentaries on Horace, some of which survives in the late antique scholia known as *Pseudo-Acro*
210	Pomponius Porphyrio writes a commentary on Horace
361	Julian "the Apostate," *The Caesars*
524	Boethius imprisoned and executed, *Consolation of Philosophy*

Selected dates in the reception of Roman satire

1380	Chaucer, *Wife of Bath's Tale*
1428	Poggio Bracciolini, *De Avaritia*
1499	John Skelton, *The Bowge of Court*

1509	Erasmus, *The Praise of Folly*
1532	Rabelais, *Gargantua and Pantagruel*
1561	Julius Caesar Scaliger, *Poetics*
1566	Thomas Drant translates Horace's *Sermones*
1590–8	Thomas Nashe, *Pierce Penniless,* John Donne, *Satires,* Everard Guilpin, *Skialetheia,* Joseph Hall, *Virgidemiarum,* Thomas Lodge, *Wit's Misery,* John Marston, *The Scourge of Villany*
1599	Bishop's ban against the publication of satires
1601	Ben Jonson, *Poetaster*
1605	Isaac Casaubon, *De Satyrica Graecorum et Satira Romanorum*
1606	Ben Jonson, *Volpone*
1642	Puritan ban of theatrical performances in London
1655	Publication of classical and neo-Latin anthology of satire, *Elegantiores Praestantium Virorum Satyrae*
1660s	Nicholas Boileau publishes imitations of Horace's satires and epistles
1673	John Wilmot, earl of Rochester, *A Satyre on Charles II*
1692	John Dryden, *Discourse Concerning the Original and Progress of Satire*
1726	Jonathan Swift, *Gulliver's Travels*
1728	Alexander Pope, *Dunciad*
1732	Pope begins writing his imitations of Horace
1749	Samuel Johnson, *The Vanity of Human Wishes*

Adams, J. N. (1982) *The Latin Sexual Vocabulary*. London.

Alden, R. M. (1899) *The Rise of Formal Satire under Classical Influence*. Philadelphia.

Anderson, W. S. (1956) "Horace, the Unwilling Warrior: Satire 1.9," *American Journal of Philology* 77: 148–66 = Anderson (1982) 84–102.

(1957) "Studies in Book 1 of Juvenal," *Yale Classical Studies* 15: 33–90 = Anderson (1982) 197–254.

(1958) "Persius 1.107–10," *Classical Quarterly* ns 8: 195–7.

(1963) "The Roman Socrates: Horace and his Satires," in J. P. Sullivan, ed. *Critical Essays on Roman Literature*. Vol. II: *Satire*, 1–37. London = Anderson (1982) 13–49.

(1970) "*Lascivia* versus *Ira*: Martial and Juvenal," *California Studies in Classical Antiquity* 3: 1–34.

(1982) *Essays on Roman Satire*. Princeton.

(1984) "Ironic Preambles and Satiric Self-definition in Horace Satire 2.1," *Pacific Coast Philology* 19: 35–42.

Anon. (1606) *The Returne from Pernassus: or the Scourge of Simony*. London.

Arber, E. ed. (1875–94) *A Transcript of the Registers of the Company of Stationers of London*. 5 vols. London.

Ariosto, L. (1976), ed. P. DeSa Wiggins, *The Satires of Ludovico Ariosto: a Renaissance Autobiography*. Athens, OH.

Armstrong, D. (1964) "Horace, *Satires* 1.1–3: a Structural Study," *Arion* 3.2: 86–96.

(1986) "*Horatius Eques et Scriba*: Satires 1.6 and 2.7," *Transactions of the American Philological Association* 116: 255–88.

(1989) *Horace*. New Haven.

Arrowsmith, W. (1966) "Luxury and Death in the *Satyricon*," *Arion* 5: 304–31.

Astbury, R. (1977) "Petronius, *P.Oxy.*3010, and Menippean Satire," *Classical Philology* 72: 22–31.

Astin, A. E. (1967) *Scipio Aemilianus*. Oxford.

Athanassiadi-Fowden, P. (1981) *Julian and Hellenism: an Intellectual Biography*. Oxford.

Austin, R. G. (1964) *P. Vergili Maronis Aeneidos Liber Secundus*. Oxford.

Bacon, H. H. (1958) "The Sibyl in the Bottle," *Virginia Quarterly Review* 34: 262–76.

Badian, E. (1972) "Ennius and his Friends," in O. Skutsch, ed. *Ennius*, 151–99. Fondation Hardt, Entretiens sur l'Antiquité classique XVII, Geneva.

Bakhtin, M. M. (1968/1984) *Rabelais and his World*, trans. H. Iswolsky. Cambridge, MA/Bloomington, IN.

(1981) *The Dialogic Imagination: Four Essays*, trans. C. Emerson and M. Holquist. Austin, TX.

(1984) *Problems of Dostoevsky's Poetics*, trans. C. Emerson. Minneapolis.

Ballaster, R. (1998) "John Wilmot, Earl of Rochester," in Zwicker (1998) 204–24.

Baratin, M. (1982) "L'identité de la pensée et de la parole dans l'ancien Stoïcisme," *Langages* 16: 9–21.

Barchiesi, A. (1994) "Alcune difficoltà nella carriera di un poeta giambico: Giambo ed elegia nell'Epodo XI," in R. Cortès Touar and J. C. Fernandez Corte, eds. *Bimilenario de Horacio*, 127–38. Salamanca.

Barr, W. and Lee, G. (1987). *The Satires of Persius*. Liverpool.

Bartsch, S. (1994) *Actors in the Audience: Theatricality and Doublespeak from Nero to Hadrian*. Cambridge, MA.

Bäumer, A. (1984) "Die Macht des Wortes in Religion und Magie (Plinius, 'Naturalis Historia' 28,4–29)," *Hermes* 112: 84–99.

Baumlin, J. S. (1986) "The Generic Contexts of Elizabethan Satire," in B. Lewalski, ed. *Renaissance Genres: Essays on Theory, History, and Interpretation*, 444–67. Cambridge, MA and London.

(1991) *John Donne and the Rhetorics of Renaissance Discourse*. Columbia and London.

Beck, R. (1982) "The *Satyricon*: Satire, Narrator and Antecedents," *Museum Helveticum* 39: 206–14.

Bellandi, F. (1974) "Naevolus Cliens," *Maia* 26: 279–99.

(1980) *Etica diatribica e protesta sociale nelle satire di Giovenale*. Bologna.

(1996) *Persio. Dai "verba togae" al solipsismo stilistico*, 2nd edn. Bologna.

(2002) "Dogma e inquietudine. Persio, Orazio e la vox docens della satira," in L. Castagna and V. Vogt-Spira, eds. *Pervertere: Ästhetik der Verkehrung. Literatur und Kultur neronischer Zeit und ihre Rezeption*, 153–91. Munich–Leipzig.

Benedetto, A. (1966) "I giambi di Callimacho e il loro influsso sugli Epodi e Satire di Orazio," *Rendiconti dell'Accademia di Archeologica* 44: 23–69.

Benjamin, W. (1970) *Illuminations*, tr. H. Zohn. London.

Bernstein, M. A. (1992) *Bitter Carnival: Ressentiment and the Abject Hero*. Princeton.

Berthet, J.-F. (1978) "La culture homérique des Césars d'après Suétone," *Revue des études latines* 56: 313–34.

Beta, S., ed. (2004) *La Potenta della Parola*. Siena.

Blanchard, W. Scott (1995) *Scholar's Bedlam: Menippean Satire in the Renaissance*. Lewisburg, PA.

Bodel, J. (1999) "The *cena Trimalchionis*," in Hoffman (1999) 38–51.

Bouché-Leclercq, A. (1899) *L'astrologie grecque*. Paris.

Bourdieu, P. (1990) *The Logic of Practice*. Stanford, CA.

Bowersock, G. W. (1982) "The Emperor Julian on his Predecessors," *Yale Classical Studies* 27: 159–72.

Bramble, J. C. (1974) *Persius and the Programmatic Satire*. Cambridge.

Branham, B., and Goulet-Cazé, Marie-Odile, eds. (1996) *The Cynics: the Cynic Movement in Antiquity and Its Legacy*. Berkeley.

Branham, B., ed. (2001) *Bakhtin and the Classics*. Evanston.

Braund, S. (1988) *Beyond Anger: a Study of Juvenal's Third Book of Satires.* Cambridge.

(1992) *Roman Verse Satire: Greece and Rome.* New Surveys in the Classics 23. Oxford.

(1995) "A Woman's Voice: Laronia's Role in Juvenal Satire 2," in R. Hawley and B. Levick, eds. *Women in Antiquity: New Assessments*, 207–19. London and New York.

Braund, S., ed. (1989) *Satire and Society in Ancient Rome.* Exeter.

(1996a) *The Roman Satirists and their Masks*: London.

(1996b) *Juvenal Satires Book 1.* Cambridge.

Braund, S. and James, P. (1998) "*Quasi Homo*: Distortion and Contortion in Seneca's *Apocolocyntosis*," in Braund and Gold (1998) 285–311.

Braund, S. and Gold, B., eds. (1998) *Vile Bodies: Roman Satire and Corporeal Discourse. Arethusa* 31.

Breton, N. and Guilpin, E. (1951) ed. A. Davenport, *The Whipper Pamphlets [1601].* Liverpool.

Brink, C. O. (1982) *Horace on Poetry.* Vol. III: *Epistles Book II.* Cambridge.

Brower, R. A. (1959) *Alexander Pope: the Poetry of Allusion.* Oxford.

Brown, P. M., ed. (1993) *Horace Satires I.* Warminster.

Brugnoli, G. (1989) "Augusto e il Capricorno," in *L'astronomia a Roma nell'età augustea*, 9–31. Galatina.

Bruns, C. G., ed. (1887) *Fontes Iuris Romani* by Th. Mommsen, 5th edn. Freiburg.

Brunt, P. A. and Moore, J. M., eds. (1967) *The Achievements of the Divine Augustus.* Oxford.

Burrow, C. (1993) "Horace at Home and Abroad: Wyatt and Sixteenth-Century Horatianism," in Martindale and Hopkins (1993) 27–49.

Butler, J. (1997) *The Psychic Life of Power. Theories in Subjection.* Stanford, CA.

(1999) *Subjects of Desire: Hegelian Reflections in Twentieth-Century France.* New York.

Camporeale, G. (1987) "La danza armata in Etruria," *Mélanges d'archéologie et d'histoire de l'Ecole française de Rome* 99: 11–42.

Carne-Ross, D. S. and Haynes, K., eds. (1996) *Horace in English.* London.

Cartault, A. (1899) *Etude sur les Satires d'Horace.* Paris.

Caston, R. R. (1997) "The fall of the curtain (Horace Sat. 2.8)," *Transactions of the American Philological Association* 127: 233–56.

Cavallo, G. (1989) "Testo, libro, lettura," in G. Cavallo, P. Fedeli and A. Giardina, eds. *Lo spazio letterario di Roma antica.* Vol. II, 307–42. Rome–Bari.

Cèbe, J.-P. (1966) *La caricature et la parodie dans la Rome antique.* Bibliothèque des Ecoles françaises d'Athènes et de Rome 206.

Ceccarelli, P. (1998) *La pirrica nell'antichità greco romana.* Pisa–Rome.

Chadwick, H. (1981) *Boethius: the Consolations of Music, Logic, Theology, and Philosophy.* Oxford.

(1999) "Philosophical Tradition and the Self," in G. W. Bowersock, P. Brown, and O. Grabar, eds. *Late Antiquity: a Guide to the Postclassical World*, 60–81. Cambridge, MA.

Charpin, F. (1978–9) *Lucilius' Satires* 2 vols. Paris.

Christes, J. (1972) "Lucilius. Ein Bericht über die Forschung seit F. Marx (1904/5)," in H. Temporini, ed. *ANRW* I, 2: 1182–239. Berlin.

Cichorius, C. (1908) *Untersuchungen zu Lucilius*. Berlin.
(1922, repr. 1961) *Römische Studien*. Leipzig/Darmstadt.
Classen, C. J. (1996) "Grundlagen und Absicht der Kritik des Lucilius," in *Satura Lanx. Festschrift für W. A. Krenkel*, 11–28. Zurich–New York.
Clauss, J. J. (1985) "Allusion and Structure in Horace, *Satire* 2.1: the Callimachean Response," *Transactions of the American Philological Association* 115: 197–206.
Clegg, C. S. (1997) *Press Censorship in Elizabethan England*. Cambridge.
Cloud, J. Duncan (1989) "Satirists and the Law," in Braund (1989) 49–67.
Cody, J. V. (1976) *Horace and Callimachean Aesthetics*, Collection Latomus 147. Brussels.
Coffey, M. (1976/1989) *Roman Satire*. London/New York/Bristol.
Coleman, K. M. (1988) *Statius Silvae IV*. Oxford.
Colton, R. (1991) *Juvenal's Use of Martial's Epigrams: a Study of Literary Influence*. Amsterdam.
Combe, K. (1995) " 'But Loads of Sh – Almost Choked the Way': Shadwell, Dryden, Rochester, and the Summer of 1676," *Texas Studies in Language and Literature*, 37.2: 127–63.
Compton-Engle, G. (1999) "Aristophanes *Peace* 1265–1304: Food, Poetry and the Comic Genre," *Classical Philology* 94: 324–9.
Connerton, P. (1989) *How Societies Remember*. Cambridge.
Connors, C. (1998) *Petronius the Poet: Verse and Literary Traditions in the Satyricon*. Cambridge.
Conte, G. B. (1986). *The Rhetoric of Imitation: Genre and Poetic Memory in Virgil and other Latin Poets*, trans. ed. C. Segal. Ithaca.
(1994) *Latin Literature: a History*, trans. J. B. Solodow. Baltimore and London.
(1996) *The Hidden Author: an Interpretation of Petronius' Satyricon*. Berkeley.
Copley, Frank Olin (1942) "On the Origin of Certain Features of the Paraclausithyron," *Transactions of the American Philological Association* 73: 96–107.
Corbeill, Anthony (1996) *Controlling Laughter: Political Humor in the Late Roman Republic*. Princeton.
Corbett, Philip (1986) *The Scurra*. Edinburgh.
Corthell, Ronald (1983) "Beginning as a Satirist: Joseph Hall's *Virgidemiarum Sixe Bookes*," *SEL* 23: 47–60.
Courtney, E. (1980) *A Commentary on the Satires of Juvenal*. London.
(1993) *The Fragmentary Latin Poets*. Oxford.
(2001) *A Companion to Petronius*. Oxford.
Cucchiarelli, A. (2001) *La Satira e il poeta: Orazio tra Epodi e Sermones*. Biblioteca di Materiali e discussioni per l'analisi dei testi classici 17. Pisa.
Curley, Thomas F. III (1986) "How to Read the *Consolation of Philosophy*," *Interpretation* 14: 211–63.
Davidson, James (1997) *Courtesans and Fishcakes: the Consuming Passions of Classical Athens*. London.
Davis, Natalie Zemon (1984) "Charivari, Honor and Community in Seventeenth-Century Lyon and Geneva," in John J. MacAloon, ed. *Rite, Drama, Festival, Spectacle. Rehearsals Toward a Theory of Cultural Performance*, 42–56. Philadelphia.

De Decker, J. (1913) *Juvenalis Declamans. Etude sur la rhétorique déclamatoire dans les satires de Juvénal*. Université de Gand: Recueil de travaux publiés par la Faculté de Philosophie et Lettres 41. Ghent.

Derrida, J. (1981) *Dissemination*, trans. B. Johnson. London.

(1986) *Glas*. Lincoln, NE.

Dessen, Cynthia S. (1996) *The Satires of Persius: Iunctura Callidus Acri* (= *Iunctura Callidus Acri* [Urbana/Chicago/London] 1968). 2nd edn. Bristol.

DeWitt, N. (1939) "Epicurean Doctrine in Horace," *Classical Philology* 34: 127–34.

Dickens, Charles (1971) *Our Mutual Friend*, ed. Stephen Gill. Harmondsworth.

Dickie, M. W. (1981) "The Disavowal of *Inuidia* in Roman Iamb and Satire," *Papers of the Liverpool Latin Seminar* 3: 183–208.

Dickison, S. (1977) "Claudius: Saturnalicius Princeps," *Latomus* 36: 634–47.

Donald, Diana (1996) *The Age of Caricature: Satirical Prints in the Age of George III*. New Haven and London.

Donne, J. (1967a) ed. W. Milgate, *The Satires, Epigrams, and Verse Letters*. Oxford.

(1967b) ed. H. Gardner and T. Healy, *Selected Prose*. Oxford.

Dronke, P. (1994) *Verse with Prose from Petronius to Dante: the Art and Scope of the Mixed Form*. Cambridge, MA.

Dryden, J. (1900) "A Discourse Concerning the Original and Progress of Satire" (1693), in W. P. Ker, ed. *Essays of John Dryden*, 15–114. Oxford.

Dufallo, B. (2000) "*Satis/satura*: Reconsidering the 'Programmatic Intent' of Horace's Satires 1.1," *Classical World* 93: 579–90.

Dupont, Florence (1985) *L'acteur-roi*. Paris.

(1993) "Ludions, lydioi: les danseurs de la pompa circensis. Exegèse et discours sur l'origine des jeux à Rome," in *Spectacles sportifs et scéniques dans le monde étrusco-italique*. Collection de l'Ecole française à Rome 172: 189–210.

Du Quesnay, I. M. Le M. (1984). "Horace and Maecenas: the Propaganda Value of *Sermones* I," in T. Woodman and D. West, eds. *Poetry and Politics in the Age of Augustus*, 19–58. Cambridge.

Eagleton, T. (1981) *Walter Benjamin, or Towards a Revolutionary Criticism*. London.

Earl, D. C. (1961) *The Political Thought of Sallust*. Cambridge.

Eden, P. T., ed. (1984) *Seneca: Apocolocyntosis*. Cambridge.

Edwards, A. T. (2001) "Historicizing the Popular Grotesque: Bakhtin's *Rabelais and his World* and Attic Old Comedy," in Branham (2001) 27–55.

Ehlers, W. W. (1985). "Das 'Iter Brundisium' des Horaz (Serm. 1.5)," *Hermes* 113: 69–83.

Eliot, T. S., ed. (1933) *Ezra Pound: Selected Poems*. London.

Elkin, P. K. (1973) *The Augustan Defence of Satire*. Oxford.

Elliott, R. C. (1960) *The Power of Satire: Magic, Ritual, Art*. Princeton.

Emerson, C. (2001) "Coming to Terms with Bakhtin's Carnival," in Branham (2001) 5–26.

Erskine-Hill, H. (1972) "Courtiers out of Horace: Donne's Satire IV and Pope's Fourth Satire of Dr John Donne, Dean of St Paul's Versifyed," in A. J. Smith, ed. *John Donne: Essays in Celebration*, 273–307. London.

Evans, H. B. (1978) "Horace Satires 2.7: Saturnalia and Satire," *Classical Journal* 73: 307–12.

Evans-Pritchard, E. E. (1965) *Theories of Primitive Religion*. Oxford.

Evenepoel, W. (1990) "Maecenas: a Survey of Recent Literature," *Ancient Society* 21: 99–117.

Everett, B. (2001) "Unwritten Masterpiece," *London Review of Books* 4, January: 29–32.

Fedeli, P. (1994) *Q. Orazio Flacco: Le Opere II, Le Satire*. Rome.

Feeney, D. C. (1991) *The Gods in Epic*. Oxford.

Ferguson, J. (1979) *Juvenal: the Satires*, New York.

Ferraro, J. (2000) in Fisher (2000) 119–31.

Fisher, N., ed. (2000) *That Second Bottle: Essays on John Wilmot, Earl of Rochester*. Manchester.

Fiske, G. C. (1920) *Lucilius and Horace: a Study in the Classical Theory of Imitation*. University of Wisconsin Studies in Language and Literature 7. Madison.

Fitzpatrick, R. S. (1979) "Juvenal's Patchwork Satires: 4 and 7," *Yale Classical Studies* 23: 229–41.

Flower, Harriet I. (1996) *Ancestor Masks and Aristocratic Power in Roman Culture*. Oxford.

Fowler, A. (1982) *Kinds of Literature*. Oxford.

Fowler, D. (2000) *Roman Constructions*. Oxford.

Fraenkel, E. (1957) *Horace*. Oxford (Italian edition [1993] trans. S. Lilla, intro. S. Mariotti, Rome).

  (1960) *Elementi Plautini in Plauto*. Florence.

Fredericks, S. C. (1975) "Juvenal: a Return to Invective," in E. S. Ramage, D. L. Sigsbee, and S. C. Fredericks, eds. *Roman Satirists and their Satire*, 136–69. Park Ridge, NJ.

  (1979) "The Irony of Overstatement in the Satires of Juvenal," *Illinois Classical Studies* 4: 178–91.

Freud, S. (1962) *Three Essays on the Theory of Sexuality*, trans. J. Strachey. New York.

  (1993) *Wit and its Relation to the Unconscious*, trans. A. A. Brill. New York.

Freudenburg, K. (1990) "Horace's Satiric Program and the Language of Contemporary Theory in *Satires* 2.1," *American Journal of Philology* 111: 187–203.

  (1993) *The Walking Muse: Horace on the Theory of Satire*. Princeton.

  (1995) "Canidia at the Feast of Nasidienus (Hor. Sat. 2.8)," *Transactions of the American Philological Association* 125: 207–19.

  (1996) "Verse-Technique and Moral Extremism in Two Satires of Horace (*Sermones* 2.3 and 2.4)," *Classical Quarterly* ns 46: 192–206.

  (2001) *Satires of Rome: Threatening Poses from Lucilius to Juvenal*. Cambridge.

Frye, N. (1957) *Anatomy of Criticism: Four Essays*. Princeton.

Galinsky, K. (1996) *Augustan Culture*. Princeton.

Gamel, M.-K. (1998) "Reading as a Man: Performance and Gender in Roman Elegy," *Helios* 25: 79–95.

Gelzer, T. (1992) "Die Alte Komödie in Athen und die Basler Fastnacht," in F. Graf, ed. *Klassische Antike und neue Wege der Kulturwissenschaft. Symposium Karl Meuli (Basel, 11.–13. September 1991)*, 29–61. Basel.

Gigante, M. (1993) *Orazio. Una misura per l'amore. Lettura della satira seconda del primo libro*. Venosa.

Glazewski, J. (1971) "*Plenus Vitae Conviva*: a Lucretian Concept in Horace's Satires," *Classical Bulletin* 47: 85–8.

Gold, B. (1992) "Openings in Horace's Satires and Odes: Poet, Patron and Audience," *YCS* 29: 161–86.

(1994) "Humor in Juvenal's Sixth Satire," in S. Jaekel and A. Timonen, eds. *Laughter Down the Centuries*, 95–111. Acta Universitatis Turkuensis 208.

(1998) " 'The House I Live in is Not my Own': Women's Bodies in Juvenal's *Satires*," *Arethusa* 31: 369–86.

Gordon, Ian (1976 [2nd edn. 1993]) *Preface to Pope.* Harlow.

Görler, W. (1984) "Zum *virtus*-Fragment des Lucilius und zur Geschichte der stoischen Güterlehre," *Hermes* 112: 445–68.

Gowers, E. (1993a) *The Loaded Table: Representations of Food in Latin Literature.* Oxford.

(1993b) "Horace, Satires 1.5: an Inconsequential Journey," *Proceedings of the Cambridge Philological Society* 39: 48–66.

Graf, F. (1997) *Magic in the Ancient World.* Cambridge, MA.

Grandazzi, A. (1997) *The Foundation of Rome: Myth and History*, trans. J. M. Todd. Ithaca, NY.

Gransden, K. W. (1970) *Tudor Verse Satire.* London.

Gratwick, A. S. (1982) "The Satires of Ennius and Lucilius," in E. J. Kenney and W. V. Clausen, eds. *The Cambridge History of Classical Literature.* Vol. II, part I. *The Early Republic*, 156–71. Cambridge.

Green, Peter (1974 [revised ed. with new intro. 1998]) *Juvenal, the Sixteen Satires.* New York.

Greer, G. (2000) *John Wilmot, Earl of Rochester.* Horndon.

Griffin, D. (1973) *Satires Against Man: the Poems of Rochester.* Berkeley.

(1994) *Satire: a Critical Reintroduction.* Lexington, KY.

Griffin, J. (1993) "Horace in the Thirties," in N. Rudd, ed. *Horace 2000: a Celebration. Essays for the Bimillennium*, 1–22. London.

Gruen, E. S. (1992) *Culture and National Identity in Republican Rome.* Ithaca, NY.

Guilpin, E. (1974) ed. D. A. Carroll, *Skialetheia.* Chapel Hill, NC.

Gunderson, E. (1997) "Catullus, Pliny, and Love-Letters," *Transactions of the American Philological Association* 127: 201–31.

(2000) *Staging Masculinity: the Rhetoric of Performance in the Roman World.* Ann Arbor.

(2003) *Declamation and Roman Identity: Paternity, Authority, and the Rhetorical Self.* Cambridge.

Gunn, Thom (1992) *The Man with Night Sweats.* London and Boston.

Haarberg, Jon (1998) *Parody and the Praise of Folly.* Oslo.

Habinek, T. (1997) "The Invention of Sexuality in the World-City of Rome," in T. Habinek and A. Schiesaro, eds. *The Roman Cultural Revolution*, 23–43. Cambridge.

Hall, J. (1969) ed. A. Davenport, *The Poems.* Liverpool.

Hammond, Brean S. (1995) " 'An Allusion to Horace', Jonson's Ghost and the Second Poets' War," in Edward Burns, ed. *Reading Rochester.* Liverpool.

Hammond, Paul (1999) *Dryden and the Traces of Classical Rome.* Oxford.

Hammond, P. and Hopkins, D., eds. (2000) *The Poems of John Dryden.* Vol. III: *1686–99.* London.

Hardie, P. R. (1993) *The Epic Successors of Virgil.* Cambridge.

Harrison, G. (1987) "The Confessions of Lucilius (Horace, Sat. 2.1.30–34): a Defense of Autobiographical Satire?," *Classical Antiquity* 6: 38–52.

Harrison, S. J., ed. (1999) *Oxford Essays on the Roman Novel*. Oxford.

Hartog, F. (1988) *The Mirror of Herodotus: the Representation of the Other in the Writing of History*, trans. Janet Lloyd. Berkeley.

Harvey, R. A. (1981) *A Commentary on Persius*. Leiden.

Haynes, H. (2003) *A History of Make-Believe: Tacitus' Histories*. California.

Hegel, G. (1977) *Phenomenology of the Spirit*. Oxford.

Hellegouarc'h, J. (1992) "Juvénal, poète épique," in *Au miroir de la culture antique. Mélanges offertes au Prés. René Marache*, 269–85. Rennes.

Henderson, J. (1989) "Satire Writes 'Woman': *Gendersong*," *Proceedings of the Cambridge Philological Society* 35: 50–80, revised and reprinted in Henderson (1999) 173–201.

(1994) "On Getting Rid of Kings: Horace, Satire 1.7," *Classical Quarterly* 44: 146–70.

(1995) "Pump up the Volume: Juvenal, Satire 1, 1–21," *Proceedings of the Cambridge Philological Society* 41: 101–37, revised and reprinted in Henderson (1999) 249–73.

(1997) *Figuring out Roman Nobility: Juvenal's 8th Satire*. Exeter.

(1998) *Fighting for Rome: Poets and Caesars, History and Civil War*. Cambridge.

(1999) *Writing Down Rome: Satire, Comedy, and Other Offences in Latin Poetry*. Oxford.

Hendrickson, G. L. (1894) "The Dramatic Satura and the Old Comedy at Rome," *American Journal of Philology* 15: 1–30.

(1926) "Convicium," *Classical Philology* 21: 114–19.

(1927) "*Satura tota nostra est*," *Classical Philology* 22: 46–60.

Hester, Thomas M. (1982) *Kinde Pitty and Brave Scorn: John Donnei's Satyres*. Durham, NC.

Hewison, P. E. (1987) "Rochester, the 'Imitation', and 'An Allusion to Horace'," *The Seventeenth Century* 2: 73–94.

Highet, G. (1941) "Petronius the Moralist," *Transactions of the American Philological Association* 72: 176–94.

(1951) "Juvenal's Bookcase," *American Journal of Philology* 72: 369–94.

(1954) *Juvenal the Satirist: a Study*. Oxford.

(1962) *The Anatomy of Satire*. Princeton.

(1967) *The Classical Tradition: Greek and Roman Influences on Western Literature*. Oxford.

Hinds, S. (1998) *Allusion and Intertext: Dynamics of Appropriation in Roman Poetry*. Cambridge.

Hodgart, M. (1969) *Satire*. London.

Hoffman, H., ed. (1999) *Latin Fiction: the Latin Novel in Context*. London/New York.

Hooley, D. M. (1997) *The Knotted Thong: Structures of Mimesis in Persius*. Ann Arbor.

Hopkins, D. (1995) "Dryden and the Tenth Satire of Juvenal," *Translation and Literature* 4: 31–60.

Horatius Flaccus, Q. (1578) *Quinti Horatii Flacci Venusini, Poetae Lyrici Poemata omnia doctissimis scholiis, & nouis aliquot annotatiunculis illustrata*. London.

(1592) *Poemata, Nouis Scholiis & Argumentis illustrata.* London.

(1606) ed. J. Bond, *Poemata, scholiis siue Annotationibus, quae breuis Commentarii vice esse possint.* London.

Hornblower, S. and Spawforth, A., eds. (1996) *The Oxford Classical Dictionary* (= *OCD*), 3rd edn. Oxford.

Hornblower, S. (1987) *Thucydides.* London.

Hubbard, Thomas (1981) "The Structure and Programmatic Intent of Horace's First Satire," *Latomus* 40: 305–21.

Huizinga, J. (1949) trans. R. F. C. Hull, *Homo Ludens: a Study of the Play-element in Culture.* London.

Huizinga, J. (1955) *Homo Ludens: a Study of the Play-Element in Culture.* Boston.

Hunter, R. L. (1985) "Horace on Friendship and Free Speech: *Epistles* 1.18 and *Satires* 1.4," *Hermes* 113: 480–90.

Hurley, D. W. (2001) *Suetonius: Divus Claudius.* Cambridge.

Inwood, B. (1995) "Seneca and his Philosophical Milieu," in C. P. Jones, C. Segal, R. J. Tarrant, and R. F. Thomas, eds. *Greece in Rome: Influence, Integration, Resistance,* Harvard Studies in Classical Philology 97. Cambridge, MA.

Jahn, O., ed. (1843) *A. Persi Flacci Satirarum Liber.* Leipzig.

Jenkyns, R. (1982) *Three Classical Poets: Sappho, Catullus, and Juvenal.* Cambridge, MA.

Jocelyn, H. D. (1972) "The Poems of Quintus Ennius," in H. Temporini, ed. *ANRW* 1, 2, 987–1026. Berlin.

(1982) "Diatribes and Sermons," *Liverpool Classical Monthly* 7.1: 3–7.

(1977a) "The Ruling Class of the Roman Republic and Greek Philosophers," *Bulletin of the John Rylands University Library of Manchester* 59: 323–66.

(1977b) "Ennius, *Sat.* 6–7 Vahlen," *Rivista di Filologia e di Istruzione Classica* 105: 131–51.

Johnson, S. (1905) ed. George Birkbeck Hill, *Lives of the English Poets,* 3 vols. Oxford.

Johnson, W. R. (1996) "Male Victimology in Juvenal 6," *Ramus* 25: 170–86.

Johnson, W. (2000) "Toward a Sociology of Reading in Classical Antiquity," *American Journal of Philology* 121: 593–627.

Jones, E. (1968) "Pope and Dullness," *Proceedings of the British Academy* 54: 231–63.

Jonson, B. (1975) ed. I. Donaldson, *Poems.* Oxford.

(1995) ed. T. Cain, *Poetaster.* Manchester.

Jordan, D. R. (1985) "A Survey of Greek Defixiones not Included in the Special Corpora," *Greek, Roman, and Byzantine Studies* 16: 161–97.

Jory, E. J. (1996) "The Drama of the Dance: Prolegomena to an Iconography of Imperial Pantomime," in W. Slater, ed. *Roman Theater and Society,* 1–26. Ann Arbor.

Justman, S. (1999) *The Springs of Liberty: the Satiric Tradition and Freedom of Speech.* Evanston, IL.

Kelly, J. M. (1966) *Roman Litigation.* Oxford.

Kennedy, D. F. (1992) "'Augustan' and 'Anti-Augustan': Reflections on Terms of Reference," in A. Powell, ed. *Roman Poetry and Propaganda in the Age of Augustus,* 26–58. London.

Kenney, E. J. (1962) "The First Satire of Juvenal," *Proceedings of the Cambridge Philological Society* 8: 29–40 (= "Juvenal erste Satire," in D. Korzeniewski, ed. *Die römische Satire, Wege der Forschung* 238: 473–95. Darmstadt).

(1963) "Juvenal: Satirist or Rhetorician," *Latomus* 22: 704–20.

Kenney, E. J., and Clausen, W. V., eds. (1982) *The Cambridge History of Classical Literature*. Vol. II: *Latin Literature*. Cambridge.

Kernan, Alvin (1959) *The Cankered Muse*. New Haven and London.

(1965) *The Plot of Satire*. New Haven and London.

Kiessling, A., and Heinze, R., eds. (1957, 6th edn.) *Q. Horatius Flaccus, Zweiter Teil: Satiren*. Berlin.

Kilpatrick, R. S. (1973) "Juvenal's 'Patchwork' Satires: 4 and 7," *Yale Classical Studies* 23: 229–41.

Kindstrand, J. F., ed. (1976) *Bion of Borysthenes: A Collection of the Fragments with Introduction and Commentary*. Uppsala.

King, Bruce (1969) *Dryden's Mind and Art*. New York and London.

Kirk, E. P. (1980) *Menippean Satire: an Annotated Catalogue of Texts and Criticism*. New York.

Kissel, W. (1981) "Horaz 1936–1975. Eine Gesamtbibliographie," *ANRW* II, 31.3: 1403–1558. Berlin/New York.

(1990) *Aulus Persius Flaccus, Satiren*. Heidelberg.

Knoche, U. (1975) *Roman Satire*, trans. E. Ramage. Bloomington and London.

Koster, S. (1990) "Der Prolog des Persius," in P. Steinmetz, ed. *Beiträge zur hellenistischen Literatur und ihrer Rezeption in Rom*, 155–63. Stuttgart.

Krenkel, W. (1970) *Lucilius Satiren*, 2 vols. Leiden.

Kroll, R. W. F. (1991) *The Material Word: Literate Culture in the Restoration and Early Eighteenth Century*. Baltimore.

Kupersmith, W. (1985) *Roman Satirists in Seventeenth Century England*. Norman.

Labate, M. (1981) "La satira di Orazio: morfologia di un genere irrequieto," in *Orazio, Satire*, 5–45. Milan.

(1992) "Le necessità del poeta satirico. Fisiopatologia di una scelta letteraria," in I. Mazzini, ed. *Civiltà materiale e letteratura nel mondo antico*, 55–66. Macerata.

Lacan, J. (1994) *Le Séminaire de Jacques Lacan*. Livre IV: *La relation d'objet*. Paris.

(1998). *Le Séminaire de Jacques Lacan*. Livre V: *Les formations de l'inconscient*. Paris.

LaFleur, R. (1981) "Horace and *Onomasti Komodein*: the Law of Satire," *ANRW* II, 31.3: 1790–1826. Berlin/New York.

Laird, A. (1999) *Powers of Expression, Expressions of Power: Speech Presentation and Latin Literature*. Oxford.

Lakoff, G. (1987) *Women, Fire, and Dangerous Things: What Categories Reveal about the Mind*. Chicago and London.

Langford, P. (1989) "Horace's Protean Satire: Public Life, Ethics, and Literature in Satires II," Dissertation Princeton.

La Penna A. (1979), "Persio e le vie nuove della satira latina," in *Persio, Satire*, 5–78. Milan (repr. in *Da Lucrezio a Persio. Saggi, studi, note* (1995) 279–343. Milan).

Lascelles, M. (1959) "Johnson and Juvenal," in F. W. Hilles, ed. *New Light on Dr. Johnson: Essays on the Occasion of his 250th Birthday*. New Haven.

Leach, E. (1971) "Horace's *Pater Optimus* and Terence's Demea: Autobiographical Fiction and Comedy in *Serm.* 1.4," *American Journal of Philology* 92: 616–32.

Leeman, A. D., Pinkster, H., and Rabbie, E. (1989) *M. T. Cicero De Oratore libri III*, vol. 3. Heidelberg.

Lefèvre, E. (1981) "Horaz und Maecenas," *ANRW* II 31.3: 1987–2029.

Le Goff, Jacques, and Schmitt, Jean-Claude, eds. (1981) *Le Charivari*. Amsterdam.

Lejay, P. (1911) *Œuvres d'Horace. Satires.* Paris, repr. Hildesheim (1966).

Lendon. J. E. (1997) *Empire of Honour*. Oxford.

Lepointe, G. (1955) "L'occentatio de la loi des Douze Tables d'après Saint Augustin et Cicéron," *Revue Internationale des Droits de l'Antiquité* ser. 3, 2: 287–302.

Levin, H. (1980) "The Wages of Satire," in Said (1980) 1–14.

Loewenstein, J. F. (1999) "Personal Material: Jonson and Book-Burning," in M. Butler, ed. *Re-Presenting Ben Jonson: Text, History, Performance*, 93–113. Houndmills/New York.

Long, A. A. (1971) *Language and Thought in Stoicism*, in A. A. Long, ed. *Problems in Stoicism*, 75–113. London.

(1986) *Hellenistic Philosophy*. London.

Lord, G. deForest (1987) *Classical Presences in Seventeenth-Century English Poetry*. New Haven.

Lott, E. (1993) *Love and Theft: Blackface Minstrelsy and the American Working Class*. Oxford.

Love, H. (2000) *The Works of John Wilmot, Earl of Rochester*. Oxford.

Lovejoy, A. O. and Boas, G. (1935) *Primitivism and Related Ideas in Antiquity*. Baltimore.

Lovisi, C. (1997) "Deux usages du serment dans l'Italie primitive," in F. Joannès and S. Lafont, eds. *Jurer et maudire. Pratiques, politiques et usages juridiques du serment dans le Proche-Orient*. Méditerranées 10/11: 175–84. Paris.

Lyne, R. O. A. M. (1995) *Horace: Behind the Public Poetry*. New Haven.

Mack, M. (1951) "The Muse of Satire," *Yale Review* 41: 80–92.

Mandelker, A. (1995) *Bakhtin in Context: Across the Disciplines*. Evanston, IL.

Mariotti, I. (1960) *Studi Luciliani, Studi di lettere storia e filosofia*. Scuola normale superiore di Pisa 25. Florence.

Mariotti, S. (1951, 1963, 1991) *Lezioni su Ennio*. Pesaro/Turin/Urbino.

(1965) "Congetture alla *Vita Persi*," *Rivista di Filologia e di istruzione classica* 93: 185–7.

Marongiu, A. (1977) "Giovenale e il diritto," *Studia et Documenta Historiae et Iuris* 43: 167–87.

Markus, D. (2000) "Performing the Book: the Recital of Epic in First-Century C. E. Rome," *Classical Antiquity* 19: 138–79.

Marsh, D. (1975) "Horatian Influence and Imitation in Ariosto's Satires," *Comparative Literature* 27: 307–26.

Marston, John (1598) *The Metamorphosis of Pigmalions Image. And Certaine Satyres*. London.

(1961) ed. A. Davenport, *The Poems*. Liverpool.

Martindale, C. (1983) "Sense and Sensibility: the Child and the Man in 'The Rape of the Lock,'" *Modern Language Review* 78: 273–84.

(1997) "The Classic of All Europe," in C. Martindale, ed. *The Cambridge Companion to Virgil*, 1–18. Cambridge.

Martindale, C., and Hopkins, D., eds. (1993) *Horace Made New: Horatian Influences on British Writing from the Renaissance to the Twentieth Century*. Cambridge.

Martindale, J. (1993) "The Best Master of Virtue and Wisdom: the Horace of Ben Jonson and His Heirs," in Martindale and Hopkins (1993) 50–85.

Marx, F. (1904–1905, 1963) *C. Lucili Carminum Reliquiae*, 2 vols. Leipzig/ Amsterdam.

Masters, J. (1994) "Deceiving the Reader: the Political Mission of Lucan *Bellum Civile* 7," in J. Elsner and J. Masters, eds. *Reflections of Nero*, 151–77. London.

Maurer, A. E. Wallace (1997) "The Form of Dryden's *Absalom and Achitophel*, Once More," in Winn (1997) 123–37.

Mazurek, T. (1997a) "Self-Parody and the Law in Horace's *Satires* 1.9," *Classical Journal* 93: 1–17.

(1997b) "Legal Terminology in Horace's *Satires*," Ph.D. Dissertation, University of North Carolina at Chapel Hill.

McCabe, R. A. (1981) "Elizabethan Satire and the Bishops' Ban of 1599," *Yearbook of English Studies* 11: 188–93.

(1982) *Joseph Hall: a Study in Satire and Meditation*. Oxford.

McGann, M. J. (1973) "The Three Worlds of Horace's Satires," in C. D. N. Costa, ed. *Horace*, 59–93. London.

McGinn, T. (2001) "Satire and the Law: the Case of Horace," *Proceedings of the Cambridge Philological Society* 47: 81–102.

Mencken, H. L. (1922) *Prejudices*. 3rd series: New York.

Merrill, W. A. (1905) *On the Influence of Lucretius on Horace*. Berkeley.

Meuli, K. (1953, 1975) "Charivari," in *Festschrift Franz Dornseiff zum 65. Geburtstag*, 231–41. Leipzig (= *Gesammelte Schriften*, ed. Thomas Gelzer, 471–84. Basel).

Migliorini, P. (1990) *La terminologia medica come strumento espressivo della satira di Persio*. Quaderni di Anazetesis 2. Pistoia.

Miller, J.-A. (1996a) "A Discussion of Lacan's 'Kant with Sade,'" in R. Feldson, B. Fink and M. Jannus, eds. *Reading Seminars I and II: Lacan's Return to Freud*, 212–37. Albany, NY.

(1996b) "On Perversion," in R. Feldson, B. Fink and M. Jannus, eds. *Reading Seminars I and II: Lacan's Return to Freud*, 306–20. Albany, NY.

Miller, P. (1998) "The Bodily Grotesque in Roman Satire: Images of Sterility," *Arethusa* 31: 257–83.

Milsom, S. F. C. (1981) *Historical Foundations of the Common Law*. London.

Miner, E. (1967) *Dryden's Poetry*. Bloomington.

Minnis, A. J., and Scott, A. B., eds. (1988) *Medieval Literary Theory and Criticism c.1100–c.1375: the Commentary-Tradition*. Oxford.

Momigliano, A. (1942) review of Laura Robinson, "Freedom of Speech in the Roman Republic," (Dissertation, Johns Hopkins University, 1940), in *Journal of Roman Studies* 32: 120–3.

Montaigne, Michel de (1993) *The Complete Essays* trans. M. A. Screech. Harmondsworth.

Moreau, P., ed. (2002) *Corps romains*. Grenoble.

Morel, J. P. (1970) "La *Iuventus* et les origines de la théâtre romain," *Revue des études latines* 47: 208–52.

Moretti, G. (1995) *Acutum dicendi genus. Brevità, oscurità, sottigliezze e paradossi nelle tradizioni retoriche degli Stoici*. Bologna.

Morford, M. P. O. (1984) *Persius*. Boston.

Motto, A. L. and Clark, J. R. (1965). *"Per iter tenebricosum*. The Mythos of Juvenal 3," *Transactions of the American Philological Association* 96: 267–76.

Muecke, F. (1985) *"Cave Canem*: the Satirist's Image," in P. Petr, D. Roberts, and P. Thomson, eds. *Comic Relations*, 113–33. Frankfurt am Main/Berne/New York.

(1990) "The Audience of/in Horace's Satires," *The Journal of the Australasian Universities Language and Literature Association* 74: 34–47.

(1993) ed. *Horace Satires II*. Warminster.

Mukherjee, N. (2000) "Thomas Drant's Rewriting of Horace," *Studies in English Literature* 40: 1–20.

Müller, K. (1995) *Petronius Satyricon Reliquiae*. Stuttgart/Leipzig.

Murley, C. (1939) "Lucretius and the History of Satire," *Transactions of the American Philological Association* 70: 380–95.

Nilsson, N. O. (1952) *Metrische Stildifferenzen in den Satiren des Horaz*. Uppsala.

Nixon, Paul (1963) *Martial and the Modern Epigram*. New York.

O'Connor, J. F. (1990–1) "Horace's Cena Nasidieni and Poetry's Feast," *Classical Journal* 86: 23–34.

O'Gorman, E. (2000) *Irony and Misreading in the Annals of Tacitus*. Cambridge.

Oliensis, E. (1991) "Canidia, Canicula, and the *Decorum* of Horace's *Epodes*," *Arethusa* 24: 107–38.

(1998a) *Horace and the Rhetoric of Authority*. Cambridge.

(1998b) *"Ut arte emendaturus fortunam*: Horace, Nasidienus, and the Art of Satire," in T. Habinek and A. Schiesaro, eds. *The Roman Cultural Revolution*, 90–104. Cambridge.

Oltramare, A. (1926) *Les origines de la diatribe romaine*. Geneva.

Pabst, B. (1994) *Prosimetrum: Tradition und Wandel einer Literaturform zwischen Spätantike und Spätmittelalter*. Cologne.

Palmer, A. (1891) *The Satires of Horace*. 4th edn. London.

Parker, H. (1997) "The Tetragonic Grid," in J. Hallet and M. Skinner, eds. *Roman Sexualities*, 47–65. Princeton.

Pennacini, A. (1983) "Retorica, diatriba cinica e satira romana," *Vichiana* 12: 282–8.

Peter, J. (1956) *Complaint and Satire in Early English Literature*. Oxford.

Petersmann, H. (1999) "The Language of Early Roman Satire: its Function and Characteristics," in J. N. Adams and R. G. Mayer, eds. *Aspects of the Language of Latin Poetry*, 289–310. Oxford.

Peterson, R. S. (1981) *Imitation and Praise in the Poems of Ben Jonson*. New Haven.

Pierce, R. B. (1981) "Ben Jonson's Horace and Horace's Ben Jonson," *Studies in Philology* 78: 20–31.

Plass, P. (1988) *Wit and the Writing of History*. Wisconsin.

Pope, A. (1963) ed. J. Butt, *The Poems: A One-volume Edition of the Twickenham Text with Selected Annotations*. London.

Powell, J. G. F. (1995) *Cicero the Philosopher*. Oxford.

Prescott, A. L. (2000) "The Evolution of Tudor Satire," in A. F. Kinney, ed. *The Cambridge Companion to English Literature, 1500–1600*, 220–40. Cambridge.

Prettejohn, E. (1999) *After the Pre-Raphaelites: Art and Aestheticism in Victorian England*. Manchester.

Price, M. (1951) *Swift's Rhetorical Art*. New Haven.

Pucci, J. (1998) *The Full-knowing Reader: Allusion and the Power of the Reader in the Western Literary Tradition*. New Haven.

Puelma Piwonka, M. (1949) *Lucilius und Kallimachos. Zur Geschichte einer Gattung der hellenistisch-römischen Poesie*. Frankfurt am Main.

Putnam, M. (1995) "Pastoral Satire," *Arion* Fall 1995/Winter 1996: 303–16.

Quinn, K. (1982) "The Poet and his Audience in the Augustan Age," *ANRW* II, 30: 175–80.

Raith, O. (1963) *Petronius ein Epikureer*. Nuremberg.

Ramage, E. (1989) "Juvenal and the Establishment: Denigration of Predecessor in the Satires," *ANRW* II 33.1, 640–707.

Rankins, W. (1948) ed. A. Davenport, *Seven Satires (1598)*. Liverpool.

Rawson, Claude (1982) "Pope's Waste Land: Reflections on Mock-Heroic," *Essays and Studies* 35: 45–65.

   (1994) *Satire and Sentiment, 1660–1830*: Cambridge.

Rawson, E. (1985) *Intellectual Life in the Late Roman Republic*. London.

   (1987) "*Speciosa Locis Morataque Recte*," in M. Whitby *et al.* eds. *Homo Viator: Classical Essays for John Bramble*, 79–88. Bristol.

Reckford, K. J. (1959) "Horace and Maecenas," *Transactions of the American Philological Association* 90: 195–208.

   (1962) "Studies in Persius," *Hermes* 90: 476–504.

   (1969) *Horace*. New York.

   (1998) "Reading the Sick Body: Decomposition and Morality in Persius' Third Satire," *Arethusa* 31.3: 337–54.

   (1999) "Only a Wet Dream? Hope and Skepticism in Horace, Satire 1.5," *American Journal of Philology* 120: 525–54.

Reeve, M. D. (1983) *Classical Review* 33: 32.

Relihan, J. C. (1984) "On the Origins of Menippean Satire as the Name of a Literary Genre," *Classical Philology* 79: 226–9.

   (1989) "The Confessions of Persius," *Illinois Classical Studies* 14: 145–67.

   (1993) *Ancient Menippean Satire*. Baltimore.

   (1996) "Menippus in Antiquity and the Renaissance," in Branham and Goulet-Cazé (1996) 265–93.

   (forthcoming) *The Prisoner's Philosophy: On the Limitations of Pagan Thought in Boethius's Consolation*. South Bend, IN.

Relihan, J. C., trans. (2001) *Consolation of Philosophy*. Indianapolis/Cambridge.

Richard, J. (1982) *Three Classical Poets: Sappho, Catullus and Juvenal*. London.

Richlin, A. (1992) *The Garden of Priapus: Sexuality and Aggression in Roman Humor*. 2nd edn. Oxford.

   (1993) "Not before Homosexuality: the Materiality of the *Cinaedus* and the Roman Law against Love Between Men," *Journal of the History of Sexuality* 3.4: 523–73.

Riikonen, H. K. (1987) *Menippean Satire as a Literary Genre with Special Reference to Seneca's Apocolocyntosis*. Helsinki.

Rimell, V. (2002) *Petronius and the Anatomy of Fiction*. Cambridge.

Rogers, P. (1982) "An Allusion to Horace," in J. Treglown, ed. *The Spirit of Wit: Reconsiderations of Rochester*. Oxford.

   (1993) ed, *Alexander Pope*. Oxford.

Rose, K. F. C. (1971) *The Date and Author of the Satyricon*. Leiden.

Rudd, N. (1966) *The Satires of Horace*. Cambridge.
  (1976) "Poets and Patrons in Juvenal's 7th Satire," in *Lines of Enquiry: Studies in Latin Poetry*, 84–118. Cambridge.
  (1986) *Themes in Roman Satire*. London.
Rudd, N., trans. (1973) *The Satires of Horace and Persius*. London.
Rudd, N., ed. (1993) *Horace 2000: a Celebration: Essays for the Bimillennium*. Ann Arbor.
Rudich, V. (1997) *Dissidence and Literature under Nero: the Price of Rhetoricisation*. New York and London.
Ruffell, I. A. (2003) "Beyond Satire: Horace, Popular Invective and the Segregation of Literature," *Journal of Roman Studies* 93: 35–65.
Said, E., ed. (1980) *Literature and Society*. Baltimore.
Sallmann, K. (1974) "Die seltsame Reise nach Brundisium. Aufbau und Deutung der Horazsatire 1,5," in U. Reinhardt and K. Sallmann, eds. *Musa Iocosa. Arbeiten über Humor und Witz Komik und Komödie der Antike*, 179–206. Hildesheim.
Sandy, G. (1969) "Satire in the *Satyricon*," *American Journal of Philology* 90: 293–303.
Sbardella, L. (2000) *Filita. Testimonianze e frammenti poetici*. Seminari Romani di Cultura Greca, Quaderni 3. Rome.
Scaliger, J. C. (1561) *Poetices libri septem*.
Schlegel, C. M. (1994) "The Satirist Makes Satire: Self-definition and the Power of Speech in Horace, Satires I." Dissertation, University of California at Los Angeles.
  (1999) "Horace *Satires* 1.7: Satire as Conflict Irresolution," *Arethusa* 32: 337–52.
  (2002) "Horace and his Fathers," *American Journal of Philology* 121: 93–119.
Schmeling, G. (1999) "Petronius and the *Satyrica*," in Hoffman (1999) 23–37.
Schmidt, E. G. (1966) "Diatribe und Satire," *Wissenschaftliche Zeitschrift Universität Rostock*, 507–15. Gesellschaftliche-sprachwissenschaftliche Reihe 15.
Schmidt, P. (1989) "Postquam ludus in artem paulatim verterat. Varro und die Fruhgeschichte des romischen Theaters," in G. Vogt-Spira, ed. *Studien zur vor-literarischen Periode im frühen Rom*, 77–134. Tübingen.
Schrijvers, P. (1993) "Horace moraliste," in W. Ludwig, ed. *Horace, l'oeuvre et les imitations. Un siècle d'interpretation*, 41–90. Entretiens sur l'antiquité classique 39. Geneva.
Scivoletti, N. (1963) "Presenze di Persio in Giovenale," *Giornale italiano di Filologia* 16: 60–72.
Scodel, R. (1987) "Horace, Lucilius and Callimachean Polemic," *Harvard Studies in Classical Philology* 91: 199–215.
Scott, I. G. (1927) *The Grand Style in the Satires of Juvenal*. Northampton, MA.
Seeck, G. A. (1991) "Über das satirisches in Horaz' Satiren, oder: Horaz und seine Leser, z. B. Maecenas," *Gymnasium* 98: 534–47.
Seidel, M. (1979) *Satiric Inheritance: Rabelais to Sterne*. Princeton.
Sellar, W. Y. (1881) *The Roman Poets of the Republic*. Oxford.
Shackleton Bailey, D. R., ed. (1985) *Horatius Opera*. Leipzig.
  (1989) "More on Quintilian's (?) Shorter Declamations," *Harvard Studies in Classical Philology* 92: 367–404.
  (1982) *Profile of Horace*. London.

Shanzer, Danuta (1986) "The Late Antique Tradition of Varro's *Onos Lyras*," *Rheinisches Museum* 129: 272–85.

Sigsbee, D. L. (1976) "The *Paradoxa Stoicorum* and Varro's *Menippeans*," *Classical Philology* 71: 244–8.

Silk, M. S. (2000) *Aristophanes and the Definition of Comedy*. Oxford.

  (2001) "Among the Blest," review of Elizabeth Cook, *Achilles*, *Times Literary Supplement*, June 29: 24.

Silverman, K. (1996). *The Threshold of the Visible World*. New York.

Skutsch, O. (1968). *Studia Enniana*. London.

  (1985) *The Annals of Q. Ennius*. Oxford.

  (1990) "Two Notes on Ennius," *Maia* 42: 25–7.

Slater, N. W. (1990) *Reading Petronius*. Baltimore and London.

Smith, G. G. (1904) *Elizabethan Critical Essays*. Oxford.

Smith, R. E. (1951) "The Law of Libel in Rome," *Classical Quarterly* 3/4: 169–79.

Smith, Rowland (1995) *Julian's Gods: Religion and Philosophy in the Thought and Action of Julian the Apostate*. London.

Smith, W. S. (1989) "Heroic Models for the Sordid Present: Juvenal's View of Tragedy," *ANRW* 33.1: 811–23.

Snyder, J. (1991) *Prospects of Power: Tragedy, Satire, the Essay, and the Theory of Genre*. Lexington, KY.

Sochatoff, A.F (1962) "The Purpose of Petronius' *Bellum Civile*: a Reexamination," *Transactions of the American Philological Association* 93: 449–58.

  (1970) "Imagery in the Poems of the *Satyricon*," *Classical Journal* 65: 340–4.

Solin, H. (1968) *Eine neue Fluchtafel aus Ostia*. Helsinki.

Speyer, W. (1969) "Fluch," in *Reallexikon für Antike und Christentum* 7: 1160–28.

Stack, F. (1985) *Pope and Horace: Studies in Imitation*. Cambridge.

Staley, G. (2000). "Juvenal's Third Satire: Umbricius' Rome, Vergil's Troy," *Memoirs of the American Academy in Rome* 45: 85–98.

Steggle, M. (1999) "Horace the Second, or, Ben Jonson, Thomas Dekker, and the Battle for Augustan Rome," in P. Franssen and T. Hoenselaars, eds. *The Author as Character: Representing Historical Writers in Western Literature*, 118–30. Madison, NJ.

Stockton, David (1979) *The Gracchi*. Oxford.

Sullivan, J. P., ed. (1963) *Critical Essays on Roman Literature: Satire*. London.

  (1968) *The Satyricon of Petronius: A Literary Study*. London.

  (1985) *Literature and Politics in the Age of Nero*. Ithaca, NY.

  (1991) *Martial: the Unexpected Classic*. Cambridge.

Summers, M. (1927) *The Works of Thomas Shadwell*, vol. v. London.

Swedenberg, H. T., Jr. (1974) *The Works of John Dryden*, vol. iv. Berkeley.

Szilágyi, J. (1981) "Impletae modis saturae," *Prospettiva* 24: 2–23.

Tave, S. (1960) *The Amiable Humorist: a Study in the Comic Theory and Criticism of the Eighteenth and Early Nineteenth Centuries*. Chicago.

Test, G. (1991) *Satire: Spirit and Art*. Tampa, FL.

Thomsen, O. (1992) *Ritual and Desire: Catullus 61 and 62 and Other Ancient Documents on Wedding and Marriage*. Aarhus.

Thormählen, M. (1993) *Rochester: the Poems in Context*. Cambridge.

Turner, Victor (1969) *The Ritual Process: Structure and Anti-Structure*. Ithaca, NY.

(1982) *From Ritual to Theatre: the Human Seriousness of Play*. New York.

(1984) "Liminality and the Performative Genres," in John J. MacAloon, ed. *Rite, Drama, Festival, Spectacle: Rehearsals Toward a Theory of Cultural Performance*, 19–41. Philadelphia.

Turpin, W. (1998) "The Epicurean Parasite: Horace, Satires 1.1.–3," *Ramus* 27.2: 127–40.

Usener, H. (1901) "Italische Volksjustiz," *Rheinisches Museum* 56: 1–29 = *Kleine Schriften* 4 (1913) 356–82.

Van Rooy, C. A. (1966) *Studies in Classical Satire and Related Literary Theory*. Leiden.

(1973) "'Imitatio' of Vergil, *Eclogues* in Horace, *Satires* Book 1," *AClass* 16: 69–88.

Venturo, David F. (1999) *Johnson the Poet: the Poetic Career of Samuel Johnson*. Newark, NJ.

Versnel, H. S. (1970) *Triumphus: An Inquiry Into the Origin, Development and Meaning of the Roman Triumph*. Leiden.

(1993a) "Two Carnivalesque Princes: Augustus and Claudius and the Ambiguity of Saturnalian Imagery," in S. Döpp, ed. *Karnevaleske Phänomene in antiken und nachantiken Kulturen und Literaturen*, 99–122. Bochumer Altertumswissenschaftliches Colloquium 13. Trier.

(1993b) "Saturnus and the Saturnalia," in *Inconsistencies in Greek and Roman Religion*. Vol. II: *Transition and Reversal in Myth and Ritual*, 136–227. Leiden.

Vice, S. (1997) *Introducing Bakhtin*. Manchester.

Vieth, David M. (1968) *The Complete Poems of John Wilmot, Earl of Oxford*. New Haven.

Vogt, G. M. (1925) "Gleanings for the History of a Sentiment: *Generositas Virtus, non Sanguis*," *Journal of English and Germanic Philology* 24: 102–24.

Von Albrecht, M. (1997) *A History of Roman Literature from Livius Andronicus to Boethius with Special Regard to its Influence on World Literature*. 2 vols. Leiden.

Wachter, R. (1998) "'Oral Poetry' in ungewohntem Kontext. Hinweise auf mündliche Dichtungstechnik in den pompejanischen Wandenschriften," *Zeitschrift für Papyrologie und Epigraphik* 121: 73–89.

Wagenvoort, H. (1956) "Ludus Poeticus," in *Studies in Roman Literature, Culture, and Religion*, 30–42. Leiden.

Walker, K. (1984) *The Poems of John Wilmot, Earl of Rochester*. Oxford.

Walsh, P. G. (1974) "Was Petronius a Moralist?," *Greece and Rome* 21: 181–91.

Walters, J. (1997a) "Invading the Roman Body: Manliness and Impenetrability in Roman Thought," in J. Hallett and M. Skinner, eds. *Roman Sexualities*, 29–46. Princeton.

(1997b) "Soldiers and Whores in a Pseudo-Quintilian Declamation," in T. Cornell and K. Lomas, eds. *Gender and Ethnicity in Ancient Italy*, 109–14. London.

(1998) "Making a Spectacle: Deviant Men, Invective, and Pleasure," *Arethusa* 31: 355–67.

Wardman, A. (1976) *Rome's Debt to Greece*. London.

Warmington, E. H. (1967) *Remains of Old Latin*, 4 vols. London.

Warmington, E. H. (1935, rev. edn. 1956, 1961) *Remains of Old Latin I Ennius and Caecilius*. London/Cambridge, MA.

Waszink, J. H. (1972) "Problems concerning the Satura of Ennius," in O. Skutsch, ed. *Ennius*, 99–137. Fondation Hardt, Entretiens sur l'Antiquité classique XVII. Geneva.

Watson, L. (1991) *Arae. The Curse Poetry of Antiquity*. Classical and Medieval Texts, Papers and Monographs 25. Leeds.

Wehrli, F. (1944) "Horaz und Kallimachos," *Museum Helveticum* 1: 69–76.

Weilen, I. (1996) "Physiognomische Überlegungen zu mens sana in corpore sano," in C. Klodt, ed. *Satura lanx. Festschrift für Werner A. Krenkel zum 70. Geburtstag*. Spudasmata 62, 153–68. Hildesheim–New York.

Weinbrot, H. (1969) *The Formal Strain: Studies in Augustan Imitation and Satire*. Chicago.

(1982) *Alexander Pope and the Traditions of Formal Verse Satire*. Princeton, NJ.

(1988) *Eighteenth Century Satire: Essays on Text and Context from Dryden to Peter Pindar*. Cambridge.

Wheeler, A. J. (1992) *English Verse Satire from Donne to Dryden: Imitation of Classical Models*. Heidelberg.

White, A. (1993) *Carnival, Hysteria and Writing: Collected Essays and Autobiography*. Oxford.

Wiesen, David S. (1964) *St. Jerome as a Satirist: a Study in Christian Latin Thought and Letters*: Ithaca, NY.

Wilkins, J. (2000) *The Boastful Chef: the Discourse of Food in Ancient Greek Comedy*. Oxford.

Wille, G. (1989) "Quellen zur Verwendung mündlicher Texte in römischen Gesängen vorliterarischen Zeit," in G. Vogt-Spira, ed. *Studien zur vorliterarischen Periode im frühen Rom*, 199–226. Tübingen.

Williams, C. (1998) *Roman Homosexuality: Ideologies of Masculinity in Classical Antiquity*. Oxford.

Williams, G. (1995) "Libertino Patre Natus: True or False?," in S. J. Harrison, ed. *Homage to Horace: a Bimillenary Celebration*, 296–313. Oxford.

Wimmel, W. (1960) *Kallimachos in Rom. Die Nachfolge seines apologetischen Dichtens in der Augusteerzeit*. Hermes Einzelschriften 16. Wiesbaden.

(1962) *Zur Form der horazischen Diatribensatire*. Frankfurt.

Winkler, M. (1983) *The Persona in Three Satires of Juvenal*. Hildesheim.

(2001) *Juvenal in English*. London.

Winn, James A., ed. (1997) *Critical Essays on John Dryden*, New York.

Winnicott, D. W. (1971) *Playing and Reality*. London.

Wiseman, R. (2002) *Laughlab: the Scientific Search for the World's Funniest Joke*. London.

Wiseman, T. P. (1988) "Satyrs in Rome? The Background to Horace's Ars Poetica," *Journal of Roman Studies* 78: 1–13.

(1998) *Roman Drama and Roman History*. Exeter.

Witke, C. (1970) *Latin Satire: the Structure of Persuasion*. Leiden.

Wolf, S. (1986) *Die Augustusrede in Senecas Apocolocyntosis*. Königstein.

Woodman, A. J. (1983) "Juvenal I and Horace," *Greece and Rome* 30: 81–4.

Woodman, T. and Feeney, D. eds. (2002) *Traditions and Contexts in the Poetry of Horace*. Cambridge.

Yon, A. (1940) "A propos du latin ludus," in *Mélanges de philologie offerts à Alfred Ernout*. Paris.

Zanker, P. (1995) *The Mask of Socrates: the Image of the Intellectual in Antiquity*. Berkeley.

Zeitlin, F. I. (1971a) "Petronius as Paradox: Anarchy and Artistic Integrity," *Transactions of the American Philological Association* 102: 631–84.

  (1971b) "Romanus Petronius: a Study of the *Troiae Halosis* and the *Bellum Civile*," *Latomus* 30: 56–82.

Zetzel, J. (1980) "Horace's *Liber Sermonum*: The Structure of Ambiguity," *Arethusa* 13: 59–77.

Zetzel, J. E. G. (2002) "Dreaming about Quirinus: Horace's *Satires* and the Development of Augustan Poetry," in Woodman and Feeney (2002), 38–52.

Žižek, S. (1999) *The Ticklish Subject: the Absent Center of Political Ontology*. New York.

Zwicker, S., ed. (1998) *The Cambridge Companion to English Literature: 1650–1740*. Cambridge.

INDEX

CAMBRIDGE COMPANIONS TO LITERATURE
Period and Thematic

European authors

UK writers

The Cambridge Companion to Chaucer,
second edition
edited by Piero Boitani and Jill Mann

The Cambridge Companion to Shakespeare
edited by Margareta de Grazia and
Stanley Wells

The Cambridge Companion to Shakespeare
on Film
edited by Russell Jackson

The Cambridge Companion to
Shakespearean Comedy
edited by Alexander Leggatt

The Cambridge Companion to Shakespeare
on Stage
edited by Stanley Wells and Sarah Stanton

The Cambridge Comanion to Shakespeare's
History Plays
edited by Michael Hattaway

The Cambridge Companion to
Shakespearean Tragedy
edited by Claire McEachern

The Cambridge Companion to Christopher
Marlowe
edited by Patrick Cheney

The Cambridge Companion to Ben Jonson
edited by Richard Harp and
Stanley Stewart

The Cambridge Companion to Spenser
edited by Andrew Hadfield

The Cambridge Companion to Milton,
second edition
edited by Dennis Danielson

The Cambridge Companion to John Dryden
edited by Steven N. Zwicker

The Cambridge Companion to Aphra Behn
edited by Derek Hughes and Janet Todd

The Cambridge Companion to Samuel
Johnson
edited by Greg Clingham

The Cambridge Companion to Jonathan
Swift
edited by Christopher Fox

The Cambridge Companion to Mary
Wollstonecraft
edited by Claudia L. Johnson

The Cambridge Companion to William Blake
edited by Morris Eaves

The Cambridge Companion to Wordsworth
edited by Stephen Gill

The Cambridge Companion to Coleridge
edited by Lucy Newlyn

The Cambridge Companion to Byron
edited by Drummond Bone

The Cambridge Companion to Keats
edited by Susan J. Wolfson

The Cambridge Companion to
Mary Shelley
edited by Esther Schor

The Cambridge Companion to Jane Austen
edited by Edward Copeland and Juliet
McMaster

The Cambridge Companion to the Brontës
edited by Heather Glen

The Cambridge Companion to Charles
Dickens
edited by John O. Jordan

The Cambridge Companion to George Eliot
edited by George Levine

The Cambridge Companion to Thomas
Hardy
edited by Dale Kramer

The Cambridge Companion to Oscar
Wilde
edited by Peter Raby

The Cambridge Companion to George
Bernard Shaw
edited by Christopher Innes

The Cambridge Companion to Joseph
Conrad
edited by J. H. Stape

The Cambridge Companion to
D. H. Lawrence
edited by Anne Fernihough

The Cambridge Companion to Virginia
Woolf
edited by Sue Roe and Susan Sellers

The Cambridge Companion to James Joyce,
second edition
edited by Derek Attridge

The Cambridge Companion to T. S. Eliot
edited by A. David Moody

The Cambridge Companion to
Ezra Pound
edited by Ira B. Nadel

The Cambridge Companion to W. H. Auden
edited by Stan Smith

The Cambridge Companion to Beckett
edited by John Pilling

The Cambridge Companion to Harold Pinter
edited by Peter Raby

The Cambridge Companion to Tom Stoppard
edited by Katherine E. Kelly

The Cambridge Companion to David Mamet
edited by Christopher Bigsby

US writers

The Cambridge Companion to Herman Melville
edited by Robert S. Levine

The Cambridge Companion to Nathaniel Hawthorne
edited by Richard Millington

The Cambridge Companion to Harriet Beecher Stowe
edited by Cindy Weinstein

The Cambridge Companion to Theodore Dreiser
edited by Leonard Cassuto and Claire Virginia Eby

The Cambridge Companion to Willa Cather
edited by Marilee Lindemann

The Cambridge Companion to Edith Wharton
edited by Millicent Bell

The Cambridge Companion to Henry James
edited by Jonathan Freedman

The Cambridge Companion to Walt Whitman
edited by Ezra Greenspan

The Cambridge Companion to Ralph Waldo Emerson
edited by Joel Porte, Saundra Morris

The Cambridge Companion to Henry David Thoreau
edited by Joel Myerson

The Cambridge Companion to Mark Twain
edited by Forrest G. Robinson

The Cambridge Companion to Edgar Allan Poe
edited by Kevin J. Hayes

The Cambridge Companion to Emily Dickinson
edited by Wendy Martin

The Cambridge Companion to Willa Cather
edited by Marilee Lindemann

The Cambridge Companion to William Faulkner
edited by Philip M. Weinstein

The Cambridge Companion to Ernest Hemingway
edited by Scott Donaldson

The Cambridge Companion to F. Scott Fitzgerald
edited by Ruth Prigozy

The Cambridge Companion to Robert Frost
edited by Robert Faggen

The Cambridge Companion to Eugene O'Neill
edited by Michael Manheim

The Cambridge Companion to Tennessee Williams
edited by Matthew C. Roudané

The Cambridge Companion to Arthur Miller
edited by Christopher Bigsby

The Cambridge Companion to Sam Shepard
edited by Matthew C. Roudané

CAMBRIDGE COMPANIONS TO CULTURE

Culture Companions

The Cambridge Companion to Modern German Culture
edited by Eva Kolinsky and Wilfried van der Will

The Cambridge Companion to Modern Russian Culture
edited by Nicholas Rzhevsky